Turning the Templar Key

The secret legacy of the Knights Templar and the origins of Freemasonry

Robert Lomas

www.RobertLomas.com
www.Bradford.ac.uk/webofhiram/
www.TurningtheTemplarKey.com

FAIR WINDS
PRESS
BEVERLY, MASSACHUSETTS

Text © 2007 Robert Lomas
This paperback edition published in 2009

First published in the USA in 2007 by
Fair Winds Press, a member of
Quayside Publishing Group
100 Cummings Center
Suite 406-L
Beverly, Massachusetts 01915-6101
www.fairwindspress.com

13 12 11 10 09   1 2 3 4 5
ISBN-13: 978-1-59233-426-1
ISBN-10: 1-59233-426-1

Library of Congress Cataloging-in-Publication Data available

Book design by Dutton & Sherman
Printed and bound in Canada

DEDICATED TO
THE FOND MEMORIES MY PARENTS LEFT ME

Other books by Robert Lomas:

Turning the Hiram Key
Turning the Solomon Key
The Secrets of Freemasonry
Freemasonry and the Birth of Modern Science

Other books co-authored by Robert Lomas:

The Hiram Key
The Second Messiah
Uriel's Machine

contents

ACKNOWLEDGMENTS

This book came about when I mentioned to Ellen Phillips, my editor at Fair Winds Press, that I had been thinking about writing a history of the Masonic Knights Templar. She thought it a great idea and encouraged me to put it to Fair Winds publisher Holly Schmidt. Holly liked it and asked if I could have a manuscript ready to publish for 13 October, 2007, the seven-hundredth Anniversary of the dawn raid which destroyed the Knights Templar.

Ellen Phillips has again proved to be an inspirational structural editor. Her light touch and helpful suggestions have guided me in shaping my ideas. Thank you, Elly, for your support, the amusing tales of your lady-bugs, greenhouses, and summer rain-storms, and for sharing some of your poems about physics. By the way, your knowledge of myth and storytelling proved invaluable too.

My grammar and spelling were laboriously checked by John Wheelwright, who told me when I was writing nonsense, or sentences without verbs, and reined in my more outrageous puns and flights of hyperbole. He remains my guardian of clarity of expression and a trusted partner, quick to spot oversights, omissions, and ambiguities. Thank you, John, for your editing, your witty conversation and your deep fund of odd facts about the world in general.

Once again John Gettings of Fair Winds Press coordinated production and managed to bring a tight set of schedules together in a calm and professional manner. I am grateful for his help and advice.

Martin Faulks, the young Freemason who inspired this trilogy of "Turning" books, has written a foreword explaining why he felt driven to hound me into writing them. Thank you, Martin, for inciting me to write about the deeper motivations of the Craft. I would also like to thank the Fratres of St. George Aboyne for introducing me to the history, living reality and philosophical depth of Templar Masonry.

Martin and Trevor Jackson of www.tracingboards.com have done a wonderful job on the cover. My agent Bill Hamilton and his assistant Corinne Chabert of A.M. Heath & Co., have been their usual professional selves and have encouraged and guided me throughout the writing process. Nick Grant, the production editor at Lewis Masonic, has also been very helpful in coordinating the UK edition.

Finally I want to thank my wife Ann and children Rhisiart, Delyth, and Geraint for their continuous support and encouragement.

FOREWORD

Robert Lomas often introduces me as his favorite stalker. This is because I have come to know him through my work with Lewis Masonic, the world's largest, oldest, and most successful Masonic publishing company. When I first came to the company, I wanted to produce a range of titles bringing Freemasonry to the attention of the general public, and I knew that a book by Robert would help bring this about. His exciting writing style, and interesting scientific spirituality, have made his writing popular with both Masons and non-Masons. Therefore, a book written by Robert would get guaranteed shelf space in all mainstream bookshops, and might create an opportunity for other Masonic authors with different writing styles to reach the general public.

So Robert was an important part of my "master plan," and, luckily, he was inspired by my idea of a range of titles written by Freemasons for the mainstream book trade. Since then, after the great success of *Turning the Hiram Key*, my dream has become reality. More and more people are getting the opportunity to read about Masonic ideas. Lewis, along with our American ally Fair Winds Press, have continued to have successes with titles like *The Rosslyn Hoax* and *The Secrets of Solomon's Temple* and *Freemasonry—The Reality* by authors whose views are different from, and even opposed to, Robert's. I am very grateful to Robert for investing his time in us and helping me open up the public discussion of Masonic subjects.

My Freemasonry has a different focus from Robert's. The wonderful thing about Masonic ritual is that it acts like an ink-blot test for the human mind. Each Freemason sees something slightly different in the workings of the Craft, depending on his situation in life, his personal background, and his level of development. I wonder if a lack of firm knowledge of our origins isn't one of the greatest gifts Freemasonry has. The ambiguity allows the ritual to speak directly: without preconceptions. To Robert, Freemasonry is a mystery to solve, a science puzzle, and a quest into the past. Indeed, it is a standing joke between Robert and myself that what I see as genuine spiritual insight, he often sees as superstition and self-delusion. But we agree that Freemasonry is a path of self-development and self-improvement, and that Masonic ritual provides a system of moral and spiritual transformation. It inspires men to look at themselves and change the way they interact with the world. It is a system of mental control and self-development comparable to Buddhism, yoga, and many other paths of self-improvement to be found around the world, but packaged in a unique western tradition.

The special thing about Freemasonry is that it is free of dogma and open to all religious persuasions. The rituals of Freemasonry are stories that tap into the basic human urge to improve one's self and make the world a better place. Freemasonry teaches that our personal characteristics are neither random nor immutable. We can change ourselves just as a builder changes his surroundings. The wisdom and inspiration contained in Masonic ceremonies allows us to reflect on ourselves and adjust our behavior and way of thinking. It's a hard path that involves the constant chipping away of our negative qualities and the cultivation of our virtues. To do this we use contemplation, speculation, ritual memorization, and constant adjustment and correction of our thoughts in daily life. A stonemason builds buildings, a Freemason builds himself into someone better and more virtuous. It is a way of becoming the best man that you can be, and of having the best effect you can on the world.

I, however, know little of history, so I was a little hesitant to produce a foreword for a book on the Knights Templar and Masonic Templarism. As I read the manuscript, though, I started to realize that this book wasn't simply about history. It looked at something much deeper: the power that stories have to inspire. I came to understand that one constant theme of Robert's books is the power of myth. He claims that the very thing that powers Freemasonry is also the thing that created it: the ability of iconic, ancient stories to continue to inspire! So get ready for a journey through some of history's most amazing tales, including Viking pirates fighting Native Americans, captured knights roasted to death for heresy, the hidden wisdom of goddess worship, and the secret history of the true cross of Jesus Christ!

Martin Faulks

PROLOGUE

Imagine it is seven hundred years ago. The Order of the Knights Templar is the most powerful international military force in the world. It has a network of Temple-fortresses in every country, but does not answer to their kings. Indeed, in many countries the kings are in debt to, and answer to, the Order.

The Grand Master of the Order is Commander-in-Chief of the strongest military force in the world, the head of a rich international banking monopoly, and the religious leader of a vast network of monks, warriors, traders, and servants housed in wealthy preceptories throughout the known world. The Order is richer than any single country, more powerful than any one monarch, and in political matters answers only to the Pope.

In Paris, the French National Treasury is controlled from the Order's Temple because the people trust the Order more than they trust the near-bankrupt King, Philip the Fair, who has borrowed large sums of money from the Order for his personal use.

The Grand Master of the Order of the Temple is held in great public regard by the rulers and people of France. During his state visit to Paris the Grand Master has recently been honoured to act as pall-bearer at the funeral of Her Royal Highness, Princess Catherine of France, sister-in-law of the King.

This is the setting for the start of our story. Now let me take you back to witness a key moment.

5:00 a.m. October 13, 1307, Paris, France As a Sergeant of the Knights Templar, you have just risen from your bed, lit a single candle, and dressed in your simple brown mantle. The flickering light of the small flame highlights the red cross on your shoulder as you kneel to pray in the solitude of your stone-walled cell.

Your job is to attend to the needs of Templar Grand Master Jacques de Molay, who is visiting the great fortress of the Paris Temple in the company of Geoffrey de Charny, the Preceptor of Normandy, and Geoffrey de Gonville, Preceptor of Aquitaine. You feel greatly honored to be the personal servant of Grand Master de Molay.

The Grand Master asked you to make sure he is awakened in good time this morning. He plans to lead the morning prayers in the Great Hall of the Paris Temple, and all the brethren of the Paris Temple are looking forward to seeing him officiate. As you approach his bedchamber, you are surprised to hear an urgent pounding on the fortified main door. Serving brothers ask who is there.

"Messengers from the King of France, urgently seeking admission," the answer rings out, and you hear the sturdy bolts being drawn on the massive door.

You rush on to make sure the Grand Master is awake for the arrival of the messengers, but you are roughly pushed aside. The air is filled with cries of rage, screams, and the occasional prayer as soldiers hack their way forward. Horrified, you recognize the arms of the King of France on their surcoats.

The Grand Master is pulled from his bed, wearing only his night shift and the lambskin breeches he never removes in front of anyone. His sixty-year-old legs are skinny and shivering beneath him as his bare feet are dragged across the stone floor. You follow the soldiers as they haul him to the Great Hall. You watch as coarse ropes are attached to his wrists, and his arms are pulled wide; he stands before a hooded figure. You are shocked that a noble priest should be treated this way—and for a moment, you think he looks like Christ as He was crucified.

The Grand Master demands to be told who dares to abuse him so. The hooded figure throws back his cowl to reveal the face of William Imbert, the Chief Inquisitor of France. Imbert orders that the Grand Master be stripped of his night clothes. Even his breeches are wrenched from him, so he shivers like a scrawny plucked chicken with his nakedness exposed to Imbert's impudent gaze. The two soldiers, holding his roped arms give no chance to preserve any modesty.

You feel proud as the Grand Master faces up to Imbert and announces that he answers only to God and his vicar on Earth, the Holy Father, Pope Clement V. He demands to know on whose authority Imbert acts. Imbert does not answer, but a figure steps forward from the shadows. The soldiers stiffen as they see it is King Philip. He says that a King of France needs no authority from any Pope to arrest and expose heretics. Imbert steps forward, takes a whip from under his robes, and lashes the naked body of the Grand Master, who screams out in shock and anger.

You cannot allow such an outrage within your Temple. You take your dagger from under your mantle and move towards the Inquisitor, determined to kill this vile offender. But the King's soldiers see you coming. You throw up an arm to ward off a blow, and feel a sword shear through the fabric of your sleeve and bite into your arm. In shock from the horror of the events and the loss of blood, you never see the sword-thrust that kills you.

The Order of the Knights Templar dies with you . . . or does it? Let's time-travel across nearly six hundred miles and five hundred years to find out . . .

March 4, 1794, Aberdeen, Scotland   The stone floor feels cold beneath the unfamiliar sandals of the Medieval pilgrim's costume you have been given to wear. The long, coarse robe hangs heavily from the cord belt at your waist, the burden on your back weighs you down, and your eyes are shaded by the wide brim of a pilgrim's hat, adorned with its traditional cockleshell.

You have worn regalia in ritual ceremonies before—after all, you have worked your way up through the ranks of Masonry until you arrive here tonight as a full Companion of the Holy Royal Arch.

But this ritual is different. If all goes well—if you prove worthy—tonight you will become a Knight Templar. It promises to be the high point of your life and the peak of your Masonic ambition.

After what seems like hours of waiting, as the distant noises of arcane rituals seep into the anteroom, you hear a movement behind you. You suppress a shiver of fear as a hoodwink, a blindfold, is placed over your eyes. The Knight Marshal leads you up to the door of the Temple and knocks. You sense the door swing silently open, and smell the warmth of many male bodies as it wafts outward toward you. You cannot yet see the Templar Encampment that you are about to enter, but you feel the pull of destiny. A voice challenges you. "Who goes there?"

But is the Order you join tonight the same as the one that perished half a millennium before? Did the Templars survive against all odds?

Today   You hold in your hand the key to this great mystery. Are you going to turn it? Let me encourage you to do so.

My name is Robert Lomas. I am a physicist, an author, a computer information systems expert, a university lecturer, and a Freemason. I am also a Masonic Knight Templar.

✳ I became a Doctor of Physics because I was born with the curiosity of an explorer and an urge to study the hidden mysteries of nature and science. I became a Masonic Knight Templar because I have an innate sense of awe at the wonder of creation, and I wanted to understand my place in the Cosmos. I became a writer and a lecturer because I wanted to share my thoughts, knowledge, and insights.

As you begin this book, I invite you to join me in a great adventure of the human spirit. Let me guide you across the bounds of time and space, through science and mystery, and together we will peer into the hearts of men and women, gods and goddesses. We will uncover secrets that have remained hidden for eleven thousand years—secrets that shaped our world and directed the destiny of our civilization.

Read ✷ In this book we'll begin our quest by uncovering the *real* Knights Templar— the men of iron and gold who yearned to die or rule for their God: the fanatics and merchant-bankers who spawned fear and awe, legends and romances. We'll follow the Templar trail to Rosslyn Chapel, and pick up the trail of the Lords of St. Clair, the ambitious family who built and ruled it. We'll take a sea voyage in search of the fabled Templar Fleet, and join Prince Henry Sinclair, the grandfather of the builder of Rosslyn, as he follows Leif Ericsson and his Viking crews to the edge of the New World. We'll trace the footsteps of the Templars to the Holy Land, and witness their Golden Age, set against the bloodshed and genocide of the Crusades. And we'll go back, back to the dawn of history, until we stand at the gates of the ancient city of Çatalhöyük. For within the thick clay walls of that Neolithic settlement lies the answer to a great mystery of humanity—an answer that is encoded in the fabric of Rosslyn Chapel and in the secret rituals of the present-day Masonic Knights Templar.

I promise you, it is truly the adventure of a lifetime. We have centuries and continents to cover, and time is short. Are you ready? Then turn the page, and let's begin with a greedy King, a frightened Pope, and a Friday the 13th that changed the luck of the whole world.

Read on →

CHAPTER I

ARE THE KNIGHTS TEMPLAR ALIVE AND WELL?

DID THEY SURVIVE?

Are the Knights Templar alive and well and meeting at a secret temple somewhere near you?

On a Friday the 13th, seven hundred years ago, the Knights Templar were struck down in a dawn raid by the King of France. Ever since that fateful and horrific day, Friday the 13th has been a source of superstition and fear. Perhaps a modern analogy of the events will make clear the enormity of what happened.

The Grand Master of the Temple controlled the richest and most powerful military machine in the world. Only the President of the United States of America now controls an equivalent amount of wealth and might. The King of France was an ambitious, but bankrupt, absolute monarch when he struck at the Templars and took them by surprise at dawn on Friday, October 13, 1307.

To appreciate the impact of what happened, think of the President of the United States coming on a State visit to London and staying in the American Embassy. Imagine that the morning after a formal banquet with the Royal family and high-ranking officials at Buckingham Palace, the American Embassy is stormed by SAS troops. The President is seized, stripped, and tortured, and the Queen appears at the torture scene to gloat in person. This is the nearest modern equivalent to the actions that took place in Paris seven hundred years ago. And it took the whole world by surprise.

I have long been fascinated by this Order and how it has become linked with Freemasonry. For well over two hundred years, there has been a Masonic Order of Knights Templar. It is known colloquially as the KTs and more formally as

Templar Masonry. The KTs are a separate Order from Craft Freemasonry, which is made of Lodges that perform (or "work" as Masons say) the basic three degrees of Entered Apprentice, Fellowcraft, and Master Mason. Before a Master Mason can become a Templar Mason, he must first complete a series of further degrees after the degree of Master, before he will be accepted. There are three routes to become a KT. These are via the York Rite, the Antient and Accepted Rite, and the Royal Order, but each ends with a ritual that allows the aspiring Mason to call himself a Knight Templar. The ritual of each of these groups of Templar Masons claims that its Order is a continuation of the original Order of Knights Templar.

In the years leading up to the seven-hundredth anniversary of the destruction of the Templars, I decided to investigate Templar Masonry, to see if any of these claims are true. I wanted to know if Freemasonry really is a secret continuation of the long-dead Order of the Templars.

Templar Fact, Templar Fiction

The reality of the Knights Templar is very different from the romantic image that powers *Da Vinci Code* mania and which took root in the public imagination after Sir Walter Scott used the Templar character of Sir Brian de Bois-Guilbert in *Ivanhoe*. The Templar Order lasted for only two hundred years, from 1118 to 1313, and it was destroyed seven hundred years ago. For all that, it remains in the public consciousness as a mystical, secretive Order. It is seen as a group of persecuted underdogs, pure idealists destroyed by an autocratic government out of self-interest. In urban myth, the Knights are reputed to have held secrets of great worth; to have been invincible in battle; to have been the custodians of the Holy Grail; to have been the guardians of the secrets of Solomon's Temple; and to have survived persecution by sailing, with their vast treasures, to found colonies in the New World of America. And many people believe that they might still exist as a secret influence on today's society.

So much for the myth, what of the reality? As with most legendary figures, the Templar reality is far removed from the myth. The bulk of the Templar brothers were staid, conservative plodders. Either they came from the lower ranks of knights, or they were simply craftsmen, servants, or agricultural laborers. Most did not travel far to join their Templar religious house; they stayed in the same area all their lives and lived near their families, like almost everyone in their time. Few were educated. Most Knights and squires could not read Latin, much less French, the lingua franca of their day (as English is in ours). The New Testament had to be rendered into their own native tongue and read aloud before they could understand it.

But not all the Templars were so ignorant. The Order had two functional branches, the fighting brothers and the fund-raisers. The fund-raisers were the educated ones, and their main aim was to collect money for the fighting brothers and the war against the Muslims. In the process, they invented the modern banking system. If we think of the fund-raising arm of the Templars as bank managers and bank clerks, we will probably get a better idea of how people in cities such as London and Paris regarded them in the early fourteenth century, just before their sudden destruction. And it becomes easier to understand how King Phillip managed to overpower them so easily. He did not strike at the fighting units, who were stationed in the East, but their Western-based servants, bank clerks, and elderly leaders

By contrast, the fighting brothers were highly trained killing machines, whose dearest desire was to lay down their lives on the battlefield while destroying the enemies of Christianity. In this way they would win a place in heaven, where they would wear the crowns of martyrs and bask in the goodwill of their patrons— Jesus, the King of Heaven, and Mary, His mother and Queen of Heaven. Education and learning was not encouraged among these knights. Their training and religious fervor encouraged them never to surrender, but to kill as many of the enemy as possible while pursuing a glorious martyr's death. They had more in common with a suicide bomber than with any modern monk.

Yet the myth of a vanished order of noble, mystical, warrior monks pervades modern literature. Why? How does a religious order forcibly disbanded seven hundred years ago maintain such a grip on the modern Western imagination? How does it provoke such animosity in the East that when an American President uses the term "crusade," he is accused of racism?

Perhaps the answer lies in the higher degrees of Freemasonry, which perpetuate the popular image of the noble Templars. This was what I set out to investigate. I have drawn on Freemasonic information, from both Craft and Templar degrees, to try to understand what happened, why and how, and to try to explain how the tolerant and inclusive modern spiritual practices of Templar Freemasonry grew out of what was, effectively, an Order with a motivation similar to that of the modern suicide bomber.

✳ The original Knights Templar ceased to exist on March 22, 1313, when Pope Clement V issued a Papal Bull dissolving the Order without ruling on its guilt or innocence. But they had been effectively destroyed on Friday, October 13, 1307, in the dawn raid by Philip the Fair, King of France. The Templars' bad luck became everyone's bad luck, and Friday the 13th has been considered an unlucky day ever since. Their last Grand Master, Jacques de Molay, was imprisoned and tortured until he confessed to heinous heresies, and then was burned at the stake in Paris, on March 19, 1314.

But when the Papal Bull abolishing the Templars was published, it was never enforced in Scotland. This was because in 1313 King Robert of Scotland, and by extension the country he ruled, was excommunicated. Robert had incurred the Pope's displeasure by murdering John Comyn, his rival for the crown, before the High Altar of Dumfries Church. This quirk of history does offer the possibility that the Templar Order might have survived in Scotland, even after it was snuffed out in the rest of Europe. But could it still exist today? Some Freemasons believe it did survive, and that it continues as a Masonic Order.

MY PATH TO TEMPLARISM

I first became interested in Templar Masonry soon after completing *The Hiram Key* (which I co-authored with Chris Knight in 1996. Soon after it was published, I was contacted by some members of the oldest Templar Preceptory (the name that Templar Masons use for their Lodges) in the British Isles, and was asked if I wanted to join them. To be accepted, it was necessary to be a member of the Holy Royal Arch of Jerusalem, which I already was, and so I was keen to learn more. Over the next two years, I progressed through the rituals of modern Templar Masonry and found it to be exciting, both in terms of its dramatic ritual and in the philosophical teaching that it inspired. (I will discuss the history of the Masonic Templar Preceptory I joined in chapter 4.)

The traditional history of the Order, given as part of the ritual of Initiation, is linked to the excommunicated King Robert and the Battle of Bannockburn, where a Templar battle force was said to have intervened to help him rout the English. This battle, in June 1314, fought between the armies of King Edward II of England and Robert I, King of Scots, decided Scotland's fate and made it an independent nation. On that day some nine thousand Scots defeated over eighteen thousand English troops, and Legend says refugee Templars helped win this victory. The Masonic story is that after the betrayal of Grand Master Molay, "a glorious martyr of a glorious Order," all over Europe the Order of the Knights Templar was persecuted, but that the Templars in Scotland were protected from persecution by King Robert and his army. Even in Scotland, though, where the Order was allowed to continue in secret, it was stripped of its public privileges and possessions.

This Masonic story flies in the face of accepted scholarship, as I will discuss, but the power of the ritual and manner of its telling, in the heart of a modern Templar Preceptory, surrounded by brother knights wearing the white mantle and red cross of the Order, tugged at the romance in my heart. My head said it was unlikely that the Templars had managed to survive as an underground organization for so long, but my Freemason's heart wanted it to be true. There was only one thing to do: conduct my own research and try to discover for myself what really happened.

My initial findings weren't encouraging. Historian Helen Nicholson, from the University of Cardiff, doesn't think the Order survived. She ends her book on the Knights Templar thus:

> Since the Masonic movement in the late eighteenth century there have also been many attempts to recreate the Templars. Obviously the original Order cannot be

recreated; its lands are lost, and its vocation would be rather out of place in modern society. Apart from the German Freemasons, a French Neo-Templar Order was founded and died out in the early nineteenth century, as did a Neo-Templar Order in England. Other such Orders exist today. These Orders have not simply been an excuse for the upper classes to dress up and play at being knights. Some of the new "Orders of the Temple" carry out charitable work, like the "Good Templars" of the Temperance movement; others have a religious aspect and can be defined as "Masonic" offering their members insights into the divine nature, or whatever . . . These new "Templar" Orders are themselves now the subject of scholarly study. It is a strange tribute to the enduring appeal of this ordinary religious Order—in existence for less than two centuries, and last seen nearly seven hundred years ago—that not only the original Order but even the myth of the Order and the "false" modern Orders which bear its name have become part of serious history.[1]

Dr. Nicholson thinks that the link between Freemasonry and the Templars was a political creation.

It was not until the eighteenth century, with the rise of secret societies such as the Freemasons, that the Templars came to the attention of the educated, upper-middle-class layman as an example of a secret society which had been destroyed because of its esoteric knowledge. Initially the Freemasons claimed no link with the Templars: it was the German Masons who in the 1760's introduced the idea that the Templars must have had secret wisdom and magical powers, which they learned while they held the so-called Temple of Solomon in Jerusalem. This wisdom and power, they claimed, had been handed down a secret line of succession to the present day masons.[2]

She adds:

The late eighteenth and early nineteenth century were a period when many upper-middle-class laymen "discovered" mysterious truths about their medieval or ancient past in order to give spurious historical authenticity to their own interests and activities. This is the period when the Welsh "neo-druids" were created, and the Scottish clan tartan kilt was invented . . . What could have been more convenient than to "discover" that the long-dead Templars had been Freemasons![3]

I will discuss the real Knights Templar—who they were and why they were both revered and despised—in chapter 3. But first, I needed to a closer look at their modern counterparts, the Masonic Knights Templar.

MODERN-DAY TEMPLARS

The original Order of the Temple survived for approximately 190 years. The oldest Lodge of Templar Masons was 213 years old in 2007. It is the Masonic Preceptory of St. George Aboyne, which meets in the Masonic Hall, Queen Street, in Aberdeen, Scotland. The Preceptories of Scotland are given numbers on the roll of the Great Priory of Scotland according to their age. The roll starts with Number 1, the oldest assembly of Templar Masons in Scotland, and it is St. George Aboyne.

Number 1 can trace its written records back to 1794. It has continuous meeting minutes for over two hundred years—in fact, for almost a quarter of a century longer than the existence of the Order it takes its name from. Could these Masonic Knights Templar be the legitimate successors of the Order of the Knights Templar? If so, what happened during the 480-year hiatus between the apparent extinction of one and establishment of the other?

What do Templar Masons do? How are they different from ordinary Craft Freemasons?

To begin to answer these questions, I must first explain what is meant by Craft Masonry. Ask a Freemason "What is Freemasonry?" and you'll get an answer that comes straight from his ritual. It is: "A peculiar system of morality, illustrated by symbols and illuminated by allegory." But this doesn't tell you enough, so I will explain further.

Freemasonry consists of three Degrees, each made up of ritual plays, which are performed (or "worked," as Freemasons put it), with each teaching a different spiritual lesson. The following is a summary of the ritual teaching that every Freemason goes through while "working" the three Degrees of the Craft.

The First, known as the Entered Apprentice Degree, equips you to develop a rational mind and to bring your intellect into balance with the irrational urges of the flesh. To aid you in this task, the ritual teaches you postures, provides a Lodge structure to focus your thinking, and gives you a set of symbols and spiritual tools. Only when you have balanced your rational mind against your bodily urges, learned how to adopt and use postures, learned to comprehend symbolism, and gained proficiency in the use of spiritual tools are you ready to move on to the Second Degree.

The Second Degree, known as the Fellowcraft Degree, helps you to balance your intellect and your emotions, so that you learn how to recognize truth and discriminate between irrational urges of the flesh and the true voice of the spirit. You are given further postures, tools, and symbols to help you to strengthen your rational mind and learn to handle your emotions, so that you are prepared for the discovery of the blazing star of truth, which is as yet only visible as darkness at your center. Here you meet the spiral symbol, which can teach you how to approach the center. The postures affect your body and feed back hormonal responses into your rational mind to help you learn how to subdue emotion. But before you can proceed to the Third Degree, you must learn to let go of your ego and self-regard.

In the Third Degree, the sublime degree of Master Mason, you must learn how to allow your ego and rational mind to die. That may sound extreme, but it is necessary so that your spirit may be reborn as the keystone of your being and support your quest to attain the vision of light which emanates from the center. The ritual of death and rebirth stills the urges of your body, your intellect, and your emotion,

Read

and brings forth your suppressed spirit. In this Degree, the circle of your being is rendered complete and perfect by acquiring mastery over its four component parts (body, intellect, emotion, spirit). When this mastery is fully achieved, a Master of the Craft has undergone a radical transformation of the mind and a regeneration of his entire nature. Now you are ready to allow the light of the center to flow through fresh channels in the brain so that the true secret of the Craft is fully internalized.

Beyond the three Degrees of the Craft (i.e., Basic Freemasonry), there are a series of other separate Orders and Degrees, each of which teaches its own individual spiritual lessons. The York Rite takes a Craft Mason and first teaches him that there is a great spiritual secret hidden in a secret vault at the center of his personal consciousness. This vault, which is a symbol of the mystery of self-awareness, is described in the ritual as a chamber which had been built beneath the first Temple by King Solomon to hide certain Masonic secrets. It was discovered when a group of Knight-Masons, working for King Zerubbabel, were clearing away the rubble while getting ready to start the construction of the Second Temple. To become a Companion of the Holy Royal Arch, a Master Mason must face the dark terror of entering this hidden vault and learn to subdue his fears. Templar Masonry takes the metaphor of the Holy Trinity and uses it to explain the threefold nature of the secret which is contained in this vault.

In modern Templar Masonry, politics and religion are forbidden topics of discussion within the meetings. So I began to wonder about Helen Nicholson's idea that the Templar Masons were linked to political activists. If they had been linked to politics in the past, they do not seem to have maintained the link. But perhaps they once were. I say this because one of the earliest accounts of the ritual of the Templar Masons, in the *Manual of Freemasonry*, was published in 1825 by a notorious political activist Richard Carlile.

> Richard Carlile . . . was to achieve national notoriety as a champion of freedom of speech and thought, a pioneer of the freedom of the press, a fierce opponent of the monarchy and supporter of republicanism, a militant atheist, and an advocate of such social novelties as vegetarianism and birth control. Indeed, Carlile can be seen as the forefather of many aspects of modern political protest.[4]

These comments are from Andrew Prescott, Professor of Freemasonry at the University of Sheffield, who researched Carlile for his Inaugural Lecture in November 2000. But did Carlile become the first person to publish the rituals of Templar Masonry because he was already a radical, or did he get his radical ideas from Templar Masonry?

If I wanted to know about the beginnings of the Masonic Knights Templar, my best starting place was to study the earliest forms of ritual attributed to them. For many years I have been collecting early rituals and storing them on a website at the University of Bradford, where I lecture (http://www.bradford.ac.uk/webofhiram/).

I had a form of early Masonic Templar ritual in my collection, which had been issued by the Grand Conclave of the Royal Exalted Religious and Military order of Masonic Knights Templar in England and Wales and dated the 6th Day of August 1812. This had been the source of the Templar ritual reproduced in Carlile's *Manual of Freemasonry* and was broadly similar to it, but Carlile's version contained more detail.

Andrew Prescott had said that Carlile's *Manual* was probably the most reliable copy of early English Masonic Templar ritual and spoke of it as an important influence on the radical political ideology of the nineteenth century, saying:

> Richard Carlile['s] . . . *Manual of Freemasonry*, which first appeared in 1825 in a volume of his journal *The Republican*, was shortly afterwards reprinted [as] a separate publication, and has remained in print ever since. Moreover, this continuous publication history is not just an accident. Carlile himself evidently thought that his *Manual of Freemasonry* represented an important contribution to radical ideology, and he went out of his way to ensure that it remained in print, even in his last years, when he was an impoverished and, to some extent, forgotten man.[5]

But how trustworthy was he as a source? I decided to begin looking at Carlile's political record.

Carlile the Radical

Richard Carlile, known to history as the Devil's Freemason, published his radical magazine *The Republican* in a singular manner, as I will explain. It was in this journal that he first printed a comprehensive account of early nineteenth-century Masonic ritual, which he later published in the book entitled *Manual of Freemasonry*. In 1817 he fell foul of a British Government edict that ordered all publishers of "blasphemous and seditious" writings to be arrested. At the time Carlile was working for a man called William Sherwin. Sherwin had started *The Republican* but it was a rather unsuccessful journal, and he was developing a second title, to be known as the *Political Register*. Carlile was short of money and contemptuous of authority, which him ideal to act as Sherwin's scapegoat. He made a deal with Sherwin to act as publisher of both periodicals and take the risk of imprisonment, so long as Sherwin wrote the radical material and paid Carlile's expenses during his incarceration. As Andrew Prescott says:

> Prison obviously seemed at this time a better bet for Carlile than starvation or the workhouse, and the arrangement with Sherwin allowed Carlile to launch himself as a radical publisher.[6]

Carlile was soon churning out a whole raft of cheap political publications. He published a magazine called *The Weekly Register* and pamphlets showcasing political parodies by William Hone. He published Robert Southey's *Wat Tyler* (which

Andrew Prescott notes was even "disavowed by its author when first published"). In Carlile's view, Britain was "a mass of Corruption, Falsehood, Hypocrisy and Slander."[7] He was soon in prison, convicted of blasphemy and sedition for publishing an article in the *Weekly Political Register* where he dared to suggest that the poor were politically enslaved.

Perhaps the most radical writer that Carlile published was Thomas Paine. Paine was a critic of religion and wanted to abolish the monarchy; he favored a democratic republic and was a major inspiration for the Fathers of the American Revolution. He wrote two famous books, *The Age of Reason* and *The Rights of Man.* He was a hero to the young Carlile, and he interested Carlile in Freemasonry when he wrote a pamphlet entitled *Origins of Free Masonry.* Carlile, who was temporarily out of prison, published it in 1818. Although I can find no proof, in the form of Lodge minutes, to prove that Paine was a Freemason, his writings on the Craft show a deep grasp of its ritual and symbolism not usually found among non-Masons. There is one clue in the introduction of Carlile's *Manual* where he says that, although he is not a Freemason himself, "the secret system which is called Craft Masonry has been communicated to me by Masons." And his main source was Thomas Paine.

Carlile was invited to speak at a public meeting at St. Peter's Field, Manchester, on August 16, 1819, along with Major John Cartwright and Henry "Orator" Hunt. The meeting was intended to get the Corn Laws (an early form of stealth tax on food) repealed, and to reform Parliament. Thousands of local people turned up to hear the speeches, and the magistrates, fearing the possibility of a riot, called in the military. They mobilized four squadrons of cavalry (600 men) from the 15th Hussars, 400 cavalrymen of the Cheshire Yeomanry, 120 cavalrymen from the Manchester and Salford Yeomanry, several hundred infantrymen, a detachment of the Royal Horse Artillery complete with two six-pounder guns, and 400 of Manchester's special constables. As Hunt stood up to speak first, this small army was ordered to break up the meeting. A hundred and twenty cavalry horses and 400 special constables charged the crowd. They killed twelve men and three women; four hundred men and over a hundred women were seriously injured. This event, infamous in the history of the city of Manchester, became known as the Peterloo Massacre.[8]

Carlile, who never got to speak, managed to escape from the field and got on the first mail coach to London. Once back home, he published a special edition of *Sherwin's Political Register* that, under the lurid headline "Horrid Massacres at Manchester," contained his eyewitness report of the events. It is obvious where his sympathies lay:

> The Yeomanry Cavalry made their charge with a most infuriate frenzy; they cut down men, women and children, indiscriminately, and appeared to have commenced a pre-meditated attack with the most insatiable thirst for blood and destruction. They merit a medallion, on one side of which should be inscribed "The Slaughter Men of Manchester", and a reverse bearing a description of their slaughter of defenceless men,

women and children, unprovoked and unnecessary. As a proof of meditated murder of the part of the magistrates, every stone was gathered from the ground on the Friday and Saturday previous to the meeting, by scavengers sent there by the express command of the magistrates, that the populace might be rendered more defenseless. The meeting was one of the most calm and orderly that I have ever witnessed. No less than 300,000 people were assembled. The Yeomanry Cavalry made their charge. They cut down men, women and children, and appeared to attack with a thirst for blood. [9]

This report was not looked on kindly by the authorities. Carlile's shop in Fleet Street was raided and he was arrested. His stock of pamphlets was confiscated, and he remained in Dorchester jail for the next three years. But he was still allowed to publish *The Republican* and to write radical, although technically legal, pieces. When he was let out in 1824, he revived his interest Freemasonry. He wrote a short article about its history for a short-lived weekly he promoted called *The Moralist*. It was not a success, but it did attract the interest of a group of ex-Masons who wanted to make a public attack on what they saw as abuses of Freemasonry.

Andrew Prescott comments that:

At the beginning of 1825, he [Carlile] wrote to William Holmes, a Sheffield shopman who himself wrote substantial quantities of atheist verse, declaring that "I am full of masonry. In a great hurry to tell you that I want a dozen of the best steel pens that you can get me . . . " In August, he wrote to other supporters declaring that "While masonry lasts you must not be sick yet, or you will be dead before it is all over. What must I feel who have to read through all this trash several times, and to write it over. The exposure could not be made without the nonsense. Besides it will form the only correct history of masonry and is important as a blow to superstition, of which Masonry is a deep rooted point. The Bible is nonsense, everything religious is nonsense, and there is no way of destroying it but by a full disclosure. I shall strike the very roots of masonry, and, in so doing, I shall un-christianize thousands . . . who, but for the Masonry subject, would not have read *The Republican*." [10]

Prescott believes Carlile was only doing what many others had done in the early nineteenth century: reprinting the private rituals of the Freemasons to incite prurient interest and sell pamphlets for profit. Carlile was expert at finding copies of the rituals, and, as Prescott says, "he made a particularly good job of the exposure." This was good news for me, because it meant Carlile had recorded as much of the rituals of the Templar Masons as he had been able to lay his hands on.

His policy of exposure made him a publishing success, and his series of articles was avidly bought by Freemason readers of *The Republican*, eager for more information about other branches of their Order. Realizing he was onto a good thing, Carlile repackaged the material as a book, but now, instead of denouncing and exposing, he moved on to the role of Masonic educator, saying:

I have omitted all those remarks which, in the Nos of the Vol. 12 of "The Republican", must have been so offensive to Masons. My great object is here to

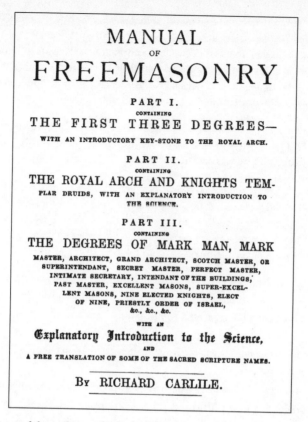

Title page of one of the earliest published accounts of the rituals of Templar Masonry (1825), by the radical Richard Carlile.

instruct Masons as well as others, and not give them offense. They ask for light. Here is light. They ask for fellowship. Here is the only basis of fellowship.[11]

Carlile kept his *Manual* in print for the rest of his life. His intense study of the rituals of Freemasonry had made him feel that his interpretation offered a key to understanding the origins of religion. Perhaps it did—as I will discuss later in this book—but more importantly, it provided a treasure-house of early ritual.

CARLILE'S EARLY MASONIC TEMPLAR RITUAL

What form did the early Masonic Templar ritual take? Carlile begins his section on the Masonic Order of Knights Templar thus:

Profane History gives us no account of these Knights anterior to the time of the Crusades; but the Revelation of Sacred History and Ancient Mystery, supposes them to have been orders in the degrees of the Temple, as they now assume to be in Masonry. The title of Hospitaller is traceable only to a provision for pilgrims journeying to Jerusalem in Palestine; while the distinction of Knights of Rhodes and of Malta was acquired in the crusade wars, by their Knights getting and defending the possession of those islands. They had two residences in London: that which is now called St. John's-square, and the Temple by the river.[12]

He relates the ritual way of opening and closing an Encampment (the name given to a Lodge meeting of Templar Masons), then goes on to reveal the ritual method of "making a Templar":

A candidate for installation is habited as a pilgrim, with sandals, mantle, staff, and cross, scrip and wallet, a belt or cord round his waist, with bread and water, and, in some encampments, a burthen on the back, which is made to fall off at a view of the cross. The whole ceremony is purely Christian, according to the vulgar notions and the literal sense of Christianity.[13]

✳ Carlile describes how the candidate is dressed: in a pilgrim's smock, with sandals on his feet, a mantle on his shoulders, a staff with a cross in his hand and a belt around his waist. He is given a roll of parchment and wallet, along with some bread and a bottle of water, and dressed and equipped as a medieval pilgrim setting off to visit Jerusalem. In some Encampments, he wears a large floppy hat with a scallop shell on the front.

✳ As the pilgrim arrives at the door of the lodge room, a trumpet is sounded, and he is challenged by an officer of the Encampment known as the Equerry. He steps outside the closed door of the lodge room to test that the candidate is ready for the forthcoming ceremony. Masons call this process confirming that the candidate is "properly prepared".

✝ The Equerry asks, "Who comes there?"

✝ The candidate answers, "A pilgrim, on his travels to the holy city, hearing of a Knights Templar Encampment, has come with a hope of being admitted."

The Equerry then asks if the pilgrim has come to the Encampment of his own free will and what he wants of this body of knights. The pilgrim, who is accompanied by a guide who prompts his answers, is instructed to say that he has crossed the wilderness of Judea and been exposed to great danger. He has been rescued by a worthy knight, who traveled with him and promised him protection and safe conduct to the holy city of Jerusalem. The pilgrim is then told to say that, following this experience, he has decided to devote his life to the service of the poor and the sick, and to pray for both his own sins and those of all people.

The candidate is next tested to prove that he is already a Royal Arch Mason (a Freemason who has successfully completed the Masonic degree of the Holy Royal Arch of Jerusalem). He does this by giving the sign and word of a Royal Arch Mason to the Equerry. He then has to confirm that while acting as a Royal Arch

Mason he has worked on the Second Temple (the Degree of the Royal Arch involves acting out the rebuilding of the Second Temple under Zerubbabel). Once this testing is complete, the candidate is told to wait while the Encampment decides what to do about his request.

Carlile says that the candidate is then allowed into the lodge room, but at the entrance he is stopped and a "rough saw" is placed against his forehead by an officer called the Second Captain. As the candidate looks around the Encampment he sees a body of knights, all wearing white mantles with red crosses upon them, also wearing white caps and bearing swords.

He taken in turn to the First Captain and the Grand Commander (the titles of officers of the Masonic Encampment) who repeat, in front of the body of knights, the test questions that the pilgrim has already answered outside the door of the lodge room. The pilgrim is then ordered to kneel on both knees, while the Grand Prelate (another officer of the Encampment) repeats this prayer:

> O Emmanuel, our great heavenly captain, look down, we beseech thee, on this encampment of thy devoted servants, and impart thy holy Spirit to the candidate now before us, that he may become a good and faithful soldier in thy service, and be worthy of thy acceptance and salvation.[14]

As the Prelate finishes this prayer, the knights chant in unison "So mote it be."

Now the Grand Commander tells the pilgrim that he has to face a trial of his faith. This will take the form of symbolic pilgrimage around the lodge room. But before this, he is taken to the West of the lodge room and told to kneel on both knees, with his face to the East. A copy of the New Testament is placed in his hands, and Carlile reports that he then repeats this obligation:

> I, ___, [The Aspirant's name is inserted here] in the presence of the Holy Trinity, and in memory of St. John of Jerusalem, that first faithful soldier and Martyr in Christ Jesus, do most solemnly promise and swear, that I will never illegally reveal the secrets of a Knight Templar to a Royal Arch Mason, nor to any person beneath the dignity of this noble order; nor aid in the installation of a Knight Templar unless five are present, myself included, under the penalty of all my former obligations.[15]

Once the candidate has taken this first part of his obligation, his pilgrim's staff is taken away, and the Grand Commander gives him a sword instead, saying:

> In the name of the Father, Son, and Holy Ghost, I arm you with this sword, as a distinguishing mark of our approbation; and I am persuaded that you will only employ it in the defense of the gospel of our Lord and Saviour Jesus Christ, against all those who may oppose the same.[16]

Now, while holding the sword in one hand and a copy of the New Testament in the other, the candidate is told to repeat these words to complete his obligation:

I swear, that, with this the sword of my faith, I will guard and defend the tomb and sepulchre of our Lord and Saviour Jesus Christ, against all Jews, Turks, Infidels, and Heathens, and other opposers of the gospel.

I do furthermore swear, that I will never knowingly draw the blood of a Brother Knight Templar, nor cause it to be drawn in wrath; but will espouse his cause, knowing it to be just, though I should endanger my own life. Even when princes are engaged in war, I will not forget the duty which I owe him as a brother. If ever I willfully violate this my solemn compact, as a Brother Knight Templar, may my skull be sawn asunder with a rough saw, my brains taken out and put in a charger to be consumed by the scorching sun, and my skull in another charger, in memory of St. John of Jerusalem, that faithful soldier of our Lord and Saviour. If ever I willfully deviate from this my solemn obligation, may my light be put out from among men, as that of Judas Iscariot was for betraying his Lord and Master.[17]

At this point in the ritual the candidate's sword is taken away, and he is given a human skull to hold instead. He then goes on to say:

Furthermore, may the soul that once inhabited this skull, as the representative of St. John the Baptist, appear against me in the day of judgment: so help me God, and keep me steadfast in this my solemn obligation of a Knight Templar.[18]

The candidate is told to place the skull in center of a triangular altar. Once he has done so, his sword is given back to him.

Carlile reports that the Grand Prelate then speaks as follows:

Pilgrim, thou hast craved admission to pass through our solemn ceremonies, and enter the asylum of our encampment by the sandals, staff, and scrip I judge thee to be a child of humility: charity and hospitality are the grand characteristics of this most Christian order. In the character of Knights Templar, we are bound to give alms to the poor and weary pilgrims travelling from afar, to succour the needy, feed the hungry, clothe the naked, and bind up the wounds of the afflicted.

As you are desirous of enlisting in this noble and glorious warfare, lay aside the staff and take up the sword, fighting manfully thy way, and with valour running thy course: and may the Almighty, who is a strong tower and defence to all those who put their trust in him, be thy support and thy salvation.

I now place in your hand a lighted taper, and admonish you to perambulate the encampment five turns in solemn meditation; and if you have any prejudice or enmity with any Christian man, as a qualification for further honours, it is necessary you should forgive, otherwise fly to the desert; and rather than appear unworthily among us, shun the knights of this order.[19]

Once the candidate has completed five circuits of the lodge room, following a route which is the shape of an equilateral triangle, he is taken to the East of the lodge room, where an altar is placed with a veiled object standing in its center. The veil is removed to show a Christian cross, and at that moment the burden, which the candidate has been carrying on his back since he first entered the lodge room, is cut away from his back and falls to the floor. As the candidate feels the weight fall away, the Grand Prelate says:

> Receive the Lord's yoke, for it is easy and light, and will bring rest to your soul.[20]

The pilgrim then removes his rough smock and is dressed in the white mantle and red cross of a Templar.

He next kneels in front of the Grand Commander, who takes a sword and lays it on each of his shoulders in turn and then on his head, with the words:

> I hereby install you a Masonic Knight Hospitaller of St. John of Jerusalem, Palestine, Rhodes, and Malta, and also a Knight Templar.[21]

The Grand Commander then takes the candidate by the hand, saying:

> Rise, Sir Knight A.B.; receive a hearty welcome into the Christian Order, which will be ever ready to defend and protect you.[22]

before he addresses the candidate thus:

> I now invest you with the paraphernalia of the order.

> First, I clothe you with a mantle. Receive it as the Lord's yoke; for it is easy and light, and will bring rest to your soul. As a habit, it is of little worth, and we promise you nothing but bread and water.

> Secondly, I invest you with apron, sash, and jewel. The emblems within the triangle, the star on the sash and the Maltese cross jewel, you will have explained in the lecture.

> Lastly, I present you with a shield and sword, which, in the hand of a valiant and Christian Knight, is endowed with three most excellent qualities. Its hilt with Justice; its blade with Fortitude; its point with Mercy; which gives this important lesson: that having faith in the justice of our cause we must press forward with undaunted fortitude, ever remembering to extend the Point of Mercy to a fallen foe.

> I shall now make you acquainted with the signs, words, and tokens, and our Grand Herald will then proclaim your installation.[23]

The signs and passwords are then given to the newly made knight, and the layout of the lodge room is explained. He is told about the Encampment and its furniture, which Carlile says are:

> First, the three Equilateral Triangles which represent the Trinity in unity, in the centre of which is placed the omnipotent and all seeing eye.

> Second, the figure of St. John of Jerusalem holding out the Cup of Salvation to all true believers.

> Third, the Cock which is a memento to Peter.

> Fourth, the Lamb.

Fifth, the Cross on Mount Calvary.

Sixth, the Five Lights of the New Testament, as emblematical of the birth, life, death, resurrection, and ascension of the blessed Redeemer.

Seventh, the Sword and Sceptre.

Eighth, the Star which appeared at the birth of Jesus.

Ninth, the Ladder with the Five steps.

Tenth, the Saw.

Eleventh, the Sepulchre and Gospels.

And Twelfth, the Cup.[24]

According to Carlile, Grand Commander then explains the significance of the seven agonies of Jesus, saying:

First, that which He experienced in the Garden of Gethsemane.

Second, being seized as a thief or assassin.

Third, His being scourged by the order of Pontius Pilate.

Fourth, the placing on His head a crown of thorns.

Fifth, the mockery and derision of the Jews by putting on Him a scarlet robe, and a reed in His hand as a sceptre.

Sixth, nailing Him to a cross ; and

Seventh, the piercing of His side.[25]

Finally, Carlile tells us, the candidate's installation as a Knight Templar is proclaimed three times by the Grand Herald, and he is offered a ritual meal of bread and wine, in commemoration of the Lord's Supper, with all the other Knights in the Encampment sharing a piece of bread and a drink from the cup of brotherly love.

In his introduction to the Second Part of the *Manual of Freemasonry*, Carlile says:

I can readily believe that Masonry has truly emanated from the ancient mysteries of Egypt and other countries . . . Indeed, I cannot otherwise account for the present character and existence of Masonry. To believe otherwise, I must believe that which I do not believe, that some one in modern times, or a hundred years ago, has understood the spirit and revelation of the Bible . . . In the degrees of Masonry, we begin with the Entered Apprentice, which signifies a beginning to learn. Then comes the Fellow-Craft, which signifies something learnt and applied under the direction of a Master. The degree of Master implies a capability to teach or to direct instruction. The Royal Arch completes the philosophic character, and is the acme of the Masonry of the present Grand Lodge. And all that the Templar degrees . . . can add, is a new form of the allegory . . .

Masonry has been considered complete in the Royal Arch Degree, and even in the Master's Degree; but the spirit of sectarianism, so difficult to be kept out of human systems of philosophy, has created new degrees, under the distinction of Christian or Cross Degrees, originating the various ancient systems of knighthood as knights of the various colored crosses, Knights Templar, Knights of Malta, etcetera. These degrees of orders of knighthood were certainly at one time engaged in active and cruel warfare with the followers of Mahomet, and were beaten in the end; but there is a higher and moral or mental distinction applicable to the whole fraternity, and that is, the better sense of symbolical philosophy, in which the cross is understood as, the great symbol of science; the enemies of the cross, as the tyrants who seek to subdue the mind of man, and subject it to superstition; and the knights, or soldiers of the cross, as the scholars of the earth chivalrously warring with ignorance and superstition, and exposing themselves to all the dangers and sufferings consequent thereon. This view leaves us a true picture of human nature; and as we go on to subdue superstition, we shall be enabled to make a beautiful development of ancient symbolical mythology, and to unlock and open the correct history of the past with the key of science, or those cross keys of physical and moral science—the keys of life and death, of heaven and hell, the key-stone of Royal Arch Masonry . . .

The advent of the Jewish Messiah, the advent of Christ, and the advent of a reasonable state of society, in which mystery and superstition shall yield to plain practical science, in the constitution of the human mind, are to be one and the same reality, the moral of the mystery of Judaism, Christianity, and Masonry . . . This is the key to the mystery of Judaism, of Christianity, and of Masonry . . .

The spirit of the warfare among the cross degrees of Masonry, means a warfare with superstition and mystery. The meaning of the church militant is lost to those who have made a mystery of Christianity, without retaining the revelation. The church militant is the church of people fighting against error, mystery, superstition, idolatry, with no other weapon than revelation, knowledge, reason, where that is sharp enough. The sword of steel should never be used but on the defensive. I claim the distinction of having been the best and most enduring soldier of Jesus Christ that the church has produced within these last fifteen hundred years, a true and trusty Knight Templar, using the right weapons in the right way.

I read from the Knight Templar, and Masonic tomb-stones, in the ruins of the Chapel of Holyrood House, at Edinburgh, that Masonry has been a pure, though mysterious, descent from the ancient mysteries; retained in letter, practised in ceremony, but not understood in revelation. In the Antiquarian Museum of that city, I saw specimens of the cross dug up in Scotland, that were wreathed with symbols of science, and evidently older than the Christian era . . . The field of ancient science, which a true knowledge of mythology opens to our view, is the only redemption we have from present superstition. Strong minds, by their own scientific perceptions, may see through superstition; but the multitude of this day is not strong of mind, and wants careful direction to abate its fears, to appease its alarms, and to unfold to its understanding of the realities of past, present, and future.[26]

This, then, is how Richard Carlile portrayed Templar Masonry in the early nineteenth century. The ceremony he describes is somewhat similar to the modern one

I underwent when I joined the Preceptory of St. George Aboyne, but Carlile has not mentioned certain unspoken key elements of the ritual that I had noticed when I was initiated, such as the symbolic role of the equilateral triangle within the Order. In Carlile's account, the triangle only receives passing mention, such as when he reports that the candidate places the human skull on a triangular altar, or is taken on a triangular route of pilgrimage round the lodge room. In modern Templar ritual the symbol of the triangle, or delta as it is often called, plays a much more important role. I decided to check through Carlile's ritual to see if there were any other mentions of the triangle. I found this statement, which describes part of the ritual of opening of the Encampment.

> The swords of the Grand Commander and the two captains are then placed in the form of a triangle, on the floor, opposite to the Grand Commander. All the other Knights sheath their swords.[27]

This was something I had not seen in modern ritual, but Carlile had recorded the ritual in England. Did it differ from Early Scottish Templar degrees? To check this, I needed to look at early Scottish ritual. But where should I look? The website of the Great Priory of Scotland seemed a good place to start, and it did give some clues.

The Early Grand Rite of Templar Masonry

The Great Priory's website has a history section, which has some information about the creation of early Templar Encampments. It says:

> In October 1779, Archibald, Earl of Eglinton, who was at that time the Grand Master of Lodge Mother Kilwinning, issued a charter for a new lodge to be formed in Dublin to be called the "High Knight Templars of Ireland Lodge". This lodge became the Early Grand Encampment of Ireland, and when Scottish Grand Lodge issued a directive in October 1800 "prohibiting and discharging its daughters to hold any meetings above the degree of Master Mason, under penalty of forfeiture of their Charter," many Scottish masons applied to the Early Grand Encampment of Ireland for charters, to work the Knight Templar degrees in Scotland.[28]

The ritual that the Early Grand Encampment of Ireland worked (acted out) became known as the E.G. Rite (for "Early Grand Rite") and was adopted in Scotland by a group called the Early Grand Mother Encampment of Scotland. I had a late-eighteenth-century copy of this ritual in my collection. It had been given to me by a venerable old Brother when I spoke at Lodge Lauden-Kilwinning in Ayrshire. The battered little ritual booklet had been privately published in Ayrshire by a Masonic Knight Templar (KT), Sir Knt. W.W. Walker. It contained a ritual of a degree of Knight Templar, called the 29th degree in the series of E.G. Rite, which was worked (acted out) under Charters issued by the Early Grand

Encampment of Ireland, itself a body which had first been chartered by Lodge Mother Kilwinning.

The Rite of "The Pilgrim"

Before a Mason can take the degree of Knight, he must first take the 28th E.G. degree, which is called The Pilgrim. Fortunately, the ritual for this degree was also included in the booklet I was given. The preamble to the 28th degree ritual says:

> The Pilgrim is the Twenty-Eighth Degree of the E.G. Rite, and is conferred in an Encampment of K.T., to which degree it is introductory, occupying, in fact, a position towards it similar, to that of the Ex. and Super Ex. towards the Royal Arch. The candidate represents a religious devotee of the Middle Ages, whose conscience being pricked by remorse for acts which were but too prevalent in those days of broil and bloodshed, resolves, by making a pilgrimage to those places in the Holy Land associated in the popular belief with the Saviour's suffering, to clear the page of his past life of all stain. He is dressed in a loose robe girt round the waist with a cord, a Palmer's hat on his head, a burden on his back, sandals on his feet, a staff in his hand, and hoodwinked [blindfolded].[29]

The password the candidate gives to prove himself a worthy pilgrim is the same one I learned to give before I was allowed to take the symbolic route of a pilgrim within a modern Templar Encampment. And this version of the ritual predated the formation of my Mother Preceptory, in 1794, by some four years. The ritual I worked, as part of a single ceremony, had stayed true to earlier workings. The 1790 ritual of the pilgrimage is familiar yet different. The titles of the officers are different, and the detailed words have changed, but the eighteenth-century pilgrim, too, meets with four officers, each of whom challenges him.

First, the Knight Marshal says:

> Pilgrim, the undertaking upon which you have entered you will find to be a difficult and a trying one, and one which will tax your powers of endurance to the uttermost. I do not say this to discourage you, far from it; for many as the difficulties are which are to be surmounted, and trying the hardships to be endured, the goal, when reached, will more than compensate for the difficulty in reaching it. And now, Pilgrim, let me recommend you to put your trust in Him, who, in His own body, offered up the expiatory sacrifice on Mount Calvary, and so wish you God speed upon your journey.[30]

The blindfolded candidate is then led around round the first leg of the conclave and various obstacles are put in his way to make his path difficult. In this way he is led to the Keeper of the First Caravanserie (the name given by the Encampment to a resting place for pilgrims). He is introduced to the First Keeper, who says this to him:

Pilgrim, I greet you. Silver and gold have I none, but such as I have give I unto you. [He then gives the candidate a little salt or some other bitter-tasting stuff before continuing.] On our pilgrimage through life we must all, if we wish to succeed, practice self-denial, and accustom ourselves to humiliation in a good cause. We must expect to taste of the bitterness of life before we taste the sweets, which can only be earned by conscious rectitude and untiring struggles in the cause of well-doing. Pilgrim, I wish you God speed upon your journey.[31]

The candidate now continues on a second leg of his symbolic pilgrimage. Further obstacles are placed in his path, so that in his blind state he stumbles. The Knight Marshal, who is leading him by the arm, makes sure he only falters and does not fall. He is led to the Second Caravanserie and introduced to its Keeper, who says:

Pilgrim, I greet you. Worldly affluence belong not us, but such as I have give I unto you. [He gives the candidate a small crust of dry bread and a cup of water to eat and drink before resuming.] Accustomed as you have been from the outset to encounter difficulty, you experience less the roughness of the way. In like manner the palate, tempered by the bitter sweets of adversity, better appreciates the comparative sweets of mediocrity. The slight advance you have made will the more encourage you to proceed, and so I wish you God speed upon your journey.[32]

The candidate is now led on the third leg of his pilgrimage, and this time no obstacles are placed in his path. He arrives at the Third Caravanserie, and is introduced to its Keeper, who says to him:

Pilgrim, I greet you. The worst of your pilgrimage is now over, and the goal for which you have striven appears in view. You have tasted the bitter though wholesome cup of adversity, and have already made some advance to a better condition. And now, such of the sweets of this life as I have give I unto you. [The Keeper gives the candidate a glass of fine wine and a piece of fresh bread, before continuing.] And now, Pilgrim, in the hope that this further advance will stimulate you to still greater exertions, I wish you God speed towards the completion of your journey.[33]

By now the candidate has returned to the West of the lodge room. Still blindfolded, he is led to the East and stood before the altar, on which is placed a human skull and a pair of crossed thigh bones at the foot of an upright cross.

The Prelate (another officer of the Encampment) then reads from the Gospel of St. John, saying:

Then delivered he Him therefore unto them to be crucified. And they took Jesus and led Him away. And He bearing His cross went forth into a place called the place of a skull, which is called in the Hebrew Golgotha, where they crucified Him and two others with Him, on either side one, and Jesus in the midst.[34]

When the Prelate has finished the reading, he asks the candidate these questions:

Q.   Who comes here?
A.   A pilgrim penitent traveling from afar, who wishes to visit the sacred places

endeared to him by his religion, and to cast the sins and follies of a life-time at the foot of the Cross where his Savior suffered.

Q. How am I to know that you are what you profess yourself to be?

A. I am in possession of the Pilgrim's pass.

Q. Then advance and give it.

A. The candidate gives the password. [Which he had been given outside the lodge room once he had proved himself by sign and word to be a Royal Arch Mason.]

At the bidding of the Excellent Commander (the Worshipful Master of the Templar Encampment) the candidate now takes an obligation to keep the secrets of the degree, under the penalty of having his skull split at the jaw should he unlawfully reveal them. Then, still blindfolded, he is instructed to kiss the skull. When he has done so, the blindfold is whipped away and he is restored to light. As he sees the brightly lit cross, his burden is released from his back. Before explaining the secret grips and passwords of the degree to the candidate, the Excellent Commander says:

> You here behold Mortality resting upon Divinity—a human skull upon the human bones. Let this ever remind you that a faithful reliance on the truths herein revealed will afford you consolation in the gloomy hours of death, and assure you inevitable happiness in the world to come.[35]

PASSING THE TEMPLAR VEILS

The Pilgrim is now entitled at some later date to take the 29th Degree of the Early Grand Rite, which is that of a Knight Templar. His does this by a ceremony known as "Passing the Veils." These Veils symbolically represent the various levels of separation from the Holy of Holies. Each Veil takes the Aspirant a step closer to the secret sanctuary at the center of the Temple, and only worthy priests may pass them. In this degree, the Veils are three in number, and are laid out with each Veil placed at the point of an equilateral triangle that is set on the floor of the Encampment. The base of the triangle lies towards the West and the apex points to the East. A Veil is placed at each corner of the triangle before the pilgrim enters. Each Veil has a guardian, or Captain, who addresses the pilgrim as I explain below.

This Degree sheds some light on the puzzle of the triangular pilgrimage, which I was curious about, as in the previous degree the three Caravanseries had been placed at the points of the triangle, which forms the layout of the Encampment. Now the three Veils were substituted for the three Caravanseries. The preamble of the degree of says:

> The Knight Templar is the Twenty-Ninth Degree of the E.G. Rite. It is the principal and ruling degree of the Black or Encampment Series. The meeting is called an Encampment, the symbol of which is a Triangle.[36]

The Pilgrim approaches the door of the lodge room and is challenged by the Herald, who asks for the password. The Herald then announces the Pilgrim to the Knight Receiver, who is inside the lodge room. The Knight Receiver also interrogates the Pilgrim and asks again for the password. He then reports to the Excellent Commander, after which the Pilgrim is blindfolded and admitted to the Encampment. The Knight Receiver leads the Pilgrim to the First Veil.

The Captain of the First Veil says, "Who comes here? Who approaches the First Veil of the Temple?"

The Knight Receiver answers, "A worthy Pilgrim, who having visited the sacred shrines and holy places, and offered up his devotions where his Savior suffered, hearing of a Knight Templar Encampment in this place, humbly solicits the privilege of finding rest with the Veils of the Temple."

The Captain of the First Veil replies "How does he expect to enter within the First Veil of the Temple?"

The Knight Receiver answers, "By benefit of the password belonging to that Veil." The Pilgrim gives the password of the 28th Degree and is told, "Enter within the First Veil."

This Veil is colored blue; being "hoodwinked" (blindfolded), the Pilgrim cannot see this, although the other Knights of the Encampment can. The candidate can only feel the cloth of the Veil brushing against him as he pushes through the gauze. The Pilgrim is then led to the Second Veil, which is colored red.

The Captain of the Second Veil says, "Who comes here? Who approaches the Second Veil of the Temple?"

The Knight Receiver answers, "A worthy Pilgrim, who having visited the sacred shrines and holy places, and offered up his devotions where his Savior suffered, hearing of a Knight Templar Encampment in this place, humbly solicits the privilege of finding rest within the Veils of the Temple."

The Captain of the Second Veil replies, "How does he expect to enter within the Second Veil of the Temple?"

The Knight Receiver answers, "By benefit of the password. belonging to that Veil." The Pilgrim gives the password of the 28th Degree and is told, "Enter within the Second Veil."

The ritual repeats again for the Third Veil, which is colored black. But as the Pilgrim is about to push through it, the Captain of the Third Veil takes his sword and rips the Veil from end to end so the pilgrim first hears the ripping sound and realizes that he does not have to push his way through it. The Captain of the Third Veil says, "At the instant when Emmanuel died, behold the Veil of the Temple was rent in twain from the top to the bottom."

The Pilgrim is now taken to the inner sanctum of the Encampment, known as the Asilium, which is veiled off from the rest of the Encampment with a white Veil. Here he kneels to take his obligation as a Knight Templar. Once this is done, his blindfold is removed, and he can see that he is kneeling within an equilateral triangle made up of twelve candles. He is given a cup of wine and told to drink a toast "to the Memory of Simon the Cyrenean." The Prelate then reads the story of Judas Iscariot from the Gospel of Matthew; he finishes by telling the candidate to snuff out the candle which is in front of him, saying: "And thus, if unworthy, may your light be put out amongst men."[37]

At this point, the ritual has more to say about the equilateral triangle, which in this version of the ritual is called a Delta. The Prelate continues reading from the Acts of the Apostles, which tells a story of Peter drawing lots to choose a replacement for Judas and the choice falling on Matthias. As the reading finishes, the Prelate orders the candidate to relight the candle, and as he does, the Excellent Commander says to him:

Pilgrim, upon being brought to light you saw the Encampment illuminated by twelve lights arranged in the form of a Delta. The lights represent the twelve apostles, the one fainter than the other representing Judas Iscariot. The form in which they are placed symbolizes the Christian idea of Deity, and is also the sign of the Encampment. You also by their aid behold this coffer with thirty Pieces of Silver, the sight of which now, and the remembrance hereafter, should ever impress upon you a sense of horror and detestation of deceit and treachery. [Pointing to the human skull and crossed thigh bones which are on the altar.] Behold these emblems of mortality, once animated like ourselves, but now have ceased to act or think; their vital energies are extinct, and all their power of life has ceased its operation. To such a state, Sir Knights, are we all hastening; therefore let us embrace the present opportunity, that when our frail bodies, like this memento, shall become cold and inanimate, our disembodied spirits may soar aloft to regions of life and light eternal.

And now, Pilgrim, by virtue of the power and authority vested in me as Excellent Commander of this Encampment, I dub and create thee a Knight of the Temple of Jerusalem. [He then touches the candidate with his sword on the head and shoulder, and the Marshal pours a little wine upon his head. The candidate is then raised to his feet, and stands before the altar.][38]

The new Knight Templar is dressed in a white mantle with a red cross on the shoulder, equipped with spurs, and given a ring. The other Knights form a circle around the Delta of candles, and the new knight stands at the center of both the circle and the Delta as he is presented with his sword of knighthood. The ceremony closes with the Herald blowing a blast on his trumpet and saying, "Hear ye, hear ye, Sir Knights all, by order of the Excellent Commander. I proclaim Sir Knight A. B. a Knight of the Order of the Temple of Jerusalem."

Before the Encampment is closed, the Excellent Commander makes the following speech to the new Knight Templar, who is still standing in the center of the lighted Delta of candles:

In conclusion, let me enjoin upon you the serious study of the history and aims of the Order of the Temple, and particularly of the Early Grand Rite, the oldest as well as the only legitimate representatives of the Templars of old, that not only might you have faith in the purity and antiquity of our Early Grand system, but be able at all times to show to our enemies that you have a reason for the faith within you. I now congratulate you upon your initiation into our Order. You can take your place as it will be shown you by the Usher.[39]

This ritual contained many of the features of the ritual which had made me a Knight Templar, and while by no means identical, was close enough to convince me that the ritual still in use in Scotland dated back to at least the eighteenth century. There were two parts to the ceremony. The first part involved a symbolic pilgrimage, and the second a reception as a knight. But there were also differences. The English ritual reported by Carlile placed much less emphasis on explaining the symbol of the Equilateral Triangle or Delta than the Scottish ritual. The Early Grand Rite of the Mother Encampment of Scotland had said that the Delta was a symbol of the Christian idea of Deity, as well as being the sign of the Encampment.

The Mystery of the Sacred Delta

I had also seen this idea of a Sacred Delta expressed somewhere else, in the ritual of the 13th Degree of the Ancient and Accepted Rite, as published by Charles McClenachan in New York in 1867. I checked it out and found this detailed explanation of its meaning, which I had noticed in the Early Grand Rite, in a historical lecture in the Masonic Degree known as The Royal Arch of Enoch:

This is the history and legend of this degree. Enoch, the son of Jared, was the sixth in descent from Adam. Filled with the love and fear of God, he strove to lead men in the way of honor and duty. In a vision the Deity appeared to him in the visible shape of a pure golden triangle, and said to him, "Enoch, thou hast longed to know my true name: arise and follow me, and thou shalt know it."

Enoch, accepting his vision as an inspiration, journeyed in search of the mountain he had seen in his dream, until, weary of the search, he stopped in the land of Canaan, then already populous with the descendants of Adam, and there employed workmen; and with the help of his son Methuselah, he excavated nine apartments, one above the other, and each roofed with an arch, as he had seen in his dream, the lowest being hewn out of the solid rock. In the crown of each arch he left a narrow aperture, closed with a square stone, and over the upper one he built a modest temple, roofless and of huge unhewn stones, to the Grand Architect of the Universe.

Upon a triangular plate of gold, inlaid with many precious gems, he engraved the ineffable name of God, and sank the plate into one face of a cube of agate.

None knew of the deposit of the precious treasure; and, that it might remain undiscovered, and survive the Flood, which it was known to Enoch would soon overwhelm the world in one vast sea of mire, he covered the aperture, and the stone that closed it and the great ring of iron used to raise the stone, with the granite pavement of his primitive temple.

Then, fearing that all knowledge of the arts and sciences would be lost in the universal flood, he built two great columns upon a high hill—one of brass, to resist water, and one of granite, to resist fire. On the granite column was written in hieroglyphics a description of the subterranean apartments; on the one of brass, the rudiments of the arts and sciences.

The granite column was overturned and swept away, and worn to a shapeless mass by the Deluge, but that of brass stood firm, and was found by Noah. Thenceforward the true name of God remained unknown until he said unto Moses in Egypt, when he ordered him to go to Pharaoh, and cause him to send forth the children of Israel out of Egypt: "I am that which I was and shall be: I am the God of thy fathers; the God of Abraham, of Isaac . . . and of Jacob. Thus shalt thou say unto the children of Israel, HE who is hath sent me unto you. I am the Lord, that appeared to Abraham, to Isaac, and to Jacob by my name AL-SHEDI but my name—I did not show them."

Moses engraved the ineffable name upon a plate of gold, and deposited it in the ark of the covenant. Moses made the name known to Aaron and Joshua, and afterwards it was made known to the chief priests. The word being composed of consonants only, its true pronunciation was soon lost, but the word still remained in the ark; and in the time of Othniel in a battle against the King of Syria, those who bore the ark were slain, and the ark fell to the ground. After the battle, the men of Israel, searching for it, were led to it by the roaring of a lion, which, crouching by it, had guarded it, holding the golden key in its mouth. Upon the approach of the High-priest and Levites, he laid down the key, and withdrew. Hence, upon the golden key worn by the treasurer, you see the initials of these words: "In are leonis verbum inveni"—"In the lion's mouth I found the word." This plate of gold was melted down, and made into an image of Dagon by the Philistines, who took it in battle.

David intended to build a temple to God but bequeathed the enterprise to Solomon, his son, and Solomon selected a place near Jerusalem; but finding overthrown columns of Enoch's temple, and supposing them to be the ruins of a heathen temple, and not wishing to select a desecrated spot, selected Mount Moriah for the site of his Temple to the true God. Under this temple he built a secret vault, the approach to which was through eight other vaults, all under ground, and to which a long and narrow passage led under the king's palace. In the ninth apartment was placed a twisted column of white marble, on which it was intended to place the ark, and in this apartment he held his private conferences with King Hiram of Tyre and Hiram Abif, they only knowing the way by which it was approached. Solomon proposed to erect a Temple of Justice, and selected as a site the spot where Enoch's temple had stood, and to that end directed that the fallen columns and rubbish should be removed. Gibulum, Joabert, and Stolkin were selected to survey the ground and lay off the foundations.[40]

So, if its ritual is to be believed, the Early Grand Rite, which is no longer worked, claims to be the oldest, as well as the only legitimate, representative of the Templars of old, and the Delta shape of the Masonic Templar Encampment is based on a tradition which goes back five thousand years to the prophet Enoch.

But is there any proof for this fantastic claim? Or is it just a nice ritual story that is enjoyable to act out? It seemed unlikely that the claim is true, because the ritual dates from about four hundred years after the destruction of the original Order.

Could a link have survived? I had to find out.

CONCLUSIONS

Its traditional history, which is given in the lectures of the Degree, says that Templar Masonry is a continuation of the original Knights Templar, and that the Masons inherited their ideas from the Templars as an underground tradition. But is there any support for this idea beyond the ritual?

The ritual currently worked in modern Scottish Templar Encampments differs from the English ritual published by Richard Carlile in the early nineteenth century. However, the modern ritual retains many references to the symbol of the triangle or Delta, which can also be found in late eighteenth-century Scottish Templar ritual. For example, it keeps the distinctive structure of a two-part ceremony, which begins with a symbolic pilgrimage and is followed by a reception as a knight.

The Early Grand Rite workings of Scotland claim that they alone are the "only legitimate representatives of the Templars of old," which Carlile's early English ritual does not. But is this a legitimate claim?

To be able to judge, I needed to know much more about the original Knights Templar. My next step had to be to look at the latest academic views on the history of the original Knights Templar. In the next chapter, you'll see what I found out. I think you'll agree that the facts are far more shocking than any legend—though many of our most enduring legends, including the Grail Quest, found their way into Templar lore. Turn the page and let's find out how.

CHAPTER 2

WILL THE REAL KNIGHTS TEMPLAR PLEASE STAND UP!

THE INVENTION OF HOLY VIOLENCE

In 1095 the Byzantine emperor, Alexius I, sent an appeal for help to Pope Urban II. The emperor's lands in Asia Minor and the Greek Christian churches in those lands had been overrun by the Muslim Seljuk Turks. Pope Urban, seeing political advantage in rescuing the Greek church, made a speech calling on Western Christian knights to make war on the Turks.

On November 27, 1095, Pope Urban II invented the concept of the crusade in a speech made to the Council of Clermont. His words were recorded by Fulcher of Chartres in the *Gesta Francorum Jerusalem Expugnantium*; here is an extract:

> The Turks and Arabs have attacked [and] occupied more and more of the lands of Christians. They have killed and captured many, and have destroyed the churches and devastated the empire [of Byzantium]. If you permit them to continue thus . . . with impunity, the faithful of God will be much more widely attacked by them. On this account I, or rather the Lord, beseech you as Christ's heralds to publish this everywhere and to persuade all people of whatever rank, foot-soldiers and knights, poor and rich, to carry aid promptly to those Christians and to destroy that vile race from the lands of our friends. I say this to those who are present, it is meant also for those who are absent. Moreover, Christ commands it.[41]

With God clearly on Urban's side, he was able to make an unusual offer to the souls of any volunteers. He went on to say:

> All who die by the way, whether by land or by sea, or in battle against the pagans, shall have immediate remission of sins. This I grant them through the power of God with which I am invested . . . Let those who . . . have been robbers, now become

knights. Let those who have been fighting against their brothers and relatives now fight ... against the barbarians. Let those who have been serving as mercenaries for small pay now obtain the eternal reward ... Accordingly undertake this journey for the remission of your sins, with the assurance of the imperishable glory of the kingdom of heaven.[42]

This was an offer few Christians could resist. They were being offered the blessing of Christ to go to the rich lands of the East to plunder, rob, and kill, with the certainty that if, by some mishap, they happened to get killed themselves, they would go straight to heaven. The plan worked. By 1099 Jerusalem was in the hands of the crusaders, and the Turks were driven back. But Alexius didn't get his lands back. Instead, four new Crusader Kingdoms, loyal to the papacy, were set up. This didn't solve the problems of the region, however, and insurgents caused all sorts of trouble. Most of the crusaders returned home, laden with plunder, while those who died in the East as victims of battle, fatigue, or disease moved on to a glorious afterlife in heaven. A few die-hard survivors, such as Hugh de Payns and Godfrey de Saint-Omer, stayed on in Jerusalem. In due course, they moved on towards the logical conclusion of Pope Urban's idea, and created a New Knighthood, the Knights Templar.

MYSTERIOUS BEGINNINGS

When did the Templars begin? It's a simple question to ask, but not so simple to answer. There are two acknowledged academic experts on the subject. One is Dr. Malcolm Barber, Reader in Medieval History at the University of Reading, the other his one-time student Dr. Helen Nicholson, now a senior lecturer in Medieval History at Cardiff University.

In his classic 1994 study of the Templars, *The New Knighthood*, Barber quotes a Russian abbot named Daniel, writing of his pilgrimage to Jerusalem in 1106. Of Galilee he said:

> This place is very dreadful and dangerous. Seven rivers flow from this town of Bashan and great reeds grow along these rivers and many tall palm trees stand about the town like a dense forest ... [It is] terrible and difficult of access for here live fierce pagan Saracens who attack travellers at the fords on these rivers. And lions are found here in great numbers.[43]

Dr. Barber says the Templars were formed to address King Baldwin of Jerusalem's problem of providing protection for pilgrims such as Abbot Daniel. But, although Daniel's fears provide a motive for creating a protective force, it does not tell us *when* the Templars were formed. Barber is candid when trying to put a date to this event, pointing out that nobody at the time thought it important enough to record.

No contemporary thought [the Templars] sufficiently significant to record their first establishment, but three chroniclers of the second half of the twelfth century, William, Archbishop of Tyre (died *c.* 1186), Michael the Syrian, Jacobite Patriarch of Antioch (died 1199), and Walter Map, Archdeacon of Oxford (died between 1208 and 1210), writing in the light of the Order's later importance, gave versions of how this came about.[44]

Barber believes William of Tyre is the most important of these three chroniclers. He was born in Galilee in 1130, but came to Europe between about 1146 and 1165. Barber respects William as an honest source, saying that he was diligent in the way he investigated events that occurred before his lifetime, and he took the trouble to read the original sources and question people who might know. But he feels William's view of the Templars was tainted by his acute dislike of their unfair exploitation of their privileges in his own time.

Barber rates Michael the Syrian as less reliable, particularly when describing matters outside his own experience and times. But it is Walter Map—the writer furthest removed in time from the events—whom he trusts least; he recognizes Map as someone for whom a good story was more important that historical fact.

The date of 1118 for the formation of the Templars comes from William of Tyre, who was writing of events which took place twelve years before he was born. William asserts that some "noble men of knightly order, devoted to God, pious and God-fearing took vows of poverty, chastity and obedience at the hands of Warmund of Picquigny, Patriarch of Jerusalem." He names the two most important as Hugh de Payns and Godfrey de Saint Omer. These men promised to devote themselves to God's service, and, to help them in this task, they were given quarters on the southern side of what William called the "Temple of the Lord." Their benefactor was King Baldwin II of Jerusalem. William said that Baldwin granted the original Templars the right to collect some tithes to provide an income, so that they could feed and clothe themselves. In return, they were asked to maintain the pilgrims' right of way along the roads and highways and protect them against the ambushes of the thieves and attackers Abbot Daniel had so eloquently described.

Malcolm Barber says that it was probably King Baldwin who persuaded Hugh de Payns and some thirty other knights to act as guardians of the highways rather than becoming cloistered monks. But they may not have needed much persuasion, as they were already becoming steeped in the concept of holy martyrdom. (More on that shortly.) Barber is skeptical of Walter Map's version of events, which he describes as a "vignette" of a simple knight devoting himself to protecting pilgrims en route to the holy sites. To offset his skepticism about the popular chroniclers' efforts to date the beginnings of the Templars, Barber has stronger evidence to offer:

Among the early grants to the Order was one by Thierry, Count of Flanders, dated 13 September 1128, which states that it was made in the ninth year from the Order's foundation. As this grant was actually made in the presence of Hugh de Payns, it must be more reliable evidence than the year 1118 given by William of Tyre.[45]

Barber points out that by the time of William of Tyre, some fifty years after the Order's foundation, the idea of nine original founders had been burned into the Order's collective memory, and it persisted throughout the thirteenth century. He describes the apse of the important Templar church of San Bevignate at Perugia (built between 1256 and 1262) as decorated with nine stars circling three crosses. He then goes on to comment that there is a suspicious symmetry about a claim of only nine members for the first nine years. He points out that the number disagrees with the figure of thirty Knights recorded by Michael the Syrian. He adds a very persuasive piece of logic: It is extremely unlikely that the Pope would have created a new order if it could only attract such small numbers.[46]

The legend says that the nine founders of the Templars were:

Hugh de Payns, a vassal lord to Hugh of Champagne;
Godfrey de Saint Omer, the son of Hugh de Saint Omer;
Andrew de Montbard, a vassal lord to Hugh of Champagne and uncle of
        Bernard, Abbot of Clairvaux;
Payen de Montdidier, related to the rulers of Flanders;
Archambald de St. Amand, related to the rulers of Flanders and Montdidier;
Gondemar, no details known;
Rosal, no details known;
Godefroy, no details known;
Geoffroy Bisol, no details known.[47]

It also says that they spent the first nine years after taking vows living quietly in the vaults beneath Temple Mount in a place called the Stables of Solomon, and hardly venturing out to commit holy violence at all.

Legend aside, Hugh *did* eventually venture out, with a view to whipping up practical support for his plans. In 1128 he went on a fund-rising trip to the West. He started in France. First he went to a wedding in Le Mans, and then on to meet the French King Henri I, who (Barber tells us) "received him with great honour and gave him great treasures, consisting of gold and silver." Then Hugh went on to England and Scotland.

His visit to England and Scotland took place in the summer of 1128 and . . . he . . . returned to Cassel in Flanders by mid September, where, together with Godfrey of Saint Omer, he received the grants of Thierry of Flanders and his vassals.[48]

During his trip to Scotland, Hugh visited Roslin near Edinburgh, and was given land by Henri de St. Clair, Baron of Roslin, to build a Preceptory (Templar community house) in the Scottish village now known as Temple. This gift of land by a Scots laird to build support houses in the West for this radical new Order started a trend among the nobility of England. It would soon form the basis of a large commercial empire that would underpin the Order's military campaigns in the East.

The climax of Hugh's fund-rising tour was his appearance before the Council of Troyes in January 1129, at which his new Order was granted a Monastic rule to govern it. This (which came to be called "the Latin Rule") was written by Bernard, Abbot of Clairvaux (later St. Bernard) and consisted of seventy-two clauses.[49] It was important for the fledgling Order, as it conferred legitimacy on it.

Early in 1129 Hugh returned to Jerusalem and led his Knights northward to try and take Damascus. The lack of logistic support during the long siege inspired him to think about how he could use the lands his Order had been given in the West to improve its fighting ability. He decided to set up a regular support network in western Europe to provide a steady flow of new Knights, money, food, clothing, and arms.[50] In 1130 he sent one of his Brother founder-Knights, Payen de Montdidier, to England, where King Stephen granted him the right to build a whole string of new Preceptories.[51]

Developing a Theology of Aggression

The Knights Templar were a new idea in Christian thought. They represented the innovative theological concept—invented by Pope Urban II and later promoted by Bernard of Clairvaux—of holy violence. Malcolm Barber points out that this idea had taken such a hold after 1050 that it became a prime aim of the papacy to redirect men's warlike impulses towards what they regarded as "higher" goals, such as killing infidels. He comments:

> By the time that the first Templars took their vows, "holy violence" had achieved a high level of general acceptance, and the idea that laymen might achieve salvation in such a cause was well established. Indeed, the crusaders believed that the indulgence granted to them by the papacy meant a direct passport to Heaven for those who were killed in battle or who succumbed to the hardships of the journey. These circumstances help to make comprehensible what at first sight seems anomalous: the development of a fighting order of monks representing what was supposedly a pacifist religion.[52]

After the granting of their Rule, the Templars went from strength to strength. They gained the support of scores of influential landowners, and donations started to arrive from all corners of the Christian world. Bernard had convinced the Pope of the Templars' worth, and suddenly they became a fashionable cause. Funds were thrust upon them by wealthy nobles who wanted a share of the "eternal reward" without having to share in the messy business of being martyred to gain it.

Almost everyone has heard of St. Bernard. But who was the man beneath the saint's halo? Bernard of Clairvaux was an important Church figure in the period after the First Crusade, a successful young cleric and abbot of the Cistercian Order.

The Cistercian Order had been founded by a group of Benedictine monks from the abbey of Molesme in 1098, just months before the taking of Jerusalem and the death of Urban II. They said they wanted to get back to the pure and original teachings of St. Benedict, the father of Western monasticism. Benedict had established what he called a rule of life, which later became a requirement for all monastic orders. It stressed the importance of communal living and physical labor, forbade members to own property, required meals to be taken in common, and insisted that unnecessary conversation be avoided.[53]

Bernard was born near Dijon in 1090, and at the age of twenty-three he decided to join the Cistercian Order. His elder brother, the Count of Fontaine, was horrified at Bernard's decision to become a poor monk. But within a year, the count also joined the Cistercian Order, along with many other members of the Fontaine family.[54]

In 1115 the twenty-five-year-old Bernard was made Abbot of a new Abbey at Clairvaux. This abbey was built by Hugh of Champagne, who also donated lands to support it. Count Hugh had long been interested in the idea of holy violence, and had taken crusaders' vows to visit Jerusalem to support the aftermath of the First Crusade. He went out to the Holy Land in 1105, returned to Champagne in 1114, and then built Clairvaux. Hugh was fascinated by the concept of holy violence and the concept of crusader indulgences, which would allow him to enjoy fighting as a knight while being sure his place in heaven was not compromised by the violence of his knightly calling. (An indulgence was basically a get-out-out-of-jail-free card. No matter how much you sinned, if you amassed enough indulgences—conferred by the Church—you would not be sent to hell.) In 1125 he returned to Jerusalem and was so impressed with the new order of holy Knights, led by his vassal Hugh de Payns, that he joined them.[55]

Even as a new entrant to the priesthood, Bernard had identified himself with the theology of holy violence, writing of the merit of a knighthood of Christ, "by which two thousand may fight securely against him who rushes to attack with two hundred thousand."[56] When Hugh of Champagne joined the Templars, young Bernard wrote congratulating him for exchanging the position as Count for that of a holy Knight.[57] Bernard obviously had no trouble mixing knighthood with monkhood, and observed that what was needed to secure the Holy Land was "fighting knights not singing and wailing monks."[58]

Not everyone was comfortable with this idea. As Barber points out, some clerics had deep misgivings and were quick to speak out. There was deep-seated hostility to the idea of any sort of monk taking part in a crusade. Henry,

Archdeacon of Huntingdon, spoke of "a certain new monster composed from purity and corruption, namely a monk and a knight," implying that he felt such a combination was against nature.[59] This monster theme was picked up and developed by Cistercian philosopher Isaac of Etoile, who in an 1147 sermon said:

> There has sprung up a new monster, a certain new knighthood, whose Order . . . may freely despoil those who are not Christians, and butcher them religiously; but if any of them fall in such ravaging, they are called martyrs of Christ.[60]

Walter Map criticized the entire theological basis for creating the Templar Order. He pointed out that Christ had told St. Peter to pursue peace, but the Templars did not follow this teaching; instead, they used violence. He noted that, while the apostles had taken Damascus, Alexandria, and most of Europe by peaceful preaching, the Templars had lost Damascus and Alexandria by fighting.[61]

How had such a strange mix of violence and piety come about, and how had it made the Templars so influential so fast? The evidence points again to the Templars' spiritual leader, Bernard of Clairvaux. He had written their guiding Rule, and actively encouraged them by writing inspirational letters about them. But how had he found them, or how had they found him?

It all goes back to King Baldwin II of Jerusalem. King Baldwin found himself with a small group of knights who wanted to stay and defend Jerusalem, but who mainly hung around Temple Mount, where Baldwin had his court. They soaked up the power of the holy places, lived in quarters he provided, and freeloaded on his hospitality. He knew he had a problem with bandits and insurgents attacking pilgrims traveling to Jerusalem and, as we know, he got the idea of making these holy knights work for their keep by policing the local roads. In 1126, with this in mind, he wrote to Abbot Bernard, the well-known exponent of holy violence, who also happened to be the nephew of one of these Knights, and asked for help in formalizing the situation.

Malcolm Barber tells us Baldwin wrote explaining that the brothers of the Temple "desired to obtain apostolic confirmation and to have a certain rule of life," and that he was sending two of the Knights, Andrew (Bernard's uncle) and Gondemar, "in order that they might obtain approval of their order from the pontiff, and incline his spirit to initiating subsidy and help for us against the enemies of the faith." He asked if Bernard could speak in favor of this new Order of Templars with the kings and nobles of Europe, probably in the hope that somebody else would feed, clothe, and arm them. As we have seen, Bernard was happy to oblige. So that is how the Templars got the Abbot of Clairvaux as their spiritual leader.

BERNARD'S BRIGADE OF MARTYRS

In 1129 Bernard wrote *De Laudibus Novae Militiae* ("In Praise of the New Knighthood"). This was a eulogy to the Templars, exhorting the Knights to conduct themselves with courage in their several stations,[62] and took the form of a letter addressed to "my dearest Hugh [de Payns], Knight of Christ and Master of the Knighthood of Christ."[63] Nearly a hundred and eighty years later, during the trial of the Templars in France, Helen Nicholson reports that one Templar said that he owned a copy of the letter,[64] and presumably used it as a source of inspiration.

In the letter, Bernard puts forward a religious reason for creating the Templars. He said they were a new type of knighthood that had grown out of the very land which Jesus had once walked. Knights of Christ were not motivated to fight by "pride, irrationality, anger, a wish for honor and glory or a greed for power but from pure motives to defend Christendom against its relentless enemies." The new Knights dressed in the simple mantle of a monk and bore the red cross of the knight who has sworn to give his life of Christ's cause. Bernard confirmed that any member of the new knighthood preserved his soul when he was killed and preserved Christ when he murdered the enemies of the Christian faith.

Helen Nicholson explains the purpose of his letter:

> Bernard's word-play and style, . . . combine to create a powerful effect: the new Order of the Temple is an exciting new development, knights who live like monks, knights who dedicate themselves to die as martyrs for Christ's sake.[65]

Did Bernard see the Templar Order as a way of enacting the prophesy of the Book of Revelations that the martyrs of Jerusalem would be resurrected after a thousand years? If he did, his choice of symbolism was apt, as the Catholic Church defines two types of martyrdom, one red and the other white.[66]

Red martyrdom is the shedding of your blood for Christ. White martyrdom does not involve the violent taking of life, but is a total offering of your life to God, by withdrawing from the world and its allurements. A white martyr willingly gives up worldly concerns and makes his or her life a perpetual pilgrimage. The mantle of the Templars combined the white martyr's habit of Bernard's Cistercians with the red cross of a knight who is willing to die for Christ.

These martyr Knights drew their strength from the very ground that Jesus had once trod. Surely with this degree of clerical support, they knew themselves to be invincible in life and death. Bernard's reasoning gave them every cause to think so. Bernard supported the ideas of an earlier saint, Augustine of Hippo, who had written a fifth-century text called *The City of God*, which said that war could be justified as long as it was waged to enforce a Christian peace.[67] This delightful piece of circular reasoning must be a great comfort to all the victims of the holy wars it inspired. Bernard developed this idea further to demonstrate that this was exactly the sort of war the Templars were formed to fight: hence they were justified in killing anybody who got in their way, because they were doing God's will. And if they happened to get killed while carrying out God's instructions, then they were granted an immediate passport to heaven and a place among the saints.

Because the papacy had already accepted the idea of holy violence in the form of a crusade, it was hard for subordinate clergy to criticize the concept—but some did. In 1150 Peter the Venerable, Abbot of Cluny, protested at the forceful attitude of the Templars with its insistence on total obedience unto death. He wrote to the Master of the Temple at that time (Evrard de Barres) and began by praising the Templars' willingness to die for Christ. He then went on to complain that one local Knight, Humbert III of Beaujeu, who had joined the Order and since returned to Cluny, should not be forced to return to the East. According to Nicholson, "Peter argued that it was more important to attack Christians who acted contrary to their faith than it was to attack pagans who did not know God." Peter also wrote to Pope Eugenius III, making a stronger claim of coercion and pointing out that Humbert had been enticed by the Templars to leave his wife in an illegal manner, and, because of this entrapment, should not be forced to remain with the Order against his own and his family's will.[68] (The Pope finally ruled in Humbert's favor, and he returned home.)

A Good Life and an Even Better Afterlife

When not being called on to kill infidels or die as martyrs, the Templars lived quite a good life. The Order did not consist only of the famous Knights; there were two lesser classes to serve the full brothers. Members of the first, known as sergeants, were recruited from what we would now call the working class, rather than the nobility that provided the Templar Knights. They undertook roles such as grooms, stewards, sentries, and general support troops. Like their betters, they wore a red cross, but their mantle was dark brown rather than white, reflecting their lack of purity compared to the Knights. The other supporting class consisted of the clerics who looked after the spiritual needs of the Knights. These priests were the only literate members of the Order and took care of record-keeping and communications, sometimes writing in very complex codes. French was the administrative language of the Templars, but their versatile priests could say the Mass in Latin, haggle with local traders in Arabic, and read the Old Testament in Hebrew and the New Testament in Greek. They served the spiritual needs of the fighting men, and were distinguished by wearing the red Templar Cross of martyrdom on a green mantle.

But life was not all wine and roses. The downside of being a Templar, as opposed to a secular knight, was that you were forced to subjugate your sex drive. This is how the Latin Rule of their Order begins:

> You, indeed, renouncing your own wills and others with you fighting for the high King for the safety of souls to that end with horses and arms, in pious and pure affection should strive universally to hear matins and the whole of the divine service, in accordance with canonical institution and the custom of the regular masters

of the holy city. For that reason it is especially owed by you, venerable brothers, since despising the light of the present life, being contemptuous of the torment which is of your bodies, you have promised in perpetuity to hold cheap worldly matters for the love of God: restored by the divine flesh, and consecrated, enlightened and confirmed in the Lord's precepts, after the consumption of the divine mystery no one should be afraid to fight, but be prepared for the crown.[69]

The Knights wore white mantles to indicate that they had placed the dark life behind them and entered the light of perpetual celibacy (the white martyrdom). But to limit temptation, they were not allowed to sleep naked. They had to wear a shirt and breeches at all times, and to make sure there was no cheating, or self-pleasuring, a light was kept burning in the dormitories throughout the night.[70]

With this sexual abstinence came an atmosphere that fostered a cult of glorious death and offered the Knights a reward in paradise, where they would become favorites of the Queen of Heaven, the Virgin Mary. Helen Nicholson comments on

A Templar Knight in full regalia.

an account of the battle of the Spring of the Cresson, which took place on May 1, 1187, pointing out that it throws a great deal of light on the attitudes of the Templars:

> The whole account is full of references which we would associate with the Templars, death as a glorious service for Christ, death as joy, non-Christians as the enemy, and a reference to the Christians' protector St. George, one of the saints venerated by the Order.[71]

St. George was a favorite of the Templars. He had been an active warrior, but was also an excellent example of a glorious martyr. He patiently suffered a horrible death at the hands of pagans for his Christian faith. He was an obvious model for the Templars to follow.[72]

Nicholson goes on to recount the story of the defeat of the Templars at the Battle of Hattin on July 4, 1187. The defeated Templars argued over who should be the first to have their head cut off by the victorious Saladin:

> A certain Templar named Nicholas had been so successful in persuading the rest to undergo death willingly that the others struggled to go in front of him and he only just succeeded in obtaining the glory of martyrdom first—which was an honour he very much strove for.[73]

She draws attention to the fact that this account plays up the glory to won by dying in Christ's name, and the honor which was given to any Templar who became a martyr. Self-sacrifice for the glory of God was an ideal that underpinned the knighthood of the Temple.[74]

> The Order of the Temple offered knights a completely different way of finding God. Templars had to commit themselves to a religious Order and vow to obey a superior without question, to live without sexual intercourse and without personal wealth, and very probably to die in action against the Muslims . . . The symbol of the red cross on the white shield . . . was a standard symbol of martyrdom in the Middle Ages.[75]

So the Order of the Templars recast Christianity from a pacifist religion, whose members turned the other cheek as they willingly offered themselves to be thrown to the lions, to a religion which claimed that it was better to die in battle than to behold the sorrows of their Christian brethren and the holy places. As Urban II put it:

> God has conferred upon you above all nations great glory in arms. Accordingly undertake this task for the remission of your sins, with the assurance of the imperishable glory of the kingdom of heaven.[76]

But to create an Order of heroic martyrs, each of whose story could be told like that of St. George, could have easily resulted in an alternative focus of spiritual power, away from the leaders of the Church. To limit this risk, Bernard's rule emphasized the community aspect of the Knights' calling to martyrdom. It instructed the brothers to act together, and individual Templars were not to be recognized as saints. Apart from the risk of creating new saintly heroes, the singling out of individuals might have encouraged others to go it alone in the rush towards martyrdom and glory, which would not have been as effective for battlefield discipline. Despite these safeguards, a few brothers were celebrated when they were martyred in brave fighting against the Muslims. Stories, such as that of Brother Nicholas, were used to inspire fresh martyrs to join the Order.[77]

THE POLITICAL BALANCE: TRADING SKILL AND ROYAL SUPPORT

The Templars arrived on the political scene after the First Crusade with a major advantage. They became an independent international military power, but they were courted rather than shunned by kings, even though the kings could not control them. This was a novel circumstance for the kings of western Europe, who ruled by Divine Right. This right was inherited from God, who had created David as the first King to bask in His Divine approval.

The Divine Royal Contract implied that monarchs were placed on their thrones by God for a specific purpose known only to the Deity. Although kings might seem to be ungodly, to question their authority was to question God's purpose. And, as we have seen from the text of Urban's call for a crusade, only someone with the authority of the Pope could raise such questions with impunity. A holy Order, free by the power of the Pope to interpret God's purpose and with an army of knights to enforce its views, had to be taken seriously by any monarch with political sense. To challenge them directly could undermine the lawfulness of a king's own right to rule in the eyes of his religious subjects

But there was another way that kings could benefit from a good working relationship with religious people. Unlike most people at the time, priests were educated, and because of their vocation it was assumed that they could be relied on to act as honest, hard-working officials.[78] The Templars, with their hierarchy of Knights, sergeants, and priests, started from a good position. And when their trading, banking, and accounting skills were thrown into the mix, it became obvious that a good relationship between a monarch and his local Templars could work for them both.

As Dr. Nicholson points out:

> The Military Orders combined the best of all worlds for a ruler who wanted servants with the godly outlook and honesty of monks, the lack of worldly connections and self-interested loyalty of the new literati, and the military skills and traditional loyalty of the warrior class. All the Military Orders were much used by nobles, monarchs and the papacy in their governments. In return, they received donations and protection.[79]

As they implemented their founder Hugh de Payns' inspired decision to create a network of support Preceptories in Europe, the Templars came to excel in their development of financial skills. It was to ensure the stability of their international operations that the Templars first developed and then began to supply financial services. To succeed with their own objectives, they had to create ways of collecting, storing and moving large sums of cash and other valuables from the West to the East. And, of course, they had to be able to track all these valuables, so they developed accounting systems.

As the Order developed early banking systems, its Brothers became papal money carriers. They were asked to act as papal almoners, were placed in charge of the Church's charitable donations to the poor, and were an obvious choice when the Church needed a skilled treasurer. Kings noted this benefit, and were not slow to approach them for similar services. For example, in 1177 Henry II of England asked Brother Roger the Templar to be his almoner, and Helen Nicholson reports that the Templars continued to appear as royal almoners in England until 1255.[80] The Templars were soon able to offer a whole range of services that were useful to kings. The crowns of both England and France used the Order almost as an arm of their royal government.

Helen Nicholson cites some canny rulers as planning ahead and promoting their own candidates to join the Templars, probably with a view to engendering loyalty from their patronage. She points out that in 1244, Henry III of England conferred a knighthood on Thomas of Curtun before he joined the Templars; Thomas was in the King's service at the time, but had made known that he planned to join the Order of the Temple. Henry invested quite a lot of money in setting Sir Thomas up as a trained and functioning knight (complete with war horses, weapons, and servants), and Dr. Nicholson feels that he must have expected Thomas to remain loyal to his benefactor even after he had joined the Templars.[81] And, from Brother Thomas's subsequent favor towards him, it seems the King was right.

As proto-bankers, the Templars lent money to kings, if it suited them to do so. In 1148, they lent money to Louis VII of France, which he then squandered on the Second Crusade.[82] In 1250, the Templars lent Louis IX enough money to ransom himself from the Sultan of Egypt, who had captured him during the Seventh Crusade.[83] (In the British Library, there is a romantic drawing of Louis languishing in prison while he waits for the ransom to arrive.[84])

The Templars often lent King Henry III of England money to see him over the many funding crises of his reign.[85] But Dr. Nicholson points out that their role was very different from that of a modern bank, which stores money, lends it, and pays interest.

The Templars were not a bank in the modern sense of the word, as their financial operations were merely a sideline, a result of their need to store and move large quantities of cash about Christendom. Money deposited with them was not pooled and reinvested, but remained in its owners' strongboxes within the Order's treasury, and could not be accessed without the owners' permission.[86]

The English Royal treasury was part of the King's household, and he employed his own officials to run it. The Templars' role in English treasury affairs was limited to supplying extra-secure deposit space for money and valuables. The English crown tried not to involve the Order in normal royal administration.[87]

In France, however, the situation was different. The Templars *were* the royal treasury. The Treasurer of the Paris Temple was also the royal treasurer. The Order collected taxes and paid the wages of royal retainers. It was not until 1295 that the King of France tried to set up an independent Royal Treasury at the Louvre. But, because of the poor state of the French economy—badly damaged by Louis IX's excessive zeal for crusading—King Philip IV had to continue to rely of the support of the Templar treasury. Things got so bad that in 1303 he had to revert to using the Templar treasury, as his own could not cope. As Helen Nicholson says, "clearly the Order was essential to the efficient running of the French royal administration."[88]

The period when the Templars flourished, from the early eleventh century to the early fourteenth century, was a period of rapid commercial and economic growth in Europe. The population expanded, new land was cultivated, new towns and cities were built. It was a good time for trade and commerce. This was a time of political stability, a period without any threat of external invasion, and even the climate cooperated, as the period was generally warm and dry. These factors all worked in the Templars' favor, and they rapidly developed economic and commercial operations to finance their military adventures in the East.[89]

THE TEMPLAR FLEET

As part of their growing trade network, the Templars began to develop a small fleet of trading vessels. By the first decades of the thirteenth century, they were operating ships outside the Kingdom of Jerusalem and sailing a regular service to Constantinople and around the Bay of Biscay. They were acquiring some fighting ships and also getting into the ship-leasing business. In 1224 Henry III of England hired a Templar ship; it was known as "the Great Ship," and its captain was Brother Thomas of the Temple of Spain. This was not just a simple merchant vessel: It was a fully fledged warship, which Henry wanted to use to fight against France. He was so pleased with it that he eventually paid the Master of the Temple in Spain 200 marks (which would be some £100,000—about $200,000—in modern money), and bought it outright. Nicholson notes that presumably the Templars in Spain had quite a few ships, if they could spare this one.[90]

The standards of navigation and ship management began to improve during the twelfth century, although before then European sailors could not venture far, not having the ocean-going skills of the Vikings, who had maintained regular trading voyages to their colonies on Greenland since the late tenth century. (The Vikings accomplished this by island-hopping across the North Atlantic using a well-tested route.[91] We'll revisit them and their seafaring skills in a later chapter.) By the 1330s western European shipbuilding skills had improved enough to create vessels that could sail out of the straits of Gibraltar, turn south, and keep going, as long as the currents and the wind stayed fair. (This is how the Canary Islands came to be mapped towards the end of the fourteenth century.) But these improvements in the sailors' art came too late to benefit the Templars. Their marine advances in the early thirteenth century had put them far enough ahead of the game to sell a fighting ship to the King of England, but a succession of reverses in their battle for the Holy Land left them with few resources for technological development in ship design. Then the defeat of the Christian forces at Acre in 1291 resulted in a massive loss of long-term investment in land and buildings for the Templars.[92] By the late thirteenth century they had few spare resources, and by the 1330s the Order had been dissolved.[93]

Over its existence of less than two hundred years, the Order changed. It began, as Henry of Huntingdon said, as a group of death-dealing martyrs, "new monsters composed from purity and corruption." At its peak, it became an Order that Helen Nicholson describes as "not interested in anything else apart from money," concerned only with generating as much income as possible from its independent economic and commercial activities.[94]

> If we think of the [later] Templars as bank managers and bank clerks we probably get a far better idea of how people in cities such and London and Paris in the early fourteenth century would have regarded them.[95]

So how did their image change from fierce warriors to urban bankers? To understand that, we have to appreciate the role and importance of holy relics and their associated myths.

How to Become Immortal: Guard the Holy Grail

Relics were important at the time the Templars were formed. It was believed that those in Heaven, such as popular saints, were able to act on Earth through their relics. If the saint's relics were venerated and well looked after, the saint would be pleased and would give supernatural aid to the guardian of the relic. But if the relic were neglected or abused, the saint would be angry and punish the abuser.[96]

Among their collection of relics, the Templars had the skull of St. Euphemia. She was a companion of St. Ursula, who led a troupe of virgins on a pilgrimage to

Germany (in some versions of the story, eleven thousand of them). They were captured by the Huns and—according to which version of the myth you believe— were either tortured and then thrown into a pit with a wild bear to be torn apart, or else burnt at the stake for refusing to take part in pagan fertility rites. (The fact so many skulls and bones from these worthy maidens made their way into various reliquaries might suggest that they were torn apart.) At all events, because she died a virgin, St. Euphemia's relics were particularly powerful, so the Templars kept her skull in the Paris Temple (and apparently it can still be seen at the Patriarchal Church of St. George in Constantinople, if you have a taste for such things). The relic consists of a large silver reliquary containing the skull of a young woman, wrapped in white linen and covered by red muslin. (The red and white wrappings, as you now know, symbolize both forms of martyrdom.) There is no record of any sign of scorching on the skull, but then neither does it show the distinctive tooth marks of a bear. So the question of how she met her end remains uncertain. And, of course, the whole story could be a romantic myth.

Helen Nicholson tells us that:

> After the dissolution of the Order, the Templars' Parisian head . . . passed to the Hospital of St. John . . . The cult of St. Ursula and her maidens was extremely widespread during the Middle Ages, and it is not surprising that the Templars had some of the relics, as every religious Order wanted to acquire such items to demonstrate its piety and holiness.[97]

She goes on to record one of the key stages in the Templars' metamorphosis from monsters to grail-knights:

> The Order regarded itself . . . as the [most important] defender of Christendom. It was so prominent in this role that the author Wolfram von Eschenbach identified the Grail Castle in his verse romance *Parzival* as Jerusalem, by making Templars its guardians.[98]

Wolfram von Eschenbach was a German narrative poet who wrote a popular version of the Grail legend at the beginning of the thirteenth century. His poem is divided into sixteen books of thirty-line stanzas of rhyming couplets. He drew his inspiration from an earlier story of the Grail written by Chrétien de Troyes in 1175. Malcolm Barber says this about it:

> The real Templars defended Jerusalem and the holy places. In Wolfram's version of the story the Grail is a stone rather than a vessel, but its central place as the object of true Christian struggle remains. The role of the Templars is explained to Parzival in the following way:

"It is well known to me", said his host, "that many formidable fighting men dwell at Munsalvaesche with the Grail. They are continually riding out on sorties in quest of adventure. Whether these same Templars reap trouble or renown they bear it for their sins. A warlike company lives there. I will tell you how they are nourished. They live from a Stone whose essence is most pure. If you have never heard of it I shall name it for you here. It is called 'Lapsit exillis.'"[99]

This walk-on part in an evolving Christian myth painted the Templars in a new light. But I couldn't help wondering, had they deliberately set out to create these myths about themselves? Helen Nicholson didn't think so:

> There has been some speculation that the Templars were involved in the development of the legend of the Holy Grail, but . . . the concept of knighthood in the Grail legends is different from the Templar ideal: the Grail knights act alone, not as part of a community.[100]

She's quite right that the Grail stories allow knights to find God without having to sacrifice their independence of action, and without having to obey anyone or give up their wealth. In addition, Muslims may also find the Grail, although they have to convert to Christianity before they can see it. (Indeed some versions of the tale make the point that Muslim converts make better grail-knights, and can be much more successful in the search than many Christians.) Dr. Nicholson believes that these concepts do not fit the Templars' ideal of fighting and killing Muslims as enemies of Christ. On the other hand, the motive for the speculation she mentions is the timing of the first recording of the Grail Myth.

As a political tool, a common belief that the Templars were the chosen guardians of the greatest treasure in Christendom could have been a useful counterbalance to criticism that a Military Order was inappropriate within what was supposed to be a peaceful religion. The Templars were closely involved in the ruling politics of France and England, and so they would have been well placed to encouraged the development of favorable "spin" for their cause. I decided to look again at the timeline of the Grail story, a matter I had first researched when preparing background material for an earlier book, *The Second Messiah*.[101]

KING ARTHUR AND THE TRAIL TO THE GRAIL

The Holy Grail is usually said to be the cup used by Jesus at the Last Supper, and is often connected to the mythical King Arthur. But when I had looked into this Grail myth, I had found that the Grail has several definitions. It can be a metaphor for an impossible task. It can sometimes be the stone upon which kings are made from men into divinely ordained monarchs. Or it can be a sacred cup used by Jesus at the Last Supper that was kept by Joseph of Arimathea after he collected the blood from the body of the crucified Christ in it. A popular version of this myth says Joseph brought the cup to Britain, where it was transmitted from generation to generation of his descendants. Today a popular interpretation is that the Grail was actually the bloodline of Mary Magdalene, through whom the holy bloodline of Christ was preserved in the form of his descendants. In fact, it seems that the Holy Grail is a very versatile myth, and can be almost anything you want it to be.

Exposure to the Grail can be good or bad, depending on the merits of the searcher. A knight without sin is furnished with food, but one of impure heart can be struck blind. Any irreverence can cause the speaker to lose the ability to talk.

When I began my research, I had expected to find that the stories of the Holy Grail and the associated stories of King Arthur and his Knights of the Round Table to be ancient folk tales, long predating the foundation of the Templars. But the truth was different.

The earliest known references to an Arthur-like character came from a fifth-century monk called Gildas, who recorded a last unsuccessful battle against the encroaching Anglo-Saxons in the West of Britain by a warlord named Aurelius Ambrosianus.[102] Four hundred years later another monk, Nennius of Bangor, wrote a history of Britain where he named the warlord "Arthur" and stated that the final lost battle had been fought at place called Mons Badonicus in 500 CE.[103] But the warlords described by Gildas and Nennius are much simpler than the complex myth of King Arthur. And the Holy Grail itself is completely missing from their narratives.

The first reference to a recognizable form of the mythical King Arthur appeared in 1138, ten years after the formation of the Order of the Knights Templar and two years after its founder, Hugh de Payns, died.[104] It was in *Historia Regum Britanniae* ("The History of the Kings of Britain") written by a secular canon (i.e., a church administrator) in Oxford named Geoffrey of Monmouth. But, although Geoffrey's version has King Arthur in it, it makes no reference to a Holy Grail.[105]

Geoffrey was a first-generation Welshman, born in 1100 in Gwent; his family had come from Brittany at the time of the Norman Conquest. He was a canon in Oxford for many years before becoming archdeacon of Monmouth and finally, Bishop of St. Asaph (in North Wales) in 1152.[106] His biographer Aneirin Jarman says:

> Geoffrey disclaims all originality and affirms that his work is merely a translation into Latin of a certain very old book in the British tongue, which had been brought to his notice by Walter, archdeacon of Oxford. Now, although Walter was a real person, contemporary with Geoffrey and without doubt known to him personally, this statement is not now generally believed to be true . . . for the conception of Arthur as a mighty emperor whose court was the centre of the world, Geoffrey alone was responsible.[107]

But what inspired Geoffrey to write this *Historia*?

> No doubt there is some truth in the view that above all else he was one who enjoyed telling a good story. It must not be forgotten, however, that he was a Breton dependent on Norman favour and offering a Norman audience a highly-coloured account of the ancient glories of the Welsh people that were at that very time resisting Norman aggression with arms . . . Geoffrey was fully conscious of the fact that the

Bretons and the Welsh were originally the same people. His book is a panegyric on his own race in the far distant past . . . The Normans . . . would feel satisfaction and pride in the thought that they were the inheritors by conquest of a land possessing such a long and splendid martial tradition.[108]

If Geoffrey's motive was clear enough, his inspiration was not. The early success of his writing and its translation into Welsh supported a verbal tradition of Arthur which grew with the telling. But the legend was not written down in Welsh again until 1300, when it was reported in *The White Book of Rhydderch*; this collection of stories, along with the later *Red Book of Hergest*, became known as *The Mabinogion*. It has Arthur, the quests, and Avalon, but not Lancelot, the Grail, or the Round Table. So almost a hundred and sixty years after Geoffrey first recorded the story, Arthur had been transformed into a great Welsh Warlord.[109] This is how a simple story can become a powerful national myth. Bu this still doesn't answer the question of where Geoffrey got his ideas. Had he really found an old document, or did he get the idea from elsewhere and want to protect his source?

I have already mentioned Walter Map, who as Archdeacon of Oxford added to the store of Arthur legends in his later writings, after publishing his history of the Knights Templar.[110] He is the only twelfth-century writer outside the Holy Land to write a history of the Knights Templar, and his source for Templar material was the Preceptory at Cowley, near Oxford, which was given to the Order during Hugh's first visit to England, about 1128. The Preceptory was extended in 1239 with the gift of considerable lands from Queen Matilda. Matilda was not only the consort of King Stephen; she was also the niece of Godfrey de Bouillon, Duke of Lower Lorraine, one of the leaders of the First Crusade, and for a year the first ruler of the crusader state of Jerusalem.

Walter Map would have been aware that the Templars held general Chapter meetings in round churches. This could well have underlain Geoffrey's writing on the legend of the Round Table, for Walter was also known to take simple facts and then build them into a good story. Walter's love of embellishment shows in his history of the Templars, where he portrays Hugh de Payns as a simple knight who took it upon himself to protect pilgrims. Walter did play Hugh as an heroic figure in the Arthurian mold. Moreover, Walter thought the Templars had declined after the death of Hugh de Payns, and had become decadent in the late 1100s.[111] Hence he may well have seen the popularity of the myth of Arthur as a way of contrasting what he saw as a decadent Order in his day with what he preferred to portray as their more heroic forebears.

Oxford seems to have been a focus of these early stories. I knew that one of the original group of Templars, Payen de Montdidier, had gone to England to establish a Preceptory there. The gift of the royal manor of Cowley by Queen Matilda of England (before marriage, Princess Mathilde of Boulogne), King Stephen's wife and the niece of Baldwin I of Jerusalem, made Oxford one of the richest and most important centers of the Templars in England during the period when Walter Map was an Archdeacon there.

Helen Nicholson records the family links that made Oxford a focus of Templar influence:

> Matilda of Boulogne, Queen of England, gave Cressing in Essex to the Templars in the spring of 1137. [Two Templar barns survive at Cressing: the largest medieval wooden structures still in daily use.] Her uncles Godfrey of Bouillon and Baldwin of Edessa had been the first two Latin rulers of the kingdom of Jerusalem, while her father Eustace had been the closest heir to the kingdom on the death of Baldwin I in 1118. Matilda had a strong dynastic interest in the kingdom of Jerusalem and wanted to support the religious Order that was helping to defend it. . . . We can only speculate as to whether her family had other links with the Templars which led her to prefer the Templars over the Hospitallers.
>
> Matilda later gave the Templars Witham in Essex and Cowley in Oxfordshire. All her donations were confirmed by her husband, King Stephen of England, who himself was the son of one of the leaders of the First Crusade. Although Stephen's predecessor Henry I of England had given Hugh de Payns money in 1128 and had allowed him to collect donations in England, it was Matilda's generosity to the Order which laid the foundations of a long and close relationship between the Templars and the kings of England.[112]

Walter Map had access to a major Templar Preceptory, and also to Templars who had known one of the original founders of the Order who had been present in Jerusalem during the formative years. Payen de Montdidier may not have deliberately set out to create a new myth, but he might easily have become a source of local interest for a keen ecclesiastical historian who loved a good story and wanted to portray him in a better light than his successors.

When Payen de Montdidier was sent by the Order to establish its base in England, Oxford became a major site because of the strong support of Queen Matilda. Walter could well have been inspired to write his history of the Templars by hearing tales of Montdidier's and his fellow founding Templars' exploits. Walter's heroic portrayal of Hugh de Payns and his motives for the founding the Templars, combined with a myth about a quest for great Christian relics, may have been just too good a tale to resist.

The Templars were very different from other Christian Orders because they promoted violence and martyrdom. And Bernard of Clairvaux had called them a new type of knighthood that had grown out of the very land that Jesus had once walked. So, from the beginning, the Templars were guardians of an important Christian relic: the Holy Land itself. But how did this story grow to include one of the greatest of all conceivable Christian relics, the mythical Holy Grail?

The earliest reference to the Grail is from William of Malmesbury, a monk and historian from Malmesbury Abbey. Writing around 1140, he said that Joseph of Arimathea came to Glastonbury, bringing both the Holy Grail and a Holy

Thorn Tree, which he planted there.[113] (Malmesbury Abbey, between Swindon and Bristol, is no more than twenty-five miles from another of Payen de Montdidier's early Preceptories, Temple Guiting near Cheltenham.) I was intrigued to notice that the earliest mention of the Grail arose at about the same time as the Arthur legends—although the two motifs were not connected until some time later—and both started in church establishments close to early Templar Preceptories. The common link seemed to be Payen de Montdidier, who built both. He had been drafted to England to promote the Templar cause, so perhaps he had caught the imaginations of local clerics with his tales of the Holy Land, and their verbal retelling became the source of Walter's old stories.

Stories about the quest for the grail did not evolve into their modern form for another few generations, until *Le Conte del Graal* ("The Tale of the Grail") was written by Chrétien de Troyes and dedicated to Philippe d'Alsace, Count of Flanders. Chrétien said he had first heard the story from Philippe himself.[114] Yet again the name of Payen de Montdidier crops up: Philippe's father was a cousin of his. If Payen had told tales of adventure and derring-do to his cousin, the Count of Flanders, who had in turn embellished and repeated them to his son Philippe, then Chrétien could well have been quite truthful when he said that he first heard the stories from Philippe d'Alsace. Chrétien had previously been closely associated with the Court of Champagne, and Maria, Countess of Champagne, had been his patron (he dedicated many of his earlier romances to her). He died in a mysterious fire before his Grail poem was completed.

As far as I could see, all the traceable early references to the legend of Arthur and the stories of the Grail came from individuals who recorded them near Templar sites associated with Payen de Montdidier, one of the original "nine" Templar Knights. There are other landmarks in the development of the story, though. One was *Roman de l'Estoire dou Saint Graal* ("Book of the History of the Holy Grail"), which was written by Robert de Boron between 1190 and 1200. De Boron said that he drew his version of the story from a "great book," the secrets of which had been revealed to him. His version linked the Graal (Grail) with Jesus and Joseph of Arimathea, and it is his version that said that Joseph used it to collect the blood of Jesus after the Crucifixion. It was also de Boron who first introduced the concept of the Round Table, which (as we have seen) echoes the shape of the Templar Preceptory.[115] Another early source is *Perlesvaus*, written between 1190 and 1212 by an anonymous author who is often said to be a Templar.[116] This version links the Templars with the story, describing them as the knight guardians of the Grail. Finally we arrive back where we started, at Wolfram von Eschenbach's *Parzival*, which is the first book to "spin" the idea that there might be a link between the Templars and the Grail Romances.

But the storytelling did not end with Eschenbach. As Helen Nicholson reminds us:

The Templars continued to appear in fictional literature throughout the Middle Ages, although usually in peaceful roles rather than fighting the Muslims. They continued to appear as defenders of the Grail Castle in German works written in the tradition of Wolfram von Eschenbach's Parzival . . . Their image in fictional literature was almost invariably good; they were holy men, dedicated to God's service.[117]

What a transformation this is from the "half-caste monsters"—unholy mixture of monk and knight! The implications of the image transformation of this myth are too important to ignore. Nicholson admits that Wolfram included the Templars in his Grail story for a political reason: He wanted his Grail castle to be Jerusalem. He wrote *Parzival* as a satire on the political conflict between Philip of Swabia and Otto of Brunswick over the imperial throne of the Holy Roman Empire.[118] Wolfram's patron, Hermann of Thuringia, was a strong opponent of Otto, and it suited his political aims if Parzival's Grail castle was guarded by the Templars, the well-known defenders of Jerusalem.[119] So by the beginning of the thirteenth century, the Templars were being linked to the Grail romance as a deliberate act of political spin, though that spin was not in fact instigated by them. After this, the legend developed through three major versions, until by 1215–35, it had became a totally Christian myth, now known as the Vulgate Cycle. (The Vulgate Cycle is more popularly known as the collection of stories of Sir Lancelot, King Arthur and the Knights of the Round Table, and their quest for the Grail.)

Relic myths, of which is Grail is a good example, had tremendous power to impress Kings and other possible donors of funds. This is shown by the actions of Louis VII of France, who in 1164 entrusted a task of magical transformation to Brother Geoffrey Fulcher of the Order of the Temple, who was leaving France for the East. He gave Brother Geoffrey a ring, which he hoped would be made into a magical talisman. Helen Nicholson quotes an English translation of the letter Brother Geoffrey wrote to French King from Jerusalem:

> Don't think that the instructions which I rejoiced to receive from your mouth when I left you have slipped your servant's mind.[120]

Geoffrey returned the King's ring with his letter. By taking it to each of the holy sites of Christendom, placing it on the hallowed ground and praying over it in memory of the King, he had created a relic of enormous religious power. This is yet another example of the magical guardianship powers of a Templar.

Later in history, the Vulgate Cycle was used by writers such as Thomas Mallory, who wrote a series of Arthurian Romances, including the famous *Le Morte d'Arthur*, in 1470. By then the Arthurian myth was well established and had settled into its present form, the form.

Whether deliberate or not, the repositioning of the Templars from an Order of violent, death-dealing martyrs, "composed from purity and corruption," as Henry of Huntingdon had portrayed them, to the guardians of one of the most powerful Christian relics (even if the Grail is a mythical creation), is a turnaround worthy of respect from any modern spin-doctor. Simply by extrapolating the popular belief in the power of relics, the Templars became respectable, and even romantic. The Holy Grail passed into common myth as a "super-relic," which could draw down the goodwill and support of Jesus to its guardians and their supporters. But there remained a dark side to this myth, that if the guardians of the Grail were perceived to have misused the power of their relics, then God would be bound to punish them. And it was this one last event that set up the Templars for immortal fame: the dramatic way in which their Order ended.

CONCLUSIONS

The first crusade was an act of political opportunism by Pope Urban II, but it established a new principle, a Holy War fought by committed Christian believers. Some of the first crusaders enjoyed this way of life, and set about forming a new creature: the religious fighting man or Christian Soldier. The Holy Violence that underpinned this concept, a theological innovation invented by Urban II and promoted by Abbot Bernard of Clairvaux, resulted in the Order of the Knights Templar, who were conceived as a brigade of martyrs, but who also spawned a vast trading and banking network to fund the fighting men in the Holy Land.

As their main religious purpose, the control of the Holy Land, became impossible, the Templars latched onto an existing Grail myth to develop the belief that they were the chosen guardians of the Holy Grail as a useful political counterbalance to criticism that an ongoing Military Order was inappropriate within a peaceful religious setup. They made skillful political use of the concept of the "Holy Relic" as a source of political power when they became closely involved in the politics of France and England.

The Templars' skillful political use of favorable "spin" created myths that lived on long after their destruction in 1307. But it was the nature of that destruction and its aftermath that I needed to look at next. Their sudden and unexpected destruction at the height of their powers had provided a fertile ground for conspiracy theories. I had read many myths about Jacques de Molay and how he cursed both King and Pope as he burned—and how they died within months of him in strange circumstances. I wanted to find out the *real* motives behind their destruction and just how complete their neutralization was. Could any of them have survived? To find out, we need to plunge into a world of politics, intrigue, greed, and murder that makes the shenanigans of today's politicians and industrial magnates seem insipid by comparison.

CHAPTER 3

FRIDAY THE THIRTEENTH AND ITS AFTERMATH

THE STRATEGIC ADVANTAGE OF A SUDDEN DEATH

As James Dean, Buddy Holly, and Marilyn Monroe have demonstrated in recent times, to die suddenly while near the height of your powers and popularity is a good long-term career move if you want to achieve iconic status. The destruction of the Templars could not have been better arranged for this purpose if it had been planned by a team of Hollywood scriptwriters. It has a villain, an evil, self-centered king who has bankrupted his county and is driven by greed. It has a weak holy man, forced into betraying his own guardians who trust him implicitly. It has noble knights tortured into false confessions, which they later retract at the cost of their lives. What more can you ask? Well . . . how about trials revealing heresy, devil worship, homo-erotic acts, and curses which bring down the mighty? Not to mention disappearing fleets and small bands of faithful knights escaping to continue their mission in exile. The destruction of the Templars has all this and more. Small wonder, then, that it has acted as a focus for romantics and conspiracy theorists for hundreds of years.

Let's begin with Helen Nicholson's view on the fall of the Templars, and then see what happened to ensure the Order's long-term place in the public's heart. Dr. Nicholson says:

> There were obvious moral lessons to be drawn from the downfall of the Templars: fortune rules all in this world, how quickly the great can fall from favour, how the poor knights of Christ became rich and proud and so met their downfall . . .
> Historians from the Middle Ages to the present day have developed a "model" of the rise and fall of the Templars: the pure ideals of the first knights became contami-

nated as the Order grew rich and became involved in politics; the Order became corrupt and greedy and increasingly unpopular, and meanwhile the West lost interest in the Crusades; so when Philip IV of France attacked the Order for its money, no one defended it and the Order fell. This "model" has gained wide acceptance despite the fact that it is false, because it provides an attractively simple explanation for the otherwise unjust and inexplicable fall of the Order.[121]

A FAMILY OF SAINTS AND BANKRUPTS

Philip IV of France (called Philip the Fair for his good looks, rather than his sense of justice) was only three years old when his soon-to-be-sainted grandfather Louis IX, a crusade junkie, died in the middle of his last fix.[122] The grandchild who later inherited the Capetian throne never really knew St. Louis, but grew up in the shadow of his pious achievements. Philip remembered the Templars' reluctance to pay his grandfather's ransom,[123] and would use that incident during his attack on them.[124] He also learned the futility of crusading as an instrument of royal policy, because his father Philip III (Philip the Bold) died after the Aragonese crusade, leaving debts of £1,299,000—nearly $2,600,000—an amount almost inconceivable at the time.[125]

So young Philip IV inherited two problems with his crown: His grandfather was a saint and his father a bankrupt. He had to learn quickly, and he did. Rather than get involved in expensive expeditions to support Papal policy, he concentrated instead on trying to solve the financial problems his father had created. His attitude had the effect of reducing the power of the Pope, and it also reduced the effectiveness of the crusade as an instrument of papal policy.

All the same, Philip affected devotion to the cult of his grandfather, probably because of its great political importance to him. By the time he inherited the French throne in 1285 his grandfather was well along the road to canonization (the process had begun under Philip III in 1273), and he would become St. Louis in 1297. To Philip the Fair, he represented French monarchy at its best, having managed to combine the roles of king, saint, and crusader in one individual. He was a hard act to follow, and the Bishop of Pamiers described Philip the Fair rather unflatteringly:

> The king is like an owl, the most beautiful of birds, but worth nothing. He is the most handsome of men but stares fixedly in silence. He is neither man nor beast, he is a statue.[126]

He was a proud king with a great faith in his dynasty and the political skill to make use of the highly superstitious inclination of his subjects. Given the widespread belief in the power of holy relics, which were venerated and believed to be able to perform miracles on behalf of their devotees, Philip was sitting pretty. He had inherited palaces full of holy relics of Louis IX, and this became a source of political strength for the seventeen-year-old King when Pope Boniface VIII made

Louis IX a saint of the Roman Catholic Church.[127] Philip's belief in the Divine destiny of the Capetian royal line would eventually drive him to defeat three Popes and to destroy the Templars.

Philip had been taught by Giles de Colonna (later Archbishop of Bourges), a learned man, forceful, and with forthright opinions on the duties and responsibilities of kingship.[128] His favorite saying, which he impressed on Philip, was "Jesus Christ has not given any temporal dominion to his church, and the King of France has his authority from God alone." When he became the grandson of a saint, this confirmed what Philip already believed about the importance of his royal lineage, and built on the foundations of self-regard that Giles de Colonna had laid down.

Philip was already aware that Popes would exploit any kingdom that accepted their authority. The financial risks of crusading, even if supported by the Pope, his father had discovered the hard way—and even his sainted grandfather had spent

King Philip the Fair—Philippe le Bel ("Handsome")—of France.

money France did not have on Eastern adventures. While recovering from a severe illness, St. Louis dedicated himself to recapturing the holy places of Christendom as a penance. His first crusade took place between 1249 and 1250 and, despite being the best-armed and -equipped and the best-provisioned ever to set out, was still a disastrous failure. It cost France £167,000 (almost $350,000) in ransom. Stephen of Otricourt, the commander of the Templar force that had accompanied Louis and suffered tremendous losses attempting to salvage the ill-conceived venture, was pressured to lend Philip the ransom payment. Louis blamed himself for this debacle, saying:

> If only I could suffer alone the opprobrium and adversity, and my sins should not recoil on the universal church then I could bear it with equanimity. But by me all Christendom has been covered with confusion.[129]

There was already a growing feeling among the nobles of Europe that crusades were an instrument of policy that were beginning to outlive their usefulness, and Louis's disaster seemed to confirm this. But despite such disillusionment, Louis announced his intention to lead another. During this period of extraordinary military demands on France, the Pope granted Louis the right to levy taxes on the French Church (a concession his grandson would take full advantage of). Louis's illness delayed the embarkation until 1270, and he died in Tunis before his army had carried out any useful military action. In 1271 his entrails were buried in Monreale in Sicily, and his bones carried back to France. These relics soon became the focus for a cult of St. Louis, which eventually resulted in his canonization.

Louis's son and heir, Philip III, was slow to learn that the days of the effective crusade were over. He took part in the abortive Aragonese crusade, which cost him his life and another £1,229,000 (about $2,500,000) of French money. He died at Perpignan amid his retreating forces, with his crusaders defeated and all their noble supporters dead. Crusading expenditure had run far beyond the upper limits of Royal income. (The annual income of the French crown was then £656,000—about $1,312,000—and the normal running expenses of the state £652,000—about $1,304,000.[130]) The crippling debt accumulated by France (around £2,500,000 or $5,000,000) would have considerable repercussions for State, Church, and Templars.

When Philip IV became king, at the age of seventeen, all his royal disposable income for the next three hundred years was needed to pay his father's debts. A teenage king would hardly welcome the news that he needed to economize for the rest of his life. Then, by the time he was twenty-six, Philip was at war with Edward I of England, who claimed the throne of France. This war created extra expenses which piled up alongside his inherited debts. The need for other sources of income was increasing inexorably. His father had come up with the idea of levying a windfall tax on the Jews in 1284. Philip continued this family tradition in 1292 and again in 1303; then in 1306 he seized all Jewish property and expelled its owners—his ultimate Jewish tax. He extended similar harsh tax treatment to the Lombard and Florentine bankers: In 1295, this tax yielded £65,000 (about $130,000).

But even these extraordinary efforts did not bring in enough money even to meet his day-to-day expenses, which were running at about £4,000 (about $8,000) a day by this time. To have sufficient coin to meet his debts, Philip had to devalue the currency. His father and grandfather had used the financial services of the Paris Temple to carry out the monetary functions of the state, but Philip decided to move his Treasury from the moderating influence of John of Tours, the Templar Treasurer there, and install his own staff at the Louvre. He must have been desperate at this time, and the Paris Temple could never have agreed to take part in what he did, since it would instantly have lost its good name for sound banking practice.

Philip's solution was to recall the coinage, melt it down, and remint coins with the same face value, but a lot lower precious metal content, in much greater quantities. This was one of the first recorded instances of hyper-inflation. The mark, originally valued at 54 shillings in 1290, had increased to 68 shillings in 1296, and by 1303 was officially valued at 104 shillings. By systematically debasing the coinage of the realm, Philip raised £1,200,000 (about $2,400,000) between 1298 and 1299 and £185,000 (about $370,000) in 1301.[131]

The Pope had granted Philip's grandfather, St. Louis, the right to levy extraordinary taxation on both the Church and the lay community during times of war, to meet the needs of the state and the defense of the kingdom. Philip revived that tradition, and taxed the Church as a convenient source of revenue to reduce his debts. But in 1302, to stop Philip's runaway taxation, Pope Boniface VIII issued a bull forbidding the clergy to give any financial subsidy to lay powers without the permission of Rome. Philip's response was to issue an order prohibiting the export of gold, silver, or merchandise from France. At a stroke, he cut off a large stream of papal revenue. His response was partly motivated by the need to protect the weak, and highly inflated, French economy, but even this did not manage to avert a major currency crisis in 1303. As the people realized what was happening, Philip was harassed by public unrest. He had to take sanctuary in the fortified Paris Temple during the currency riots.[132]

To counter Philip's attack on papal revenues, Boniface issued a decree that all princes were subject to his rulings in matters temporal and spiritual. Philip publicly burned that papal bull. To make sure his subjects understood that he did not accept the Pope's jurisdiction, he announced his action to the people of Paris with a mighty fanfare of trumpets.

Boniface could not overlook this act of rebellion, and summoned the French clergy to Rome to discuss how to preserve the traditional freedoms of the Church. Philip responded by calling a national assembly of clergy, and lay administrators of the Church, in Paris. They passed a resolution to stand by their monarch, in defense of his rights. Philip then ordered the seizure and confiscation of the lands and properties of all the churchmen who had obeyed the Pope's edict to go to Rome. The Templars supported the King, and he considered them trustworthy enough to use the skills of John of Tours, treasurer of the Paris Temple, to handle the financial sequestration (seizure of church property). The move certainly improved the wealth of the French crown.[133]

Boniface responded by publishing the bull *Unam sanctam*, asserting that not only was every human being subject to the rule of the Pope, but they also had to appear in Rome if so ordered. Now the battle of the egos was really hitting its stride. The eighty-four-year-old Boniface VIII had a weak spot, though. In his earlier incarnation as Cardinal Benedict Gaetani, he'd chalked up a colorful history of sexual adventures, and Phillip was aware of this. So he accused the Pope of gross sexual misconduct. Boniface was bisexual, having kept a married woman and her daughter as his mistresses, as well as attempting to seduce a number of handsome young men, with some measure of success. He was quoted as saying that the sex act was "no more a sin than to rub your hands together." However, while he may well have practiced adultery and sodomy, it seems very unlikely that Boniface went as far as keeping a tame demon in his ring to come out and sleep with him at night, as Philip claimed. He would never have had the spare time, or enough room in his bed.[134]

Boniface sent emissaries to France to insist that the French clergy conform to his instructions, and a vigorous argument occurred before the King publicly pledged to stand by all churchmen who supported the independence of France against the Pope. By now the proceedings were becoming farcical, with the King intercepting the papal bull that should have excommunicated him (but didn't, because he prevented its publication). At this point, Boniface lost his sense of humor completely, and using the rather dubious authority of the Donation of Constantine, declared the French throne vacant and offered it to the King of Austria.

Neither side would back down, but Philip had a master stroke up his royal sleeve. On the morning of September 7, 1303, he hired enough mercenary "French patriots" to hold an impromptu riot outside the gates of the Pope's residence at Anagni. He also bribed a papal retainer to open the gates and allow the "patriots" inside, where they rushed about shouting "Live the King of France, die Boniface." They kept the Pope prisoner for three days. Soon after returning to Rome, Boniface died of a seizure.[135] Philip did not attend the funeral.

PHILIP'S PUPPET POPE

The Church was in a political mess at the time of Boniface's death. The Church of Rome was founded on the political dogma that the Pope is the supreme ruler of the world, pontifical supremacy then being a fundamental article of the Roman Catholic religion. This brought to a head the conflict with Philip, who did not accept any limitation of his kingly role. The Church's crusades had reduced many kingdoms to poverty without reclaiming the Holy Land. The days of secular rulers rushing forward to pour men and money into papal adventures were fast disappearing. This was a problem Boniface's successor would have to face; another would be dealing with Philip.

That successor, Pope Benedict XI, initially gained Philip's approval by removing the sentence of excommunication that Boniface had issued against him. But as Benedict settled into the papacy, he tried to restore the authority of the Holy See. Philip had no intention of reopening the battle for temporal supremacy that he felt Boniface had already lost, so he arranged to have Benedict poisoned in 1305.[136] Then came the problem of selecting a new Pope. The suggestions of the French cardinals counterbalanced those of the Italian cardinals, and a stalemate ensued within the Conclave (the gathering of cardinals that elected the next Pope) for ten months. To break it, Philip's agents suggested that one side should select three candidates, from which the other side should choose a Pope. Bertrand de Gotte, Archbishop of Bordeaux, a man who had many reasons to dislike both Philip and the Italian Cardinals, was selected as the compromise candidate by both sides.

The Cardinal of Prato advised Philip that Bertrand was an ambitious and malleable character who could serve the King's purposes and, when the King spoke to him, would see where his own best interests lay. Philip set up a private meeting with Bertrand at the abbey of St. Jean d'Angely in Gascony. He told the ambitious prelate that it was within his power to make Bertrand Pope, but if he were to do so there would be six conditions attached to the deal. These were:

1. A perfect reconciliation between himself and the Church.
2. Admission to the Roman Catholic communion for himself and his nominees.
3. The tithes of the clergy of France to be given to him (Philip) for five years to pay for his war in Flanders.
4. The persecution and destruction of the memory of Pope Boniface VIII.
5. James and Peter Colonna to be made cardinals.
6. To combine the Crusading Orders (the Knights Templar and Hospitallers of St. John) under Philip's command, and sequester their funds to raise money to solve his currency crisis. (This amalgamation had been proposed before, but now had considerable attractions for Philip, especially if he could take over the joint assets of both orders.)

The King of France was about to undermine the authority of the papacy for the next fifty years—the period that would be known to history as the Avignon Period. Philip did not trust Bertrand, but agreed to make him Pope if he would cooperate. However, he was not prepared to allow any papal candidate out of France, so it was at Lyons rather than Rome that Bertrand was crowned Pope Clement V on December 17, 1305.[137]

The King's agenda, now that his regular taxation of the Church was assured, was to gain control of the redundant military crusading orders, and to use their financial assets to restore his economy. But Templars, because of their great wealth and their connections with most of the noble families of France, could prove a serious obstacle to his plans. He must have felt that he needed to limit their power before the Pope had a chance to use them against him, so he was quick to call in the Pope's promise to consider combining the Christian Military Orders. Only six months after his coronation, on June 6, 1306, Clement wrote to William de Villaret, the Master of the Hospital (Knights Hospitaller), and to Jacques de Molay, the Master of the Temple (Knights Templar), calling them to meet him in France and discuss the combining of the two orders.[138]

De Villaret, the Master of the Hospital, was astute enough to avoid the trip, pleading he could not be spared from an attack on Rhodes. De Molay, who was defending Limassol when the message reached him, could have made a similar plea, but he did not foresee the danger to his Order. In a disastrous miscalculation, he chose to obey Clement's order. He delegated the defense and embarked for La Rochelle aboard a fleet of eighteen ships. He also took with him sixty of his most distinguished knights, 150,000 florins of gold, and twelve pack-horses laden with unminted silver.[139] A tempting morsel indeed to set before a king short of money to consolidate his debased coinage! Or did he perhaps hope to buy Philip's favor with the bullion?

The Paris Temple had been a major center of Templar financial operations in north-west Europe since the time of St. Louis and was a large establishment, encompassing many buildings, outside the walls of the city, to the north. The Templar treasury had once carried out French state financial operations,[140] until in 1295 Philip took back that function to the Louvre and systematically debased the currency. By 1306 Philip had a strong motive for gaining control of Templar assets if he was to rebuild the debased French coinage, and he was going to need a new source of precious metals suitable for coining. The Templar treasury was such a source.

John de Tours was the second successive man of that name to be treasurer of the Paris Temple. He was appointed in 1302, and fragments of the surviving accounting records show he used an early type of double-entry accounting. The Templar treasurers had developed their methods of administration to finance crusades. Their techniques involved secure storage of deeds and wills, the safe-keeping of valuables, and the accounting of payments for the management of estates. They provided a ready means for a government to maximize its taxation revenue. The kings of Europe had quickly realized that the Templars had the financial infrastructure they lacked, and the Templars were happy to cooperate in providing primitive banking facilities. To service this need, the establishment of the Paris Temple had expanded.

Although it no longer exists, we know that the original building was a typical Templar round church—similar to the Temple Church, which still stands just off

Fleet Street in London—later extended with rectangular choirs. Around 1270, as its financial importance grew, this structure had grown to over 150 feet high with four floors.[141] It had grown into a grand and fortified building, though its fortifications were there to protect the valuables stored, not to provide the base for a military force.

ACCUSATION, TORTURE AND ROYAL LARCENY

In June 1307 King Philip the Fair greeted Templar Grand Master Jacques de Molay warmly, receiving him and his pack-horse train of silver with the greatest marks of distinction and favor. With a great show of pomp and ceremony, de Molay deposited the Order's portable store of treasure within the Temple precincts, watched by the debt-ridden and financially beleaguered King.

But Philip had what he regarded as a plausible case for moving against the Templars and was planning to accuse them of heresy. On September 14, 1307, sealed letters were sent to all the governors and royal officers throughout France, with orders to arm themselves on the 12th of the following month, to open the letters that would follow in the night, and act according to the instructions they contained. Meanwhile the intended victims had no suspicion of their fate—indeed, on the eve of his arrest de Molay was one of four pallbearers at the funeral of the King's sister-in-law, the Princess Catherine: a very great honor.[142] The King's directions to his officers were to seize the persons and the goods of the Templars; to interrogate, torture, and obtain confessions from them; to promise pardon to those who confessed; and to menace those who opposed them.

In October 1307, in the cold gray glimmer of dawn on Friday the 13th, Philip's seneschals swooped down on the French Templars and the head of the entire Templar Order. With the perfect vision of hindsight, it seems remarkable that the senior members of the Order received no forewarning. Many junior French clerks and officials must have seen the multiple copies of the instructions, but they must have been either totally loyal to Philip or totally terrified of reprisals. (The charges involved may have helped preserve their silence, because actively assisting accused heretics would have attracted the attention not just of Philip's soldiers but also of the tame monks of Philip's homegrown French Inquisition, who would be in charge of interrogating the Order.)

The stronghold of the Paris Temple could have caused Philip considerable problems if the Grand Master had received warning and reacted quickly. But there was no strong defense, even though the Temple was a fortified building, and it appears the Order was so unprepared to defend it that it was garrisoned only with elderly and sick brothers; at least one of the knights arrested there that morning was a leper.[143] Thus Philip took possession of the Paris Temple, detaining Grand Master de Molay, the Preceptor of Aquitaine, and the Prior of Normandy in the process.

It is said that the eighteen-ship Templar fleet had heard rumors of the impending raid, and so set sail from La Rochelle, laden with fighting knights and treasure before the dawn strike, but this seems unlikely. Helen Nicholson pointed out that the port of La Rochelle was an important link in the Templars' trading chain, and its function provides a simpler explanation:

> Coin was carried from the West to the East. This meant that the Templars needed ships to carry their coin, as well as agricultural produce, horses and personnel for the East. They also provided a secure carrying service for pilgrims—safer and cheaper than hiring a commercial carrier. These would have been heavy transport vessels rather than warships. Much of the surviving evidence for Templar shipping comes from the relevant port records or royal records giving permission for the export of produce. At La Rochelle on the west coast of France during the twelfth century the Templars were given several vineyards and produced wine for their own consumption and for export. . .
> the records of the port of La Rochelle show that the Templars were exporting wine by ship . . . these would have been transport vessels rather than warships, and the Templars probably hired them as they needed them, rather than buying their own.[144]

This raises two points that offer clues to what might have happened to the famous "fleet." The King's sealed orders had been sent out after the Templar Grand Master had arrived in France,[145] the date on the orders being September 14, 1307.[146] The implication of this is that the Grand Master of the Templars had been in France at least a month before the mass arrests. And there would be no reason for so many of the Templars' limited number of hired transport ships to remain in port. Indeed, in early autumn, the Templar vintners of La Rochelle would be needing the cargo space to export the new vintage of wine they had produced. And remember that the Templar "fleet" was nothing like a modern battle flotilla.

> After 1312 the Hospital of St. John was mainly involved in sea-based warfare and had an admiral in command of its marine operations, but only had four galleys (warships), with other vessels. It is unlikely that the Templars had any more galleys than the Hospitallers. The ships would have been very small by modern standards, too shallow in draught and sailing too low in the water to be able to withstand the heavy waves and winds of the open Atlantic, and suited for use only in the relatively shallow waters of the continental shelf. What was more, they could not carry enough water to be at sea for long periods.[147]

THE MANY CONFESSIONS JACQUES DE MOLAY

De Molay made his first confession to the charges of heresy soon after his arrest, but, as it was obtained under torture, it proves nothing. The fact that a number of different confessions are attributed to de Molay perhaps says more for the skill of Philip's torturers—and his spin doctors— than it does about the breadth and depth of wrongdoing on de Molay's part.

Jacques de Molay, the last Grand Master of the Knights Templar.

The objectives of the dawn raid were clear from Philip's sealed orders: The directions sent by the king to his officers had been to seize the persons and the goods of the Templars; to interrogate, torture, and obtain confessions from them; to promise pardon to those who confessed; and to menace those who denied.[148]

De Molay is said to have made a verbal confession before the University of Paris on Sunday, October 15, 1307.[149] This was only two days after his arrest so, if true, he had rapidly been persuaded to speak. Some two weeks later, on Tuesday, October 24, he wrote a letter of confession where he admitted denying Christ and the Cross but vehemently denied any homosexual activities.[150] Early the following year the Master and the Prior of Normandy and the Preceptor of Aquitaine were taken to Chinon, where they again confessed to denying Christ and the Cross at an audience with Pope Clement. Clement recorded this in a private letter he wrote to Philip dated December 30, 1308.[151]

Clement was outraged by Philip's attack on the Templars, but was forced to admit the King's legal right to do so under the terms of an earlier papal directive which had ordered all Christian princes "to give all possible assistance to the Holy Office of the Inquisition." And Philip could also invoke his sainted grandfather: In 1249 Louis IX had ordered his barons to deal with heretics according to the full dictates of their duty to the Pope.[152]

The attack on the Templars was directly against Clement's interests. It showed the world that Philip didn't need his consent to act against an Order that was supposed to be directly under papal protection. Philip then went further, holding an assembly of state at Tours in May 1308 and obtaining its approval of his royal right to punish heretics without need of the Pope's consent.[153] Clement, threatened by this move, tried to escape to Rome, via Bordeaux. Unfortunately, his baggage train, his treasures, and His Holiness himself were stopped on the King's orders, and from 1309 onwards Clement became a prisoner of Philip.[154]

To play for time, the Pope set up a papal Commission to investigate the guilt of the Order. On Wednesday, November 26, 1309, de Molay was brought before it at Vienne. Yet another of his confessions was read to him, which this time admitted all the charges, including homosexuality. He again vehemently denied the charges of homosexual abominations, and had to be told by the bishops of the commission to moderate his behavior. The following day, when he had regained his composure, de Molay made this statement to the commission:

> If I, myself, or other knights, have made confessions before the bishop of Paris, or elsewhere, we have betrayed the truth—we have yielded to fear, to danger, to violence. We were tortured by our enemies.

He offered to remove his shirt to show the assembled bishops the marks that the torture had left on his body.[155] Three months later De Molay demanded to be brought before the Pope following a public accusation of 546 Templars at Paris on March 28, 1310. Philip simply refused him.[156]

Encouraged by the King, the Pope now drew up an act of accusation against the Templars, which included the following: At the time of their reception into the Order, the Knights were made to deny Christ and the Virgin birth. In particular, they had to declare that Christ was not the true God, but a prophet who was crucified for his own crimes and not for the redemption of the world. They also were accused of spitting and trampling on the cross, especially on Good Friday.[157]

On October 1, 1311, Pope Clement and 114 of his bishops met to decide the Templars' fate. The bishops, the majority drawn from outside France, refused to find the Templars guilty, and so Clement closed the Council and continued to do nothing. The following February Philip went to visit Clement and had a private discussion with him. The result was that on March 22, 1313, Clement abolished the Templar Order on his sole authority, without ruling on its guilt or innocence. The General Council reconvened on April 3, and, in the presence of the King and his royal guards, the Pope read his bull of abolition. By May 2, 1313, the Order of Knights Templar ceased to exist.[158]

The law of heresy under which Philip claimed to have acted allowed the Christian prince who carried out the interrogation of a heretic the use of various sanctions such as imprisonment, confiscation, the stake, etc. He was also allowed to recover his expenses from the heretic's property, in order to cover the costs of the investigation and imprisonment of the suspects.[159] Philip's costs conveniently managed to absorb all the Order's assets in France.

Jacques de Molay, the Grand Master of the Templars, Geoffrey de Charny, Prior of Normandy, Hugh de Peyraud, Templar Visitor to France, and Guy de Auvergne, the Preceptor of Aquitaine, remained in prison. Clement set up a papal Commission under the Bishop of Alba and two other cardinals to pronounce their sentence. Philip wanted maximum publicity for this show-sentencing, so he ordered a stage to be set up in front of the Church of Notre Dame in Paris. The Archbishop of Sens, with the three papal Commissioners, took their places on this stage on March 18, 1314. An immense crowd gathered to hear the fate of the four senior Templars, and a hush fell over the square as the prisoners were brought on stage. The Bishop of Alba read out the most recent and damning of their many confessions, and pronounced their sentence: Eternal imprisonment. He was proposing to go on to explain to the crowd that their crimes amounted to "a bitter thing, a lamentable thing, a thing which is horrible to contemplate, terrible to hear, a detestable crime, an execrable evil, an abominable work, a detestable disgrace, a thing almost inhuman, indeed set about from all humanity," as Philip had described it in his letter of September 14, 1307.[160]

However, at this point he was interrupted by Grand Master de Molay, who insisted on speaking to the assembled crowd. The mood of the crowd was such that the cardinals dared not interfere as he made this speech:

> It is just that, in so terrible a day, and in the last moments of my life, I should discover all the iniquity of falsehood, and make the truth triumph. I declare, then, in the face of heaven and earth, and acknowledge, though to my eternal shame, that I have committed the greatest of crimes; but it has been the acknowledging of those which have been so foully charged on the order. I attest, and truth obliges me to attest, that it is innocent. I made the contrary declaration only to suspend the excessive pains of torture, and to mollify those who made me endure them. I know the punishments which have been inflicted on all the knights who had the courage to revoke a similar confession; but the dreadful spectacle which is presented to me is not able to make me confirm one lie by another. The life offered me on such infamous terms I abandon without regret.[161]

De Molay was supported by Geoffrey de Charny, and amidst great confusion the Commissioners stopped the proceedings and reported to Philip. The King's response was immediate: Without any papal authority, he condemned both outspoken Templars to the flames. The following day a pyre was erected on an island in the Seine, and the two men were roasted slowly over a hot, smokeless fire. The heat was applied first to their feet, spreading slowly to their more vital parts, and the fetid smell of their burning flesh infected the surrounding air, adding to their torment.[162]

To their last breaths, both Templars continued to shout the innocence of their Order. As he slowly roasted to death, de Molay cursed both Clement and Philip, summoning them both to appear within forty days before the Supreme Judge. Even when his face was black with the flames and his tongue swelled so that he could not speak, de Molay's lips still moved in condemnation until they were shrunk back to his gums. Fat, water, and blood dripped out of his finger ends until his strength was gone, and with his lower body fully consumed, he fell forward from his support into the fire.

> When death finally ended their misery the spectators shed tears at the view of their constancy and during the night their ashes were gathered up to be preserved as relics.[163]

This dramatic climax ensured the Order iconic status and started a whole new chapter in its story. The last Templar Grand Master and his senior officers died on March 19, 1314, but the Order's new place in history was only just beginning. Dr. Nicholson remarks about the aftermath of their destruction:

> The supposed Templar involvement in the Grail legend reinforced the Order's supposed connection with secret societies and esoteric knowledge. Upper-middle-class secret societies such as the Hermetic Order of the Golden Dawn and high-profile occultists such as Aleister Crowley made much of the Templars as supposed bearers of magical knowledge and hidden truth. This has now become holy writ among modern occultists and neo-pagans . . . These new Templar Orders are themselves now the subject of scholarly study. It is a strange tribute to the enduring appeal of this ordinary religious Order—in existence for less then two centuries and last seen nearly seven hundred years ago—that not only the original Order but even the myth of the Order . . . [has] become part of modern history.[164]

Conclusions

It seems that Philip IV of France had clear political motives when accusing the Templars of heresy, and his views were not shared in other countries. He was personally almost bankrupt, and canon law allowed the goods and chattels of convicted heretics to be seized by the state—which is to say, him. Whatever the moral pros and cons of the Templar Order, the motive for their destruction appears to be pure, unadulterated greed.

The period of the trial and final execution of the Templar leaders left a lot of time—almost seven years—in which they could have planned an underground continuation of the Order, and the failure of Pope Clement to rule on their guilt or innocence left a lot of scope for the growth of revisionist ideas and myths about the extent of their esoteric knowledge.

The story of the Templars' fall did seem to leave enough unexplained gaps for their rituals and knowledge to have passed into Freemasonry. So it was obvious that my next task must be to look at the modern-day Templar Masons and see if I could find the route by which Templar rituals and beliefs could have been transmitted to the Freemasons. In the next chapter, we'll pick up the Templar trail amid the secret Temples of the Freemasons.

CHAPTER 4

DID THE KNIGHTS TEMPLAR BECOME FREEMASONS?

MY INTRODUCTION TO TEMPLAR MASONRY

In chapter 1, I traced Templar Masonry back to 1779, and discovered that it was intertwined with the story of one of the oldest and most venerated Lodges in Scotland, "Mother Kilwinning." The Masonic legend says that the Lodge of Kilwinning was founded by King Robert the Bruce in 1314, immediately after the Battle of Bannockburn. This was less than seven years after King Philip's dawn raid on the Knights Templar in Paris in 1307, and it was plausible for many refugee Templar knights to have still been around. Did they help the Scottish King, and were they rewarded by being allowed to hide themselves in Scotland, disguised as Freemasons?

The Lodge of Kilwinning is certainly one of the oldest in Scotland, and hence in the world. It is affectionately called "Lodge Mother Kilwinning" because of its role as the "mother" Lodge of all the "daughter" Lodges that were formed much later. (Freemasons use the terms "mother Lodge" and "daughter Lodge" to describe the formation of new Lodges by Masons who already belong to other Lodges—like an older Lodge giving birth to a new one.)

In 1779 an early Templar Lodge, now known as the Early Grand Encampment of Ireland, was born as a "daughter Lodge" of "Mother" Kilwinning. This soon developed into what became the founding Templar group in Scotland, and it came to be called the Early Grand Mother Encampment of Scotland. Its ritual was broadly similar to the modern ceremony that I had participated in when I became a Masonic Templar. But then I still knew little about the history of the Masonic Knights Templar, so I set out to learn more.

I decided to begin by looking at my own Preceptory: St. George Aboyne, in Aberdeen. (Preceptory is the Masonic term for a Lodge of Knights Templar, Priory for a Lodge of Masonic Knights of Malta; a ritual meetings of either body is called an Encampment.) St. George Aboyne awards two Masonic degrees. The first is Knight Templar; the second is Knight of Malta, and this is awarded only to Knights Templar in good standing.

St. George Aboyne is acknowledged as the oldest Templar Preceptory in Scotland, and has been given the number 1 on the roll of the Great Priory of Scotland, the body that controls Templar Masonry in Scotland. In 1994 the Venerable Preceptor at the time, George W.C. Davie, sponsored *A Brief History of the Knights of the Temple and the Priory of St. George Aboyne* to celebrate its bicentenary. The book was written by a historian from Aberdeen University, Elizabeth Boyd, who was given access to all the Order's records.

In the foreword, George Davie says:

> The Fratres [Knights] of St. George Aboyne felt we should in some way mark our bicentenary celebrations and it was decided that this would be in the form of a short history of Templar Masonry and the St. George Aboyne Preceptory in particular.
>
> That we exist after 200 years is due to the efforts and support of our predecessors: We hope through the endeavours of the present Officers and Fratres that the Preceptory will continue to prosper and in time commemorate another 100 years.[165]

Liz Boyd then begins with an outline of the history of the Templars, with particular reference to their activities in Scotland. She also looks at Bonnie Prince Charlie and the Jacobite (Stuart) links with Scottish Freemasonry:

> In September 1745 at Holyrood, Bonnie Prince Charlie is credited as being installed as the Grand Master of the Templars: The evidence for this is very flimsy and cannot be substantiated. What is more likely is that the Prince was installed as the Grand Master of the Royal Order of Scotland, as the purported regalia worn is similar to that of the Royal Order in the 18th Century.[166]

Liz Boyd also makes the interesting point that it was not until after the formation of the Grand Lodge of Scotland, in 1736, that Masonry was forced to use the same ritual in every Lodge; before then, the rites that characterized Freemasonry varied widely, each Lodge jealously guarding its own. When Grand Lodge was formed, the higher degrees were brought under its control and a common basic ritual agreed upon.

> Early entries in various minute books detail the workings of the Higher degrees by the Craft Lodges. In order to ensure that these degrees were kept secret from all but the chosen few, the Lodge would be opened and closed in due form for each Degree, the people to whom it was not relevant leaving appropriately. In some recorded entries a Lodge could be opened and closed two or three times in one evening. It was not until the late 1790's that Grand Lodge forbade the bestowing of the higher

Degrees due to a series of acts of Parliament, pertaining to Secret Societies, which effectively made anything above Master Mason illegal.[167]

The Masonic Lodge that would eventually become the Preceptory of St. George Aboyne began its existence as a Friendly Society. Liz Boyd observes that many Lodges were set up with dual purposes, as Operative Lodges (assemblies of working stonemasons) and Friendly Societies (groups that collected regular dues so they could help out their members and their families in hard times). When she looked at the original minute book of Lodge St. Nicholas of Aberdeen, No. 93, she was surprised to find that it also contained the rules and regulations of its associated Friendly Society.

The St. George Friendly Society began operation in 1792 in the city of Aberdeen, founded by members of St. James Lodge and St. Luke Lodge (both Operative Lodges based in Aberdeen, and now defunct). On November 3, 1794, the members of St. George Friendly Society were granted a Charter by the Grand Lodge of Scotland to work as a Masonic Lodge. Liz Boyd could not find any minutes from the early days of St. George Lodge, but she was able to examine its Accounts Book, which contained details of candidates. She observed that most candidates were previously members of the Mariners or Weavers Craft Guilds.

By 1808 St. George Lodge had become so popular that it formed a daughter Lodge called The Aboyne Lodge, which was disbanded in 1837.

> The early records of the St. George Lodge are very patchy, however retrospective entries of the Royal Grand Conclave Roll Book date from August 16th 1795. The first recorded Royal Arch Degrees were worked earlier in that year: It is safe to assume that members of the Lodge were qualified to work the Templar Grades at the time of the Charter being granted. Certainly, the Founder Members of the St. George Encampment in London were advanced through the Templar Grades by the St. George Lodge in 1795.[168]

This added two items of interest to my knowledge of the origin of my Preceptory: First, that the members of the St. George Lodge were working both the Royal Arch and the Templar degrees in 1795, and, second, that an early Templar encampment in London (also called St. George) was created by the members of St. George, Aberdeen, taking the would-be London Templars through the necessary rituals to make them Masonic Knights Templar.

Seditious Secret Societies?

Professor Andrew Prescott notes that towards the end of 1798 seditious societies, bound by secret oaths and harbingers of a French invasion, were seen around every corner.[169]

> This atmosphere created a groundswell of support for the passage in July 1799 of one of the most sweeping of the legislative measures introduced by Pitt's govern-

ment to forestall the threat of revolution. This act, "An act for the more effectual suppression of societies established for seditious and treasonable purposes; and for the better preventing treasonable and seditious practices", to give its full name, was, almost by accident, to form the mainstay of the relationship between freemasonry and the state in Britain for nearly two hundred years, until its repeal by the Criminal Justice Act of 1967.[170]

At the time of this Act, there was one Grand Lodge in Scotland and two Grand Lodges in England. All were potentially at risk of breaching the proposed Secret Societies Act and becoming proscribed organizations, even though their oaths were not seditious. As it became clear that the Bill would be passed into law, Lord Moira, the Acting Grand Master of the Grand Lodge of England (known as the Moderns), and the Duke of Atholl, Past Grand Master Mason of Scotland and Grand Master of the Ancients' Grand Lodge, with other senior Freemasons met with the Prime Minster, William Pitt the Younger.

Prescott points out that Pitt did have some cause to worry about the loyalty of certain Freemasons, saying:

> The government had worrying information which suggested that the masons needed to be more vigilant. Among the documents which had been shown to the secret committee was a letter sent to the Home Office by John Waring, a catholic priest at Stonyhurst, who described how an Irishman named Bernard Kerr had told him he was "a freemason, a Knight Templar, and belonged to a society of people who called themselves United Englishmen." Kerr had shown him the printed rules of the United Englishmen, which he kept in a large portfolio together with his papers of admission as a Knight Templar . . . [Also] many of the United Irishmen were freemasons and many features of their organisation, such as the use of oaths and secret signs, were drawn from Masonic models.[171]

A plot, centering on a Masonic Lodge in Leeds, was uncovered by a lawyer named James Green, who reported it to the Government. Green had visited a Lodge in Leeds, and had been involved in seditious political conversation at the supper held after the Lodge meeting by a Freemason who was also a member of the United Irishmen. Green discovered that there was to be a major meeting of the United Irishmen to be held, under cover of a Masonic gathering, at Paisley in Scotland. Green said:

> Now my Lord, if your Grace will approve of it, as I am in the higher orders of masonry, and as I have every reason to believe that I can be of signal service in this matter, I will very readily undertake to conduct matters as occasion may serve so as to nip the evil in the bud, or let it run to such a length as may come to a riper maturity, and tho' there are too many rotten of the Craft fraternity, I can with great truth aver that the general part of the mass are strictly loyal.[172]

To get around these difficulties, the Prime Minster accepted that the Grand Lodges would operate a system of self-regulation. The Grand Secretaries would

Coat of arms of the Grand Conclave of Masonic Knights Templar in England and Wales (1812).

record details of the time and place of meeting of all approved Lodges in the country, together with a declaration that the Lodges were approved by the Grand Master. Each Lodge had in turn to keep a book in which every member was to declare "that he is well affected to [i.e., supports] the constitution and government of this realm, by King, Lords, and Commons, as by law established." This book was to be open for inspection by local magistrates. In this way, the Grand Lodges were made responsible for policing Freemasonry; Lodges whose names did not appear on the return made by the Grand Secretaries would be deemed criminal conspiracies.[173]

The portion of the Act of Parliament says:

> Nothing in this act contained shall extend, or be construed to extend, to prevent the meetings of the Lodge or society of persons which is now held at Free Masons Hall in Great Queen Street in the County of Middlesex, and usually denominated The Grand Lodge of Freemasons of England, or of the Lodge or society of persons usually denominated The Grand Lodge of Masons of England, according to the Old Institution, or of the Lodge or society of persons which is now held at Edinburgh, and usually denominated The Grand Lodge of Free Masons of Scotland, or the meetings of any subordinate lodge or society of persons usually calling themselves Free Masons, the holding whereof shall be sanctioned or approved by any one of the above mentioned lodges or societies.[174]

This Act caused many problems with the Lodges in Scotland, as the exemptions initially proposed by the Prime Minister only covered the two English Grand Lodges. The exemption for the Scottish Grand Lodge was only inserted during the committee stage of the bill. This led to a dispute between the Scottish Grand Lodge and its most senior Lodge, Mother Kilwinning. The Master of Lodge Mother Kilwinning wrote to William Fullarton, the Member of Parliament for Ayrshire, and protested that the bill referred only to the Grand Lodge in Edinburgh, while "another, more ancient and equally respectable, and remarkable for its attachment to the laws and constitution of the country (themselves) was taken no notice of." They requested Fullarton "to make the necessary application, and through the proper channel, to have that lodge, and those holding charters from her, likewise exempted from the operations of this Bill."[175] In effect, the Act made the Grand Lodge of Scotland in Edinburgh the sole arbiter of what degrees could be worked in Scotland. Before the Act, Archibald, Earl of Eglinton, the Grand Master of Lodge Mother Kilwinning, had issued a charter for a Lodge in Dublin by name of the "High Knight Templars of Ireland Lodge."[176]

The British Government's worry that John Waring's evidence showed the Masonic Templar degrees to be a possible recruiting ground for the United Irishmen coincided with a dramatic rise of interest in Templar Masonry in Scottish Craft Lodges. To avoid suspicion, the Grand Lodge of Scotland issued a directive in October 1800 "prohibiting and discharging its daughters to hold any meetings above the degree of Master Mason, under penalty of forfeiture of their Charter."[177] This did not stop the Lodges from working the higher and Templar degrees, but it did have the effect of encouraging many Scottish masons to apply to the Early Grand Encampment of Ireland for charters, to work the rituals I outlined in chapter 1. This was not a satisfactory situation.

SIGNS, SEALS, AND SELF-PROMOTION

In 1805 The Early Grand Encampment of Ireland issued a charter to Alexander Deuchar to form a Knights Templar group in Edinburgh. It was to be known as the "Edinburgh Encampment No. 31," though Deuchar later renamed it the "Grand Assembly of Knights Templar in Edinburgh." To comply with the Secret Societies Act, he approached the Duke of Kent, Grand Master of the Order in England, who in 1811 granted a charter to set up the "Royal Grand Conclave of Scotland." Naturally, Deuchar was named Grand Master, and was all set to take control of the Templar Order in Scotland.

The Great Priory of Scotland says this about the Royal Grand Conclave:

> Deuchar's motives in turning to England rather than to Ireland are not clear. He may have had genuine doubts about the validity of the Irish charters, or he may have been working to raise the prestige of the Edinburgh Templars. Whatever his reasons,

he was unsuccessful in his attempt to bring all the Scottish Templars into the Royal Grand Conclave. A large section, chiefly in Ayrshire, held to their Irish charters, and were organized under Robert Martin in 1826 as the "Early Grand Encampment of Scotland." Until the beginning of the twentieth century both these Grand Bodies existed.[178]

Liz Boyd reports that the minutes of St. George Lodge from 1810 show that an application was made to the Early Grand Encampment of Ireland for a Charter to work the Royal Arch. This was granted on March 6, 1810. The minutes of September 14, 1813, show that the Early Rite Encampment of the Lodge of St. George applied for membership to Deuchar's Royal Grand Conclave of Scotland. She notes that the application did not succeed, as there is no record of their admittance in the Royal Grand Conclave books. She goes on to say that a main criterion "for admittance to the Royal Grand Conclave was that associated bodies would not recognise any Lodge, Chapter or Encampment working the Templar Grades, who were working them under a Master Mason Charter."[179] This was because Deuchar did not want to recognize the Early Grand Encampment of Ireland, which drew its authority to work the Templar degrees from Mother Kilwinning. He argued that it was trying to usurp his position and was suspicious of any groups who supported it.

Liz Boyd is convinced that he refused the St. George Encampment because they were working Templar Grades under their Lodge Charter of 1794, which did not specify that the higher Degrees could be worked. This could have caused trouble under the Secret Societies Act. But in 1817 St. George Knights Templar Encampment made an application to merge with the Aboyne Encampment, which already held a Charter from Deuchar's Grand Conclave to work the Templar degrees as an independent body.

> The Aboyne Encampment was originally part of the Lodge of the 6th North British Militia, which was chartered in 1799 and dissolved in 1839. This Lodge was sometimes (confusingly) known as the Aboyne Lodge as Lord Aboyne was the Commander in Chief of the Regiment and had been Grand Master Mason of Scotland 1802–1804. The Regiment was later known as the 55th Aberdeenshire Regiment of the North British Militia, and subsequently the 3rd Battalion of the Gordon Highlanders which was eventually dissolved in 1885. As a regular Militia unit, it was stationed in varying parts of the country, including Liverpool, Dover and the Tower of London. In 1812 they were stationed at Dalkeith which was then a separate town on the outskirts of Edinburgh. Under the sponsorship of Lord Aboyne, application was made to be admitted to the Royal Grand Conclave of Scotland. This was accepted and "The Aboyne Encampment" as it was then styled, was formally admitted as Number 21, on the roll on the 6th July 1812.[180]

One of the minutes from the records of the Aboyne Encampment of May 27, 1816, tells the story:

The Aboyne Encampment having had previous communication with a Body of Irregular Sir Knights Templar in Peterhead and its vicinity, holding under an illegal charter or paper from the Early Grand of Ireland, and having received a petition from them to take them under our protection and make them regular under the Royal Grand Conclave of Scotland. The Sir Knights having taken into their serious consideration that it would be for the particular good of the Order came to the resolution of sending Sir Frances Donald Commander and Sir Alexander Walker, Secretary to Peterhead to swear them in to the Royal Grand Conclave and Aboyne Encampment . . . to grant them a letter of separation to enable them to meet at such time as they could receive one from the Grand Conclave.

This time, the St. George Encampment was successful with their application, and so their fifty or so members became part of the Royal Grand Conclave.[181]

I wondered what had caused Alexander Deuchar to embark on such a divisive course, and ultimately found the answer: Deuchar was a seal-maker by trade, and he had set up the Royal Grand Conclave as a means of self-promotion. He decided he was unlikely to become Grand Master Mason of Scotland, so he created a grand role for himself by appealing to England and taking advantage of the Secret Societies Act. This had not endeared him to the rank and file of Scots Freemasons, and he now went further by admitting non-Masons to the Conclave and changed its ritual to make this possible (previously only Royal Arch Masons in good standing had been allowed to join.) He probably saw this as a way of increasing revenues, but the Encampments would not accept these non-Masons as members, so they never made them Templar Masons.[182]

Liz Boyd comments that the Royal Grand Conclave was in serious difficulties by 1836, chiefly because Alexander Deuchar's style of leadership was not popular. As a result, many Encampments did not bother to pay their annual dues, creating further hardship for the Conclave. There was also a backlash in Edinburgh. On July 19, 1850, a number of Royal Arch Masons from the city sent a letter to the St. George Aboyne Knights, asking them to admit them to the Order and then aid them in setting up their own Encampment, in line with the original ritual. This was agreed and done, and in this way St. George Aboyne helped protect and preserve the early Masonic ritual in Scotland.

The Royal Grand Conclave died out in the 1840s and was replaced by a Chapter General, which only dealt with the Royal Arch, leaving no obvious governing body for Templar Masonry except The Grand Encampment of Scotland. I have already mentioned that this body was a direct descendant of the Grand Encampment of Ireland, which had first been chartered by Lodge Mother Kilwinning. The role of St. George Aboyne in the rise of the Grand Encampment was forgotten and ignored. To ensure its continued survival, the Sir Knights of St. George Aboyne took what Liz Boyd describes as "the unusual step of petitioning the Grand Conclave of England for recognition." The English did not re-charter the St. George Aboyne Preceptory under the English Constitution, but simply acknowledged its continuing existence and seniority.

St. George Aboyne was an irregular Encampment as far as the other governing bodies of Templar Masonry in Scotland were concerned. So in 1901 it decided to approach the Chapter General of Scotland to enquire if it could be received into that body, which had grown from the Grand Encampment of Scotland. The Fratres (Sir Knights) of St. George Aboyne swore the Oath of Allegiance to the Chapter General, and became No. 4 on the roll of that organization. In 1907 the present Grand Priory of Scotland was created by merging the Chapter General with the original Charter of the defunct Royal Grand Conclave. St. George Aboyne was finally recognized, and became No. 1 on the roll of the new Grand Priory and moved into its present premises in the Masonic Hall at Crown Street in Aberdeen, where it remains to this day.

This was the history of my own Preceptory, which had introduced me into Templar Masonry. But interesting as that history is, it does not extend back as far as the original Knights Templar. Indeed, the Great Priory of Scotland says:

> The tradition that the Masonic Order of the Temple is the legitimate descendant of the Crusading Order is not supported by documentary proofs.[183]

But it does point out that Templar Masonry is older than St. George Aboyne, Encampment No 1:

> A reference of interest to Scottish Templars is from the Bye-laws of the Old Stirling Lodge agreed upon in 1745, where the list of fees payable reads—"Excellent and Super-excellent, five shillings, and knights of Malta, five shillings." In the possession of the same Lodge are the Stirling "Brasses," which would appear to be not later than middle eighteenth century, and on which are rudely engraved "Knights of Malta" and "Night Templar".[184]

The Great Priory also notes that:

> In the month of December 1778 the Lodge of Scoon and Perth conferred the "six sundry steps of Masonry" on the Office-bearers of St. Stephens Lodge in Edinburgh, viz.: "Past the Chair, Excellent and Super Excellent Mason, Arch and Royal Arch Mason and, lastly, Knights of Malta."[185]

But even these fifty extra years of Templar Masonry tradition in Scotland don't reach anywhere near far back enough to provide a clear link to the original Knights Templar. The Great Priory has to be correct that there is no documented link with Templar Masonry and the original Templar Order.

I had not yet reached a dead end, however. Liz Boyd, the official historian of St. George Aboyne, had mentioned a clue to an earlier Masonic Templar tradition. She had said that Bonnie Prince Charlie had been credited as being installed as the Grand Master of the Templars, but it was more likely that he had been installed as the Grand Master of the Royal Order of Scotland. So the next thing I had to investigate was the Royal Order of Scotland.

THE ROYAL ORDER OF SCOTLAND

Robert Freke Gould published a three-volume work called *The History of Freemasonry* in 1883. Later, he became a founding member and eventually Master of Quatuor Coronati Lodge. Gould reported:

> The oldest records in the possession of the Grand Lodge of Edinburgh [concerning the Royal Order of Scotland] are those of an Anglo-Dutch Provincial Grand Chapter established . . . on July 22 1750.[186]

The History of Freemasonry remained in print throughout Gould's life (he died in 1915) and was then "revised, edited and brought up to date" by Dudley Wright in 1931. This edition says:

> There is a tradition among the Masons of Scotland that, after the dissolution of the Templars, many of the Knights repaired to Scotland and placed themselves under the protection of Robert Bruce and that, after the battle of Bannockburn, which took place on St. John the Baptist's day (in summer), 1314, this monarch instituted the Royal Order of H.R.M. and Knights of the R.S.Y.C.S.[187]

It is this association with the Royal Order of Scotland that helped the Lodge of Kilwinning establish its reputation as "Mother Kilwinning."

Gould goes on to say that:

> There is presumptive evidence that a Provincial Grand Lodge met in London in 1696 and indubitable evidence to show that in 1730, there was a Provincial Grand Lodge of the Order in South Britain, which met at the Thistle and Crown, in Chandos Street, Charing Cross, whose constitution is described as being of "Time Immemorial."[188]

The date of 1696 makes this the earliest Masonic claim to a link with the Knights Templar. Gould describes the official history of the Royal Order of Scotland thus:

> The Royal Order is composed of two parts, The Heredom of Kilwinning and The Rosy Cross. The former took its rise in the reign of David I, King of Scotland and the latter in that of King Robert the Bruce (1274–1329). . . . The Order of Heredom of Kilwinning had formerly its seat at Kilwinning and there is reason to suppose that it and the Grand Lodge of St. John's Masonry were governed by the Grand Master. The introduction of the Order into Kilwinning appears to have taken place about the same time, or nearly the same period, as the introduction of Freemasonry into Scotland. . . . The office of Grand Master is vested in the person of the King of Scotland (now of Great Britain) and one seat is invariably kept vacant for him in

whatever country a Chapter is opened, and cannot be occupied by any other member. Those who are in possession of this Degree and the so-called Higher Degrees [The degrees of Templar Masonry] cannot fail to perceive that the greater part of them have been concocted from the Royal Order.[189]

Gould seems to suggest that the Royal Order is the earliest form Templar Masonry. But where does the Order itself say it comes from? Their governing body is quoted as saying:

There are no reliable records tracing the history of the Order from its alleged revival in 1314 to the middle of the eighteenth century, when it appears to have flourished in France about the year 1735–1740 under the adherents of the Jacobite Cause, who being refugees from Scotland practiced these Degrees no doubt for the purpose of maintaining a common bond of union among them in a foreign land. It is stated that in 1747 in a Charter which was in existence in 1840, granted by Prince Charles Edward Stuart to the Masonic Lodge at Arras, he described himself as Sovereign Grand Master of the Order of "Rose Croix de Herodim de Kilwinning."[190]

Clearly, I now needed to look at the ritual of the Royal Order of Scotland. The earliest version I had in my collection was printed in 1844, by C. Blackledge in the county of Warwick. It is from that ritual that I will summarize the working of the two degrees.

The Rites of the Royal Order

As we have seen, there are two degrees worked within the Chapters of the Royal Order of Scotland. The first is called Heredom of Kilwinning. (In Masonic legend, Mount Heredom is another name for Mount Moriah in the Kingdom of Judea, where Moses is believed to have acted as Grand Master of the First or Sacred Masonic Lodge, which founded the rituals of the Order.) The second degree is called the Rosy Cross.

The ceremonies are carried out within a guarded lodge room, which is known as a Chapter. The outer guard is called the Junior Grand Guardian. The officer in charge of the proceeding is called Tirshatha and sits in the East of the Chapter. Outside the lodge room door, the candidate is first tested in the signs, words, and tokens of the first three degrees of Craft or St. John's Masonry. These are the degrees of Entered Apprentice, Fellowcraft, and Master Mason. Having proved himself, the candidate enters from the North of the Chapter, symbolically indicating that he is coming from a place of darkness. He wears the normal dress and apron of a Master Mason.

Once inside the Lodge, he is given a question-and-answer summary of the origins of the degree he is asking to join. I summarize:

The candidate is told that the highest and most sublime Degree of Masonry is the Royal Order of Heredom of Kilwinning. It was first established on the holy top of Mount Moriah in the Kingdom of Judea. Later it was re-established at Icolmkill (the Gaelic name for the island of Iona), in the West of Scotland, and afterwards at Kilwinning, where the King of Scots first sat as Grand Master. This was done in order to correct the errors and reform the abuses that had crept in among the three degrees of St. John's Masonry.

To gain admittance into the Order, the candidate must display Temperance, Fortitude, and Justice. A Brother of the Order is identified by a Sign and five points. He must also know the points of Fellowship on which Hiram Abif was raised, and the Master Mason's word. Having proved himself in this, he is given a new name and a title. The title is Giblim, and the name, Adoniram. He is then asked what he seeks, and has to reply "A Word which was lost, and which by your assistance I hope to find." He is then asked if he will travel, and has to reply that he will travel from east to west, from north to south, until he finds that Word. The members of the Chapter all agree to join him on his travels, and they form a procession which travels in a series of straight paths within the lodge room from North to West to South, repeating the series three times. The pilgrimage consists of tracing out three triangles on the floor of the Chapter. Once he has completed this pilgrimage, the candidate recites an obligation, which is in doggerel verse.

A RITUAL IN EIGHT PARTS

The candidate is now given a Characteristic, which is to remain his motto and guiding principle, while forever after distinguishing him in the Order. Then he is given a series of short lectures, called sections, which instruct him in the basic ideas of Freemasonry.

In the first section, he is taught the names of the nine muses: Calliope, Clio, Euterpe, Melpomene, Terpsichore, Erato, Polyhymnia, Urania, and Thalia. Then he is taught the nine orders of Angels in the celestial harmony: Cherubim, Seraphim, Thrones, Dominions, Principalities, Powers, Virtues, Archangels, and Angels. Next, he learns the importance of the number seven in forming a just and perfect Lodge and the seven liberal arts: Grammar, Logic, Rhetoric, Arithmetic, Geometry, Music, and Astronomy. Next, he is taught the importance of the number five in forming a Fellowcraft Lodge, which is explained first in terms of the five orders of Architecture—Tuscan, Doric, Ionic, Corinthian, and Composite—and then in terms of the five points of fellowship, a familiar piece of ritual to all Master Masons. Finally, the number three is introduced as the number of Masters required to rule a Lodge, then as a rule of reasoning (there are three terms in a syllogism by which we discover truth: the major and the minor proposition, and the conclusion), and finally as a symbol of divinity: There are three sides in an equilateral triangle, which is an emblem of the Three Persons in the Holy Trinity: Father, Son, and Holy Ghost—One God.

In the second section, the candidate is taught the importance of the Stone which the Builders rejected, which he is told has now become the Chief Stone of the Corner, or the most perfect pattern for Masons to try their Moral jewels upon. He is also reminded of the Masonic virtues of Brotherly Love, Relief, and Truth.

Section four deals with Noah's Ark and the Seven Wonders of the World, which the candidate is told are: the Tower of Babel; the Pyramids of Egypt; the Statue of Jupiter by Phidias at Olympia in the Peloponnese; the Temple of Diana at Ephesus; the Tomb of Mausolus, King of Caria; the Pharos or Lighthouse at Alexandria in Egypt; and the Colossus at Rhodes. Next, he is told the stories of Bezaleel, Maher-shallal-hashbaz, and King Cyrus the Great. Bezaleel was the inspired workman who made the Holy Tabernacle (where the Divine Shekinah resided and the ark of the Covenant was deposited), which afterwards became the model of King Solomon's Temple. It conforms to a pattern delivered on Mount Horeb by God to Moses, who afterwards became Grand Master of the Lodge of Israel. Maher-shallal-hashbaz was the son of a Prophetess, as we read in the Prophecies of Isaiah, chapter VIII. And Cyrus the Great was founder of the Persian Monarchy, conqueror of Asia, and restorer of the Holy Temple.

Next, section five tells the candidate that Enoch and Elijah never died. He is told that Enoch was the fifth after Seth, and the seventh from Adam, who prophesied of the flood and general conflagration; and lest the Arts and Sciences should slip from the knowledge of men, he erected two pillars, the one of brick, the other of stone, on which these Arts were engraven, to the end that if the pillar of stone should be destroyed by fire, the pillar of brick might remain, and if the pillar of brick was destroyed by water, that of stone might remain, and which, we are told by Josephus, were to be seen in his day in the Land of Syria. And then the candidate is told about Elijah the Tishbite, who after working many miracles in the presence of the Kings and Princes of Israel in order to bring them back to the worship of the true God, was translated to Heaven in a chariot of fire. This section is summed up by telling him that Freemasons should commemorate three great events. These, he is told, are the Creation of the World, Noah's Flood, and the Redemption of Man.

In section six, the candidate is told about the history of the Royal Order, and that it was formed on the top of Mount Moriah in the Kingdom of Judea. He is told that Mount Moriah was holy because it was where Abraham, at the command of God, offered up his son Isaac, that it was where King David made prayers and offerings to appease the pestilence, and also because it was the site of the prayer and offerings that King Solomon made at the dedication of the Holy Temple. He is then taught that only Mount Calvary is equal to Mount Moriah in holiness. The lecture then moves on to the topic of the Bright Morning Star, known as the Shekinah, whose appearance he is told was the first and highest honor ever conferred on Freemasons. This honor was the descent of the Divine Shekinah, first at the consecration of the Holy Tabernacle, and afterwards at the dedication of the

Temple of the Lord by King Solomon, placing itself on the Ark or Mercy-seat of the Holy of Holies, covered by the wings of the Cherubim, where it continued to deliver its oracular responses for fourteen generations, after which it was removed because the Israelites were unfaithful to their God.

In section seven, the candidate is told about the Middle Chamber of King Solomon's Temple, where all Freemasons receive their wages, and how they must practice Fidelity, Hospitality, and Taciturnity before they can be admitted. He is told that in this Middle Chamber he will find the Mosaic Pavement, the Blazing Star, and the Tasseled Border. These are then explained: the Mosaic Pavement represents the Law delivered by God to Moses on Mount Sinai; the Blazing Star represents the Glory of God appearing on Mount Sinai at the deliverance of that Law; and the Tasseled Border represents the ornaments of a virtuous life, living in conformity to that Law. Next, he is told that the only equal to King Solomon's Temple in the world is the mystical Temple of Christ's body, which can also represent the Middle Chamber, and that he must learn Faith, Hope, and Charity to be allowed to enter. He is then told about the furniture of the Middle Chamber, which is the Tressel-board, the Perpend-ashlar, and the Broaching-turner. Each is then explained. The Tressel-board is the way of Salvation laid out to us in the Book of Glad Tidings. The Perpend-ashlar is the Great Architect of the Church who called Himself the Rose of Sharon and the Lily of the Valley. And the Broaching-turner represents Divine Grace penetrating his hard and stony heart.

Section eight explains the Square, Level, Plumb-rule, and Compasses as they are taught in the Craft.

At this point in the ceremony, the candidate has been taken on a physical pilgrimage, walking three times around an equilateral triangle within the Lodge, and on a mental pilgrimage through all the teachings of the Craft. He is now told that he has become a Royal Brother of the Order and is prepared to pass on to higher honors. He is taken to a part of the lodge room that is called the Tower of Refreshment and which is approached by a series of odd steps. The Tower is guarded by an officer of the Chapter known as the Guarder. He challenges the candidate and asks him for his name and title, and then asks him what he seeks. The candidate replies that he searches for the Word that was lost. The Guarder closes the candidate within the Tower and leaves him to meditate on the Word in darkness and silence. After a period of reflection, the door to the Tower is opened and the candidate is asked a series of ritual questions, which are answered on his behalf by the Guarder. They summarize the teaching about Masonry of the previous sections. When this exchange is complete, the candidate is given a Word and Sign and freed from the Tower. He is then taken across a drawbridge back into the chapter room, where he climbs up a winding shaft to the Sphere, which represents the open sky, adorned with stars. There, he is asked the riddle of Zerubbabel, which is stronger, wine, women, or the King? (The answer is: Truth is strongest.)

The final part of the ceremony explains to the candidate, now called a Right Worthy Brother, that he has performed a long, perilous, and mystical journey, with scenes in it that can scarcely with propriety be depicted to mortal eyes, and because of the knowledge gained on the pilgrimage, he can be admitted to the Cabinet of Wisdom, which he is told is an Ox's stall beneath a Blazing Star appearing in the East.

That concludes the First Degree of the Royal Order. Although the ritual working is very different from the degree of Pilgrim, the symbolic intent is identical. Before a candidate for the Order is ready to be made a Knight, he must first complete a long, dangerous journey, and in both cases it is a journey around the perimeter of an equilateral triangle or delta, which is finally revealed to be a secret symbol of divinity. Only when this pilgrimage is complete is the Pilgrim ready to be presented to be made a Knight. In Templar Masonry he becomes a Knight Templar, in the Royal Order a Knight of the Rosy Cross, which is the title of the second degree.

Ritual of the Rosy Cross

The ritual of the Rosy Cross is a much shorter ceremony. The preamble says:

> The tradition connected with the Rosy Cross or second Degree of the Royal Order, is that King Robert the Bruce having received great service from a party of Masons who had fought under him in the Battle of Bannockburn on Summer St. John's Day, 1314, conferred on them the civil rank of Knighthood, with permission to them to accord it in their Grand Lodge to those faithful and patriotic Brethren who might succeed them, so that the Degree is, strictly speaking, a civil Order granted to Scottish Masons. Originally none were entitled to it but Scotsmen, or perhaps their allies, the Irish, and there were only sixty-three members. That number has been since much extended, and Masons of other nations are allowed to participate in the honor provided they shall first have taken the Degree of Heredom of Kilwinning in a Chapter holding of the Grand Lodge of the Order.

The candidate is first tested in the signs, tokens, and words of a worthy Brother of the Royal Order before he is admitted to the Chapter. He is clothed as a Brother of the Royal Order. There is an altar in the center of the lodge room on which is placed a Bible, open at the Book of Malachi, on which are placed a square and compasses with the points facing the West. To the North of the Bible is placed a sword and to the South a trowel. The candidate is announced as:

> A worthy Brother of Heredom, who requests the Grand Lodge to confer on him the honor of Knighthood of the Rosy Cross, as a reward for his faithful services.

He is taken to the Altar, where he kneels on both knees, taking the sword in his right hand and the trowel in his left. Both his hands rest on the Bible, and the Knights of the Chapter form a circle around him. He takes his obligation as a Rosicrucian Knight.

The Banner of the Order is waved three times over the candidate's head. Once this has been done, the worthy Brother, who remains kneeling, is made a knight by being given three light strokes of the Grand Sword on his shoulders by the Provincial Grand Master, who says:

> By virtue of the special powers vested in me, I create and constitute you a Knight of the Rosy Cross, to enjoy, under all the Obligations you have contracted, the prerogatives belonging to this honourable Order. Rise Sir [Christian name and Characteristic].

The candidate then rises and is invested with his regalia before standing and facing East to listen to the lecture of the degree. The lecture explains the ceremony and says this about the purpose of the degree:

> The Knighthood of the Rosy Cross was established to remind its member knights of the tree [the Cross] that bore the lovely Sharon rose, which was Jesus.

ROSY CROSS TO TEMPLAR CROSS

But how is this connected to the Templars? In his *History of Freemasonry* Gould says of the Royal Order:

> Whatever may have been the origin and foundation of the Royal Order of Scotland, its claim to be the oldest, if not, indeed, the only Masonic Order of Knighthood, is presumably valid.[191]

The ritual of Heredom of Kilwinning claims to be a summary of all the important events which figure in previous Craft teaching, as far as the Royal Arch, with an additional section dealing with the role of Jesus. It contains the same triangular pilgrimage path as the Pilgrim degree of the Early Encampment, and contains a description of the meaning of the triangle that agrees with both the ritual of Templar Masonry and the ritual of the Ancient and Accepted Rite. The apparent anomaly of the lack of Masonic content in the ritual of Templar Masonry is explained by the Great Priory of Scotland's own version of its history, which says:

> During the period when Sir David Milne was Grand Master [mid-nineteenth century], an attempt was made to re-constitute the Order upon a non-Masonic basis. As part of this plan, a Priory was set up in London, and a number of prominent men were admitted to the Order. All were Freemasons, but it is thought that at least one non-Masonic or Chivalric Knight was created in Edinburgh about 1847. Also, as a result of this plan the ritual was entirely re-written to give a close resemblance to the little that was known of the ancient Templar ceremonies. The non-Masonic phase lasted only for about twelve years, but we have received from it the fine and distinctly Scottish ritual which we practice today.[192]

But many common elements remain within Templar Masonry that can be traced back to Craft Lodges. For example, the importance of the Triangle, the pilgrimage as preparation for knighthood, and the separation of the Pilgrim and Knight degrees. It does, of course, pose the question of where and when Templar Masonry began. I have traced the roots of my mother Preceptory back to 1792 in Aberdeen. And I have traced the Royal Order of Scotland, with a broadly similar degree structure, although a very different set of ritual workings, to London in 1696, almost a hundred years earlier. I have long accepted the principle that common elements between widely divergent rituals are most likely to be the oldest sections. Looking at the early Templar Masonry ritual and early Royal Order Ritual, it seems that both draw on a common inspiration. But while the Royal Order contains the teachings of the Craft and the Royal Arch, with elements of symbolism and pilgrimage that draw on Christian philosophy, Templar Masonry retains little of the Craft beyond its rituals of opening and closing.

I was now curious to see if I could trace this common inspiration. Could it really have been the original Knights Templar? I decided to look for the earliest recorded instances of Templar Masonry.

Gould reproduces a pamphlet published in Edinburgh in 1788, which says:

> Of the real higher degrees, there are two regular Chapters in the Kingdom of Scotland—one in the North, the other in the West, who hold their convents in Aberdeen and Glasgow.[193]

Gould comments that the degree of Knight Templar doubtless had its origin in some form of the Scots degrees. He divides Templar Masonry into two types. These are the non-Christian degrees, which he says are under the control of the Chapters, and the Christian degrees, which are under the charge of Encampments. He specifically mentions the degrees practiced in the St. George Aboyne Encampment as a good example of these. He confirms Liz Boyd's view that in its early days, the St. George Aboyne Encampment moved with the Aberdeenshire Militia to Dover in 1812, the Tower of London in 1814, to Liverpool in 1815, and back to its present home in Aberdeen in the same year.[194]

Gould also confirms that Lodge Mother Kilwinning warranted Templar Masonry in Ireland, before the Secret Societies Act forced them to deny any involvement under the penalty of being declared an illegal organization, as I discussed earlier. He records:

> The Jurisdiction of the Grand Lodge of Ireland was invaded by Mother Kilwinning in 1779, whose Grand Master, the Earl of Eglinton, granted a Warrant in that year to "the High Knights Templars of Ireland, Kilwinning Lodge," Dublin. The members of this Lodge . . . were working the Knight Templar Degree . . . as early as December 27, 1779 . . . From this Lodge arose the Early Grand Encampment of Ireland, which chartered over fifty Encampments—some having been for Scotland and England— whilst the present Kilwinning Preceptory, Dublin, is an offshoot of the year 1780. When the rights of this Knight Templar Organization were disputed or questioned, their Sublime Commander (John Fowler) maintained that their Warrant was

"holden from the Royal Mother Lodge of Kilwinning of Scotland, the true source from which any legal authority could be obtained" and it was declared that "the documents to support this statement are in the archives of the Chapter, ready for the inspection of such Knights Templar as choose to examine them."[195]

J.S.M. Ward reports the earliest occurrence of Templar Masonry at Stirling in his book *Freemasonry and the Ancient Gods*. He says:

> The Lodge at Stirling had a chapter of "Cross-legged Masons," or Templars, as early as 1590, and worked various higher degrees also, including Rose Croix, Royal Arch, and Knight Templar up to 1736.[196]

On the role of Lodge Mother Kilwinning in Templar Masonry he notes:

> Up to 1799 Mother Kilwinning worked Templary . . . In 1813, however, they had ceased to practise these higher degrees, and even denied that they ever had, the reason being apparently that the Grand Lodge of Scotland had in 1800 threatened that any Lodge which worked these higher degrees would lose its charter. Had this happened the members of Mother Kilwinning might have found themselves liable to prosecution under the Secret Society Act of 1799, for the exception therein made in favour of Freemasonry might not have been considered to cover them once their own Grand Lodge had struck them off the list. They preferred to lose their higher degrees rather than their craft.[197]

My next step was to see if I could find earlier references to Templar Masonry anywhere else. Ward had noted other sites of Templar Masonry, saying:

> In England we find that Bristol, Bath, and York all have old Masonic Templar Preceptories, and were the sites of medieval Templar Preceptories.[198]

But the earliest record of Templar Masonry in Bristol I could find was in A.G. Mackey's *Encyclopaedia of Freemasonry*:

> There is at Bristol in England a famous Preceptory of Knights Templar, called the Baldwyn, which claims to have existed from time immemorial . . . The earliest record preserved by this Preceptory is an authentic and important document dated December 20, 1780.[199]

This is about the time that St. George Aboyne began.

What about York? Gould notes that on May 27, 1778, the Grand Lodge of All England met in York Minister. The minutes note:

> The Royal Arch Brethren whose names are undermentioned assembled in the Ancient Lodge, now a sacred Recess within the Cathedral Church of York, and then and there opened a Chapter of Free and Accepted Masons in the Most Sublime Degree of Royal Arch. The Chapter was held and then closed in usual form, being adjourned to the first Sunday in June, except in case of Emergency.[200]

Gould goes on to record:

On June 2, 1780, the Grand Chapter resolved that "the Masonic Government, anciently established by the Royal Edwin and now existing at York under the title of The Grand Lodge of All England, comprehending in its nature all the different Orders or Degrees of Masonry, very justly claims the subordination of all other Lodges or Chapters of Free and Accepted Masons in this Realm." The Degrees were five in number, viz. the first three, the Royal Arch and that of Knight Templar. The Grand Lodge, on June 20, 1780, assumed their protection and its Minute-book was utilized in part for the preservation of the records of the Royal Arch and Knight Templar Degrees . . . the draft of a certificate preserved at York for the five Degrees of January 26, 1779, to November 29, 1779, is the earliest official document known in Great Britain and Ireland relating to Knights Templar in connection with Freemasonry.[201]

None of these references was taking me back far enough. They all seemed to be clustered around the end of the eighteenth century. But where did this sudden blossoming of interest in the Templars spring from? It's hard to believe that it was simultaneously invented all over Britain from nothing. Then I happened to read a new book by Neville Barker Cryer, *York Mysteries Revealed*, which looked at the history of Freemasonry in the city of York. Barker Cryer had discovered that a Guild of St. George Masons had been authorized by the Mayor and Bailiffs of the city in May 1447. Their license permitted the members to have a common seal. They were given the right to meet in St. George's Chapel near York Castle, a building that had belonged to the Knights Templar but had passed to the Crown on their suppression. The Guild of St. George Masons were permitted to elect a Master and eight wardens as well as own corporate property. This operative group survived until 1462, when they combined with the Guild of St. Christopher.[202]

The first recorded working of Templar Masonry in York, however, did not occur until much later. Barker Cryer records that:

In the 1730s there appear two lodges in London which claim to practice a new form of Masonry in what was called the "Rite de Bouillon" . . . That rite embraced the usual three degrees with 4. Ecossais or Scottish Master, 5. Novice and 6. Knight of the Temple or Templar.[203]

He also comments:

Speculative Masons were meeting in York around 1740 and were practicing what was apparently some form of [Royal] Arch ceremony . . . the way ritual was developing in York . . . [made their] Jacobite sympathies evident.[204]

This was a clear statement of the political implications of certain branches of Freemasonry, which suddenly threw light on a comment by Liz Boyd had made that "in September 1745 at Holyrood, Bonnie Prince Charlie is credited as being installed as the Grand Master of the Templars: The evidence for this is very flimsy and cannot be substantiated." I had wondered why a Stuart pretender (claimant) to the crown of England should want to be associated with Templar Masonry, but Ward had inadvertently suggested a reason when he reported:

> The Duke of Antin, in his speech in Paris in 1714, says that the nobles who agreed to support Bruce were admitted Freemasons in Kilwinning when James, Lord Steward of Scotland, was made Grand Master.[205]

Was there a deliberate attempt to tap into Masonic loyalty to the Stuart cause? Neville Barker Cryer seemed to have found evidence of this. Many Templar Encampments had been warranted by the Early Irish Encampment, which had grown out of the charter Mother Kilwinning had issued in 1779 to an Irish Lodge to work Templar Masonry. Barker Cryer comments on the political danger of this link between Ireland and Templar Masonry, something I covered when discussing the Secret Societies Act. He says:

> In the 1740s there was real nervousness about the intentions of the Stuart House and the assistance that they might receive from foreign powers. Not least was there a real concern lest one of the Stuart ploys might be to attempt an attack on England from an Irish base. This was no time for claiming an Irish ancestry for suggested re-formations of English Masonic ritual and practice.[206]

Although the origins of Templar Masonry still remained obscure, what was becoming clearer was that this branch of Masonry had grown in popularity during a period of major concerns about Hanoverian-Stuart rivalry for the crown of Britain. And Templar Masonry was on the losing Jacobite (Stuart) side.

With this new insight, I reread Gould and found that he had also noticed it. He ascribes the paternity of the Royal Order of Scotland to a single man:

> Andrew Michael Ramsay, a devoted follower of Prince Charles Edward Stuart and a famous fabricator of certain Rites inaugurated in France between 1735 and 1740, through the propagation of which it was hoped that the fallen fortunes of the Stuarts would be revived.[207]

He also points out what Liz Boyd had commented on, the report that:

> Prince Charles Edward Stuart, in 1747, issued his famous Arras Charter, in which he claimed to be Sovereign Grand Master of the Royal Order of Scotland.[208]

But he also notes that not until 1845, long after the Jacobite threat had totally receded, was the King of Scots formally declared to be the hereditary and permanent Grand Master of the Royal Order.[209]

CONCLUSIONS

The evidence says that both Templar Masonry and the Royal Order had their roots in Scotland. Both seem to be linked into the Stuart cause. The earliest instance of the Royal Order appeared in London after James II had been driven from power, but was still alive, as a focus for his supporters in exile. Later actions by the Stuarts, in the form of the Declaration of Arras, seem to suggest that they realized the value of the Templar links as a draw for potential insurgent supporters, and so Templarism became interwoven with support for the Stuart cause.

My next step had to be to see what I could uncover about possible survival strategies for the original Order of Templars that would have allowed them to bring the elements of Templar Masonry to Scotland. We know the Templars were skilled strategists, and they had a vast arsenal of resources at their command. But were they able to save themselves by rebuilding their lost Order within Freemasonry?

CHAPTER 5

SURVIVAL OR REVIVAL?

HOW TEMPLAR LORE MIGHT HAVE PASSED TO THE FREEMASONS

We have seen that the original Order of Knights Templar was destroyed back in 1307, in a dawn raid in Paris led by the rapacious King of France, Philip the Fair. But at many times in history, different groups of Freemasons have claimed that the arcane knowledge of the Templars has been preserved within secret Masonic traditions. Are they all lying, or do they know something non-Masons don't? After researching the options, as a Mason and a Masonic Templar, I was able to list four main Masonic claims to a Templar heritage. These have been produced by various Masonic writers over the last three hundred years or so, but each has claimed that items of Templar knowledge were deliberately transmitted into Freemasonry.

Here is a summary of each of the claims, showing the routes by which the Templars' knowledge passed into Freemasonry:

1. Via the knights of the Order of Christ in Portugal, and their offshoots in Spain. These groups are certainly descended from the Knights Templar. However, they have never been connected with Freemasonry, and have remained completely Roman Catholic.
2. The traditional history of the Continental Masonic Rite of the Strict Observance says there was a group of knights who accepted Pierre d'Aumont as the successor of Jacques de Molay. This Masonic Order once had a strong following in Germany and Scandinavia, but has now almost died out.

3. There was a group of French knights who accepted Jean Marc Larmenius as the successor to de Molay. This document of transmission is held at Mark Mason's Hall in London.
4. The founding legends of the Royal Order of Scotland and the Templar Masons say that groups of English and Scottish knights acknowledged neither of the above successions and were already established in Britain.

According to these founding legends, the English route came via the Masonic Lodges at Bristol, Bath, and York. All these places have early Masonic Templar Preceptories (although not as old as St. George Aboyne), and all are sited close to where mediaeval Templar Preceptories once stood.

The Scottish route has two versions:

1. The Mother Kilwinning Scottish legend, associated with King Robert the Bruce, which is preserved in the ritual of the Royal Order of Scotland and places the St. Clair family (more about them later) at the center of Templar Masonry.
2. The Emigrant French legend, associated with the Highlands and Aberdeen, which features in the founding legend of St. George Aboyne. This says that the Templar Grand Master of Auvergne, Pierre d'Aumont, fled to Scotland in 1307. Accompanied by two commanders and five knights, he landed on the Isle of Mull, where they disguised themselves as operative Masons. On St. John's Day, June 21, 1313, they formally re-established their Order and elected Pierre d'Aumont their Grand Master. As their local cover depended on being seen as Masons, they called themselves Freemasons and adapted their Templar rituals to make symbolic use of the tools of a Mason's Craft. They moved to Aberdeen in 1361, and from there Freemasonry spread throughout Europe.

TEMPLARS AS MASONS, MASONS AS TEMPLARS

I decided to look at each of these claims in turn, and started by reading the work of J.S.M. Ward, a Freemason writing in the early twentieth century. In *Freemasonry and the Ancient Gods* he says:

> There are at least three possible lines of Templar transmission: English, Scotch, and French. Moreover, all may be independent of each other. We must remember that the Order was divided into three classes (1) Knights, (2) Templar Priests, (3) Serving Brothers. This last class was divisible into two classes (a) men-at-arms, and (b) craftsmen. Many of this class were wealthy and in a position to help their former masters. Neither they nor the priests appear to have been persecuted, the whole fury of Philip being concentrated upon the unfortunate knights.[210]

He says that some masons among the craftsmen for the Templars were great builders. Ward assures us that Comacine Masons at this date were not "illiterate workmen." A surviving contract says that John Wood, "Masoun," was allowed "borde for himself as a gentilman and his servant as a yeoman." This is how Ward describes them:

> The Comacines were a college of architects rather than a trade union of stonemasons. Now this is a most essential point, for over and over again those who endeavour to prove that the speculative side of Freemasonry is no older than the eighteenth century base their chief arguments on the fact that ordinary ill-educated workmen in the Middle Ages could not have appreciated, much less evolved, the speculative side of Freemasonry . . . Under Charlemagne, and even before him, the Comacines began to migrate across Europe, and they followed the missionaries of the Church. The legends which associate the craft with King Athelstan may be more correct than most have believed.[211]

The Templars had their own priests and their own masons who, Ward tells us, were not persecuted by King Philip.

The Order had many concealed estates scattered around Europe, and thousands of knights escaped the purge. A simple way for Templar knights to disappear would be to enter the Masonic brotherhood, with the help of their former servant craftsmen. With the threat of a cruel death hanging over them, Ward says, "I am sure they would have quickly humbled their pride and become convinced of the advisability of joining the Craft." He goes on to add:

> The Pope issued a Bull in November, 1307, to the various European sovereigns, stating that the heads of the Order had already confessed the truth of the crimes of which they had been accused, and sent instructions to Edward II of England to arrest all the Knights Templar in his kingdom.
> The English King at first refused, and told the Pope that the Templars were "faithful to the purity of the Catholic Faith." But Edward was negotiating for a marriage with Isabella of France, and his future father-in-law exerted such pressure that Edward gave way . . . In obedience to a second papal Bull, he seized their property, but would not arrest or torture them.
> This delay was important, as it must have enabled many of the knights to escape into obscurity, warned by what was happening in France of the fate which threatened them. It would be from these that the Masonic Templar succession would probably derive.[212]

This is Ward's explanation for the Masonic Templar Encampments of Bristol, Bath, and York: That, because of the delay in arresting the Templars in England, the Knights of the English Preceptories merged into the background and carried on their traditions for four hundred years in secret, to finally reemerge on December 20, 1780—four hundred and sixty-seven years later, when the earliest Templar Mason Preceptories began to appear. This implies a continuous secret tradition lasting unsullied and in secret for around nineteen generations. And not once in this time did they accidentally reveal themselves, not until the Grand Lodge of England was strong enough to protect them!

He goes on to develop the idea for the rest of the British Isles:

> In September 1309 the Papal Commission arrived in England, and insisted on the Templars being arrested, and they were taken to London, Lincoln and York for trial.

But many had escaped, and particularly in the north, where the Sheriff of York was reproved for allowing them "to wander throughout the land."

> Scotland, then nominally under English rule, and Ireland were included in the same orders, and the knights from both countries were taken to Dublin for trial. In view of the disturbed state of Scotland at this time, it is unlikely that very many Scottish Templars were captured, and the tradition in the Royal Order of Scotland as well as that of the [Masonic] Templar preceptories may well have a solid foundation.[213]

THE PRISONER'S DILEMMA

Moving on to consider the claims of French Freemasonry to be the true custodians of the Templar tradition, Ward says:

> The tradition of the French is that Jacques de Molay, whilst in prison before his martyrdom in 1313, determined to carry on the Order secretly, in spite of its suppression by the Pope, and he therefore assigned his full power and authority to Johannes Marcus Larmenius as his successor. Larmenius, growing old, drew up the *Charta Transmissionis* and transmitted his power to Theobaldus, and, after this, each succeeding Grand Master appended his acceptance on the original document, down to and including Bernard Raymond in 1804.[214]

Brother F. Crowe discovered this document and presented it to the Grand Priory of the Temple in England, and in Ward's time it hung in the Council room at Mark Masons' Hall, and it is still at Mark Masons' Hall today.

The Charter is written in abbreviated Latin and is mediaeval in tone. Some of the document is in cipher and the rest in French. The signatures vary considerably in style and wording. Ward produced his own transcription of the charter in English:

> I, Brother John Mark Larmenius, of Jerusalem, by the Grace of God and by the most secret decree of the venerable and most holy Martyr, the Supreme Master of the Knighthood of the Temple (to whom be honour and glory), confirmed by the Common Council of the Brethren, being decorated with the highest and supreme Mastership over the whole Order of the Temple, to all who shall see these Decretal letters, I wish health, health, health.
>
> Be it known to all both present and future, that, my strength failing on account of extreme age, having taken full account of the perplexity of affairs and the weight of government, to the greater glory of God, and the protection and safety of the

Order, the brethren and the Statutes, I the humble Master of the Knighthood of the Temple have determined to entrust the Supreme Mastership into stronger hands.

Therefore, with the help of God, and with the sole consent of the Supreme Assembly of Knights, I have conferred and by this decree I do confer for life on the eminent Commander and my dearest Brother Theobald of Alexandria the Supreme Mastership of the Order of the Temple, its authority and privileges, with power according to conditions of time and affairs, of conferring on another brother, having the highest distinction in nobility of origin and attainments and in honourable character, the highest and Supreme Mastership of the Order of the Temple, and the highest authority. Which may tend to preserving the perpetuity of the Mastership, the uninterrupted series of successors, and the integrity of the Statutes. I order, however, that the Mastership may not be transferred without the consent of the General Assembly of the Temple, as often as that Supreme Assembly wills to be gathered together, and, when this takes place, let a successor be chosen at the vote of the knights.

But, in order that the functions of the Supreme Office may not be neglected, let there be now and continually four Vicars of the Supreme Master, holding supreme power, eminence, and authority over the whole Order, saving the right of the Supreme Master; which Vicars should be elected among the Seniors, according to the order of profession. Which Statute is according to the vow, commended to me and the brethren, of the very holy our above said Venerable and most blessed Master, the Martyr, to whom be honour and glory. Amen.

I, lastly, by the decree of the Supreme Assembly, by Supreme authority committed to me, will, say and order that the Scots Templars deserters of the Order be blasted by an anathema, and that they and the brethren of St. John of Jerusalem, spoilers of the demesnes of the Knighthood, on whom God have mercy, be outside the circle of the Temple, now and for the future.

I have appointed, therefore, signs unknown, and to be unknown to the false brethren, to be orally delivered to our fellow-knights, and in what manner I have already thought good to deliver them in the Supreme Assembly.

But these signs must only be revealed after due profession and knightly consecration according to the Statutes, rights, and uses of the Order of fellow-knights of the Temple sent by me to the above-said eminent Commander, as I had them delivered into my hands by the Venerable and most holy Master the Martyr (to whom honour and glory). Be it, as I have said, so be it. Amen.

I John Mark Larmenius gave this Feb. 13, 1324.
I Theobald have received the Supreme Mastership, with the help of God, in the year of Christ 1324.
I Arnald de Braque have received the Supreme Mastership with the help of God AD 1340.
I John de Clermont have received the Supreme Mastership with the help of God AD 1349.
I Bertrand Guesclin &c. in the year of Christ, 1357.
I Brother John of L'Armagnac &c. in the year of Xt. 1381.
I humble Brother Bernard of L'Armagnac &c. in the yr. of Xt. 1392.
I John of L'Armagnac &c. in the yr. of Xt. 1418.

I John Croviacensis [of Croy] &c. in the yr. of Xt. 1451.

I Robert de Lenoncoud &c. AD 1478.

I Galeas Salazar a most humble Brother of the Temple &c. in the year of Christ
  1496.

I Philip de Chabot . . . AD 1516.

I Gaspard Cesinia

Salsis de Chobaune &c. AD 1544.

I Henry Montmorency . . . AD 1574.

I Charles Valasius [de Valois] . . . Anno 1615.

I James Rufelius [de] Grancey . . . Anno 1651.

I John de Durfort of Thonass . . . Anno 1681.

I Philip of Orleans . . . AD 1705.

I Louis Auguste Bourbon of Maine . . . Anno 1724.

I Bourbon-Conde . . . AD 1737.

I Louis Francois Bourbon-Conty . . . AD 1741.

I de Cosse-Brissac (Louis Hercules Timoleon) . . . AD 1776.

I Claude Matthew Radix-de-Chevillon, senior Vicar-Master of the Temple, being attacked by severe disease, in the presence of Brothers Prosper Michael Charpentier of Saintot, Bernard Raymond Fabre Vicar-Masters of the Temple, and Jean-Baptiste Auguste de Courchant, Supreme Preceptor, have delivered these Decretal letters, deposited with me in unhappy times by Louis Timoleon of Cosse-Brissac, Supreme Master of the Temple, to Brother Jacque Philippe Ledru, Senior Vicar-Master of the Temple of Messines, that these letters in a suitable time may thrive to the perpetual memory of our Order according to the Oriental rite. June 10th, 1804.

  I Bernard Raymond Fabre Cardoal of Albi, in agreement with the vote of my Colleagues the Vicar-Masters and brethren the Fellow-Knights, have accepted the Supreme Mastership on November 4th, 1804.[215]

It seems straightforward enough—problem solved, continuity established, the end. But, as I was finding so many times when pursuing the Templars, it turned out to be another dead end. In his German-language *History of Freemasonry* in 1863 (translated into English in 1866) a German Masonic writer, J.G. Findel, had published a critique of the Charter, rejecting it as a fake. Findel rejects the Charter on the grounds:

1. That the Latin is not typical of the fourteenth century;
2. That no Grand Master could nominate his successor;
3. That the deed is unnecessary;
4. That the institution of four Vicars-General was unnecessary;
5. That the level of hate shown against the Scotch Templars shows it to be an eighteenth-century work aimed at the higher Masonic Degrees.
6. That the signature of Chevillon leads to the same conclusion, for this deed was without any doubt prepared under the rule of his predecessor, Cosse-Brissac (1776–92); it must have been delivered over to Chevillon in the

hottest fury of the Revolution of 1792, when anything smacking of aristocracy, and these Templars into the bargain, were suffering persecution. For, if this document, and all the signatures accompanying it, were genuine, France, since the fourteenth century, would have seen many *tempora infausta* (times of calm), which would have afforded those Grand Masters, as well as Chevillon, at the period of the Revolution, the opportunity of adding any remark they chose to their signatures; which was not the case, for each signature is the counterpart of the other, Chevillon's alone excepted, that and Brissac's being the only genuine ones, and the very deviation of the former from the counterfeit signatures proving it to be a genuine one.

7. The manner in which the names of these Parisian Templar Masters succeed each other is incorrect.

But Ward disputes Findel's rejection of "The Charter," concluding:

My own feeling is that the document is genuine, though I hesitate to fly in the face of the accepted theory that it is a forgery. Though I was a history scholar of my college, I should hesitate to declare the document genuine solely on my own authority, though I venture to think that it looks quite as genuine as many fourteenth and fifteenth century MSS. whose authenticity is unquestioned. The view of Sir George Warner seems to me, however, to outweigh those of our Masonic students who declare it is a forgery. I suggest that they are influenced by the characteristic fault of many Masonic students who are so nervous of declaring that anything connected with Freemasonry is older than the eighteenth century, that they prefer to declare any evidence on the other side as forged or based on imagination.

This attitude, however, has had its day, and the new Masonic generation will, I think, no longer be content to fix their eyes on the eighteenth century only.

But, if genuine, this document . . . might, however, explain certain Templar traditions, and Templar influence in Masonry, but mainly on the Continent, though, no doubt, Continental Masonry might have influenced English, and particularly Scotch Freemasonry.

So far as I can trace them, the descendants of the Paris Templars have become extinct, though when that happened I cannot say. This body was apparently still in existence up to about 1850 . . . The tale told in the Charter is a perfectly reasonable one. If the remnants of the knights in France wished to carry on the Order as a secret and mystical society, the method therein said to have been adopted was probably the best possible.[216]

I found it rather puzzling that Brother Crowe was able to buy this great Templar treasure so easily on the open market. He apparently came by it thinking it an early Masonic Knight Templar Certificate, not the definitive Charter of Templar power that Ward claims it is. You may recall that Dr. Helen Nicholson, in her definitive history of the Templars (*The Templars: A New History*), also rejected the theory of a direct line of succession between the original Order and the Masonic Templars. Her view was:

It was not until the eighteenth century, with the rise of secret societies such as the Freemasons, that the Templars came to the attention of the educated, upper-middle-class layman as an example of a secret society which had been destroyed because of its esoteric knowledge. Initially the Freemasons claimed no link with the Templars: it was the German masons who in the 1760s introduced the idea that the Templars must have had secret wisdom and magical powers, which they had learned while they held the so-called Temple of Solomon in Jerusalem. This wisdom and power, they claimed, had been handed down a secret line of succession to the present-day masons! [217]

Findel and Nicholson both reject the Charter's authenticity, so I decided to look elsewhere for a way to explain how the "mystic secrets" of the Templars might have gotten into Freemasonry.

THE KILWINNING HOAX?

A favorite explanation in Scotland is the story told by the ritual of the Royal Order. As we have seen, one of the oldest Masonic Lodges in Scotland is based in the town of Ayr, alongside the grounds of Kilwinning Abbey, and is known throughout the Masonic world as Mother Kilwinning. It calls itself the Mother Lodge of Scotland. It is certainly ancient (I will discuss this more fully later)—but is it really linked to Robert the Bruce and a Masonic Order created as a home for disenfranchised Knights Templar after the Battle of Bannockburn, as what is often known as the Kilwinning legend claims? I had already discovered (see Chapter 4, page 81) that Templar Masonry in Ireland was linked to Irish Nationalism, and this had caused political problems for Mother Kilwinning during the period of the Secret Societies Act of 1799.

I have already quoted from the work of Robert Freke Gould, the famous Masonic historian. Gould was born in 1836, and as a young man was commissioned as a lieutenant in the 31st Huntingdonshire Regiment of Foot. He had been a member of three Masonic Lodges before he was out of his twenties. He was initiated into a military Lodge, Royal Navy Lodge No. 429, Ramsgate, as an eighteen-year-old officer; at twenty-one he joined the Friendship Lodge while serving in Gibraltar; and he became Master of Northern Lodge No. 570 at the age of twenty-seven, while serving in China. In 1886 he wrote his *History of Freemasonry*, which was reprinted in many editions until his death in 1915. Thereafter, it continued to be regarded as a definitive work and went on being reprinted until 1951. In this book Gould looked at the links between Templar Masonry in Ireland and Lodge Mother Kilwinning. He tells in detail a story I have already introduced:

> The Jurisdiction of the Grand Lodge of Ireland was invaded by Mother Kilwinning in 1779, whose Grand Master, the Earl of Eglinton, granted a Warrant in that year to "the High Knights Templars of Ireland, Kilwinning Lodge," Dublin. The members of

this Scottish Lodge fully considered that they were justified in working the Knight Templar Degree by virtue of their Charter and actually did so as early as December 27, 1779. Other Degrees were also wrought by the same body, such as the Royal Arch in 1781 and the Prince Rose Croix in 1782, whilst the Chair, the Excellent and the Super Excellent Degrees came in for a share of their attention. From this Lodge arose the Early Grand Encampment of Ireland, which chartered over fifty Encampments—some having been for Scotland and England—whilst the present Kilwinning Preceptory, Dublin, is an offshoot of the year 1780. When the rights of this Knight Templar Organization were disputed or questioned, their Sublime Commander (John Fowler) maintained that their Warrant was "holden from the Royal Mother Lodge of Kilwinning of Scotland, the true source from which any legal authority could be obtained" and it was declared that "the documents to support this statement are in the archives of the Chapter, ready for the inspection of such Knights Templar as choose to examine them." The Charter, however, simply authorized the formation of a Lodge . . . The erection of this daughter Lodge encouraged, however, the belief in Kilwinning being a centre of the Higher Degrees. In 1813 application was made to the Mother Lodge to authorize the transfer of a Black Warrant from Knights of the Temple and of Malta, in the Westmeath Militia, to Brethren in the same Degree serving in the Shropshire Militia . . . It was to their intercourse with Brethren belonging to regiments serving in Ireland towards the end of the last century, that Scotch Lodges owed their acquaintance with Knight Templarism. This order, then known as Black Masonry, was propagated, to a large extent, through Charters issued by the High Knights Templar of Ireland, Kilwinning Lodge—a body of Freemasons in Dublin, who were constituted by Mother Kilwinning in 1779.[218]

Gould also confirms that by 1865, after the changes and restrictions brought in by The Secret Societies Act, Lodge Mother Kilwinning was denying any links with Templar Masonry:

Lodge of Kilwinning, in reply to the Sir Knights of the Shropshire Militia, repudiated the existence of any maternal tie between herself and any Society of Masonic Knighthood and confessed her inability to "communicate upon Mason business farther than the Three Steps" (see Freemasons' Magazine, February 18, 1865, p. 114).[219]

Gould investigated the Kilwinning Legend, and quotes Bro. Alexander Lawrie, author of a History of Freemasonry in 1804, as saying:

That Free Masonry was introduced into Scotland by those architects who built the Abbey of Kilwinning, is manifest, not only from those authentic documents, by which the existence of the Kilwinning Lodge has been traced back as far as the end of the fifteenth century, but by other collateral arguments, which amount almost to a demonstration . . . The Barons of Roslin, as hereditary Grand Masters of Scotland, held their principal annual meetings at Kilwinning, but whether the English received it from the Scotch Masons at Kilwinning, or from other brethren who had arrived from the Continent, there is no method of determining.[220]

However, Gould is skeptical about some elements of this origin story: "Legends are stubborn things when they have once forced themselves into a locality," and he thinks "It is improbable that the popular belief in Hereditary Grand Masters, with a Grand Centre at Kilwinning, will ever be effectually stamped out."[221] But it sounds as though he would have liked to try!

He has a preference for the idea of Freemasonry beginning at York, and throws in this idea to link Kilwinning and York:

> The two legendary centres of Masonic activity—York and Kilwinning—were comprised within the ancient Kingdom of Northumbria. Northumbria extended from the Humber to the Forth, and from the North Sea inland to the eastern offshoots of the Pennine Range. Its western limit in the country now called Scotland is more uncertain, but would probably be fairly represented by a line drawn from the Liddel through Selkirk or Peebles to the neighbourhood of Stirling.[222]

He goes on:

> The casual occurrence of the ENGLES leaving their name to this land has bestowed on our country a foreign designation; and—for the contingency was nearly arising—had the Kingdom of Northumbria preserved its ascendancy in the octarchy, the seat of dominion would have been altered. In that case, the lowlands of Scotland would have formed a portion of England; York would have stood forth as the metropolis of Britain, and London had been but a remote mart for her port and her commerce . . . A plausible theory, [is] that the Italian workmen imported by Benedict Biscop and Wilfrid, may have formed Guilds—in imitation of the Collegia, which perhaps still existed in some form in Italy—to perpetuate the art among the natives, and hence the legend of Athelstan and the Grand Lodge of York. But unfortunately, Northumbria was the district most completely revolutionised by the Danes, and again effectually ravaged by the Conqueror.[223]

But what does Gould think is claimed in the Kilwinning Legend? This:

> That the lodge was presided over about the year 1286 by James, Lord Steward of Scotland, a few years later by the hero of Bannockburn [Robert the Bruce], and afterwards by the third son of Robert II [Earl of Buchan], are some of the stories which were propagated during the last century, in order to secure for the lodge the coveted position of being the first on the Grand Lodge Roll, or to give countenance to its separate existence as a rival grand lodge . . . However . . . difficult it might then have been to reconcile conflicting claims, we are left in no doubt as to the precedence given to the Lodge of Edinburgh in the Statutes of 1599, Kilwinning having distinctly to take the second place.

And why does he think the claims were made?

> It is most singular . . . that neither the records of the Edinburgh or Kilwinning Lodges allude in the slightest degree to these regulations, and . . . it [the copy of the St. Clair statutes, which I will discuss later in this book] was unknown in 1736, and during the struggles for priority and supremacy waged by the Grand Lodge and

Mother Kilwinning . . . its production as evidence would have at once settled the points in dispute. In 1861 the late Earl of Eglinton and Winton . . . presented the Grand Lodge with a copy of Memorials of the Montgomeries, Earls of Eglinton . . . [to] Lord Eglinton . . . the Scottish craft owes the discovery of this valuable code of Masonic laws and decisions. There cannot be a doubt as to the authenticity of the MS., and . . . its preservation in the repositories of the noble house of Montgomerie was in all probability owing to that family's former connection with the Masonic court of Kilwinning, is fully warranted by facts.[224]

(This quote is confusing, as Gould starts by claiming Edinburgh as the first Lodge of Scotland, an assumption that appears to be borne out by the text that follows. But then he takes up a position firmly on the fence by agreeing that Kilwinning is indeed the Mother Lodge. For the moment, I decided to set this confusion aside until I knew more about the circumstances. The matter did become clear eventually, but only after a great deal of research, as I will explain later.)

Gould returns to the question of a possible link between Templar Masonry and Mother Kilwinning and quotes Bro. David Murray Lyon, writing in 1863:

The lodge [Mother Kilwinning] was never more nor less than a society of architects and artisans incorporated for the regulation of the business of the building trade, and the relief of indigent brethren, until the development, early in the eighteenth century, of speculative masonry. So imperceptibly has the purely operative character merged into the condition of a purely speculative one, that the precise date of such change cannot with any certainty be decided upon.[225]

But he feels Lyon is overstepping the mark when he claims the Baron of Roslin was hereditary Grand Master of Masons:

Lyon, was not, in 1863, so fully conversant with all the facts relating to Masonic history as in later years, and especially when writing the admirable work with which his fame will be inseparably connected; for we find him mentioning the appointment of the Baron of Roslin to the Grand Mastership by James II . . . There is, doubtless, something in the suggestion that Kilwinning may have been originally the chief centre of Scottish Freemasonry, the removal of the Masonic court to Edinburgh being due to causes which can be explained; but there is also much weight in the argument, that if Kilwinning ever was the headquarters of Freemasonry, as one or more of the legends declare, it is not likely that the lodge would have so quietly accepted a secondary position in 1599, and by its representative agreed that its authority should be restricted to Western Scotland. True, in 1643 it styled itself The Ancient Lodge of Scotland; but that was only an indication of the vanity of its members, and a claim to which others might have had recourse with just as much reason. The Schaw Statutes effectually dispose of all such pretensions, and whilst admitting Kilwinning into the trio of head lodges, place it immediately after its metropolitan rival.

Gould also reports the earliest written evidence for the existence of Mother Kilwinning Lodge:

The oldest minute-book preserved by the lodge is a small quarto, bound in vellum, and contains accounts of its transactions from 1642 to 1758.[226]

As to its links with the Templars, he reports these claims:

The Royal Order of Scotland . . . is stated to have originated in the reign of David I, King of Scotland (1124–53), but the ritual of the Order states that it was first established at Icolmkill and that, afterwards, at Kilwinning, Robert Bruce took the chair in person. There is an oral tradition that, in 1314, when this monarch again reinstated the Order, he admitted all known Knights Templar into the Order. It is also claimed that Robert Bruce gave power to the Grand Master of the Order for the time being to confer the second Degree, an Order of Civil Knighthood, known as the Rosy Cross, a power not inherent in the general body, but given specially to the Grand Master and his Deputy, which can only be conferred by them or by Provincial Grand Masters appointed by them. In the earlier days of the Order the number of Knights was limited to sixty-three, all of whom must be Scotsmen, but that number has long since been exceeded and is now practically limitless, both as regards numbers and nationality.

This Order of Knighthood is said to have been instituted by Robert Bruce after the battle of Bannockburn and to have been conferred by him upon certain Brethren who assisted him upon that memorable occasion. Thus the revivification of the Degree of Heredom and the creation of the Order of Knighthood were simultaneous and it is asserted further that the Royal Order of Scotland and the Masonic Fraternity of Kilwinning were governed by the same head.[227]

Gould goes on to quote the French Masonic writer Claude Antoine Thory, writing in *Acta Latomorum: A Chronology* in 1815, who said about the Royal Order:

On the 24th June, 1314, Robert Bruce, King of Scotland, instituted, after the battle of Bannockburn, the Order of St. Andrew of the Thistle, to which was afterwards united that of Heredom for the sake of the Scottish Masons, who composed a part of the thirty thousand men with whom he had fought the English army consisting of one hundred thousand. He formed the Royal Grand Lodge of the Order of Heredom at Kilwinning, reserving to himself and his successors for ever the title of Grand Master.[228]

All this stuff fitted with the dates of the Templars, which I established in the previous chapter. But all these stories seemed to simply be quoting the traditional history of the Royal Order as it is contained in the ritual. I think Gould shares this view, because he also quotes Bro. David Murray Lyon as saying:

As regards the claims to antiquity and a royal origin that are set up in favour of this Rite, it is proper to say that modern inquiries have shown them to be purely fabulous . . . The Fraternity of Kilwinning never, at any period, practised or acknowledged other than the Craft Degrees; neither does there exist any tradition worthy the name, local or national, that can, in the remotest degree, be held to identify Robert Bruce with the holding of Masonic Courts, or the institution of a secret society, at Kilwinning.[229]

Whatever may have been the origin and foundation of the Royal Order of Scotland, its claim to the oldest, Masonic Order of Knighthood is valid. Gould says there is presumptive evidence that a Provincial Grand Lodge of the Royal Order met in London in 1696, and indubitable evidence to show that, in 1730, a Provincial Grand Lodge of the Order in South Britain met at the Thistle and Crown, in Chandos Street, Charing Cross, London. Its constitution is described as being "of Time Immemorial."[230]

In 1747 Prince Charles Edward Stuart is said to have issued his famous Arras Charter, in which he claimed to be Sovereign Grand Master of the Royal Order.[231] So he bought into the legend, but perhaps he had political motives. His action was designed to make political capital from a speech made by a Scots Stuart supporter who had been exiled in France, Andrew Michael Ramsay: the next witness I need to consider.

ENTER CHEVALIER RAMSAY

Chevalier Andrew Michael Ramsay held the French Masonic office of Orator and Grand Chancellor in 1737, when he made a speech, directed at the Grand Lodge of England but delivered in his Lodge in Paris. Ramsay had been born at Ayr, in Scotland in 1668, so by now he was nearly seventy. The speech was his last public intervention in Masonry (he died in 1743), and his Masonic influence ended with it. I doubt he had any intention of inducing the surge in popularity of Templar Masonry that occurred after his death.

Ramsey's French Lodge had been consecrated in 1730 and applied for a constitution as a Provincial Grand Lodge in 1735, so at the time of his oration, it was newly authorized to act as a Provincial Grand Lodge. Here is a brief summary of his speech (for a fuller discussion of it and it consequences, see *The Secrets of Freemasonry*[232]).

1. The Crusaders created the Order of Freemasonry in the Holy Land during the period of the Christian Wars in Palestine.
2. Its objective was to unite individuals of every nation
   (a) To restore the Temple in the city of Jerusalem and maintain and extend the true religion there; and
   (b) To return to the basic principles of the sacred art of architecture.
3. The Masonic mystery is a continuation of the mysteries of Ceres, Isis, Minerva, Urania, and Diana.
4. The Masonic mystery is a continuation of the old religion of Noah and the patriarchs.
5. Freemasonry comes from remote antiquity and was restored, rather than started, in the Holy Land.

6. To thwart Saracen spies, the Crusaders agreed on secret signs and words to recognize each other.
7. The Crusaders adopted symbolic ceremonies to initiate candidates and advance members from lower Grades.
8. When kings, princes, and lords returned from Palestine to their own countries, they established Masonic Lodges.
9. This is how Lodge Mother Kilwinning was formed in 1286.
10. The main order of chivalry was St. John of Jerusalem. (This order is preserved within Templar Masonry in the form a the higher Templar degree of Knight of Malta and St. John.)

Ramsay implied that the Lodge of Kilwinning is important to the beginning of Scottish Freemasonry, and that the Craft was a universal Order from the start, as its first Lodges were formed by returning Crusaders. Ramsay claimed that the Masonic mystery had its roots in the religion of Noah and the Patriarchs. His affirmations soon became articles of faith.

Freemasonry was, at this time, a new introduction to the Continent. In 1725 the Lodge of St. Thomas had been founded in Paris, under a warrant from the London Grand Lodge issued to John Ratcliffe, Earl of Derwentwater. But Ramsey's Oration claimed the Order dated from time immemorial, could impose its own authority, and that its origins were lost in legend. Ramsay phrased his personal views in the language of certainty, and they were accepted blindly. His romantic association with the Crusades inspired the Continental imagination. And Ramsay hinted at Jacobite connections within French Freemasonry to enhance the attraction of his ideas in France.

Ramsey's discourse inspired the creation of many so-called High Grades of Templar Masonry, and his ideas gave rise to a Masonic tradition known as the Ecossais, or Scots, Lodges. These Lodges later manipulated their Craft Grades to fit Ramsey's hypothesis, and also added High Grades to their rituals. This is the source of many of the Templar degrees which became known as the Ancient and Accepted Scottish Rite.

In 1754 the Rite of the Strict Observance was founded, linked closely to the name of Baron von Hund, who was received into Masonry in 1742. A year later, he claimed, the Earl of Kilmarnock created him a Knight of the Temple.

There was a gap of some seventeen years between Ramsey's statements and the start of the Strict Observance in 1754. But in this period, isolated Grades were formed. These were the Petit Elu, or Lesser Elect (known as the Kadosh Grades) in 1743; the Primordial Rose-Cross Jacobite Chapter of Arras in 1747; and the Jacobite Grade of Ecossais Fidèles in 1748. Finally, in 1750, the Mother Scottish Lodge of Marseilles was founded.

Gould thought Ramsey's ideas were pure fiction. Gould also got philosophical about the role of Mother Kilwinning, making comments such as "waters take tinctures and tastes from the soils through which they run, so the Masonic customs, though proceeding from the same source, vary according to the regions and circumstances where they are planted. Neither the traditions not the usages of the Craft have come down from antiquity in a clear unruffled stream."[233] I have to agree with him. Gould concludes that it is quite impossible to decide when the Legend of the Craft, and other Masonic traditions that are enshrined in the Old Charges, were introduced into Scotland—but I don't agree with him about that, as I will show in the next chapter.

Conclusions

I had now looked closely at the four major routes that have been suggested to explain how the Templars ended up becoming Freemasons, and found that none could be sustained.

It looks as if the Kilwinning legend might not be the link between the Templars and Freemasonry that I had hoped it might have been. But was Gould really right to say that Mother Kilwinning only invented the Templar link to position itself higher up, or even at the top of, the roll of the Grand Lodge of Scotland? That sounds cynical even to my cold physicist's heart. And did Lord Eglinton really create a whole system of Templar Encampments in Ireland quite by accident?

It was quite possible that Gould was right, but the whole myth seemed to be far too consistent not to be a deliberate creation. Too many accidents made me suspicious. Or was I drifting into the realms of conspiracy theory with that thought? I decided I might be, but if it *was* a conspiracy, it wasn't the Templars who had been weaving the myth. I decided to take up Gould's challenge and try to find out when Masonic traditions were introduced into Scotland.

And I had now identified a place where I wanted to start my search, the East Lothian village that was home to the St. Clairs, the Barons of Roslin. So now let us explore the village of Roslin, its Chapel, its castle and the powerful family who created it.

CHAPTER 6

ROSSLYN CHAPEL AND THE GENESIS OF FREEMASONRY

WHAT'S IN A NAME?

Some seven miles south of Edinburgh, in East Lothian, the small village of Roslin contains both Roslin Castle and Rosslyn Chapel. (And, no, I haven't misspelled village, castle, or chapel.) Over the centuries, and especially in our time, the highly ornate Rosslyn Chapel has gained great fame as a center for arcane and secret knowledge, and has been considered to be pretty much everything from the seat of the exiled Templars to the hiding place of Mary Magdalene and the Holy Grail. In this chapter, we'll see if we can uncover some of the truth about Rosslyn Chapel, including how it came by a different spelling from its castle and village. What's in a name, anyway?

Well, I'm sure you were told as a child just how much a name can matter. Let me remind you of an old fairy tale: the one about a beautiful girl who is given the task of spinning straw into fine gold cloth by the king of her land. If she does not do it, she will be killed. As the girl sits weeping in front of the straw and the spinning wheel, an ugly goblin appears and offers to turn it into golden cloth if she will grant him just one small favor. The girl agrees, and the goblin spins all the straw into wonderfully fine gold cloth. The girl marries the king. But when their first child is born, the goblin appears in her bedchamber and demands she carry out her promise to grant him the favor—to give him her firstborn child. The queen cries and pleads, but he stands firm. She even offers him half her kingdom, but the goblin insists that she give him the child. Again she pleads to be allowed to repay him some other way, and the goblin says that if she can tell him his real name, then he will let her keep the child and bother her no more. To cut a long story short, the queen finds out the goblin's name, and when he turns up to claim her child, she says his name and he flies away. And, of course, the king, queen, and little prince live happily ever after. The name of the goblin was Rumpelstiltskin, but that is bye the bye; the moral of the story is that if you know the true name of a magical being, you can control it.

What has this got to do with Roslin? Well, Rosslyn/Roslin puzzled me, because I was unsure of its real name, and I felt that if I could understand why the name of the chapel was different from the name of the village it stood in, then I would learn something useful about its purpose. Let me explain.

The name of Rosslyn Chapel had been regularly cropping up in connection with early Scottish Freemasonry along with that of the Barons of Roslin, the St. Clair (or Sinclair) family.

More than thirty-seven collegiate churches were built in Scotland between the reigns of James I and James IV (1406–1513). They were secular foundations intended to spread intellectual and spiritual knowledge, and the extravagance of their construction depended on the wealth of their founder.[234] Rosslyn Chapel, of the Collegiate Chapel of St. Matthew, was founded by Sir William St. Clair of Roslin.

While researching a previous book, I had been puzzled by the fact that the name of the chapel that William St. Clair built is spelled Rosslyn, yet the village alongside it is spelled Roslin. The local government tourist information site gives this explanation:

> Aptly named from the Gaelic "ross" meaning promontory and "lyn" meaning a waterfall or pool, the area lies beside the North Esk and is seven miles by coach from Edinburgh, and eleven by rail.[235]

When I first saw this translation I was suspicious of it, though. The word *ross* did not exist in my Gaelic dictionary.[236] But there were a number of variants on *ros*, all spelled with a single "s." Here are the entries I found:

ros: (noun masculine) a rose
ros: (noun masculine) knowledge
ros: (verb transitive) defeat, miscarry
ros: (noun masculine) seed
ros: (noun masculine) a promontory

Likewise, there was no word *lyn* in my Gaelic dictionary, though this is not really surprising, since there is no letter "y" in the Scots Gaelic alphabet. (This alien letter in a purportedly Gaelic word was what aroused my suspicions in the first place.) Most of the Gaelic alphabet is the same as English, but has only eighteen letters: five vowels (a, e, i, o, u) and thirteen consonants (b, c, d, f, g, h, l, m, n, p, r, s, t).[237] There is only one word similar to *lyn*, which is *linn*. Here is the dictionary definition:

linn: (noun feminine) a generation, age, ministration, incumbency or time in office, race, offspring.

One thing is now obvious: The name Rosslyn is not Gaelic, but the name Roslinn is (when used as a girl's name, both Roslin and Roslinn are accepted spellings.)[238] When I inquired at Rosslyn Chapel why it didn't have the same Gaelic name as the village, I was told that the current spelling with the double "s" and the "y" was devised by the Sixth Earl of Roslin in the 1950s as a way of making the place sound more Celtic. He also painted the carvings with silica fluoride of magnesium to try to preserve them, but his action only increased their rate of decay. In the same way, he changed the name from something that had a meaning in Scots Gaelic to something that looked vaguely Welsh but was not.

If the Earl had simply intended the Chapel name to sound more Celtic, then the Welsh form "Rhosllyn" would have sounded the same and satisfied his desire for a more Celtic spelling, and have translated into "Lake on the Moor." Not surprisingly, the Welsh words that sound the same do not describe the location any more than the Irish do. To the Sixth Earl, "more Celtic" seems to have meant "more Welsh-looking," possibly to suggest links to the legends of King Arthur, Merlin, and the tales of the Knights of the Round Table, which appear in the Welsh story collection known as the Mabinogion. Or perhaps he didn't realize that there was a difference between the Welsh and Gaelic branches of the Celtic languages, and erroneously assumed he was making it look more like archaic Scots Gaelic. As the Sixth Earl spoke neither Gaelic nor Welsh and lived in the Thames Valley, which is much closer to Wales than Scotland, perhaps this not surprising.

Being Welsh, I know that Celtic place names always have a meaning. (In fact, some of the longer ones, such as the Welsh village of Llanfairpwllgwyngyllgogery-chwyrndrobwllllandysiliogogogoch, contain a full description of what the place looks like and what its purpose is. That one translates as "Mary's church by the rapid whirlpool near the hollow white hazel tree opposite the red cave of St. Silio.") The most common Gaelic words for promontory are *roinn*, *rubha*, *maoil*, and *ceanntire*, and for waterfall are *eas*, and *leum-uisge*. So a reasonable translation of "promontory by the waterfall" would be "Roinnease." An additional meaning for *ross*, which only occurs in Irish place names, is "wooded promontory," so only if the name had Irish connections (or the Sixth Earl had used an Irish Gaelic dictionary by mistake) might that form have been used.

There is a central problem with all these possible translations, however. The chapel is on a grassy slope which runs down to the castle, on the outskirts of the village. It is a good mile from the nearest river, and not near a lake or any other body of water. It is not, and never has been, on a promontory by a waterfall.

I was well aware, though, that, when combining English equivalents of Gaelic words to form place names, relying on dictionaries could result in odd translations, so I decided to seek advice from someone who had better knowledge of the Scots Gaelic than I do.

In 1996 I had been introduced to Tessa Ransford, at that time the director of the Scottish Poetry Library in Edinburgh, who was married to a Gaelic speaker from the Isle of Skye. She regularly met a large number of people who had a detailed knowledge of the language, and she commissioned poems in Gaelic. I wrote to Tessa and said that as far as I could see, the only Gaelic translation of the chapel's name that seemed to make sense was "knowledge passed down the generations." After a few days, she called me back and told me that I had missed a significant overtone in the word *ros*. She said it usually carries the meaning of, more specifically, "ancient knowledge," so the translation she suggested as best fitting the Gaelic words was:

Roslinn: Ancient knowledge passed down the generations.

As you recall, the chapel's website claims that it was "a secular foundation intended to spread intellectual and spiritual knowledge." In addition, the St. Clairs were reputed to have maintained a large library and a scriptorium—a workroom for creating copies of manuscripts—at Roslin Castle, and the castle was established before the adjoining village and the Chapel. (I will return to this later.) So, from this knowledge of the site's history, it appears that Tessa's translation is a good fit. Consequently, I decided to take a closer look at Rosslyn Chapel itself to see what it could tell me about Freemasonry.

EVIDENCE IN STONE

The earliest documentary evidence for the existence of Freemasonic rituals is found on the south wall of Rosslyn Chapel. The chapel's website quotes Father Richard Augustine Hay, writing in the eighteenth century, as an historian of Earl William the chapel-builder. Hay discusses William's motive for building it and the method of design and construction:

> It came into his [William's] mind to build a house for God's service, of most curious work, the which that it might be done with greater glory and splendour he caused artificers to be brought from other regions and foreign kingdoms and caused daily to be abundance of all kinds of workmen present as masons, carpenters, smiths, barrowmen and quarriers . . . the foundation of this work he caused to be lain in the year of our Lord 1446, and to the end, the work might be more rare, first *he caused draughts* [plans] *to be drawn upon eastland boards* [imported Baltic timber], *and he made the carpenters carve them according to the draughts thereon and he gave them for patterns to the masons, that they might cut the like in stone* and because he thought the masons had not a convenient place to lodge in . . . he made them build the town of Roslin that is now extant and gave everyone a house and lands.[239] [Italics mine.]

While this building work was going on, King James II of Scotland was deeply involved in the Wars of the Roses, which got him killed at the siege of Roxburgh Castle in 1460. James Kennedy, Bishop of St. Andrews, became Guardian of Scotland and until he died in 1465 ruled in the name of the nine-year-old James

III. When James's mother died in 1463, Robert, Lord Boyd became the young King's guardian, and he arranged for the twelve-year-old James to be betrothed to Princess Margaret of Denmark, daughter of Christian I, King of Denmark, Norway, and Sweden (they were married in 1469). However, King Christian was too poor to afford a proper dowry, so he pledged the Earldoms of Orkney and Shetland—at the time governed by William St. Clair—to the crown of Scotland as security for payment of his daughter's dowry.

William Thompson, in his *History of Orkney*, says of this event:

> The pawning of the islands in 1468 by a Danish king short of ready cash to provide an adequate dowry for his daughter on the occasion of her marriage to James III of Scotland marks a decisive point in the history of Orkney. But, however important this sordid transaction was, it was just one step in a very lengthy process of Scottish penetration.[240]

King Christian never managed to raise enough cash for the dowry, and so Orkney and Shetland, held as a Jarldom (Earldom) from Norway by the St. Clairs since 1358, was forfeit and became crown lands of Scotland.[241] In 1480 William was forced to surrender the Jarldom. The loss of Orkney broke the power base of the St. Clair family, and the family's political influence waned. I will show later that Roslin Chapel, as it was then known, proved to be the final flowering of the mighty St. Clairs.

The Chapel was a tremendously ambitious project. The entire surface of the building, inside and out, was to be carved with incredibly ornate detail. Father Hay tells us that William personally supervised all the decoration. The implication of his words is that none of the strange tableaux carved into the structure are there by either accident or by the whim of individual masons with a sense of humor. (Though it appears that William himself had one: There is a carving of a fox wearing clergyman's robes, standing in a pulpit lecturing a congregation of chickens, which tells us something about what Sir William thought of the priests of the Church.) As I explored the chapel, I found one carving of particular significance. It is a small tableau on the external southeastern corner that I believe is the earliest documentary evidence of ritual myths used in what is today known as speculative Freemasonry.

This tableau shows a man kneeling in a strange posture: His feet are placed in the form of a square, in his left hand he holds a bible, he is blindfolded, and he has what Freemasons call a running noose (a hangman's noose) around his neck. Alongside him stands a bearded man, robed as a Knight Templar, holding the noose. This strange pair are placed between two pillars. But for the medieval clothing of the kneeling man and the adjacent Templar, this could be a depiction of a modern Masonic First-Degree ceremony. Once I had realized how many points of similarity there are between this carving and a modern Freemasonic First Degree, I often commented on this when giving Masonic lectures. Eventually, I published the evidence in a book called *The Second Messiah*. On many occasions, I was asked to debate this evidence in Masonic Lodges on American and British radio, and in the course of these debates the Librarian of the Grand Lodge in London suggested that my conclusion, that this tableau was evidence of Masonic ritual in use in Scotland in the mid-fifteenth century, could be explained away as simple coincidence.

Why was my claim so controversial? The problem is that the tableau was carved in Scotland over five hundred and fifty years ago—about two hundred and seventy years before it is claimed that the Craft (of Freemasonry) was founded in England! By publishing this information, I caused a tremendous fuss in English Freemasonry. The Librarian's view was taken up and expounded by various Masonic writers who rushed to agree that these similarities were simply coincidence: Freemasonry could not possibly have come from such an outlandish place as Scotland. But is such a bizarre "coincidence" reasonable? As a scientist, this was a question I was well placed to address.

The Numbers Can't Lie

Among other things I do, I teach Statistics at my own University. And in one of my regular lectures, I look at the wider scope of statistical analysis in helping to understand evidence. So, as a demonstration, I decided to undertake a complete analysis of the suggestion that the similarities between William St. Clair's authorized carving and the modern First Degree of Freemasonry were pure chance.[242] The statue at Rosslyn shows a number of features that are now considered to be Masonic. It shows what appears to be a Templar Knight carrying out what would now be called the First Ceremony of Freemasonry. Could all this really be coincidence?

My counter-claim—that the rituals of Freemasonry did indeed originate in Scotland hundreds of years before they arrived in England—can be tested using standard techniques of hypothesis-testing. Let me explain the statistical reasoning that led me to conclude that Freemasonic myths, as still used in modern rituals, existed in the time of William, the eleventh Baron of Roslin and builder of Roslin Chapel. We'll start by reviewing my analytical process.

There are seven points of congruence (agreement) between the carving and the modern Masonic ceremony. These are:

1. The man is blindfolded. This is unusual in medieval statues, and the only example I could find elsewhere was the figure of "Blind Justice." I could find no other blindfolded figures carved in Rosslyn Chapel itself.
2. The man is kneeling. This is fairly common in medieval carvings, and there are other kneeling figures in Rosslyn.
3. The man is holding a Bible, or at any rate a book with a Christian cross on its cover, in his left hand. There are a number of other carvings showing figures holding books or scrolls within Rosslyn.

4. The man has a noose around his neck. There are few known figures shown with nooses around their necks. The best known is the statue called "The Dying Gaul." There is one other figure in Rosslyn that has a noose, and that is the figure of the hanged man, which represents the angel Shemhazai. In Biblical legend, Shemhazai's sins caused God to send the Flood. He was so afraid to face God that he hanged himself between Heaven and Earth, with his face away from God. However, Shemhazai is carved with a noose about his feet. There is no other noose carved in Rosslyn.

5. The man has his feet in the posture that is still used today by Masonic candidates. This is a very unusual position and does not occur in any other carvings in Rosslyn.

6. The ceremony is being carried out between two pillars, as it is in a Masonic Lodge.

7. The noose is being held by a man clearly dressed as a Knight Templar.

So what is the chance of all these factors coming together by chance? To find out, I set up a Null Hypothesis that it was pure coincidence that all these elements linking Templarism and Freemasonry occurred in the same carving, and then set out to test the probability of the idea. (My Null Hypothesis took the Grand Lodge Librarian's claim and set out to try to prove it true.) To play fair, I made sure that I gave the highest possible probability that it was just a coincidence. Here's what I found:

1. The probability that the figure is blindfolded by chance is 0.5, as it can only be blindfolded or not blindfolded. This is a worst-case probability that gives the Null Hypothesis the best chance of succeeding, as there is no other blindfolded figure in Rosslyn.

2. The probability that the figure is kneeling by chance is 0.5, as it again can only be kneeling or not kneeling.

3. The probability that the figure is holding a Bible by chance is 0.5, as there are again only two possibilities. Holding any sort book or a scroll, or not.

4. The probability that the figure has noose around its neck by chance is 0.5, even though it is the only figure in Rosslyn with a noose around its neck. Again, I am giving the Null Hypothesis the best possible chance of succeeding.

5. The probability that the figure has his feet in a Masonic posture (which the ritual says is the only way a candidate will be admitted to Freemasonry) by chance is 0.5, again because he can have them that way or not. No other figure in Rosslyn holds its feet in this strange symbolic way, so again the Null Hypothesis is being given the full benefit of any doubt.

6. The probability that the ceremony is taking place between two pillars by chance is 0.5, because the alternative would be not to place the two pillars there.

7. The probability that a Templar is holding the noose by chance is 0.5, and this is generous towards the Null Hypothesis, because the rope could be hanging loosely from the neck or held by somebody who is not a Templar. In the modern Masonic ceremony, the rope is held by the senior deacon while the candidate takes his oath on the Bible, and for the rest of the ceremony dangles freely.

I now needed to consider the possibility of all these seven probabilities occurring at the same time. If you have ever studied statistics, you will recall that to find the composite probability, in these circumstances, you have to multiply the separate probabilities together. So the highest possible probability of the Null Hypothesis being true is:

$(0.5)^*(0.5)^*(0.5)^*(0.5)^*(0.5)^*(0.5)^*(0.5)$, which works out as 0.0078.

This means that there are only eight chances in a thousand that all these elements linking Freemasonry to Templar Masonry to Sir William St. Clair—and thus, to Scotland—are there by coincidence. This probability is less than both the standard 95-percent confidence level of one in 20, and the 99-percent confidence level of one in 100. There is only one chance in 128 of the links being coincidental. On this evidence, then I must reject the Null Hypothesis.

That leaves me with a strong claim that there *was* some link between speculative Freemasonry, the St. Clairs, and the Knights Templar at the time the statue was carved. But my statistics can't tell me what that link is.

The facts say that William did not mix all these disparate elements by accident. From my analysis, I conclude that he almost certainly meant to have all those factors together when he approved the piece. The same "landmarks" survive into modern Freemasonry, which claims to have preserved them from "our ancient brethren." So I was curious about how these myths might have begun to be told among Masons. William died in 1484, nine years after the City of Edinburgh granted formal recognition to Masons in the city. We'll pick up the trail of the St. Clairs in a later chapter. But first, let's follow William St. Clair's original masons and see what became of them.

PLAQUES, COUNCIL MINUTES, AND CHURCH BUILDERS

In *The Origins of Freemasonry* Professor David Stevenson notes that:

> The seal of cause of the Incorporation of Masons and Wrights of Edinburgh was granted in 1475, while in Aberdeen and Glasgow masons, wrights (carpenters) and coopers were grouped together in incorporations which received their seals in 1527 and 1551 respectively. These seals should not, however, be taken to mark the beginnings of organisation by the crafts concerned; rather it would usually be the case that craft organisation had existed and evolved for generations, with the granting of a seal representing the culmination of the process, even though it is often the first point at which the organisation becomes visible to the historian.[243]

This implies that Masonic organizations needed to exist in a city for some time before they could become recognized by its Burgh (borough) Council, although Stevenson does not suggest how long that period might be. All the same, from 1446 onwards, once William had established a strong base for the large contingent of operative Masons in Roslin (the village, you recall, is said to have been built to house the many Masons he clearly employed to create the ornate stonework of the Chapel), they were well placed to begin this process in the Edinburgh area. In the case of Edinburgh, the move from a strong Masonic presence to the grant of a seal took about thirty years.

What happened to the large group of Masons William had assembled when he died in 1484? Rosslyn Chapel's official website says:

> After Sir William died in 1484, he was buried in the unfinished Chapel and the larger building he had planned was never completed.[244]

In other words, the building work dried up and the operative Masons had to move on. Where did they go? Stevenson tells us that the next Scottish city to grant a seal of incorporation to its Masons was Aberdeen. If I assume the process of creating the appropriate political environment for the grant of a seal takes about thirty years, as it did in Edinburgh, then what was happening in Aberdeen thirty years before its Lodge was incorporated in 1527?

Once again Professor David Stevenson, who is not a Mason, is a useful source. He spotted a wall plaque on the west front of King's College, Aberdeen, bearing a Latin inscription that he translates as:

> By the grace of the most serene, illustrious and ever-victorious King James IV: On the fourth before the nones of April in the year one-thousand five-hundred the Masons began to build this excellent college.[245]

That date is significant for Freemasons, and Stevenson quotes research which explains that April 2 is traditionally accepted as the date on which the building of Solomon's Temple began some 2,500 years earlier.[246] He adds:

> This, however, does not explain the peculiar wording of the inscription. It mentions the king as patron of the project but states that 2 April was the date on which the masons started work. It is surprising that an inscription of this sort should specifically mention the craftsmen responsible for the work at all and yet here they are standing alongside the king.[247]

Clearly by 1500, the Masons of Aberdeen were becoming an important social power. Gould and Stevenson agree that references to Freemasonry can be found in Aberdeen from around 1483 (this was the year before William was buried in Roslin Chapel, as it was then known, and around the time that building work on the Chapel would have been winding down). What is evident is that there was work for skilled Masons in Aberdeen at this time. Aberdeen council's website makes the point about the work carried on St. Nicholas's Kirk:

The church's present structure on Union Street dates mainly from the 18th and 19th centuries, but it incorporates portions of the 12th-century church and stands on the site of the 15th-century building, which was one of the largest and most prestigious burgh churches in Scotland.[248]

Gould, writing in 1886, says:

The eventful history of the ancient Lodge of Aberdeen deserves a volume to itself . . . The original formation of a lodge at Aberdeen ranges back into the mists of antiquity, and wholly eludes the research of the historian . . . [But] the records of the burgh of Aberdeen present us with a greater combination of materials for a national history—glimpses of the actual social position of the people, as seen in a system of jurisprudence in legal pleadings, as exhibited in various professions and trades, pageants, and sports, and styles of manner and dress—than is generally to be found in similar sources. Their historical importance has long been acknowledged by those who have had access to them. They comprehend the proceedings of the Council, and of the Baillie and the Guild Courts from 1398, to 1745, with the exception of the years from 1414 to 1433, there is no hiatus in the series.[249]

The first written reference so far found to a Lodge of Masons occurs in the records of Aberdeen Burgh Council in the Scots language. The minutes taken on June 27, 1483, say:

It was rehersit be Dauid Menzes, master of the kirk wark, that it was appoyntit betuix the masownys of the luge efter that thai war accordit vpon certane controuersy betuix thaime that gif ony tym tocum ony of thaim offendit til vther for the first faute he suld gif xx s. to Sanct Nicholace wark and, gif thai fautit the thrid tym, to be excludit out of the luge as a common forfautour.[250]

This paraphrases as:

The council decided that David Menzies, the master of the Church work, was appointed to rule of the Masons of the Lodge [consisting of six members, whose names are duly recorded at the end of the minutes], and who were to pay 20 shillings to the Parish Church (Saint Nicholas Kirk) for the first and second offences respectively, in the event of either of them raising any debate or controversy. [It seems there had been disputes before, which they had been involved in.] If they were at fault for a third time, they were to be excluded from the Lodge as a common wrongdoer.

It seems that, even then, it was a common practice to give two warnings, and to inflict a series of fines, before insisting on exclusion for a third offence.

Gould adds that this was recorded as a bylaw, and was approved by the aldermen and Council, the masons being obligated to obedience *be the faith of thare bodiis* (by the faith of their bodies). Two in particular were labeled as offenders, and were cautioned that, should either of them break the rule they had agreed to, he that *beis fundyn in the faute thairof salbe expellit the luge fra that tyme furtht* (was found at fault would thereby be expelled the from the Lodge from that time forward).[251] David Stevenson has investigated the same record.

In Aberdeen in 1483 the burgh council was involved in the settlement of a dispute between the six "masownys of the luge," and fines were laid down for offences, with provision for the exclusion of masons from the lodge (presumably thus incurring loss of employment) in case of repeated offences . . . these late fifteenth-century references to the lodge coincide with a period of building activity: The choir of St. Nicholas was rebuilt.[252]

Gould had hunted out a number of other minutes from around this period. He notes that on November 15, 1493:

Three masons were hired for a year by the Aldermen and Council, to *abide in thar service, bathe in the luge and vtenche, and pass to Cowe, than to hewe and wirk one thar aone expensis, for the stuf and bigyne of thar kirk werke* [abide in their service both in the lodge and in public and go to the village of Cowe to cut and work at their own expense the stones and blocks of the Church work].[253]

Stevenson picks up on the same point, saying:

This Aberdeen lodge was under the supervision of the master of kirkworks, being a permanent or semi-permanent institution attached to the burgh church of St. Nicholas, and these late fifteenth-century references to the lodge coincide with a period of building activity: the choir of St. Nicholas was rebuilt. Indeed, the lodge building may only have been erected at about this time. It is said that in 1485 the burgh bought the lodge from a burgess of Montrose for 100 merks [marks], and it may be that he had built it for masons he was employing to work on the church but that the council was now taking it over. In 1493 three masons bound themselves to remain and abide in the "luge" and work there and elsewhere. Five years later a mason bound himself "to mak gude seruice in the luge" and outside it, and two others swore "to remane at Sanct Nicholes werk in the luge" and elsewhere, not leaving without permission.[254]

The Scots *bathe in the luge and vtenche*, which Gould had highlighted, was an unusual phrase, but he had not commented on it. I noticed that Stevenson had translated it as "both in the lodge and elsewhere." It occurred to me that if I used data-mining techniques on this unusual phrase, I might find other useful things. I knew that the University of Dundee had created an online Dictionary of the Scots Language,[255] and as part of the groundwork for that project had digitized many early Scots documents, including the Aberdeen Burgh Council Minutes. I used their database to search for this phrase, and found another interesting sentence in their records from 1493. It said:

Alexander Stute, masonis, hirit be the aldirman for ane yer to remane and abide in thar seruice, batht in the luge and vtenche.[256] [Alexander Stuart, a Mason, is named here to serve as an alderman for the one year, both in the lodge and elsewhere.]

The Dundee database confirmed what both Gould and Stevenson had said, that 1483 is the earliest written record of a Masons' Lodge, at least in Dundee's digitized database. But it also added the interesting detail that ten years later a Mason of that Lodge became an Alderman of the Burgh (rather than simply being taken on as an employee, as Gould had found to be happening ten years earlier). There is considerable evidence from the seventeenth century that the Lodge of Aberdeen had members who were not working Masons, but this record suggests the process of Lodge members becoming important members of Aberdeen society began a lot earlier.

There is a sentence in the council records of November 22, 1498, which says that Mathou Wricht (one of the Masons mentioned in the extended 1483 entry) had been referred to in an entry (November 22, 1498) as agreeing, "be his hand ophaldin, to make gude seruice in the luge" [by token of holding up his hand to make good service in the Lodge] "the said day that Nichol Masone and Dauid Wricht oblist thame be the fathis of thar bodiis, the gret aithe sworne, to remane at Sand Nicholes werk in the luge . . . to be leile trew in all pontis" [the said day that Nicholas the Mason and David the Wright obligated themselves to be faithful with their bodies, the great oath being sworn, to continue at the work of St. Nicholas in the Lodge and to be loyal and true in all points]. Gould had also seen this passage in the minutes, and commented:

> The foregoing furnish early instances of the use of the word Lodge (Luge), and assuredly the context in each case—by the penalty of exclusion—suggests that something more was meant than a mere hut or covered building. Even in the fifteenth century, at Aberdeen, it would appear that the Lodge was essentially a private building, and strictly devoted to the purposes of masonry. To work in a lodge was the privilege of free masons, cowans and disobedient members being excluded.[257] [In Masonic terms, a cowan is a worker in rough stone, such as a dry-stone waller, who does not know how to shape and work stone as a Mason does.]

That the winding down of building work at Roslin coincided with the growth of a permanent Lodge attached to St. Nicholas's Kirk in Aberdeen is unlikely to be coincidence. Skilled masons were not so thick on the ground in fifteenth-century Scotland that there would have been enough local masons in Aberdeen to populate this new Lodge or undertake the work required.

Father Hay commented on this shortage in remarking that:

> He [William] caused artificers to be brought from other regions and foreign kingdoms and caused daily to be abundance of all kinds of workmen present as masons, carpenters, smiths, barrowmen and quarriers.[258]

Having settled these immigrants in Roslin for a job that lasted for the best part of forty years, William had managed to create an indigenous workforce of skilled masons, who had become first-generation Scots by default. It is not unlikely that they would prefer to seek work in Scotland rather than return to lands that their fathers or even grandfathers had left forty years before. And, if they wanted work in Scotland, Aberdeen was where the action was.

I can't prove this hypothesis by tracing names, because while the Burgh of Aberdeen does record names of some of the masons who formed this first Lodge (in particular Alexander Stute [Stuart], who became an alderman ten years later), Roslin does not have records of masons who were made redundant as the work there stopped. But I have shown, by statistical analysis, that any mason who did move to Aberdeen from Roslin had worked on a building that shows evidence of Masonic ritual and symbolism within its stone-carved fabric—and that evidence was hewn by brother-masons. Is this northern exodus the origin of the ancient Lodge of Aberdeen? To test this idea, I would need to find other evidence of early Masonic ritual or symbolism.

First, though, I wanted to take a closer look at another possibility, the Emigrant French legend, which I introduced in Chapter 5 (page 103). Could this have happened? Was Alexander Stuart, Master Mason of the Lodge of Aberdeen and Alderman of Aberdeen Burgh Council, the successor of Pierre d'Aumont and a Grand Master of the continuing Knights Templar?

Conclusions

As far as the origins of the speculative Craft of Freemasonry in Scotland is concerned, I could find no direct link to the Templars. (Masons distinguish between "operative" Lodges, which are made up of working stonemasons, and "speculative" Lodges, made up of men who come together to speculate, work rituals, and reflect on the spiritual meaning of Masonic teachings.) The speculative Lodges all developed after the building of Roslin Chapel, which shows the earliest evidence of ritual practices and the existence of Masonic myth. The earliest documented Lodge appeared in Aberdeen soon after the work at Roslin ended and the Masons who had worked on the St. Clair Chapel were dispersed.

Now I needed to look more closely at the legend that claimed that Templar refugees established Freemasonry in Aberdeen. This would involve me in a trip to the Scottish island of Mull, and then across the narrow strait to the abbey of St. Columba on the Isle of Iona. I would walk along the Street of the Dead and speculate about the lives of High Kings and Saints, before returning to the mainland to visit St. Nicholas Kirk in ancient Aberdeen to study the men who built it. This is what the next chapter is about.

CHAPTER 7

THE TEMPLAR ESCAPE
TO SCOTLAND

THAT MISSING TEMPLAR FLEET AGAIN

The idea proposed by J.S.M. Ward in *Freemasonry and the Ancient Gods* has an intrinsic appeal. It explains the disappearance of the Templar Fleet; it provides a legitimate route for the transmission of Templar secrets and the continuation of the Order; it explains how Freemasons came to be custodians of the Templar legacy; and finally it explains the recognized antiquity of Freemasonry in Aberdeen. All in all, it has a lot to offer. But is it true?

According to Ward:

> Pierre d'Aumont, Grand Master (sic) of Auvergne, accompanied by five knights and two commanders, fled to Mull disguised as Operative Masons, and, agreeing to continue the Order, chose d'Aumont as Grand Master, assumed the name of Freemasons, and adopted many of their symbols. In 1361 they moved to Aberdeen, and thence Freemasonry spread throughout Europe.[259]

But there are problems with this explanation. When I looked at the myth of the eighteen-ship Templar battle-fleet that supposedly sailed from La Rochelle, laden down with knights and treasure, the evening before the dawn raid, it soon became clear that no such fleet existed. The eighteen ships which brought Grand Master Jacques de Molay and his officers to France were trading vessels and would not have stayed in La Rochelle but gone on about Templar trading business. However, a senior Templar officer might have been at sea when the dawn raid took place, and wisely decided not to return. The story of a Preceptor and five knights escaping by sea to the west coast of Scotland and eventually ending up in Aberdeen had enough plausibility to make it worth looking at; all the same I was wary, remembering what Malcolm Barber had said about a long-lasting historical trend in *The New Knighthood*:

> So great is the appeal of a comprehensive explanation of history that writers have been attracted to it ever since, undeterred by lack of evidence. In recent times, through the media of television and paperbacks, the message that the Templars fulfilled this pivotal historical role. Lack of evidence has never been a serious problem for such writers.[260]

In the light of Barber's warning, I couldn't help thinking that the area where Auvergne is situated is completely landlocked, so why would its Preceptor be at sea, or even have access to any Templar vessel? Nonetheless, this idea is well established:

> The fleet of eighteen ships that had brought de Molay and his entourage from Cyprus to La Rochelle had also disappeared. Painstaking detective work by a variety of modern authors . . . all tends to confirm with hard historical fact the traditions passed down in French Freemasonry, that the treasure of the Templars was sent for safekeeping to Scotland. We know that the St. Clairs of Roslin were members of the secret group that had founded and directed the Order throughout its history.[261]

The voyage from La Rochelle in France to Tobermory on the Isle of Mull is about 700 nautical miles. At an average speed of, say, two knots, it could be accomplished in under two weeks. The whole course is over the shallow seas of the continental shelf, so such a voyage was a technical possibility with the type of vessels the Templars used.

Anybody who has read Robert Louis Stevenson's adventure story *Kidnapped* knows what to expect from the Isle of Mull, because Stevenson set his classic tale there. The island is wild, windswept, beautiful, and damp; it is about 25 miles long and 35 miles wide at its north–south and east–west maximums; and it lies in the Atlantic ocean off mainland Scotland's west coast, near the Argyllshire port of Oban. With over 300 miles of coastline, Mull has many natural harbors, the most famous being Tobermory. And just off Mull to the west lies Iona, where St. Columba established a monastery of the Celtic Church (which had a tradition of remaining aloof from Roman Catholicism) and which has the one of the oldest Christian burial grounds in western Europe. The more I looked at Ward's idea, the more plausible it began to look—so there was only one thing to do: visit Mull and Iona for myself and see if I could find any evidence.

Oban, where I stayed while I waited to catch a ferry, looks out towards Mull. It has a strong Masonic tradition, and the Coliseum-like McCaig's Tower, a magnificent folly on the hill overlooking the harbor, was paid for by the Freemason and philanthropic banker John Stuart McCaig. (Its purpose was to provide continuous work for the local operative Masons, and McCaig kept adding to it until his death in 1902.) Once I arrived in Oban, I made contact with the local Masonic Lodge, Oban Commercial Lodge No. 180, in Albany Street, and asked the brethren about possible Templar links in the area. They came up with two ideas:

1. They suggested it was worth having look at the Cathedral of St. Columba on the island of Iona, as it had a collection of what were said to be Templar gravestones.
2. One brother pointed out that the church at Kilmartin also had a collection of what were reputed to be Templar stones in the graveyard.

Since it was on the mainland, I decided to start by driving down to Kilmartin, so the following morning I headed south out of Oban. Kilmartin is a small village in a valley crammed full of ancient rock carvings, standing stones, and Neolithic mounds. It has a few guest houses, a pub, an excellent restaurant, a village shop, a fascinating museum at Kilmartin House,[262] and some private houses. The church is on a terrace to the east of the valley, overlooking a series of cairns and standing stones. The guidebook told me the current church was built in 1834–5 to replace a church from 1798, and that the first church on the site had been built in 1304. What's more, my brother Mason from Oban was right: The church and grounds did hold a large collection of medieval grave slabs, most of which featured knights and images of swords. In the churchyard, there were some ancient gravestones with knights on them, others with just swords, and some with both knights and swords, alongside a number of later Masonic graves dating from the seventeenth century.

The downside was that the stones, although they featured images of knights in armor, appeared to portray images of secular knights. (The distinctive feature of Templar grave images, like those in the Templar Church in London, is that the knights are shown with legs crossed in a particular way. Only Templars were so depicted, secular knights being traditionally shown with straight legs, or occasionally with legs crossed at the ankles.) Even so, I could see why this legend could have resonances: The church was established just around the time the Templars were raided in France, and the churchyard was full of images of medieval knights and also contained seventeenth-century Masonic graves. Recently, the images of the knight and sword stones have been placed on the Web by a modern Neo-Templar organization.[263] At first sight these stones did appear to be Templar, though, as I will explain, I came to doubt this. However, I could easily see how the existence of a local stone-carving tradition focusing on knights and swords (many Templar gravestones did simply show the shape of the sword of the grave's occupant) could tap into the romance of the French emigrant legend—and the presence of Masonic graves could only enhance this tale. Were the French Masonic myth and the founding myth of the Royal Order, both widely publicized in Ward's work in the 1920s, the inspiration for the Templar legend's retelling? In a 1989 exposé of the Craft, *The Temple and the Lodge*, written by two non-Masons, these stories appeared once more:

> It was only idle curiosity that led us to enter the churchyard [at Kilmartin]. But there . . . were rank after strictly regimented rank of badly weathered flatstones. There were upwards of eighty of them. Some had sunk so deeply into the ground

that the grass was already growing over them . . . Many of the stones, particularly those of later date and better condition, were adorned with elaborate carvings—decorative motifs, family or clan devices, a welter of Masonic symbols. Others had been worn completely smooth. But what interested us were those that bore no decoration save a single simple and austere straight sword . . . It was this stark anonymous sword that marked the earliest of the stones, those most badly worn, weathered and eroded . . . It seemed we had found the Templar graveyard we were seeking.[264]

The writers were eager to identify the stones as Templar grave markers:

During the course of our research, we had explored most of the ruins of Templar preceptories still surviving in England, and many of those in France, Spain and the Middle East. We were familiar, almost to the point of satiation, with the varieties of Templar sculpture, Templar devices, Templar embellishment—and, in the few instances where they could still be found, Templar graves. Those graves displayed the same characteristics as the graves in Kilmartin.[265]

Their conclusion was that, by implication, these were the anonymous graves of Pierre d'Aumont, Templar Grand Master of Auvergne, and the two commanders and five knights whom J.S.M. Ward had mentioned in his earlier work. But how had they come to be in a remote glen in Argyll? Later in the same exposé, their answer is revealed:

Shortly after the initial arrests, the Master of Auvergne *is known to have come to England.* . . . Any mass exodus of knights, especially if it included the Order's treasure as well, would almost *certainly have involved the Templar fleet*—that fleet which vanished so mysteriously, and about which so little is known. Indeed, the Templar fleet may hold the answers to many of the questions surrounding the last days of the Order. It may also point to a possible Templar presence in Argyll.[266] [Italics mine]

It's a nice romantic story, but, as the Kilmartin gravestones may not date from 1300 (only the site of the church does), and they don't seem to be quite Templar in style, it also seems unlikely that the non-existent, treasure-laden, Templar fleet was the means of transport their original occupants used. There is, however, plenty of evidence, in the form of dated Masonic graves, to show that the Craft of Freemasonry existed in Argyll in the seventeenth century. But this is not really a great surprise, because, as we shall see, the Lodge of Edinburgh has continuous minutes of its meetings dating back to 1599. And there has been a Lodge in Argyll, Lodge St. .John and the Isles No. 50, which dates back well before the formation of the Grand Lodge of Scotland in 1736. Oh, well! Perhaps Mull and Iona would provide more evidence.

OVER THE SEA TO MULL

My trip across Mull to Iona was thrilling and spectacular. As I write this, I have on my desk a white pebble, as described by St. Columba, inscribed with a black cross, which I was given while on the island. (Weighing it in my hand brings back the skirling cries of the gulls whirling and twisting overhead, as I stood at the top of the Street of the Dead with my newly acquired white stone clutched in my right fist.) The story of the white stone is told by Adamnan, the ninth abbot of the monastery of Iona in 679–704. He wrote a life of Columba, the Saint of the Celtic Church, who had founded the monastery in 52 CE. Adamnan tells how Columba took a white stone from a river and blessed it for the working of certain cures, and this stone, contrary to nature, on being dropped into water, floated like an apple.[267] To this day, the Iona Community takes pure white pebbles from Iona, incises them with the cross of St. Columba, and stains the cross black. It was just such a white stone that I was given, and now keep on my desk as a memento of that beautiful island.

Iona is a spectacularly remote, rugged island, dominated by the graves of the Scottish kings and St. Columba's Abbey. Columba had been exiled from Ireland and lived out his later years in Scotland. A great man for founding monasteries, he set up those of Derry, Kells, Durrow, Lambay, Swords, Drumcliff, Glencolumcille, and Tory Island in Ireland, before moving to Scotland and founding Hinba (Jura), Tiree, and Loch Awe, before finally settling down on Iona.[268]

My arrival at St. Columba's most important site was memorable. Having crossed the Ross of Mull, I walked up from the ferry landing at Port nam Mairtear—Martyrs' Bay. Moving away from the cluster of houses by the landing, I saw the present abbey building dramatically outlined against the clear blue sky. But to reach it, I had to pass along Sraid nam Marbh—the Street of the Dead. I walked up the slope towards this burial ground of ancient kings. Here, it is said, the Lords of the Isles, from Somerled Mac Gillebride down to the Clan MacDonald Chieftains, are buried, somewhat incongruously, alongside John Smith, the late Leader of the British Labour Party.

The land I was walking over was the famous *Relig Odhrain*—the burial ground of kings. If I accept the testimony of the medieval *Chronicles of the Kings of Alba*, then on that sunny summer day, I walked by the graves of the Pictish King Bruide, the Irish High Kings Artgal and Niall Frossach, the Norse Kings Olaf Cuaran, Godred Olafsson, and Uspak Hakon, and two hundred years of Scots Kings from Kenneth MacAlpin down to Macbeth.[269] The sense of history on Iona is powerful and heady. George MacLeod, the founder of the Iona Community that now cares for the Abbey, described Iona as a "thin place, a place where only a tissue paper separates the material from the spiritual worlds."[270]

The Venerable Bede, in his history of the church in Britain in the late seventh century, recorded the founding of the Abbey of Iona:

> Columba arrived in Britain in the ninth year of the reign of the powerful Pictish king, Bridius, son of Meilochon (Mailcuin) [565 CE]; he converted this island [Britain] to the Faith of Christ by his preaching and example, and was granted the island of Iona on which to found a monastery. Iona is a small island, with an area of about five hides according to English reckoning, and his successors hold it to this

day. It was here that Columba died and was buried at the age of seventy-seven, some thirty-two years after he had come into Britain to preach.[271]

Adamnan, who became Abbot of Iona in 679, wrote the original *Life of St. Columba*, and this is how he described Columba's death:

Now there was once one of the brothers who spoke frankly in the venerable man's presence, saying to the saint, "To celebrate your obsequies after your death, it is thought that the whole population of these provinces will row across and fill this island of Iona." Hearing these words, the saint then said, "My little child, the event will not prove to be as you say. No promiscuous throng of people will be able to come to my obsequies. Only the monks of my community will perform my burial and grace my obsequies."

The almighty power of God caused these prophetic words of his to be fulfilled immediately after his passing. For during those three continuous days and nights there occurred a great storm of wind, without rain, and such was its force that it prevented anyone from crossing the Sound by boat in either direction. And after the blessed man's burial was completed, the storm was at once stilled, the wind ceased, and the whole sea became calm.

Let the reader, therefore, judge in what great and special honour before God our patron is held, at whose prayer, when once he lived in mortal flesh, God granted that storms were stilled and that seas became calm; and again, when he had need, on the occasion mentioned above, gales of wind arose and the seas, at his will, were stirred up by the winds; but afterwards, as was said above, on the completion of his burial rites, they were changed to a great calm.[272]

Iona became an iconic site of Celtic Christian power in Scotland, and it grew into a place of pilgrimage. It was far from Rome and never acknowledged the authority of the Pope, so it would have made an ideal place for persecuted French Templars to seek sanctuary. As John Marsden, who edited the illustrated translation of Adamnan's *Life of St. Columba*, explained:

> The influence and importance of Iona burgeoned through [the next] hundred years . . . [after 597 CE] Multitudes of pilgrims thronged to the holy island of Iona. The bodies of kings were borne down its Street of the Dead to lie in the *Relig Odhrain*. Iona became renowned as the great centre of Celtic learning and its name was revered . . . [It] was the lodestone of the "white martyrdom."[273]

Marsden also notes that Iona was a traditional burial site of the Pictish, Norse, and Scottish kings long before Columba arrived. He tells of a dark legend connected with the founding of the Abbey, when the pagan burial ground was sanctified by the human sacrifice of a monk named Odhrán. He was buried alive as an act of sacrificial martyrdom:

> The sinister legend of the interment of Odhrán has attached itself to the foundation on Iona. The Irish *Betha Coluim Cille* includes the story—with dark pagan over-

tones—of the ritual burial of the still-living Odhrán at the foundation of the monastery:

[Columba] said, then, to his people, It would be well for us that our roots should pass into the earth here. And he said to them, It is permitted to you that some one of you go under the earth of this island to consecrate it. Odhrán arose quickly, and thus spoke: If you accept me, said he, I am ready for that. O Odhrán, said [Columba], you shall receive the reward of this: no request shall be granted to anyone at my tomb, unless he first ask of thee. Odhrán then went to heaven.

The oldest burial place on Iona still bears the name of Odhrán, a dedication arguably older than the Columban foundation . . . Although Odhrán was an histori-cal personality, he had no historical connection with Columba and his name is nowhere listed amongst the brothers who accompanied Columba to Iona. It would have been wholly characteristic of Adamnan to [try to] confound any legend linking ritual "burial alive" with the foundation of Iona.[274]

What ever else it is, Iona remains a powerful repository of myths. It is the last resting place of saints and warriors—and, once again, my brother Masons in Oban were right: There is a collection of stones decorated with the images of knights and swords beside the Abbey. When I visited, many were stored in an outbuilding near the cloisters, and they were impressive. Fortunately, in 1881 James Drummond had carried out a detailed survey of these stones, and had published the list along with detailed drawings of them. (His book, *Sculptured Monuments in Iona & the West Highlands*, had been reprinted in 1994, so I was able to buy a copy.[275]) Unfortunately for the French Templar emigrant legend, there were no cross-legged knights and no Masonic symbols. Then, as I sat reading Drummond's book in the lounge of the Caledonian MacBrayne ferry returning to Oban, I found the answer to something that had puzzled the writers of the 1989 Masonic exposé I mentioned earlier, when claiming evidence of Templar graves at Kilmartin:

There were even some women's graves. It seemed we had found the Templar graveyard we were seeking. The sheer existence of the ranked graves in Kilmartin must surely have elicited questions from visitors other than ourselves. Who *were* the fighting men buried there? Why were there so many of them in such an out-of-the-way place? What explanations were offered by local authorities and antiquarians? The plaque at the church shed only meagre light on the matter. All it said was that the earliest of the slabs dated from around 1300, the latest from the early eighteenth century. "Most," the plaque concluded, "are the work of a group of sculptors working around Loch Awe in the late 14th-15th Centuries." *What* group of sculptors? If they were known to have constituted a "group" in any formal or organized sense, as clearly seemed to be the case, surely something more must be known about them. And was it not rather unusual for sculptors to congregate in "groups", unless for some specific purpose or under some specific aegis—that of a royal or aristocratic court, for example, or of a religious order? In any case, if the plaque was vague about who had carved the stones, it was worse than vague about who had been buried under them. It said nothing.[276]

I found that Drummond offered a simple explanation for the use of the sword on tombstones when he says of the Iona gravestones:

> The sculpture on the monuments . . . is generally looked upon as of a merely orna-
> mental character, but as we study them the designs show an earnest symbolism, full of
> deep meaning and suggestiveness, many of them hinting at the history of a life, or
> some of the characteristic habits of the deceased . . . After the cross, the sword is the
> object most frequently represented, and naturally so among a warlike and brave race;
> having studied these representations carefully, I cannot but think that the actual sword
> would be placed upon the stone and outlined, the other ornamentation designed
> round it. The form of the handle varies according to locality. The sheath seems also
> occasionally highly ornamented. Of this there are specimens at Iona and Kiels. At Iona
> there are three or four different designs of handles, but none of them so elegant as
> those at Kiels and St. Michael Glassary. In some cases the belt is also given, showing
> how the buckles were attached . . . On an early slab at Iona the centre has a cross the
> whole length of the stone, at one side a sword, at the other a galley . . . [foremost
> among] the womanly symbols . . . is the shears. This has by some been thought typical
> of the fates, as cutting the thread of life. But I think there can be no doubt as to its real
> meaning when thus represented. It is frequently figured in the Nunnery at Iona, and
> on one stone two pairs are carved, touchingly hinting at two sisters or friends buried
> under the same stone. But there is surer evidence than even this on a slab at
> Kilchenzie. Here is a pair of shears beside a sword, and this inscription opposite, HIC
> JACET KATERINA, the rest being illegible; the husband's name being effaced.[277]

It turns out that Drummond had solved the puzzle of the origin of the Kilmartin stones, and many similar ones in the West Highlands, after studying fourteen different sites ranging from Kilmory to Kilmichael Glassary, all sporting gravestones carved with swords and knights.

> As to the style of art upon these monuments, many and conflicting opinions have at
> various times been advanced as to where and how it originated . . . Sufficient for my
> purpose to call the art Celtic, for surely no other name could so well characterise an
> art so peculiar to Iona, where the class of monuments seems to have originated, and
> from which, as from a school of design (which I believe it to have been), its educated
> priests and monks were scattered over its dependencies in the West Highlands,
> among the now solitary churchyards in which these beautiful memorials are still to
> be found. In connection with this subject a very common idea prevails among the
> modern Highlanders that the monuments are all taken or stolen from Iona.[278]

This idea of Celtic Christian tradition, which built on earlier local pagan symbolism, makes a lot more sense than the *émigré* Templar theory. But Drummond has also managed to date the period during which these stones were carved to between 1380 and 1500.

> The date of these slabs is a more perplexing matter but should my conjecture as to
> the Macdonnell of Isla one be correct, that gives us 1386. Then there is the tomb-

stone of the four Priors, the design of which is altogether more florid and modern looking, having the date 1500. Something between these two dates I should suppose pretty near the period, although I believe a few of those I have drawn are of earlier date. We must remember also that the same sort of design and execution might go on for centuries in lonely localities so little disturbed, as far as art was concerned.[279]

So despite the superficial excitement of finding gravestones carved with swords and knights, it turns out that the French Templar emigrant legend is no more than a romantic myth. But if the Templars didn't flee to Mull and tie up in Tobermory with a fleet of eighteen treasure-laden ships, then it also means they wouldn't have been able to move to Aberdeen in 1361, and so would have been unable to spread Freemasonry throughout Europe, as J.S.M. Ward had claimed. But we have already seen from the Burgh Council records of Aberdeen that by the late fifteenth century, at least one member of the "luge" (Lodge) had become an alderman. The process of Masonic respectability had begun, and by the mid-seventeenth century, the Lodge of Aberdeen had many respectable and even noble citizens among its ranks. If this wasn't due to the *émigré* Templars, how did it happen?

ABERDEEN—THE OLDEST LODGE IN THE WORLD

As Robert Gould said in the first edition of his *History of Freemasonry*, "the eventful history of the ancient Lodge of Aberdeen really deserves a volume to itself."[280] I agree, but a brief summary of what he recorded is all I have room for here. As we have already seen, the records of the Burgh of Aberdeen offer rare glimpses of the early history of the Lodge and some of its members. These records extend to sixty-one folio volumes, averaging about 600 pages each, and, apart from the years 1414–1433, there are no gaps.

The first volume (1399) contains an account of an early contract between the "comownys of Ab'den" (the common people of Aberdeen) on the one part, and two "masonys" (masons) on the other part, which was agreed on the Feast of St. Michael the Archangel. The work contracted was for "xii durris and xii wyndowys, in fre tailly" (12 doors and 12 windows in full total), and the work was to be delivered in good order at any quay in Aberdeen.[281]

Jumping ahead a century, on November 15, 1493, three masons were hired by the Aldermen and Council to spend a year:

> in thar service, batht in the luge and vtenche, and pass to Cowe, thar to hewe and wirk one thar aone expensis, for the stuf and bigyne of thar kirk werke, and thai bane sworne the gret bodely aithe to do thax saide seruice and werk for this yer, for the quhilkis thai sal pay to ilk ane of the said masonis xx merkis vsuale money of Scotland alarnelie, but al accidents of trede.

Here is a version in more modern English:

in their service, both in the lodge and thereabouts, and to pass to the village of Cowe, there to hew and work at their own expense the building work of the church and be sworn to devote their bodies to this work for the coming year. For carrying out satisfactory work they are to be paid 20 marks in Scottish currency, but nothing for faulty work.

As I mentioned earlier, one of these masons was Mathou Wricht (Matthew Wright) He seems to have been an active member of the Lodge, because he is also mentioned in a decree of 1483, and again in November 22, 1498.

In fifteenth-century Aberdeen, "the luge" (Lodge) was a private building strictly devoted to the purposes of masonry (stonework). To work within the company of this Lodge was the privilege of Freemasons. Cowans (rough stone workers) and disobedient members were excluded. Interestingly, it was a covered building, which meant it could not be overlooked or spied upon, and it was "tyled or healed," which means it was guarded by a Mason with a drawn sword. This is one earliest mentions of the words "Tyler" and "Heal" (or Hele) in connection with Freemasonry.[282]

On February 1, 1484, the Burgh Council ordered that all Craftsmen should bear their tokens on their breasts on Candlemas Day. Candlemas Day is a religious festival to celebrate the ritual purification of Mary in the Temple, forty days after the birth of Jesus, and also the presentation of Jesus in the Temple in Jerusalem. The link with the Temple made it an important feast for the Masons, who would carry the tokens of their Craft (wearing their work aprons, they would carry compasses and set-squares, which were the tokens of their trade) through the streets of the city in procession.

On January 23, 1496, it was agreed that every craft should have its own standard. This was a banner, which showed images to identify the craftsmen who would parade behind it. At a time when few people could read, these banners would display pictures of the tradesmen's tools and workplaces, so people watching the procession could identify them. For example, the Free-Gardeners would have a picture of Adam working in the garden of Eden, the Free-Carpenters would have a saw cutting into wood, and the Free-Masons would have a banner showing the compasses and set-squares they used to mark out their work and the hammers and chisels they used to cut the stone.

At this time, the masons would have been only one of the many groups of skilled craftsmen, called guilds, who were recognized by the City Council. There would be guilds of bakers, cobblers, carpenters, haberdashers, cloth-makers, shoemakers, apothecaries, and many more, as well as the masons. Each guild would have a system of training apprentices to pass on its skills, and each would have a means of registering its members and recording which ones were Masters, who could be trusted to carry out work, and who could be responsible for training the next generation. After 1496 each of these guilds of experts could parade through the city of Aberdeen with the banner of their guild fluttering proudly before them. Then in May 22, 1531, the Provost and Council agreed to another official parade through the city:

in honour of God and the blessit Virgin Marye, the craftismen, in thair best array, keep and decoir the processioun on Corpus Cristi dais, and Candilmes day, every craft with thair awin baner, with the armes of thair craft thairin . . . last of all, nearest the Sacrament, passis all hammermen, that is to say, smythis, wrichtis, masonis, cuparis, sclateris, goldsmythis and armouraris.[283]

Or, in more modern English:

in honor of God and the blessed Virgin Mary, the craftsmen, dressed in their best clothes, shall on Corpus Christi day [celebrated on the first Thursday after Trinity Sunday, ranging from May 21 to June 24] and also on Candlemas Day, hold a procession lead by a copy of the Bible. Each Craft will be led by its own banner, which will carry the symbols of their Craft, and the guilds of all the hammermen [those who used hammers in their trades], that is the Smiths, Wrights, Masons, Glaziers, Ladder men, Goldsmiths and Armourers, shall be allowed to follow closest to the Bible. [It was considered a great honor to be allowed to parade close to the Bible]

According to a rule of October 4, 1555, a visitor was chosen every year by each of the crafts to be sworn before the "Provost and Baillies in judgment." His duty was to see that all the statutes and ordinances were faithfully kept, and that:

thair be na craftisman maid fre man to use his craft except he haf seruit as prentise under ane maister Mire yeiris, and be found sufficiee and qualifeit in his craft to be ane maister. [284]

[That no craftsman is to be made a "free" man and allowed to practice his craft until he has served his time as an apprentice under a skilled Master. He must be tested and found to be able to demonstrate the skills of his craft and be qualified to apply before he can become a Master.]

The prefix "free" was applied to those Scottish craftsmen who were free to exercise their trades because they had served an apprenticeship and completed their master piece. A craftsman's master piece was an example of his skill that would show to peers that he was skillful enough to be accepted as a Master craftsman. Traditionally in Masonry, the craftsman would have to take a piece of rough stone, called rough ashlar, and work it into a perfect cube. This cube would be tested for its perfection, using the set square and compasses, and if it was judged to be a perfect cube, it would be accepted as a "Master piece" and the man who made it would become a Master Mason and Free to work in his trade in his own right. This is how the terms Free Mason, Free Gardener, Free Carpenter and the like arose, as well as the term "masterpiece." Today, of all the free trades, only the term "Freemason" survives, though it now describes a member of a Masonic order rather than a working stonemason.

The first cathedral church of St. Nicholas in Aberdeen stood for only about 200 years. Bishop Alexander had it demolished because it was too small for a cathedral. He had the present kirk (church) built in 1357, and in the late fifteenth century, a choir was added. (These are the kirkworks, which I have already mentioned in connection with the early minutes about a Lodge of Masons. The large number of Masons' marks that can be found in St. Nicholas's from the foundation upwards show that it was built by Free Masons, entitled to mark their work. (A Free Mason was awarded a distinctive mark by his Lodge, and he was allowed to carve that mark somewhere on his work, rather like a signature.) Masons' marks have also been found on other Aberdeen churches, such as Greyfriars in Queen Street, founded in 1471, and in King's College and Chapel, which were founded in 1494. There are also Masons' marks on the Bridge of Dee, which was started in 1505 and finished in 1527.

There is a local Aberdeen tradition which says that a mason named Scott, with several assistants from Kelso, was employed in 1165 by Matthew Kininmonth, Bishop of Aberdeen, to build St. Machar's Church.[285] Scott and his associates are said to have founded the Aberdeen Lodge.

It is possible to argue that this ancient Lodge of Aberdeen is not the one described in the Burgh Records of 1483, but in those early days, there was never more than a single Lodge in each town or city, and it would have a monopoly on the rights and privileges of the trade. It was later secessions, such as that of the Edinburgh Journeymen in the seventeenth century, that gradually led to the formation of more than one Lodge in a city. So the likelihood of there being some other Lodge is small.

The Seal of Cause of the masons and wrights of Aberdeen was confirmed on May 6, 1541, under the common seal of the Burgh, and then included the coopers, carvers, and painters.[286] From this confirmation the brethren in Aberdeen date the institution of their Lodge, and the Grand Lodge of Scotland, on granting a warrant to it on November 30, 1743, acknowledged that year as the period of its formation. The Lodge charter says "that their records had by accident been burned, but that since December 26, 1670, they have kept a regular Lodge, and authentic records of their proceedings." The members may as well claim to have "kept a regular lodge" from 1483 as from 1541, although their Lodge is officially acknowledged as "before 1670."

The Lodges in Scotland, England, and Wales are supposed to be numbered in order of their founding, with the oldest occupying Number One on the Roll, but in fact they have often been numbered at the whim of various Grand Master Masons, as they responded to the political pressure of ascendant Lodges. However, the 1736 assignment (at the formation of the Scottish Grand Lodge) of thirty-fourth place on the Masonic roll of Scotland to the "Luge of Aberdeen" seems absurd. (It is now recognized as Number 1 *bis* 3 on the Roll of the Grand Lodge of Scotland.) Inferentially, from the Burgh records, it dates from a far more remote period than is shown by its minutes, and even restricting its claims to the limits imposed by the rules of membership of the Grand Lodge of Scotland in 1737, it has eventually emerged that there are no more than two or three Lodges entitled to take precedence above it. But several bodies, chartered late in the eighteenth century, were listed above it on the first register of Grand Lodge. After 1736 the Lodge of Aberdeen made a dignified protest, but failed to get a lower roll number. As Gould says, "had members not been more concerned to preserve and extend brotherly love and concord, rather than haggle for precedence, there might have been a rival Grand Lodge formed in the North of Scotland, as well as by Mother Kilwinning in the South."[287]

Gould notes that a grant was made in favor of Patrick Coipland of Udaucht as warden "over all the boundis of Aberdene, Banff, and Kincarne," by no less an authority than King James VI in 1590. This is an important point, as it shows that another local nobleman, who was not a member of the St. Clair family, was made a hereditary Grand Master (or Warden) of Masons in Aberdeen. The original deed is contained in the Privy Seal Book of Scotland. The terms of the grant are:

1. that the Laird of Udaucht possessed the needful qualifications to act as a warden over the "airt and craft of masonrie";
2. that his predecessors had of old been wardens in like manner;
3. the said Patrick Coipland having been "electit ane chosin to the said office be common consent of the maist pairt of the Master Masounes within the three Sherriffdomes";
4. the King graciously ratifies their choice, constitutes Coipland "Wardane and Justice ovir them for all the dayes of his lyif;" and the King empowers him to act like any other warden elsewhere, receiving all fees, etc., holding courts, appointing clerks and other needful officers, etc.

The grant is dated September 25, 1590.[288]

The written records of the Lodge of Aberdeen date only from 1670— probably because previously they had not kept any written minutes of their meetings. Only after the reforms brought in by William Schaw, which I will discuss later, did Lodges begin keeping records, and to try to cover up this omission, Brethren would often claim that their older records had been lost to fire or some such calamity. But if the Lodge of Aberdeen did not keep written records in its early days, the Burgh Council of Aberdeen did, and it is from these records that it is possible to show that the Lodge of Aberdeen is the oldest documented Lodge in the world.

When the Brethren of Aberdeen did start to keep written records, they wrote them in a book measuring about 12 inches by 8, each leaf having a double border of ruled lines at the top and sides, the writing being on one side only. This book is kept at Crown Street Lodge Rooms. The volume originally consisted of about one hundred and sixty pages. According to one of the minutes of February 2, 1748, the box-master, Brother Peter Reid, was ordered to have the minute book rebound, as it had been damaged by the iron clasps that held its leaves. Whatever talents Bro. Reid may have had, bookbinding was not one of them. Instead of having more pages inserted, as he had been instructed, he removed all but thirty, and arranged those in a random order. But the "Lawes and Statutes" of 1670 remain unshaken, even if stirred up. The "Measson Charter," which outlines the general laws, the roll of members and apprentices, and the register of their successors are all still there. There is also a volume known as the Mark Book: a register of the names and marks of each member and apprentice. By 1670 the Lodge had only 12 operative members (i.e., working stonemasons) out of a total of 49 members. The other 37 included four noblemen, three church ministers, an advocate, nine merchants, two surgeons, two glaziers, a blacksmith, three slaters, a professor of mathematics, two wig-makers, an armourer, four carpenters, and several gentlemen.[289] The transformation from a Lodge of working operative Masons to a Lodge of speculative gentleman Masons was well under way.

CONCLUSIONS

As far as the origins of the speculative Craft of Freemasonry in Scotland are concerned, I could find no direct link to the Templars. The legend of the French Templars fleeing with eighteen fighting ships laden down with treasure to the island of Mull, and then littering the Western highlands with Templar graves, had no substance.

I was, however, able to find out that the earliest Lodge had appeared soon after the work at Roslin ended, when the Masons who had worked on the chapel were dispersed. And the Records of the Burgh Council of Aberdeen show that the Masons who carried out the kirkworks (church-building) at St. Nicholas's in the late fifteenth century began a movement towards social acceptance of Freemasonry by the great and the good that was well established by the mid-1600s. This has largely been ignored by previous Masonic historians, although not by non-Mason David Stevenson in his recent history.

The mystery of the hereditary Grand Mastership of the Lords of Roslin over the Free Masons was deepened by the knowledge that another laird, Patrick Coipland of Udaucht, had exercised similar rights in Aberdeenshire, and evidence for it is recorded in a non-Masonic source. And yet the myth that the Templar fleet, its treasure, and its magical seafaring skills somehow benefited the St. Clairs of Roslin is pervasive. Having disposed of the French Templar emigrant legend, perhaps I needed to look at the other aspects of this mysterious fleet to see if they made more sense. The next legend I needed to investigate was that of Prince Henry St. Clair and how he sailed the Atlantic on board the missing Templar fleet and hid its treasure in the Americas. Who was this seafarer prince? And how was he connected to the Templars—and the mystery of Roslin (Rosslyn) Chapel?

CHAPTER 8

THE LEGEND OF PRINCE HENRY ST. CLAIR

THE FLIGHT OF THE TEMPLAR FLEET

The legend of the flight of the Templar fleet to Scotland and its subsequent utilization by the Barons of Roslin is persistent. It is summed up on the Clan Sinclair website, which says:

> The [Knights Templar] . . . who went to Scotland [after October 13, 1307] are said to have sailed in more than a dozen ships, carrying their treasure. There their fate became bound up with that of the family of St. Clair.[290]

✳ It goes on to describe exactly how this Templar fleet became bound up with the Sinclairs via the person of "Prince" Henry St. Clair of Orkney, whom it describes thus

> Henry Sinclair was the Baron of Roslin near Edinburgh . . . he became Lord Chief Justice of Scotland and Admiral of the Seas. Burke's Peerage and Gentry agrees that he was Baron of Roslin, Earl of Orkney, and Lord of Shetland, "who on 2 August 1379, was formally invested by Haakon, King of Norway, as Jarl of the Orkneys, ranked next to the Royal House before all the Scandinavian nobility. As Admiral he discovered Greenland, lived in much state at Roslin, and was killed in battle in Orkney 1404." . . . Henry was descended from Rogenvald the Mighty, first Earl of Orkney, on both sides of his family.

> According to Fredrick J. Pohl,

> by inheritance from Henry's mother and confirmation of the King of Norway, Henry became the first Sinclair Earl of Orkney . . . This made him the premier Jarl of Norway and the crowner of its king . . . He had the right to various royal privileges, including

wearing a crown. He held Orkney from the King of Norway, yet was also a leading Scottish noble. This dual loyalty and the geographical position of his Jarldom of Orkney with its 200 islands and 5,000 square miles on the sea lanes between the two countries made him in effect all but an independent king . . . not content with success-fully bringing Orkney, Shetland, and perhaps Faroe under his control, Henry built a fleet of ships larger than the navy of Norway. He gained adherents from the princely Zeno family of Venice, who were great sailors and who made available to him the new invention of cannon. He and the Sinclair family have often been associated with the Knights Templar, who were also great sailors . . . His grandson William, first Sinclair Earl of Caithness, immortalized [his voyages] in stone at Rosslyn Chapel, near Edinburgh.[291]

This view that the Templars were a great maritime force is picked up by Tim Wallace-Murphy and Marilyn Hopkins, who expand the claim in *Templars in America*:

Protection of the pilgrimage routes and the transport of their own men and materi-als to the Holy Land, as well as the transport of pilgrims, led to the creation of a large and well-disciplined fleet, much of which was built in the shipyards of Venice. The order became long-term allies of the Most Serene Republic of Venice, and their combined naval might helped to sustain the Christian kingdom of Jerusalem against the growing power of its Muslim enemies.[292]

But historian Helen Nicholson thinks differently. On the size and nature of the Templar Fleet, she says:

The hierarchical statutes attached to the Templars' Rule, dating from the twelfth cen-tury before 1187, refer to the Order's ships at Acre (Section 119) but do not state how many ships the Order owned. After 1312 the Hospital of St. John was mainly involved in sea-based warfare and had an admiral in command of the marine opera-tions, but it only had four galleys (warships), with other vessels. It is unlikely that the Templars had any more galleys than the Hospitallers. The ships would have been very small by modern standards, too shallow in draught and sailing too low in the water to be able to withstand the heavy waves and winds of the open Atlantic, and suited for use only in the relatively shallow waters of the continental shelf. What was more, they could not carry enough water to be at sea for long periods.[293]

She adds:

A post-Second World War addition to the story [of the Templars] is that the Order owned a huge fleet of ships which discovered the New World and brought back silver, with which it built Chartres Cathedral. Anyone with any knowledge of the Order would ask why, if the Order had so much silver, it did not use it to raise soldiers to fight in the Holy Land, recover the holy places and win the gratitude of Christendom.[294]

Wallace-Murphy and Hopkins develop this conspiracy myth by asserting that the Templar Fleet and the silver it carried passed to the control of the St. Clairs of Roslin in 1307:

The fleet of eighteen ships that had brought de Molay and his entourage from Cyprus to La Rochelle had disappeared . . . the treasure of the Templars was sent for safe-keeping to Scotland.[295]

Dr. Nicholson offers a simpler explanation of what could have happened to these ships:

There has been some debate among scholars as to whether any actual transfer of coin took place, but the latest view is that coin was actually carried from the West to the East. This meant that the Templars needed ships to carry their coin, as well as agricultural produce, horses and personnel for the East. They also provided a secure carrying service for pilgrims—safer and cheaper than hiring a commercial carrier. These would have been heavy transport vessels rather than warships. Much of the surviving evidence for Templar shipping comes from the relevant port records or royal records giving permission for the export of produce . . . This was not a fleet in any modern sense . . . the Templars probably hired them as they needed them rather than buying their own.[296]

So the simple explanation for what happened to the fleet of eighteen ships which brought Jacques de Molay to France is that, once they had delivered their cargo, they just sailed away on their normal trading business. But this has not stopped a mighty myth arising around Henry St. Clair, the ninth Baron of Roslin. This needed a closer look.

THE LEGENDARY "PRINCE" HENRY OF ORKNEY

The late Professor Gwyn Jones of Cardiff University was an expert on Viking history and northern myth. He is famous for his translation of the body of Welsh heroic tales known as *The Mabinogion* as well as his standard academic text *A History of the Vikings.* He explains how the name St. Clair was first adopted by a group of pillaging Vikings led by Rollo, son of Rognwald, Jarl of Moray, in memory of a treaty which granted them the rich lands of Normandy:

The Norsemen were about to achieve a considerable unexpected success . . . the cession of Upper Normandy to Rollo and his following in 911 . . . Icelandic sources . . . identify him with Ganga-Hrolf, Hrolf the Walker, the son of Rognwald earl of Moer, who in defiance of Harald Fairhair's ban plundered in the Vik, suffered outlawry, and after spending some time in Scotland proceeded to France, where he founded the dukedom of Normandy . . . Until 910 we are . . . much in the dark about Rollo's movements . . . but he had evidently been operating in France for a number of years and had grown to prominence before the Viking outburst of that year. In 911 he commanded the army which unsuccessfully besieged Chartres, and later is found back on the lower Seine. By now this was an area . . . [with] one perdurable asset . . . its rich and orchard soil . . . Presumably the king of the West Franks made the overtures, while Rollo was clear-headed enough to welcome them. By the treaty of St. Clair-sur-Pete he was confirmed in the lordship of the spacious and strategically important territories whose modern titles are Seine Inférieure, Eure, Calvados, Manche, and part of Orne.[297]

✳ So Rollo the Viking, an outlaw subject of Harald Fairhair of Norway, became the first Norse Duke of Normandy and an ancestor of William the Conqueror. He abandoned his faith in the Goddess Freya and became a follower of the Virgin Mary. He also gave up the democratic way of ruling through a meeting of subjects, known as a "Thing," and fervently embraced the Franks' feudal system of subjection and domination. Rollo saw Christianity as a way to centralize power in the ruler, and one which gave him a cast of supporting bishops to add the supernatural threat of hellfire to enforce his authority. This way of ruling was a clear move away from the accountability of the *Lawthing*, and other Viking rulers, back in Scandinavia, soon realized its advantages. The decline of the Old Norse gods, and the spread of the religion of Christ paved the way for a new type of Norse society: a new order that granted political power to bishops and absolute power to rulers. This trend towards centralization, and reduction in accountability, would eventually have disastrous consequences for some Viking lands, as we will see. Gwyn Jones explains how Rollo the Viking became a Christian king:

> Rollo did homage to King Charles the Simple and promised to defend the land entrusted to him. In 912 he was baptized, and though his followers must have varied considerably in their attitude to his new religion, the political wisdom of his decision is undoubted . . . He strengthened the towns' defences and gave the countryside good peace . . . but from the beginning Norman society had an aristocratic and incipiently feudal character . . . . Neither Thing nor hundred is heard of in Normandy. Its rulers early had their eye fixed on domination.[298]

But this rather brutal political reality does not figure greatly in the myth of "Prince" Henry of Orkney. The legend of Henry tells a different story, at least as recounted by Tim Wallace-Murphy and Marilyn Hopkins. Let's start with their explanation for the change of surname from Moer or Moray to St. Clair:

> Rollo and his senior officers were solemnly baptized in the miraculous waters of a fountain fed by a spring named in honor of Saint Clair, who was martyred there in 884 . . . [Rollo then took the Saint's name, for reasons I will discuss later.] The use of the family name of St. Clair can be traced to the reign of the fourth Duke of Normandy, Richard II . . . As Rollo and Gisele [the daughter of Charles the Simple of France] had no children, Rollo remarried . . . [he had a son] known as William Long-Sword. [Who] was succeeded by Richard I [Duke of Normandy], whose daughter, Emma, married King Ethelred the Unready of England. Another of his daughters married Geoffrey, Count of Brittany, while a third, Matilda, became the wife of Eudes, Count of Chartres. Not content with joining with the royal house of Saxon England and the family of the Count of Brittany, Rollo's family married into the aristocratic families of . . . Champagne. They were also linked to the ducal House of Burgundy . . . the Capetians [Kings of France] and . . . to Godefroi de Bouillon, the first Christian ruler of the Kingdom of Jerusalem.[299]

Pretty good going for a Viking outlaw. But, as Gwyn Jones has told us, the Norman branch of the Moray family had their eyes fixed on domination from the start of their adventures in the south. So perhaps it is not surprising that they formed strategic alliances by marrying off their Viking maidens.

This is noted and subsumed into myth:

> The lands of Normandy, important though they may have been, do not of themselves explain this headlong charge by some of the oldest families in Europe into matrimonial alliances with the Vikings. When you study the genealogies of these families, you find that they made repeated dynastic alliances with one another.[300]

Perhaps the novelty of marrying striking blond Valkyries whose father was strong enough to have taken the lands of Normandy as the ransom for lifting the siege of Chartres, and whose ships still controlled the major trade route of the Seine,[301] played no part in it? Simple political motives never play any part in the mythical history of the "Lordly Line of the High St. Clairs," as Wallace-Murphy and Hopkins dub Hrolf's descendants. But they were Norse outlaws who came from a Trondheim-based family, and they had been devotees of the Goddess Freya for generations. The Christian rulers of the petty kingdoms of France would have looked down on them as pagans, and Hrolf (Rollo) was astute enough to recognize that a change of religion could pay political dividends.[302]

The late Professor Hilda Ellis Davidson of Cambridge University explained what the Norse, including Hrolf, believed about a supreme Goddess:

> The literary sources tend to give the impression of one supreme and powerful goddess who might be regarded as wife or mistress of her worshipper. If he were a king, her cult would become part of the state religion, and she would receive official worship as part of the state religion along with the leading gods. In Scandinavian tradition the main goddess appears to be Freyja.[303]

Temples to Freya were extremely important to the Norse Jarls who built them. They believed that their political power depended on protecting these sacred buildings. When Olaf Tryggvason wanted to overthrow Jarl Hakon of Halogaland, the *de facto* King of Norway in the late tenth century, he did it by breaking down the image of Freya from the temple where Hakon worshipped. Tryggvason dragged the image of the goddess out from her temple behind his horse, eventually breaking it up and burning it to dishonor his rival.[304] The rulers of France, on the other hand, drew their power from the Divine Right of Kings underpinned by the Christian Church.

Rognwald of Moray, Hrolf's father, built a temple to Freya in Trondheim that was eastward-facing and had two pillars at its entrance. This was discovered when this temple was excavated during repairs to the floor of a medieval church dedicated to the Virgin Mary, which later Christians built on top of it.[305] Hrolf thus came from a culture that understood the power of a divinity to reinforce the right of a king to rule, but he was astute enough to recognize that being a consort of Freya cut no ice in Normandy. So Hrolf, consort of Freya, became Rollo the newborn Christian, baptized in "the miraculous waters of a fountain . . . named in honor of St. Clair." And, of course, there was no political calculation here by the river-wise Viking; he was simply overwhelmed by the theological arguments and fell on his knees before the assembled bishops, asking for redemption.

Or perhaps not. Wallace-Murphy and Hopkins have a different explanation:

> Something else is at work here—something that is difficult, if not impossible, to explain by the accepted standards of history. The breeding, or should we say interbreeding, of these families resembles the creation of bloodstock in the farming sense more than normal human behavior . . . There is an esoteric legend that has persisted for centuries that . . . a group of families in Europe have a long-held oral tradition that they are all descended from the twenty-four high priests of the Temple of Jerusalem of the time of Jesus. To keep their bloodlines pure, they restricted their matrimonial alliances, wherever possible, to other families claiming the same descent . . . the priestly class . . . was hereditary and drawn from the tribe of Levi . . . the Cohens, [are] an even more exclusive group . . . [who were] strictly enjoined to marry only within the wider Cohen family . . . [to] preserve an unbroken . . . genealogical link to . . . Moses.[306]

So far so good. This belief does have some measure of truth in it. The study of genetics has revealed that the male Cohens do carry a distinctive gene, and the genealogy of the Bible traces the line of the priestly male Cohen gene down through Abraham, Moses, David, Solomon, Zerubabbel, and Joseph[307] to Jesus himself:

> A particular Y-chromosome type termed the "Cohen modal haplotype," is known to be characteristic of the paternally inherited Jewish priesthood and is thought, more generally, to be a potential signature haplotype of Judaic origin.[308]

But this idea is developed beyond the strategic marriages of the daughters of Hrolf, who take on all the surnames of the ruling families of France and England, to a "lordly line of high St. Clairs." Let Wallace-Murphy and Hopkins speak for themselves about this secret group:

> [These] families . . . preserve the true teachings of Jesus . . . and are dedicated to bringing about "the Kingdom of Heaven upon Earth." . . . [they] outwardly followed the prevailing religion . . . but kept their hidden teaching alive by passing it down orally through the generations . . . Richard II, the fourth Duke of Normandy, had three sons: Richard III, who became the fifth duke, Robert the Devil, and Mauger the Young . . . . Mauger had three sons: Hamon, Walderne, and Hubert. Hamon and Walderne were both killed at the battle of Val-des-Dunes . . . Two of Walderne's children, Richard and Britel, became reconciled with William the Conqueror and played a part in the conquest of England, where they were later given estates. This left two other children, William and Agnes. They were both quite young when their father was killed at the battle of Val-des-Dunes, for which William never forgave William

the Conqueror . . . Known as William the Seemly because of his courage and courtesy, he was chosen . . . to escort Princess Margaret to Scotland, where she was to marry Malcolm Canmore, King of the Scots. As a reward he was granted the barony of Roslin. The first St. Clair born in Scotland, Henri de St. Clair, was confirmed by King Malcolm as Baron of Roslin and also Baron of Pentland.[309]

They go on to explain:

Royal dynasties come and go . . . The fate of certain aristocrats who attain "royal favor" is even more transient and ephemeral . . . [But] there is one aristocratic family who never sought a throne, yet were always close to the seats of power as advisors to kings, and who have wielded virtually unbroken power and influence of a subtle and all-pervasive kind from the last years of the ninth century until the final decade of the second millennium. Their history is one that is of as much interest to students of British or Scottish history as it is to those fascinated by the medieval Knights Templar or to historians of pre-Columbian exploration of America. [They are] known as "the Lordly Line of the High Sinclairs," . . . [and are] true Viking stock, descended from Rognwald, the Earl of More, in Norway.[310]

The problem with this powerful story is that the Cohen Y-chromosome marker, which this secret group is claimed to be preserving, is only passed down the male line. So how does a lineage founded in the marriages of a group of Freya-worshipping Norse women become the guardian of the "true teachings of Jesus"? The only contribution from the St. Clair line was Viking maidens with lots of mitochrondria, but no Y-chromosomes. Perhaps they made good marriages to royal husbands who really *were* a part of this Cohen lineage, but this is never made clear. I did wonder if the political reality might not be something rather simpler. It couldn't just be the astute use of religious endorsement to centralize political power, could it? I decided to look more closely at the historical background.

THE VIKING ORDER: THRALLS, CHURLS, AND JARLS

In 2005 Jared Diamond, a professor of geography at UCLA, published a study of the reasons why some societies collapse while apparently similar ones do not. One of the cases he studied was the Viking colonies in the North Atlantic. His work looked at what the Vikings did in Orkney, Shetland, the Faroes, Iceland, Greenland, and North America. His great sweep through Viking history gave me a new insight into the background to the myth of Prince Henry St. Clair. Diamond prefaced his examination of the Vikings with an overview of the beginnings of civilization, to set them in context. It is a powerful statement worth quoting in full, although I recommend reading his book, *Collapse*, if you want to really understand the Vikings:

All the basic elements of medieval European civilization arose over the previous 10,000 years in or near the Fertile Crescent, that crescent-shaped area of Southwest

Asia from Jordan north to southeastern Turkey and then east to Iran. From that region came the world's first crops and domestic animals and wheeled transport, the mastery of copper and then of bronze and iron, and the rise of towns and cities, chiefdoms and kingdoms, and organized religions. All of those elements gradually spread to and transformed Europe from southeast to northwest, beginning with the arrival of agriculture in Greece from Anatolia around 7000 B.C. Scandinavia, the corner of Europe farthest from the Fertile Crescent, was the last part of Europe to be so transformed, being reached by agriculture only around 2500 B.C. It was also the corner farthest from the influence of Roman civilization: unlike the area of modern Germany, Roman traders never reached it, nor did it share any boundary with the Roman Empire. Hence, until the Middle Ages, Scandinavia remained Europe's backwater.[311]

Diamond pointed out the Viking lands had two natural advantages. These were, first, easy access to the furs of northern forest animals, seal skins, and beeswax, which were considered to be luxury goods in the rest of Europe; and second, a rich coastline, full of natural harbors that made sea travel potentially faster than overland travel. This environment encouraged societies to develop marine technology. Around 600 CE, the Earth had a period of global warming, which favored agriculture in the north of Europe. Diamond notes that better designs of the plough enabled food production to increase, and this in turn brought about a population explosion in Scandinavia.

But only about 3 percent of the land area in Norway can be used for agriculture, and by 700 CE., that land was coming under increasing pressure. With no new farms available at home, Norway's growing population expanded overseas. And this was where their growing expertise in ship-building paid off. As Diamond explains:

> [They] quickly developed fast, shallow-draft, highly maneuverable, sailed-and-rowed ships that were ideal for carrying their luxury exports to eager buyers in Europe and Britain. Those ships let them cross the ocean but then also pull up on any shallow beach or row far up rivers, without being confined to the few deepwater harbors . . . [this trade] paved the way for raiding. Once some Scandinavian traders had discovered sea routes to rich peoples who could pay for furs with silver and gold, ambitious younger brothers of those traders realized that they could acquire that same silver and gold without paying for it . . . [Ships developed for trade] could also be sailed and rowed over those same sea routes to arrive by surprise at coastal and riverside towns, including ones far inland on rivers. Scandinavians became Vikings, i.e., raiders . . . Chiefs who lost in the struggle against other chiefs at home were especially motivated to try their luck overseas.[312]

Gwyn Jones paints a similarly perceptive picture:

> Take self-confidence and professional skill, add resource, cunning, no nonsense about fair play, a strong disregard for human life and suffering, especially the other man's, and you have a good soldier. Give a ship's crew or a mounted commando of such men a leader in whose intelligence, tactics, valour, profitability, and record of success they can trust, and you have a good unit. Multiply the units, find them a →

general like the famed Halfdan or Hastein, Ganga-Hrolf or Olaf Tryggvason, or a monarch like Svein Forkbeard or Knut, and you shake kingdoms. It is not surprising that the Vikings prospered overseas as much as they did: the surprise is that they did not prosper more.[313]

The practice of "viking" (trading, raiding, piracy and pillage) began as a summer diversion for a group of extremely hierarchical subsistence farmers eking out a living on the high northern coast of western Europe. There were three classes in Viking society: the thralls, who were slaves; the peasants, who were freemen; and the jarls, the noble warriors who ruled them all. *?Churls*

✱ The Viking creation myth claimed that all these classes were bastard children of the god Heimdall, who wandered around Scandinavia seeking hospitality and impregnating trusting housewives while their husbands slept. The first couple who gave him shelter were Ai and his wife Edda. Edda was old and ugly, but nevertheless Heimdall slept with her, and in due course she gave birth to a son who was ugly and short with thick knuckles and clumsy fingers. Ai and Edda called him Thrall, and he grew up and married an ugly bandy-legged girl called Bir (which means Slavery) and had a series of children. Their boys were called Nosey, Horsefly, Byreboy, and Roughneck, and their daughters Fatty, Beanpole, and Lazybones. These children and their descendants did all the dirty, heavy, back-breaking work on the farms. They were considered less than human, and were bought, sold, and treated like cattle.

As Heimdall traveled on, he stayed with another couple, a weaver called Afi and his wife Amma, who was a skilled seamstress. Once again, Heimdall slept with the wife, and in good time, she gave birth to a son who was named Churl (which means freeman). Churl was fresh-faced, with a ruddy complexion and bright eyes. He grew up and married a sturdy woman called Snor. They had many children. The boys were called Strongbeard, Holder, Smith, and Husbandman. The daughters were named Capable, Prettyface, and Maiden. Churl taught his sons all the skills of farming and how to build houses, barns, wagons, and ships. Snor brought up her daughters to hold the keys to their households, to look after their husband's wealth, and to provide food and clothes for her family. From these children, all the free men of the Norse were descended.

Finally, Heimdall came to a magnificent hall, where he met Fadir and his beautiful blonde wife Madir. Fadir was a weapon-maker and Madir was the most perfect housewife ever born. She spread a feast before Heimdall before taking him into her bedroom. Nine months later, she gave birth to a son who was named Jarl (which means warrior). Jarl was fair-haired, tall, strong, and sharp-eyed. Soon after Jarl began to toddle, his divine father returned and taught him to shoot a bow and arrow, throw a spear, and defend himself with shield and sword. As he grew, Jarl learned to ride a horse, hunt with hounds, and swim like a fish. When the boy was of age, Heimdall returned once more to the hall of Fadir and Madir and gave him the name of Rig, taught him the secret art of writing with runes, and told him to take control of his hereditary estates. So Jarl went out into the world and took what was his by right from those who were too weak to defend themselves. He returned home laden with plunder and married Erna (which means "lively"), who was slim, fair, and wise. Together they had twelve sons, who were the ancestors of all the rulers of the Viking lands. At least, this is the story told in The Song of Rig. And it explains why the Vikings had slaves who were little better than beasts and often valued less. It also explains why there were peasants who were skilled in many trades, and why there were warriors who were meant to spend the long days of summer plundering the rich but ill-defended lands to the south.[314]

Gwyn Jones agrees with Diamond that geography and climate put pressure on the population to seek new sources of food and wealth.

> The limitations imposed on both crop and animal husbandry in parts of Scandinavia in early times by sea, mountains, latitude and cold, especially in respect of Norway and upper Sweden were always constrictive . . . Domiciled in this . . . region was a vigorous and fast-breeding race whose numbers increased considerably from the seventh to the tenth century. Their social habits were shaped to increase . . . that men like girls, concubines, mistresses, and that those who can afford them frequently acquire them . . . According to Adam of Bremen, every Swede whose means allowed had two or three wives, while the wealthy and high-born set themselves no limit.[315]

This Viking appetite for the mechanical delights of procreation, no doubt inherited from the genetic contribution of Heimdall, is confirmed by the writings of Ibn Fadlan. He was a Muslim scholar known as a "truth-teller" because of his reputation as a reliable reporter, and he took great interest in the ways of the people he met. In 922 CE, as part of an Arab embassy visiting the local king, he was visiting a port on the River Volga that was a major trading center for a Norse group known as the Rus. He described being invited into the houses of the Norse-Rus merchants:

> [On] the shores of the Volga . . . they build big houses of wood . . . each holding ten to twenty persons more or less. Each man has a couch on which he sits. With them are pretty slave girls destined for sale to merchants. A man will have sexual intercourse with his slave girl while his companion looks on. Sometimes whole groups will come together in this fashion, each in the presence of the others. A merchant who arrives to buy a slave girl from them may have to wait and look on while a Rus completes the act of intercourse with a slave girl.[316]

ENTER THE LONGSHIPS

But what made this luxurious lifestyle possible? Jones agrees with Diamond that it was Norse skill in ship-building and navigation.

> The quick-in quick-out Viking raids which began in the 790s, and still more the voyages of settlement to the lesser Atlantic islands which began somewhat earlier, were

Real

sea-borne and could hardly be undertaken until northern shipwrights had brought the sailing-ship to some . . . state of excellence . . . The necessary command of techniques was attained about the middle of the eighth century.[317]

In contrast to the lumbering cargo ships that the Templars used as troop carriers and trade vessels, Gwyn Jones tells us the Viking ship was:

> . . . an inspired combination of strength and elasticity . . . the power to cross seas and oceans did not exhaust her excellence as a raider . . . An exceedingly shallow draft, rarely exceeding three and half feet, allowed her to penetrate all save the shallowest of rivers, gave her mastery of harbourless shelving beaches, and facilitated the rapid disembarkation of men at the point of attack. By turning into the wind and making off by oar she was almost immune from pursuit by the clumsier sailing-ships of the lands she preyed on . . . the ship which carried the Norsemen overseas, whether to the British Isles, the Frankish Empire, or to the Atlantic Islands, Iceland, Greenland, and America was a sailing ship: her oars were an auxiliary form of power for use when she was becalmed, in some state of emergency, or required manoeuvring in narrow waters, fjords or rivers. This was true of raiding ships and carriers alike, though the ratio of men to space would naturally be higher in the raider.[318]

Now, Jones and Diamond, both tell a story of an early Viking discovery and attempt at colonization of North America. It was already clear that from about 800 CE onwards the Vikings had ships good enough to reach Canada, but what of their skills in navigation? Could they have maintained trade routes across the Atlantic without knowledge of either charts or compass? Gwyn Jones thought they could:

> First and foremost . . . [the captain] would commit himself to latitude sailing. This is no haphazard affair . . . If sailing from Bergen in Norway to [the Viking settlement

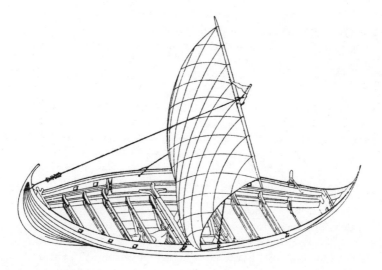

A typical Viking longship.

in] L'Anse-aux-Meadows in Newfoundland . . . he would move thirty miles or so North of Bergen to the landmark of Stad, because this had the same degree of latitude as his landfall in Greenland. If now he sailed due west he would find himself after the right count of days passing north of Shetland, therefore south of the Faroes at a recognisable distance from them. On the same course he would next traverse the ocean well to the south of Iceland and know where he was, not by the measurement of miles, but by observing the birds and sea-creatures associated with those waters . . . This part of the voyage would take seven days. It would take him almost as long again to sight the east coast of Greenland, about eighty miles north of Cape Farewell . . . [Once round] he would be following a well-described coastal route till he reached Herjolfanes.[319]

Jones also expands on the idea that the sophistication of the Viking longship, which made it a useful trading tool, also made it a potent weapon of war. It was the longship that made it possible for the Norse to take advantage of the weakly defended petty kingdoms of the British Isles.

Norse freebooters plundered and slew at Lindisfarne and Jarrow in Northumbria, Morganwg [Glamorgan] in South Wales, Lambey Island north of Dublin in Ireland, in Kintyre and the Isle of Man and at the sacred island of Iona . . . In 799 they raided various islands lying off Aquitaine in France.[320]

The Viking movement was rooted in simple human motives. The Norse had needs and ambitions which the limited size of their coastal lands could not support. They had the will, strength and marine technology to satisfy these needs at the expense of their weaker southern neighbors. They wanted land to farm, wealth to enjoy luxuries and fame to become heroes. These were the simple drivers of the Viking phenomenon: land, wealth and fame. The ways they could achieve these goals were trade, colonization, piracy, and war. Jones describes Scandinavia as "like a mighty hive . . . which, growing to too full of people, threw out some new swarm."[321] But there was another factor at work during the period when what are now Norwegians, Danes, and Swedes were fighting to establish distinct Scandinavian kingdoms:

In wars of succession losers lose all, making a shift abroad welcome to all parties . . . the earliest Norse incursions into Shetland, Orkney and thereafter the Hebrides . . . circa 780, appear to have been peaceful and carried out by men concerned not with plunder but with a search for pasture land. Vikings seeking a base came later.[322]

Jones goes on to expand this idea when discussing the first Norse Jarls of Orkney:

Northern tradition is insistent that in the years after . . . [the battle of] Hafrsfjord [in 900 CE] . . . considerable numbers of Norwegians fled from the tyranny of king Harald to Shetland, Orkney, and the Hebrides, and from there practiced viking in reverse. Instead of spending their winters in Norway and their summers raiding in the British and Atlantic islands, they now lived out west and did their raiding back in Norway. True to his nature and his lifelong strategy [Harald] now used his command of the sea-lanes to tackle the trouble at its source, sailed with his fleet to the Atlantic islands, and put all he caught to the sword in Shetland, Orkney, and the Hebrides. He is reported to have harried on the mainland of Scotland, and to have sailed south to Man. Having extirpated his enemies, Harald laid claim to both Shetland and Orkney, then bestowed them on the family of Jarl Rognwald of Moer. The first earl of Orkney was Rognwald's brother Sigurd, notorious for his assaults on Scotland; the second, Rognwald's base-born son Einar, ruthless, capable, one-eyed, an archetypal turf-cutter and middling poet.[323]

I will return to the question of the Viking Jarls of Orkney and their role in the legend of "Prince" Henry when I have looked at the whole question of the exploration of North America by the Vikings.

The Lure of the Unsailed Western Seas

The vast possibilities of the North Atlantic were tremendously attractive to the Vikings.

> The presence of a vast and for the most part unsailed ocean to the west of Norway and the British Isles was a constant challenge to the land-hungry, wealth-hungry, fame-hungry Vikings . . . As soon as they had ships fit for its waters it was a challenge they accepted.[324]

The Faroe Islands bask in the relative warmth of the Gulf Stream in the North Atlantic at 62° N, to the northwest of Scotland and about halfway between Iceland and Norway. The 18 islands in the group have 687 miles of coastline to offer harbors for longships. They had been discovered by Irish monks in 700 CE. Abbot Dicuil, writing in 825, reported them to be only two full days' sailing from Britain, but complained that Norse pirates had since killed the hermit monks and replaced their anchorite cells with sheep folds.[325] Newly aspiring hermits had been forced to sail farther west in search of solitude, and it was common gossip around the Irish monasteries by 790 that really serious hermits had discovered a land which had a day that was six months long. It ran from the vernal to the autumnal equinox, with the rest of the year black as night twenty-four hours a day, dark and dreary enough to mortify even a Celtic Christian soul. But the Irish have always loved talking, and Gwyn Jones is sure they told the Vikings about islands to the west.

> It was intelligence gleaned in Ireland, The Western Isles, Orkney and Shetland which led the Norsemen to the Faroes. Once Irish priests reached Iceland in the 790s news of this discovery spread rapidly. And none would more readily lend an ear than the Norsemen, their minds on homes for their families, pasture for their animals, havens for their ships.[326]

Nobody is quite sure which Viking hero first sailed to Iceland. Gardar Svavarsson, Naddod the Viking, and Floki Vligerason all have their devoted saga-writers. But the romantic favorite has to be Naddod, who was such a hot-headed menace that he was driven out of Norway in 785, picked up on the wings of an Atlantic storm, and driven before the gale to Iceland, where he promptly founded a settlement. What is clear is that Iceland was a completely settled and stable republic with its own *Lawthing* to elect and control its rulers by 930.[327] After the battle of Hafrsfjord, when King Harald Fairhair drove out his rivals for a united Norway, Iceland started to get crowded. The real Vikings needed more pasture, more harbors, and less government. One such was Eirik (Erik) the Red. In 982, he was driven out of Norway for killing too many of his rivals. He sailed to west to Iceland, to Haukadal, where his temper again got the better of him and he killed a few more Icelanders. The *Lawthing* exiled him for three years, and so, for want of anything better to do, he set off north but accidentally got blown west by bad weather and discovered Greenland.

Gwyn Jones describes what happened next:

> For three years he explored the region between Herjolfanes and Eiriksfjord, and with his crew marked out sites of farms and homes to be. Marked, too, that the land was rich in animals: bears, foxes, caribou; that the Skaergaard bred sea mammals; and that wherever there was water there were fish. And everywhere birds that had never known the fowler's snare. So it was with a determination quickly to return and colonize it that he sailed back to the Breidafjord when his period of banishment was over. Not too inaccurately in respect of the fjords of the south-west he called the country Greenland, believing that no place is the worse for an attractive name.[328]

By now the Vikings were living on the side of the Davies Straits across from Canada at a point where it is less than two hundred miles wide. This was no distance for a Viking longship, and it didn't take long for a Viking mariner to reach mainland America. Considering one of the main drivers for Viking exploration was fame, it is rather sad that we have largely forgotten about the voyage of Bjarni Herjolfsson. Admittedly, he was much less of a self-publicist that Columbus, but at least he reached the mainland of Canada rather than simply stopping short in the West Indies. Herjolfsson was an Icelander. He had been on a trading trip to Norway over the winter of 985–6, so he missed all the excitement when Erik returned to Iceland with wondrous tales of the new green land he had discovered. Bjarni's father, Herjolf, had sold up in Iceland and set off with Erik as part of a fleet of twenty-five ships intending to colonize Greenland.[329]

Bjarni decided to follow his father. As Gwyn Jones puts it, he set off pilotless, chartless, and compassless for the southwestern fjords of Greenland. Three days into his journey, Bjarni's ship hit a patch of appallingly bad weather, a combination of alternating fog and erratic high winds. So not only could he not use landmarks on the receding Iceland to fix his bearings, he also didn't know where the gales were taking him. He was blown well past Greenland, and when the weather cleared he found himself near a low-lying forested land. He may not have known where he was, but knew it wasn't the mountainous Greenland. He decided to sail north for a couple days, when he reached another place which didn't fit the description of Greenland. It was an area of high glaciated mountains, and Bjarni thought is was "good for nothing." Fortunately, at this point the wind moved off-land, and he was able to turn the bows of his longship back into the Atlantic. After four days of fair winds, he finally reached Herjolfsnes in Greenland and was reunited with his father.[330]

VIKING AMERICA

It was another fifteen years before Leif, Erik the Red's eldest son, made his first landings in the New World. The Greenland Saga (*Grœnlendinga Saga*) tells how hard it was to set up a functioning colony in Greenland, with few ships to carry materials from Europe to support the colonists. It is hardly surprising that it was not until the Greenland colony was stable and able to feed itself that the Greenlanders found enough spare time to investigate his findings.[331] Gwyn Jones explains that Bjarni's account was accepted, but there were simply no resources available to investigate Markland, Woodland, and Vinland, as he called them:

> There was no question of them not believing him. Medieval geography favoured the notion of more land to be found beyond Greenland and, more practically, when men climbed high mountains they could see the far distant land itself or the cloud formations they associated with land.[332]

The implication of these facts is that Norse sailors were exploring the lightly populated coasts of North America with a view to colonization about a hundred years before Christian Europe came up with the idea of Holy Violence as a way to justify colonizing the heavily populated Holy Land. This does rather negate the idea that Columbus discovered America in 1492. But exactly where did the Vikings get to? It was an Icelander, Thorfinn Karlsefni, who set up the first trading colony on Vinland in the early years of the eleventh century. Gwyn Jones says:

> While there is general agreement that the Norsemen reached North America, agreement does not extend to how far south they reached. An increasing weight of opinion has now settled for southern Baffin Island as Helluland, Labrador south of Nain as Markland, but Vinland, Wineland, where the voyagers are said to have found grapes and wheat growing wild, is a different story. The St. Lawrence Estuary, Baie de Chaleur, New Brunswick, Nova Scotia, New England, Massachusetts, Rhode Island, Long Island Sound, Virginia, Georgia, and Florida have been argued for with acumen and eloquence . . . Maybe it was as a result of far-ranging voyages . . . that tales of grape-clusters, self-sown wheat, and kindly winters enriched the Norse tradition of Vinland; maybe longer voyages and later travellers blurred the outlines of Leif's landing and Karlsefni's settlement . . . Bishop Eirik sailed there in a year variously stated to be 1112, 1113, 1117, and, most probably, 1121, with what result we do not know. As late as the

middle of the fourteenth century men were still sailing there, presumably to fetch timber and furs. The Icelandic Annals record that in the year 1347 a ship with seventeen or eighteen Greenlanders on board was storm-driven to Iceland as they sought to return to their own country from Markland. But after that there was silence.[333]

Jared Diamond agrees with this, and goes further:

The coast of northeastern North America . . . lies thousands of miles from Norway . . . all Viking ships destined for North America sailed from the westernmost established colony, Greenland. Even Greenland, though, was far from North America by Viking sailing standards. The Vikings' main camp on Newfoundland lay nearly 1,000 miles from the Greenland settlements by a direct voyage, but required a voyage of 2,000 miles and up to six weeks by the actual coast-hugging route that Vikings took for safety . . . To sail from Greenland to Vinland and then return within the summer sailing season of favorable weather would have left little time for exploring . . . Hence the Vikings established a base camp on Newfoundland, where they could remain for the winter, so as to be able to spend the entire subsequent summer exploring . . . Scholars tended to . . . doubt that the Vikings ever reached the New World, until the debate was finally settled when archaeologists located the Vikings' Newfoundland base camp in 1961 . . . at Anse-aux-Meadows on the northwest coast of Newfoundland. Radiocarbon dating indicated that the camp was occupied around AD 1000.[334]

Because of the abundance of native grapes, the Vikings called this area Wineland, which is recorded in the sagas as Vinland. Vinland was much farther south than Greenland, which made its climate so much milder. A longer grazing season meant that cattle could be kept outdoors all year, instead of having to be fed hay in barns in the winter, as they did in Greenland—and this removed the need to harvest and store hay. The land was heavily forested, providing timber for ship-building. There were plenty of lakes, and these, as well as the surrounding coastal seas, swarmed with fish. Edible fauna included caribou, deer, and nesting birds with clutches of eggs. The Newfoundland colony began to export timber, grapes, and animal furs to Greenland.[335]

Then something went wrong with this land of plenty, and the settlement was abandoned. Diamond reports that the archaeological excavations were disappointing, because the Norse left nothing of value:

The site was not abandoned hastily, but as part of a planned permanent evacuation in which all tools and possessions of value were taken back to Greenland. Today we know that North America was by far the largest and most valuable North Atlantic land discovered by the Norse; even the tiny fraction of it that the Norse surveyed impressed them. Why, then, did the Norse give up on Vinland, land of plenty?[336]

The answer was simple: They were driven out by the local inhabitants, with whom they failed to establish good relations. Diamond notes that when the Vikings first met a group of nine Native Americans they killed eight, while the ninth escaped to warn the rest. The escaper soon returned with his friends and family in a fleet of canoes and killed Eirik the Red's son Thorvald with an arrow in his belly. The Vinland Saga, quoted by Diamond, attributes these last words to him:

> This is a rich country we have found; there is plenty of fat around my belly. We've found a land of fine resources, though we'll hardly enjoy much of them.[337]

And Diamond quotes another saga writer as saying:

> The [Viking] party then realized that, despite everything that the land had to offer there, they would be under constant threat of attack from its former inhabitants. They made ready to depart for their own country [i.e., Greenland].[338]

The failure of the Vinland colony didn't stop the Greenlanders from raiding the North American coast line for timber and iron. Diamond points to widespread archaeological evidence in the form of bits of smelted copper, smelted iron, and spun goat's wool found scattered around the Canadian Arctic. He comments that "the most notable such find is a silver penny minted in Norway between 1065 and 1080 during the reign of King Olav the Quiet, found at an Indian site on the coast of Maine hundreds of miles south of Labrador, and pierced for use as a pendant." As late as 1347 the Greenlanders were still occasionally visiting North America and not thinking it unusual.[339]

DECLINE AND FALL IN GREENLAND

Although the Vikings didn't realize it, Greenland was a far more fragile environment than Norway. Its soils were thinner and less stable, its climate colder, its winters longer, and the vegetative recovery of overgrazed land took much longer than they expected. Also there was a critical difference in sea temperature. Norway, Orkney, Shetland, the Faroes, and Iceland all sit in the warm Gulf Stream. The west coast of Greenland, where the two Norse colonies were established, is in the cold West Greenland Current.[340]

The two main settlements, were both on the Western coast of the island but, rather confusingly, were known as the Western settlement, which was in the North, and the Eastern settlement, which was in the South. The Western settlement, which peaked at a population of about 1,000, was dominated by the Sandnes estate.[341] (The estates were large farms or ranches, which took their names from their owners.) The Eastern settlement, of about 5,000 people, boasted a cathedral and was dominated by the Gardar estate, from which the cathedral took its name.

The Norse colony of Greenland might have been a success. The Vikings had potentially a much broader food base than the Inuit, because they were livestock farmers. Diamond makes four key points about the reasons for the final collapse between 1360, when the Western colony failed, and 1440, when the last members of the Eastern colony died.

1. The colonies were set up during a period when the climate was warm. But a severe bout of global cooling began in 1200, and by the mid-1400s, the Earth was much cooler. This made farming much harder, especially on an exposed northern island like Greenland.
2. The Norse saw Greenland as just another Norway in the west. They brought a system of dairy farming and a clerical lifestyle which worked for Norway but not for the harsher, thinner, more fragile soil of Greenland. For years, they were ruled by Norwegian-bred bishops who insisted on importing finery, and even bells for their churches, rather than using precious resources and cargo space for much-needed necessities
3. These church leaders despised the Inuit (Eskimos) for not being European and for worshiping pagan Gods. Because of this bias, the Norse never did learn the survival techniques used by the Eskimo hunters, and treated them as sub-humans to be killed on a whim. The Inuit moved in as the Norse finally died of starvation, huddled in their finely furnished cathedrals with their neglected longship hulls lying rotting and decayed on the now-hostile shores. They waited for relief from Norway or Iceland, but it never came.
4. The political power of Greenland society was concentrated in the hands of the chiefs and clergy. The land belonged to them, the ships belonged to them, and they controlled and limited the trade with Europe.

As Diamond comments:

They choose to devote much of that trade to importing goods that brought prestige to them: luxury goods for the wealthiest households, vestments and jewellery for the clergy, and bells and stained glass for the churches . . . they allocated their few boats . . . [to hunt] the luxury exports (such as ivory and polar bear hides) with which to pay for those imports.[342]

✳ The move away from the Norse tradition of *Lawthings* (meetings of Freemen to decide on matters of government) towards the new Christian notion of a king's divine right to rule (supported by the myth of the Donation of Constantine, which gave bishops the power to crown kings) meant that there was little accountability on the part of the leaders of the Greenland colony. Secure in the support of its bishop and clergy, the chiefs overgrazed their lands to farm as much wool as possible to pay for luxury imports. This had the additional advantage that independent farmers on overgrazed land were forced into tenancy and ended up in hock to the chief. If leaders had used their control of shipping to import more iron and timber from Markland, and had learned Inuit boat-building and hunting techniques, they might well have survived. Or if they had chosen to build replacement ships rather than import vestments, they might have been able to flee back to Norway. But Diamond points out that these types of innovation would have threatened the power and prestige of the chiefs and the newly established Christian clergy, which owed allegiance to the ecclesiastical hierarchy of mainland Europe. As he explains:

> Much of what the chiefs and clergy valued proved eventually harmful to the society. Yet the society's values were at the root of its strengths as well as of its weaknesses. The Greenland Norse did succeed in creating a unique form of European society, and in surviving for 450 years as Europe's most remote outpost. . . . Ultimately, though, the chiefs found themselves without followers. The last right that they obtained for themselves was the privilege of being the last to starve.[343]

The climate change that took place after 1200 is often overlooked. The voyages of exploration by Erik the Red, his son Leif, and Thorfinn Karlsefni took place when the climate of the northern land and seas was fairly mild. By 1347 this climate change, combined with a period of maritime decline in Norway, was already making it difficult to maintain the long and dangerous sea route to Greenland. Disarray and power struggles in Scandinavia also worked against Greenland. As Gwyn Jones explains:

> Over much of Europe the glaciers were advancing, the tree-line fell lower, vegetation and harvest were diminished by the cold, and the alpine passes were sealed for longer periods. The northern coast of Iceland grew increasingly beleaguered by drift ice; and off Greenland as the sea temperatures sank there was a disabling increase in the ice which comes south with the East Greenland Current to Cape Farewell, and then swings north to enclose first the Eastern and then the Western Settlement.[344]

But, in the period after the collapse of the Western colony, in the final struggling years of the Eastern colony, there was a golden opportunity for a return to the old Viking ways of piracy for any Jarl who had ocean-going ships at his disposal. The beleaguered clergy of Greenland would pay well in furs and walrus ivory to any smuggler who could slip a cargo of fine vestments into a vessel traveling the trade routes that were forbidden them by the King of Norway. Perhaps this was where the legend of "Prince" Henry of Orkney arose? Let's see.

A New Look at "Prince" Henry of Orkney

The modern growth of interest in Henry, the first St. Clair Jarl of Orkney, was launched in a most unlikely way, with the publication of a book by science-fiction writer Frederick Pohl. In 1967 Pohl was editing four science-fiction magazines, one of which, *IF*, won the Hugo award for best professional science-fiction magazine from 1966 to 1968. Pohl is not only a wonderful storyteller in his own right, but his success in fostering new science-fiction writers for *IF* shows he had the ability to recognize a good story even if it was written by somebody else. He used this talent for story-spotting when he came across the story of an obscure Scottish Earl who was reputed to have sailed to America with a Venetian admiral.

This is how the back flap copy of Frederick Pohl's biography, *Prince Henry Sinclair: His Expedition to the New World in 1398* puts it:

✱ It is one of the anomalies of human history that despite our passion for knowledge, we are still in doubt as to who actually "discovered" the North American continent. According to author/historian Frederick J. Pohl, the glory should go to none other than Prince Henry Sinclair, Earl of Orkney, who set off on a voyage of discovery for "a very great country" and dropped anchor in Guysborough Harbour, Nova Scotia, on June 2, 1398, almost a century before Columbus's and Cabot's historic voyages.[345]

Pohl's book is a retelling of the story he found in a document known as the Zeno Manuscript. Its full title, as listed in the bibliography of Pohl's book, is *The Discovery of the Islands of Frislandia, Eslanda, Engronelanda, Estotilanda, and Icaria; Made by Two Brothers of the Zeno Family, Namely, Messire Nicolò, the Chevalier, and Messire Antonio. With a Map of the Said Islands* translated in Venice, 1558. This document tells of two Venetian sailors, Nicolò and Antonio Zeno, who sail the islands of the North Atlantic with a nobleman called Zichmni. Zichmni owned some islands called Porlanda off the south coast of Frislanda, and ruled the duchy of Sorant, or Sorand, on the south-east of the same island. A year before the story begins, Zichmni defeated the ruler of Frisland, the King of Norway, and he was busy conquering the island. Zichmni hired Nicolò as a pilot, and the Venetian proved such a valiant seaman that Zichmni ennobled him as a reward for his part in the conquest of the island.

Pohl translates Sorano as Roslin and Zichmni as d'Orkney, which as far as he was concerned fixed the identify of Prince Zichmni as Earl Henry Sinclair of Orkney.[346] The rest of the book decodes the Zeno manuscript as the tale of Henry's voyage to America at a date Pohl fixes, from assumptions about Christian place-naming conventions, as 1398.[347]

I have already discussed the problem of translating the name Roslin, but in Pohl's book I found the original of the translation I found on so many tourist websites. You will recall it puzzled me because it used letters which do not occur in the Gaelic. So the mystery of the odd translation was solved: It was a myth created by Frederick J Pohl. He says:

The name of the castle perfectly describes its position. A "ross" is a promontory or peninsula. A "lynn" is a pool or waterfall. The aptness of the name Roslin (Rosslyn) becomes apparent as one walks over the arched bridge and hears directly beneath it the torrent from the marshes tumbling down over the rocks to rejoin the river below.[348]

Neither the name nor the description of the site are accurate, and it would seem that Pohl based his translation on the *Chambers Twentieth Century Dictionary* entry for "Linn, lin, a waterfall: a cascade pool: a deep ravine [OE

A map of the world the Vikings knew.

hlynn, a torrent, combined with Gael. *linne . . .* pool.]" From this romantic visualization I suspect Pohl may never have visited Roslin. He paints an equally romantic picture of the nativity of Henry:

> ✳ In 1345, a boy, the first child of his parents, was born to the lord of the castle. The custom among French-speaking families like his was to give the infant his birth drink, his *boisson natale,* immediately. A few moments after his birth, the hero of our story was no doubt fed a spoonful of toddy, warm, sweet, strong—a taste of his native Scotland.
>
> Soon after, while his sixteen-year-old mother was still confined to bed and as yet not churched, his seventeen-year-old father, Sir William St. Clair, Lord of Roslin, Warden of the Southern Marches, Lord of the Lands of Carden and Pentland Moor, Sheriff of Lothian, Baron of Cousland, Great Master Hunter of Scotland, proudly carried the swaddled baby through the courtyard, across the ancient drawbridge, and over the causeway, up the road to St. Matthew's Church. There he was baptized without delay to save his infant soul from an eternity in limbo in case he died. He was christened Henry.[349]

I love Pohl's science-fiction writing, and his book *Prince Henry Sinclair* is a delight to read. It is a romantic quest to "peer into a distant past where time's dark, destroying hand has been so efficient in destroying traces," and Pohl admits an initial despair, which is overcome by the thrill of searching "with patience" until "good luck intervenes." He describes the task he has set himself:

> These pages record the quest for a fourteenth-century man—to establish, if possible, the facts of his life, to identify the land to which he sailed, and to trace the exploring he did therein; and also to ascertain whether that land to which he and his men sailed was indeed a "New World" and was the land that, a century later, everyone except Columbus began to realize was exactly that.[350]

It is a romantic *tour de force*, more novella than non-fiction. Unfortunately, Pohl's love of a good story and his gift for romantic storytelling runs away with him, and he quotes uncritically from anything that any antiquarian said about Henry, however unreliable. But his sense of a good story never fails him. For that reason alone, his book is worth reading, but it does not reflect the reality of history—instead, it's more like the spin of later supporters of the St. Clair family.

Henry: The Last Viking Jarl

Brian Smith, who is the archivist for the Shetlands Island Council and curator of the Shetland Museum, is an expert on the history of Orkney and Shetland. He has investigated the claims of Frederick Pohl about Henry Sinclair, and he pointed me to an article he wrote for the *New Orkney Antiquarian Journal* in 2002—the full text is also available on the internet—in which he made the following comments about Pohl's book (which he admits he too enjoyed reading):

> Frederick Pohl, give him his due, wasn't very manic: he was just a big romantic. His longest work on the subject is more or less in the form of a novel. Pohl believed just about everything that the seventeenth century antiquarians said about Henry, however foolish. He also . . . [made] absurd speculations about the place-names in the Zeno text.

Brian has strong views about Henry Sinclair:

> No contemporary document or commentator ever suggested that Henry Sinclair was an explorer, and there is no hint in any fourteenth century Italian record that the Zeno brothers had the adventures described in their descendant's narrative. Less than fifty years after Henry's death his grandson commissioned a genealogy of the Sinclair family, full of praise of his ancestors' achievements. Did he mention his grandfather's alleged maritime exploits? He did not.

He goes on to say:

> My impression of Henry Sinclair, from looking at the documents that have survived about him, is that he was a minor figure. He played little or no part in the politics of his native country or of Norway. His name doesn't appear in the records of the Scottish parliament or exchequer, and he only figured in Norwegian affairs on a few ceremonial occasions. One historian has claimed that he was "a powerful earl of Orkney very much in the old tradition", and that he was "very active in his northern earldom and integrated with the people of the earldom and their customs." I can find no evidence at all for such claims . . . The story is a modern myth, based on careless reading, wishful thinking and sometimes distortion.[351]

So what was the origin of the Zeno manuscript? After the debate, I stood on a windy, winding street in Kirkwall and asked Brian about it. He said it was simply "a hoax by Nicolò Zeno," whom he described as "one of the most blatant and successful hoaxers in the history of the art." He went on, "He even left us his signature in his text. Of the 26 Greenland place-names on his map, 25 appear on earlier maps. The exception is the name of the monastery that Nicolò Zeno allegedly found there." Brian grinned out from under his unruly mop of hair. "Zeno gives it the name of a saint who never existed. The saint's name? St. Thomas *Zeno*bius!"

So where does this leave my quest to understand "Prince" Henry Sinclair and his use of Templar Treasure and maritime skills? Pohl's book makes no mention of Freemasonry, the Templars, or hidden treasure; these seem to be later additions to the Henry myth. But there was one other source I needed to consult: Willie Thompson, a native Orcadian who has been Rector of Kirkwall Grammar School since 1971 and has spent his life collecting the material for his definitive *History of Orkney*. What had he to say about the matter. He was of the opinion that Henry St. Clair was quite independent in attitude:

> The fourteenth century brought about a regression to the independence and violence of saga days. A contraction of royal power in both Scotland and Norway created something of a vacuum. Scotland was weakened by prolonged English wars, by the imprisonment of David II (1346–1357), and by the ineffectual rule of Robert II (1371–1390) and Robert III (1390–1406). At the same time Norway's population, like that of Scotland, was much reduced by the Black Death, its trade was in the grip of the Hanseatic League and its shipping in decline, while by the end of the century its interests were being drawn eastwards by the politics of Scandinavian union. This was the time when Earl Henry I was free to rule Orkney like a jarl straight out of saga in a brief outburst of independence which Sinclair genealogists later transformed into a period of legendary magnificence.[352]

But it seems Henry did not gain the hereditary earldom of Orkney as a matter of course. He was not the first choice, and King Hakon had to be forced into accepting him:

> Rule by Erngisl Suneson, Alexander de Ard and direct government by sysselmen [Royal Bailiffs] all having failed, Norway arrived at the granting of the earldom to Henry Sinclair by a process of elimination. By his installation on 2 August 1379 at Marstrand, a little island off the west coast of Sweden, Norway was reluctantly forced to admit that there was no one else capable of ruling Orkney. Henry's very detailed installation promise was essentially a treaty between two mutually suspicious, even hostile parties . . . . Henry received the earldom as a feudal grant in return for military service and he was responsible for the defense of the islands, yet he was forbidden to construct castles or other fortifications—a promise he proceeded to ignore with the building of the massively strong Castle of Kirkwall.[353]

One thing was clear, though: Henry had a strong marine presence and was not above indulging in some traditional Viking piracy, as he showed when he killed his cousin Malise Sperra, who had a stronger claim to Orkney, even though Malise was then King Hakon's governor on Shetland. Thompson explains:

Although Earl Henry had no further trouble from Alexander de Ard, he was involved in a violent quarrel with his other cousin, Malise Sperra, whose power base was in Shetland where his father's family owned large estates . . . In 1389 both Henry and Malise were in Norway where they both witnessed the accession document of Eric of Pomerania, and Malise's seal shows that he was now a royal councillor, a position which implies that he had been given a royal appointment, most probably the governorship of Shetland. Perhaps it was intended that Malise's promotion should be a counter to Henry's dubious loyalty, but it created a dangerous rivalry . . . Immediately on their return from Norway, Malise and seven of his followers were killed in Shetland by Earl Henry in circumstances which are far from clear. The very presence of an Earl of Orkney in Shetland is surprising since it was long separated from the Orkney earldom.[354]

Thompson joins with Brian Smith in discounting the Zeno manuscript as confused and mythical:

> This strange story is full of difficulties, having been transcribed five generations later by a descendant who edited original documents he did not fully understand, thus the identification of people and places is largely a matter of speculation . . . [However] it would be unwise to dismiss out of hand the account of Earl Henry I's voyage of exploration and the tales of Orkney fishermen who were storm driven to the coasts of America a century before it was "discovered" by Christopher Columbus.[355]

So where does this leave my picture of "Prince" Henry St. Clair? Far from being a noble and loyal supporter of the King of Norway who was rewarded with the gift of the hereditary Earldom of Orkney, it appears he was a pushy intruder who was a long way down the order of succession for Orkney but, by political maneuvering and brute force, got his own way. He took advantage of the weakness of Norway to steal Shetland from his cousin, and established his own pirate stronghold at Kirkwall in defiance of Norway's King Hakon VI. He clearly had dynastic ambitions for his family, as he went out of his way to consolidate his hold on the Northern Isles. As Thompson explains:

> Orkney had been plunged into all the troubles of a divided inheritance and disputed succession by the dynastic accident that all Earl Malise's children had been female. By another dynastic accident, all came miraculously right for the Sinclairs in the end. Isabella of Strathearn, Henry's mother . . . inherited all the divided property which she eventually passed intact to Earl Henry II. This property now included large estates in Shetland inherited from Malise Sperra, so for the first time since 1194 Orkney earls had a substantial holding in Shetland . . . . Henry I took steps to avoid any such disputes after his own death. In 1391 he granted lands in Aberdeenshire to his brother, David Sinclair, in return for rights in Orkney which David would inherit from their mother, and he similarly bought out the rights of his own daughter, Elizabeth, by a grant of land in Banff. Evidently he put great store on the Orkney property and was willing to give away lands elsewhere in order to keep it intact.[356]

Read

Read

Willie Thompson records Henry's death in Orkney as occurring around 1400, while his son was young and inexperienced, but old enough to inherit. The exact circumstances of his death are unknown. The romantics say he died in a last great battle with pirates; the prosaic say he was lost at sea. Either way, he set sail from Kirkwall and was never seen again. His death marked a change in direction for next generation of the St. Clair family, who became more interested in their Scottish lands:

> When Henry I was killed and his son succeeded it was the first time in over a century that there was no interregnum as a result of a minority or a disputed succession. But far from bringing continuity, the accession of Earl Henry II (c. 1400–1420) marked an important point in the development of a Scottish-orientated society . . . In contrast to Henry I's "Viking Jarl" image, Henry II was a purely Scottish nobleman; no visits to Orkney are recorded.[357]

What Tim Wallace-Murphy and Marilyn Hopkins describe as "the vision of Earl Henry St. Clair, for his expeditions to North America were part of a strategy to found a commonwealth based on tolerance, far from the oppressive hand of Holy Mother Church," seems to be at odds with the facts. Henry was a political opportunist who managed to add extensive Norse lands in Orkney and Shetland to his existing Scottish holdings in Caithness, Aberdeenshire, and Roslin. But even after discarding the dubious evidence of the Zeno narrative, there are other possible St. Clair links with America which still need to be looked at. In their book Wallace-Murphy and Hopkins state unequivocally:

> The carvings in Rosslyn Chapel, which was founded in 1446 and completed in 1482, ten years prior to Columbus's voyage in 1492, consist of depictions of maize [corn], aloe cactus . . . *trillium grandiflorum*, and *quercus nigra*, all native American plants that were completely unknown in Europe at the time of the chapel's construction. These carvings, commissioned by Henry's grandson, Earl William St. Clair, were probably based upon drawings of Native American plants brought back to Europe by Henry at the end of the first voyage.[358]

Knowledge of exotic plants from North America is certainly something that could be evidence of voyages to the New World. But there might be a simpler explanation. One possibility is rooted in Henry's reputation for acting with the ruthless decisiveness of a Viking Jarl.

"'Tis a Noble Thing to be a Pirate King"

Wallace-Murphy and Hopkins inadvertently offer a clue to that alternative explanation when they claim that:

> Financial pressure was being endured by the kingdom of Norway at that time [of Henry's appointment to the Earldom of Orkney]. Her ability to trade was severely

circumscribed by the Hansa, whose monopoly over Baltic trade placed a complete stranglehold on all of Norway's efforts in the East and whose imports of fur from Russia were in direct and powerful competition with the export of furs from the Norwegian colonies in Greenland, Markland, and Vinland. This perilous situation was exacerbated by bands of pirates who infested the North Sea and exerted a devastating effect on Norwegian shipping elsewhere . . . Under the circumstances . . . the need of a strong man as earl who could . . . put a stop to piracy was all too apparent . . . Henry seemed the ideal candidate on these grounds alone.[359]

Their comments about the effects of the Hanseatic League are accurate, but the Viking colony in Vinland had been abandoned some three hundred years before 1379—although the Greenland colonies continued to raid the North American coast for timber and iron. There is no evidence for a permanent colony in Markland, and the latest radiocarbon date for the short-lived Vinland colony is around 1000.[360] It is the reference to Henry being in a position to put a stop to piracy which suggests a possible origin for the rumors that he imported goods from America, which Wallace-Murphy and Hopkins say is implied by the carvings in his grandson's chapel at Roslin.

The Norse colony of Greenland lasted for 450 years, from its founding by Erik the Red in 981 to its final death-throes in the 1440s. The Greenlanders were an intensely hierarchical society who considered themselves Norwegian Christians,[361] and Jared Diamond points out how the chiefs and clergy continued to import European luxuries to the bleak northern climate of Greenland.[362] The trading ships of the fourteenth century took a week or more to sail from Norway to Greenland, and many were lost on what could be a very dangerous voyage. The Greenlanders were lucky if more than a couple of European trading ships visited each year. Diamond has calculated that each individual would have received only about seven pounds of cargo per year, if it had been shared out equally. But it wasn't: Most of the available cargo capacity was devoted to materials for churches and luxuries for the elite. Studies of the Greenlanders' skeletons shows that the thralls (slaves) were left to eat blubber, which they obtained from seals killed with wooden spears.[363]

As we have seen, Henry St. Clair gained control of Orkney and Shetland at a time when the controlling feudal power of Norway was weak.[364] It was the time when Greenland's Western settlement collapsed, and the Eastern settlement began to struggle. They had few resources to build ocean-going ships, and their existing vessels were aging. Increasingly, they had to depend on Norway to export both essentials and luxuries—and the ruling elite preferred to import luxuries. This state of affairs was well-known in Norway from the writings of a priest called Ivar Bardarson, who was sent by the bishop of Bergen on a visit to Greenland to collect outstanding tithes. He wrote the story of his visit in a document he called A

Description of Greenland.[365] He reports that the "Skatlings" (Inuit) had laid waste Sandnes estate and Stensnes Church, and all the population were dead.

This gruesome account was first published in Norway in 1362, and Henry St. Clair had spent some time in Norway, lobbying for the Earldom of Orkney, in 1379.[366] If he had any sense of political opportunism—and we know he did—then he would have spotted a chance. The King of Norway had sent out a relief vessel to Greenland in 1368, but the ship never got there.[367] Diamond reports Norwegian records of just four further voyages to Greenland between 1381 and 1406:

> All by private ships whose captains alleged that their destination had really been Iceland and that they had reached Greenland unintentionally as a result of being blown off course. When we recall that the Norwegian king asserted exclusive rights to the Greenland trade as a royal monopoly, and that it was illegal for private ships to visit Greenland, we must consider four such "unintentional" voyages as an astonishing coincidence. Much more likely, the captains' claims that to their deep regret they had been caught in dense fog and ended up by mistake in Greenland were just alibis to cover their real intentions. As the captains undoubtedly knew, so few ships by then were visiting Greenland that the Greenlanders were desperate for trade goods, and Norwegian imports could be sold to Greenlanders at a big profit.[368]

So, let us sum up. Henry St. Clair had enough naval force at his disposal to be able to kill his cousin by sending a fleet to Shetland; he was believed to have enough influence over the frequency of incidents of piracy to be bought off by the King of Norway; and he had enough contempt for Norwegian authority to build an illegal castle at Kirkwall. Match this to his historical reputation for behaving like a "Viking Jarl," and a picture of a self-made pirate king emerges. And this particular pirate king would not have been averse to using his maritime resources to cut a deal with the elite of the struggling Eastern settlement.

Exchange with Greenland may have been the source of the images of North American plants that eventually found their way onto the walls of Rosslyn (then Roslin) Chapel, as well as the root of Henry's legendary access to treasure. The latest carbon date for the Eastern Settlement is 1435, and it was obtained from a woman's dress excavated from Herjolfsnes churchyard. So at the time of Henry's rise to power in the Northern islands, there was plenty of profit to be made before the last ship returned from Greenland in 1410.[369]

CONCLUSIONS

I have found no evidence that Henry I St. Clair, Earl of Orkney, was a custodian of Templar secrets or a guardian of Templar treasure. He seems instead to have been an opportunist warlord with a taste for piracy and an ambition to amass land. The myth of his discovering America is false, but it is based on a real history

I think right Hes Not...!

of Norse voyages to the New World and the successful exploration of parts of the coast of the American continent hundreds of years before Columbus.

Using images celebrating knowledge of this western "land of plenty" would not have been unreasonable for later St. Clairs. Indeed, the development of a myth of Henry I of Orkney as a great leader and explorer, in the mode of Erik the Red, may well have become politically useful to the St. Clair family. Could it be that St. Clair political spin led to a blossoming of a myth that the Templars founded Freemasonry using their lost treasure?

This idea is repeated often in the Masonic press, as this excerpt from a recent book on the search for their lost treasure, shows:

> It has always been comfortably non-threatening to have a group of stonemasons as one's antecedents. It now looks as if . . . Freemasonry is the ingenious creation of some remarkably clever people, most likely from the Court of Champagne . . . The same people who designed Freemasonry probably also devised . . . the Knights Templar . . . Just who were these people? What was it that made them able to design such highly-esteemed fraternities? In this modern world of ours, such talents would make them kings of the entertainment business with riches beyond imagination.[370]

The myth of the Templars as a powerful naval presence, particularly in books dealing with the St. Clairs of Roslin, is also tenacious, as this quote from a 2006 book shows:

> The meteoric rise of the Cistercians was quickly matched by that of the Templars . . . The Templars were supposed to exist to fight Muslims in the Holy Land but they very quickly became much more than holy soldiers. They built a powerful navy and began to indulge in trade.[371]

How had this story arisen, and why had it persisted so long? Had Freemasonry repeated and enhanced the legend? If so, then a closer look at the earliest documented links between the St. Clairs and Freemasonry would be a logical step. This had to be my next move. I needed to go back to the secret archives of the Masons to see if I could find out how the how the roguish St. Clair family became respected patrons of Freemasonry's arcane Craft.

1. Roguish (1) of, relating to or acting like a rogue/mischievous
2. Rogue- Some who cheats, deceives, and takes advantage of others

CHAPTER 9

THE ST. CLAIR GRAND MASTERS

▶ ANCIENT KNOWLEDGE PASSED DOWN THE GENERATIONS

"Prince" Henry St. Clair of Roslin and Orkney might not have been the inheritor of either the Templar fleet or its treasure that legend has made him out to be. All the same, his family is indisputably and intimately connected to Freemasonry. The idea that the St. Clair family of Roslin are hereditary patrons of Freemasons is deep-rooted. Was there something in this legend—that the oldest chivalric Order of Freemasonry (The Royal Order of Scotland) was founded after a military intervention at the Battle of Bannockburn by a member of the St. Clair family, who was also Templar Preceptor of Scotland? Was this how they became hereditary patrons of the Craft of Freemasonry? Well, let's see.

✱ The St. Clair family of Roslin has been associated with Freemasonry since the early seventeenth century. The earliest documents that connect them to Freemasonry are what Robert Freke Gould, in his *History of Freemasonry*, referred to as "the St. Clair Charters." In these charters, an assortment of Masonic groups and other trades make a claim that the St. Clairs (or Sinclairs, as the family was beginning to spell its name) of Roslin were their hereditary patrons.

▶ There are two different St. Clair Charters, written twenty-eight years apart, and they make different claims. Gould comments on the dating.

✱ The first charter could not have been written immediately after the Union of the crowns of England and Scotland (March 24, 1603), having been signed by William Schaw, master of work, who died in 1602; and its probable date is 1601–2, the names of the deacons of the masons at Edinburgh affording some assistance in identifying this period. The second, long assigned to 1630, and so dated in many of the transcripts, was evidently promulgated in 1628, according to the internal evidence which has been so well marshalled by Mr. Lyon.[372]

But what did the charters say? They were written in the Scots language, but (with the aid of Dundee University's dictionary of the Scots language) I have summarized them both in modern English. (The full Scots versions can be found in Appendix 1 of *The Secrets of Freemasonry*.[373])

THE FIRST ST. CLAIR CHARTER

Be it known to all men by this letter that we Deacons, Masters and Freemen of the Masons within the realm of Scotland with the express consent and agreement of William Schaw, Master of Works to our Sovereign Lord, confirm that from age to age it has been observed amongst us that the Lairds of Roslin have ever been Patrons and Protectors of us and our privileges. We acknowledge that our predecessors also obeyed and acknowledged them as Patrons and protectors but recently, through sloth and negligence, the Lairds of Roslin have been deprived of their just rights and our fine Craft has been deprived of any patron, protector and overseer. This has created much corruption and imperfection, both amongst ourselves and in our Craft, and as a result many people have formed a bad opinion of us and our Craft. Many great enterprises have failed because of bad behaviour that has not been corrected. This has come about by the deliberate exploitation of faults and by failure of honest Masons to correctly practise their Craft. When controversies break out among our brethren the lack of any Patron and Protector is a great problem. We have to appeal for judgement to the normal processes of law to remedy our grievances and to keep us in good order. We speak for all the brethren and craftsmen of the realm when, for the advancement and good government of our Craft, we consent that William Sinclair of Roslin and his heirs shall be allowed to purchase from the hand of our Sovereign Lord the freedom to rule over us and our successors for all time and to act as patrons and judges over all practitioners of our Craft within this realm. We acknowledge the said William Sinclair and his heirs as our patrons and judges under our Sovereign Lord without restrictions on his power of judgement over us and call on him to appoint and authorise judges to rule our Craft under the powers that it pleases our Sovereign Lord to grant to him and his heirs.

It was signed by both William Schaw, Master of Works, and by various Lodges, which I will discuss later.

Some Masonic writers claim a hereditary Grand Mastership of *all* Scottish Freemasonry for "the Lairds of Rosling." But Gould reads it differently:

> The two deeds are altogether silent as to the Grand Mastership of the Craft being hereditary in the St. Clairs of Roslin, yet that distinction has been claimed for this family . . . The late Sir David Brewster observes: "It deserves to be remarked that in both these deeds the appointment of William Sinclair, Earl of Orkney and Caithness, to the office of Grand Master by James II of Scotland, is spoken of as a fact well known and universally admitted."[374]

The first charter speaks of the consent of certain "Deacons Maistres and freemen of the Masons" within the realm of Scotland, but that consent, approved by James VI's Master of Works, is to allow William St. Clair to buy the position of patron and judge from the King. Gould adds:

> Whilst the first deed records a statement, that the "Lairds of Rosling" had previously exercised such a privilege for very many years, the Masonic body must have valued their patronage very slightly, to have required another deed to be executed in less than thirty years. The second being obtained from the "hammermen"—blacksmiths and others—as well as the masons, and though it is not mentioned in the text, the "squaremen" were likewise a party to the agreement, these including the crafts of coopers, wrights (or carpenters), and slaters, who were represented on the charter by their deacons from Ayr.[375]

So who, in addition to William Schaw, signed the first charter? The other signatures were notaries, acting on behalf of the members of the Lodges of Edinburgh, St. Andrews, Haddington, Atchison's Haven, and Dunfermline. (These Lodges had to use notaries because the Masons themselves were illiterate.) The second charter is additionally signed by the notaries from Glasgow, Dundee, and Stirling, and also by representatives of Masons and other crafts at Ayr.

In the first charter a particular group of Masons, with the support of the King of Scotland's Master of Works, joined together to request the restoration of a long-time patron for their craft. But Aberdeen did not join in with this request. This may have been because they already had a different hereditary patron of their own: Patrick Coipland of Udaucht.

The Masons of Aberdeen would not have been given royal permission to elect a warden to rule over them and to settle disputes if there had already been a hereditary Grand Master of Masons for the whole of Scotland. I have already pointed out that the Burgh Council of Aberdeen fulfilled the role of patron and judge in 1483 when it employed the only Lodge of Masons in the district to work on St. Nicholas Kirk. St. Nicholas was a collegiate church that had been established by the Provost and Magistrates of Aberdeen in 1441 and so naturally fell under their rule. As Masonry spread out from the city into Banff and Kincardine, however, it would have been improper for Aberdeen Council to settle wider disputes, and so the expanding Masonic system needed a warden with a broader base of support. Hence the vote to seek royal approval to allow Patrick Coipland to purchase that right from the Crown.

Nevertheless, the First St. Clair Charter confirms that the King's Master of Works (who had authorized the appointment of Patrick Coipland) thought there had also been a hereditary regional warden in the south of Scotland. The Lodges who signed the First Sinclair Charter were all from a radius of thirty miles around Edinburgh. They were the Lodges of Edinburgh (in Edinburgh), St. Andrews (thirty miles across the Firth of Forth from Edinburgh), Haddington (twenty miles east of Edinburgh), Atchison's Haven (ten miles east of Edinburgh, near Prestonpans), and Dunfermline (fifteen miles across the Firth of Forth from Edinburgh). Their claim of past patronage and protection from the Lairds of Roslin and obedience by Masons to them may simply have referred to a local arrangement, like that in Aberdeen, when the growth of the Masonic Lodges spread beyond the jurisdiction of the city council.

And Gould comments that Kilwinning Lodge, based in Ayrshire, did not sign this first charter,[376] even though the lands surrounding the Abbey at Kilwinning had once belonged to the St. Clairs. This omission strengthens the probability that any arrangement with the St. Clairs was a regional one. If they were hereditary Grand Masters of *all* Scottish Masons, then Schaw could not have supported them, as to do so would have undermined the position of Coipland, whom he also supported.

So the first St. Clair Charter implies that before 1602 the Masonic writ of the St. Clair family did not run any farther that Fife and Lothian. And even this was in dispute: Why else would the local Masons need to issue a charter asking the King's Master of Works to confirm the arrangement? But this raises a question: Why did the Masons dotted around the Firth of Forth suddenly feel that they needed to claim an ancient right to have the Baron of Roslin act as their general warden?

David Stevenson is not a Freemason, but he is Emeritus Professor of Scottish History at the University of St. Andrews, and has been described as "one of the most distinguished and prolific historians of Scotland."[377] I was fortunate to share a platform with Professor Stevenson in London in 2002. After we had given our separate lectures, the conference organizers took us out to dinner. I found David a charming and witty companion over the dinner table. His deep knowledge of Scottish history was worn lightly, but he was never at a loss to answer even my most abstruse questions. In *The Origins of Freemasonry* he points out, the reign of James VI was a time of profound change for Freemasonry:

> By the late sixteenth century the Craft was in fact on the verge of a remarkable development which would make it different . . . one man saw that some aspects of the traditional heritage of the craft of masonry linked up a whole series of trends in the thought and culture of the age, and worked to introduce them in the craft.[378]

WILLIAM SCHAW—THE ARCHITECT OF THE CRAFT

The man responsible for this flurry of activity was William Schaw. He was born around 1550 in Clackmannan, near Stirling. His father, John Schaw of Broich, had been keeper of the King's wine cellar.[379] By the age of ten, William was employed at court as a page to Mary of Guise. Mary had been Queen consort to King James V and, as the mother of Mary Queen of Scots, had also acted as regent when the young Mary married the Dauphin of France. Through her favor for the Roman

Catholic faith, which she also impressed on her daughter, she eventually provoked the religious rebellion of John Knox, founder of the Reformed Church of Scotland, which in turn ultimately led to her daughter's execution.

Mary of Guise died in June 1560, and her accounts record William Schaw's name on the list of her retainers for whom mourning clothes were purchased. That same year, his father John was charged with murdering the servant of another Laird.[380] William next appears in Scottish records when he signed the Negative Confession, a document which James VI and his courtiers had to agree to in order to assure the Reformed Church that the King and his retinue were not trying to bring back the Catholic Faith. William Schaw was a Catholic, but seems to have been flexible enough in his attitude to stay out of trouble with the Protestants, although when he was put in charge of the King's building program Kirk leaders complained that the King was favoring Catholics. Professor Stevenson says of Schaw:

> Like a number of other Scots in court circles, though remaining a Catholic he avoided actions that might provoke persecution, probably attending Protestant services from time to time.[381]

Schaw became James VI's Master of Works towards the end of 1583. About a month after his appointment, the King sent him on a delicate political mission to France, suggesting that he had diplomatic as well as building skills.[382] This was confirmed when the King chose Schaw to help entertain the ambassadors of the King of Denmark, who came to Scotland to try to negotiate the return of Orkney and Shetland to the kingdom of Denmark.[383] Schaw must have gotten along well with the Danes, because in 1589 James sent him back to Denmark to escort his new bride, Anne of Denmark, back to Scotland. He went on to become Queen Anne's Chamberlain and her favorite. The inscription on his monument in Dunfermline Abbey says:

> Queen Anne ordered a monument to be set up to the memory of a most admirable and most upright man lest the recollection of his high character, which deserves to be honoured for all time, should fade as his body crumbles into dust.

Stevenson believes that Schaw was intending to reorganize the Mason Craft under a number of regional wardens, and used the precedent of Aberdeen to establish the principle.[384] However, some eight years later, Schaw changed direction. He took on an expanded role as General Warden of the Mason Craft of Scotland. Schaw invented this post with the approval of a number of unnamed "maister maissounis" who attended a meeting on the Feast of St. John at the Lodge of Edinburgh 1598. The news was proclaimed to the Masons of Scotland by the First Schaw Statute. It contained 22 clauses. Here is my paraphrase of it from the original Scots:

1. All the good ordinances concerning the privileges of the Craft, which were made by our predecessors of good memory, to be observed and kept; and especially to be true to one another, and live charitably together as becomes sworn brethren and companions of the Craft.

2. To be obedient to our Wardens, Deacons, and Masters in all things concerning the Craft.

3. To be honest, faithful and diligent in our calling, and upright with the masters or owners of the work which we undertake, whatever be the mode of payment.

4. No one shall undertake work, be it great or small, unless he is able to complete it satisfactorily, under the penalty of forty pounds [Scots], or the fourth part of the value of the work, according to the decision of the General Warden, or the officers named in the 2d item, for the sheriffdom where the work is being wrought.

5. No Master shall supplant another under the penalty of forty pounds.

6. No Master take an uncompleted work unless the previous Masters be duly satisfied, under the same penalty.

7. One Warden be elected annually by every Lodge, by the votes of the Masters in the Lodge, with the consent of the General Warden if present, as they see fit, to have charge thereof, and should the latter be absent, then the results of such elections must be communicated to General Warden, that he may send his directions to the Wardens-elect.

8. No Master shall have more than three apprentices during his lifetime, unless with the special consent of the officers previously mentioned of the sheriffdom in which the additional apprentice shall dwell.

9. Apprentices must not be bound for less than seven years, and no apprentice shall be made brother and fellow-in-craft, unless he has served an additional seven years, save by the special license of the regular officers assembled for that purpose, and then only if sufficient trial has been made of his worthiness, qualification and skill. The penalty is forty pounds, beside the penalties to be set down against him individually according to the order of the Lodge.

10. Masters must not sell their apprentices to other masters, nor dispense with their time by sale to such apprentices, under the penalty of forty pounds.

11. No Master is to receive an apprentice without informing the Warden of his Lodge, that his name and date of reception may be duly booked.

12. No apprentice to be entered but by the same order.

13. No Master or fellow-of-craft to be received or admitted except in the presence of six Masters and two entered apprentices, the Warden of that Lodge being one of the six, the date thereof being orderly booked, and his name and mark inserted in the said book, together with the names of the six

1. Supplant - to supersede (another) esp. by force, cunning etc.

Masters, the apprentices, and intender. Provided always that no one be admitted without an assessment and sufficient trial of his skill and worthiness in his vocation and craft.

14. No Master is to engage in any Masonic work under charge or command of any other craftsman.

15. No Master or fellow-of-craft is to receive any cowans [workers in rough stone] to work in his society or company, or to send any of his servants to work with them, under a penalty of twenty pounds for each offence.

16. No apprentice shall undertake work beyond the value of ten pounds from the owner thereof, under the penalty aforesaid, and, on its completion, a license must be obtained from the Masters or Warden in his own neighborhood, if more is desired to be done.

17. Should strife arise amongst the Masters, servants or apprentices, they must inform the Wardens, Deacons or their Lodges within twenty-four hours thereof, under ten pounds penalty in case of default, in order that the difficulties may be amicably settled. Should any of the parties concerned therein refuse to accept the award made, they shall be liable to be deprived of the privileges of their Lodge, and not be permitted to work during the period of their obstinacy.

18. Masters and others must be careful in taking all needful precautions as to the erection of suitable scaffolding, and should accidents occur through their negligence, they shall not act as Masters having charge of any work, but for ever afterwards be subject to others.

19. Masters are not to receive apprentices who have run away from their lawful service, under penalty of forty pounds.

✳20. All members of the Mason Craft must attend the meetings when lawfully warned, under the penalty of ten pounds.

✳21. All Masters present at any assembly or meeting shall be sworn by their great oath, not to hide or conceal any wrong done to each other, or to the owners of the work, as far as they know, under the same penalty.

22. All the said penalties shall be collected from those who break any of the foregoing statutes, by the Wardens, Deacons and Masters, to be distributed as they see fit according to good conscience, and by their advice.

These Statutes, were signed "William Schaw, Maistir of Wark, Warden of the Maisonis," [Master of Works, Warden of the Masons] on December 28, 1598.

His first clause refers to a system of regulations known to Masons as the Antient [Ancient] Charges. The remainder deal with how the Lodges shall be ruled and governed, and how the work of Masons should be managed. But there are two particularly interesting items. One is Clause 18, the first health and safety directive ever issued to the building trade, which imposes a stern penalty on any

Master Mason who did not ensure that his workers were properly secured when working in the dizzy heights of a great cathedral or a Scottish grand house. Today's factory inspector would not quarrel with the intentions and sanctions of this sixteenth-century Masonic legislation.

The other interesting item, Clause 7, concerns how the Master of a Lodge should be chosen. He was to be elected each year, and Schaw, as General Warden of the Craft, reserved the right to issue instructions to the Craft via its elected officers.

This Statute is a far-sighted and fair document that simplified the general management of Masons in Scotland. It took account of the ancient traditions of the order and respected existing rituals; it made proper provision for safe working practices; and it provided regular democratic feedback from the Master of the Lodge. It was issued with the endorsement of the Master Masons who had attended the Feast of St. John meeting in Edinburgh in 1598.[385] This document also contains the first instance of Lodges being instructed to keep written records of their proceedings. (Interestingly, the oldest set of continuous Lodge minutes in existence is those of Edinburgh St. Mary's Chapel, and it starts immediately after this meeting with Schaw.)

This first Schaw statute tells a lot about early Freemasonry: The Scottish brethren met in Lodges; these Lodges were ruled by Masters or Wardens; there was a system of meetings at a higher level than the Lodge; Lodges were obliged to keep written records of their activities, and they were honor-bound to observe the ancient practices of their Craft. All these things have survived down to modern Freemasonry, and this is the earliest written evidence of their introduction.

Schaw's achievement was formidable: He single-handedly formalized the present-day system of Masonic Lodges. A Lodge is not just the building where Masons meet; it is also the body of men who make up that group. It has its own traditions, hierarchy, and records to prove what it has decided, but remains a democratic unit inherited from a time when democracy was not yet supposed to have been invented.

Mother Kilwinning Makes a Stand

There is more to this story, however, because, as we have seen, a well-established Lodge existed out on the west coast of Scotland. Known today as Mother Kilwinning, it was based on the coast of Ayr, in the grounds of Kilwinning Abbey. The Wardens of Mother Kilwinning Lodge were used to issuing charters to other groups of Masons to form themselves into new Lodges, and they claimed ancient rights over the Mason Craft in Ayrshire. Schaw's First Statute did not recognize the place that Kilwinning felt it was entitled to in his newly created Masonic ranking, and the Masons of Kilwinning were annoyed that their Masonic status was not recognized.

They sent Brother Archibald Barclay to present a case that they should have a role in this new way of ruling the Craft. Bro. Barclay was successful, because Schaw soon issued a new set of statutes confirming that Lodge Kilwinning was to be allowed to keep its ancient practice of electing its officers on the eve of the winter solstice. The objection raised by Kilwinning was so powerful that the following year, 1599, on the Feast of St. John, Schaw issued his Second Statute from one of the King's palaces, Holyrood House. It confirms the statements in the First Statute, but goes on to assign a formal status to the self-assumed authority of Kilwinning Lodge in Ayrshire. Here is my paraphrase of the original Scots:

1. The Warden is to act within the bounds of Kilwinning, and other places subject to that Lodge, and shall be annually elected on the 20th day of December, within the Kirk at Kilwinning, as the head and second Lodge of Scotland, The Warden General to be informed who has been elected.

2. The Lord Warden General, considers that it is expedient that all the Scottish Lodges should prospectively enjoy their ancient liberties as of yore, confirms the right of the Lodge of Kilwinning, second Lodge of Scotland, to have its warden present at the election of wardens within the bounds of the surrounding wards of Cliddisdaill, Glasgow, Ayr and Carrick, and also to convene these wardens to assemble anywhere within the district (embracing the west of Scotland, including Glasgow), when and where they are to submit to the judgment of the warden and deacon of Kilwinning.

3. The Warden General, for reasons of expediency, confirms the rank of Edinburgh as the first and principal Lodge in Scotland, that of Kilwinning being the second, as is manifest from all ancient writings; and the Lodge of Stirling to be third, according to their ancient privileges.

4. The Wardens of every Lodge shall be answerable to the Presbyters within their sheriffdoms, for the masons subject to their Lodges, the third part of the fines paid by the disobedient being devoted to the goodly use of the Lodge where the offences were committed.

5. An annual trial of all offences shall be made, under the management of the Warden and most ancient Masters of the Lodge, extending to six persons, so that due order be observed.

6. The Lord Warden General ordains that the Warden of Kilwinning, as second in Scotland, shall select six of the most perfect and worthy masons, in order to test the qualification of all the fellows within their district as to their craft and science in the ancient art of memory. The said Wardens shall be duly responsible for such persons as are under them.

7. The Warden and Deacon of Kilwinning, as the second Lodge, is empowered to exclude and expel from the society all who persist in disobeying the

ancient statutes, and all persons disobedient either to kirk, craft, council, and other regulations to be hereafter made.

8. The Warden General requires the Warden and Deacon (with his Quartermasters) to select a skilled notary, to be Ordinary Clerk or Scribe, by whom all deeds are to be executed.

9. The acts heretofore made by Kilwinning masons must be kept most faithfully in the future, and no apprentice or craftsman is to be either admitted or entered but within the kirk of Kilwinning, as his parish and second Lodge; all banquets arising out of such entries to be held within the said Lodge of Kilwinning.

10. All fellow-craftsmen at their entry and prior to their admission must pay to the Lodge the sum of £10, with 10s. worth of gloves, which shall include the expense of the banquet; also that none shall be admitted without a sufficient test and proof of their ability in the art and craft of memory, under the supervision of the Warden, Deacon, and Quartermasters of the Lodge, as they shall be answerable to the Warden.

11. Apprentices are not to be admitted unless they pay £6 towards the common banquet, or defray the expenses of a meal for all the members and apprentices of the Lodge.

12. The Wardens and Deacons of the second Lodge of Scotland (Kilwinning) shall annually take the oath of fidelity and truth of all the Masters and fellows of craft committed to their charge; that they shall not keep company nor work with cowans [dry-stone workers, not trained as masons], nor any of their servants or apprentices, under the penalties provided in the former acts.

13. The Warden General ordains that the Lodge of Kilwinning, being the second Lodge in Scotland, shall annually test every craftsman and apprentice, according to their vocations, and should they have forgotten even one point of the art of memory and science, they must forfeit 20s. if fellow-crafts, and 11s. if apprentices, for their neglect. Fines to be paid into the box for the common good, in conformity with the practice of the Lodges of the realm.

The regulations are signed by William Schaw.

The document ends with an important certificate from William Schaw, which proves that it was intended exclusively for the Masons under the jurisdiction of the Kilwinning Lodge, for it is addressed to the Warden, Deacon, and Masters of that Lodge, and testifies to the honest and careful manner in which Archibald Barclay, the Commissioner from the Lodge, had discharged the duties entrusted to him. Bro. Barclay had taken a commission from Kilwinning Lodge to the Warden General and the Masters of the Lodge of Edinburgh, but, "by reason of the King being out of the Toun [town]," and no Masters but those of the Lodge of Edinburgh being convened at the time, the deputation did not succeed in obtaining all that the members asked.

The chief requests of the Lodge were to obtain additional powers to preserve order, which the Craft required for the conservation of their rights, and especially to secure from King James VI a recognition of the privileges of the Lodge, including the power of imposing penalties upon the "dissobedient personis and perturberis of all guid ordour." These Schaw promised to obtain.

✸ THE MASON WHO WAS KING ✸

✸ With this clarification of the most important of the ancient ordinances, that Masons should learn and practice the "art of memory," and the adjustment to the pecking order between Edinburgh, Kilwinning, and Stirling, Schaw seemed to have settled Freemasonry into a stable structure. But he had greater ambitions for his fledgling organization. Now that he was accepted as Warden General, he wanted the King to become Grand Master of the Order and award a Royal Charter to confer status on the Craft forever. But he had one problem: The Masons would not accept a non-Mason as their Grand Master—even if that non-Mason was a king.

✸ If James VI was to become Grand Master Mason of his own kingdom of Scotland, he would first have to be initiated into Freemasonry (which Masons call being "made a Mason"). This was confirmed to be a Scottish tradition by the fact that Sir Anthony Alexander and his elder brother Lord Alexander had to be initiated together into the Lodge of Edinburgh in July of 1634, when Anthony became Warden General and Lord Alexander Master of Works respectively. But this was far in the future. Schaw's immediate problem was to choose one of the proud and prickly Lodges of Scotland to initiate a king. Certainly he now knew better than to ask Edinburgh, Kilwinning, or Stirling. But he must have realized that whatever his choice was, it would cause problems. Fortunately, he had a friend who was a member of James's court and a Freemason.

Read: (Book) The Master Game Pg. 305-10

Read

In 1584, William Schaw had helped to design a house for Lord Somerville with his close friend Alexander Seton (later Earl of Dunfermline), who was a member of Aberdeen Lodge. The master mason who did the actual building was a man called John Mylne,[386] and in 1601, when Schaw was looking for a Lodge to initiate the King, Mylne was Master of the Lodge of Scoon and Perth.[387] It was at Scoon (the modern spelling is Scone)—at Moot Hill, a mound within the grounds of the royal palace there—that the Kings of Scots had traditionally been crowned for hundreds of years. So here was an answer for Schaw's dilemma: This Lodge met in a suitable place for a king to be made a Mason.

Today, a painting of the initiation ceremony of King James VI hangs on the wall of the Lodge of Scoon and Perth. Is it a fictitious portrayal? The official entry for Scoon and Perth on the Roll of the Grand Lodge of Scotland says only that the Lodge existed "before 1658." This date refers to its charter, which is a set of rules to explain how the Lodge was to be governed. Although this document is accepted as evidence of the existence of the Lodge, its content is usually ignored outside Scotland. It claims to be a record of the event depicted on the Lodge room wall and says that the James VI, King of Scotland, was made a Mason in 1601.

> In the reigne of his Majesty King James the sixt, of blessed Memorie, who, by the said John Mylne was by the king's own desire entered Freeman, Meason and Fellow-Craft. During his lifetime he mantayned the same as ane member of the Lodge of Scoon, so that this lodge is the most famous lodge within the kingdom.[388]

Far be it for me to suggest that Schaw might have felt that having the King initiated in Perth was fair retribution for the public squabbling over precedence among the self-proclaimed "senior" Lodges of southern Scotland. (The Lodge of Aberdeen, meanwhile, was quietly going about its Masonic business under the rule of Patrick Coipland and his heirs and keeping well out of the squabbling). But I can't help wondering if he saw some ironic justice in his choice.

John Mylne and his family went on to play an important role in Scottish Masonic history. No less than three generations of them (all with the Christian name of John) held the Mastership of the Lodge of Scoon and Perth between the late sixteenth century and 1658, when the Scoon Charter says the mastership passed to James Roch. This Charter, dated December 24, 1658, also suggests a reason why the Lodge would have played along with Schaw's attempt to win a royal charter. By making King James a Freemason. From the earliest days of the Lodge of Scoon and Perth, John Mylne (the second of that name) had actively tried to obtain the patronage of the King. Gould reports it as saying:

> It speaks of the "Lodge of Scoon" as being second in the nation, priority being given to Kilwinning, and a singular reticence is observed as to Edinburgh . . . The same record states that, according to the knowledge of "our predecessoris ther cam one from the North countrie, named Johne Mylne, ane measone or man weill experted in his calling, who entered himselff both frieman and burges of this brugh." In process of time, because of his skill, he was preferred to be the king's master mason, and he was also master of the lodge. His son, "Johne Milne," succeeded him in both offices, "in the reigne off his Majestie King James the Sixt, of blessed memorie, who, by the said second Johne Milne, was (by the King's own desire) entered Freeman, measone, and fellow-craft." [389]

Read

That second John Mylne, who initiated King James, also carved a famous statue of the King in Edinburgh in 1616. In 1631, he was appointed Master Mason to James's son Charles I, and in 1636 retired from that office and was replaced by his eldest son, also named John Mylne. This John had been made a Fellow Craft of the Lodge of Edinburgh in 1633. He was to take part in a Masonic meeting in Newcastle in 1641, where Sir Robert Moray stepped into the pages of Masonic history as the first Mason documented as having been initiated on English soil. The grandson of the man who initiated James VI initiated Sir Robert Moray.[390] (Moray went on to found the Royal Society, still one of the most important scientific societies in the world today. I told his story in *Freemasonry and the Birth of Modern Science*.)

Schaw's political purpose for enlisting the Mylne family's aid in having the King initiated into Freemasonry was now clear. To complete his designs for the expansion of the Craft, Schaw needed the King to be a Mason to engender Masonic loyalty. James VI loved ritual, masques, and dressing up. He already knew and trusted John Mylne as his personal Master Mason. From all accounts, James would have delighted in the ceremony when he was initiated into the ancient mysteries of the Mason Word. With the King now a Mason, Schaw had everything in place to propose a Royal Grand Master Mason for the Craft—to be followed with the issue of the Royal Charter to confirm Schaw's authority as Lord General Warden of the Craft. However, the Masons of Lothian and Fife had different ideas. Led by the Lodge of Edinburgh, they claimed a different patron, William St. Clair, Laird of Roslin. The idea of a Lodge in Perth becoming "the most famous Lodge within the kingdom" obviously did not appeal.

THE RISE OF WILLIAM ST. CLAIR

When Schaw circulated his second statutes, he seemed to be on the verge of obtaining royal patronage for the privileges of the Craft. Had he done so, he would have consolidated his own position as sole controller of the building craft in Scotland. But the opposition of the Edinburgh Masons forced him to backtrack. This powerful group insisted that he support a document which we now know as the First St. Clair Charter. And soon afterwards the chance was lost entirely when Schaw died and the King moved to England. In *The Origins of Freemasonry* Stevenson says:

> [The publication of the First St. Clair Charter] can be seen as indicating . . . that Schaw was forced to change his plans [for obtaining a Royal Charter] to take account of claims of the Craft.[391]

Schaw had shown that he could be manipulated to a certain extent when he allowed Bro. Archibald Barclay to pressurize him into confirming the claims of Kilwinning in her role as a minor Grand Lodge. Stevenson comments:

> Archibald Barclay doubtless had need of Schaw's statement that he had acted honestly and carefully, for when he returned to Kilwinning he had to report that he had failed to get the lodge declared first in the land. The fact that the seventeenth-century minutes of the lodge never refer to the Second Schaw Statutes may well be an indication that the lodge, far from being proud of the statutes as they declared their lodge the second in the country, spurned them for not making it the first . . . the question of the precedence of lodges is one feature that distinguishes the Second Schaw Statutes from the First.[392]

When Schaw deferred to Mother Kilwinning in the second set of statutes, the other Lodges recognized that Schaw could be put under pressure and made to adjust his ideas. Knowing this could only have encouraged them to push him further.

Schaw himself must have felt that getting John Mylne to initiate King James would be a move towards uniting the Lodges of Scotland under the Grand Mastership of the King, and possibly also settling the issue of precedence by creating a new First Lodge of Scotland. If the Lodge of Scoon and Perth became the Royal Grand Master's Lodge, this would undermine all the jockeying for position that had gone on earlier. It is clear from its 1658 Charter that the Lodge of Scoon did not support the Lodge of Edinburgh's claim to be the First Lodge of Scotland. In Schaw's second statutes in 1599, Edinburgh had been named as First Lodge, Kilwinning was officially number two, and Stirling was third in seniority (it is rather ironic that the Lodge of Scoon and Perth is today No. 3 on the current roll of the Grand Lodge of Scotland). But John Mylne had found a different way for Scoon and Perth to take precedence over all other Lodges. By initiating the King, he must have thought, as Schaw did, that he would outflank them all.

But things didn't quite work out as Schaw expected. The other Lodges now put pressure on him. The Lodges in the East of Scotland—Edinburgh, St. Andrews, Haddington, Aitcheson's Haven, and Dunfermline—drew on the opening statement of Schaw's First Statute to make their own choice of Grand master, William St. Clair (Sinclair) of Roslin. As Stevenson comments, the choice of St. Clair had an air of desperation about it:

> Schaw's death in 1602 and the move of the king to England on the Union of the Crowns the following year may have disrupted attempts to win the king's support. A further difficulty may have been that, though in William Sinclair the masons had found a gentleman of ancient lineage willing to be their patron, they had not found a respectable or influential one. The character of William Sinclair of Roslin, indeed, provides the strongest argument in favour of accepting that the First St. Clair Charter's claim that the Sinclairs of Roslin had well-established rights as patrons of the craft represented a genuine tradition, not one invented to help gain approval for a newly chosen patron. If the masons had had a free choice in seeking a suitable patron to advance the craft's interests they would never have chosen the laird of Roslin![393]

The William who figures in the First St. Clair Charter was the great grandson of William St. Clair, 12th Baron of Roslin, 11th Baron of Pentland, 9th Baron of Cousland, 3rd Earl of Orkney, 1st Earl of Caithness, 1st Baron of Dysart, and the builder of Rosslyn Chapel. The 12th Baron Roslin had been the second most powerful man in Scotland until 1471, when he suddenly split up his holdings.

The fifteenth Baron, the William of the First St. Clair Charter, was a Catholic who kept quarreling with the Kirk (Church) of Scotland. He used Roslin Chapel (as it was then known) to have one of his children baptized in 1589 despite the fact that the Kirk did not recognize Roslin as a parish church. William was unperturbed by the outcry, but the minister who conducted the service was forced make a public plea for forgiveness.[394] A year later, the presbytery of Dalkeith accused Sinclair of "keiping images and uther monuments of idolatrie" in Roslin. The Kirk officials had to postpone interviewing him, however, as he had been arrested and charged with threatening the King's person.[395] When he was freed, the Kirk pursued him, insisting that Roslin should not be used as a place of worship, as William was suspected of holding illicit Catholic worship there. They insisted that William force his tenants to attend the parish Kirk. They also suggested that he set an example and become an elder of that Kirk. William declined, saying he was "insufficient" for the position. He proved his point soon afterwards when he was forced to make a public confession of fornication with local barmaid; to add insult to injury, he told the Kirk he could not remember if all of his bastards had been baptized or not. For his acts of unlawful carnal knowledge he was ordered to do a public penance that involved sitting on the repentance stool. He refused, unless he was supplied with a quart of good wine to help him pass the time.[396]

To judge from the number of summons naming him and requiring him to keep the peace and refrain from attacking numerous individuals, Baron William seems to have been fond of both brawling and wenching. Father Hay, the historian of the St. Clair/Sinclair family whom I mentioned earlier, described him as "a lewd man, who kept a miller's daughter for the purpose of fornication."[397] He eventually had to run away to Catholic Ireland with his mistress, because the political climate became too much for him; he left behind his more upright Protestant son, also called William.

This lewd fornicator was the man whom the Masons of Scotland preferred as their patron, rather than let the Lodge of Scoon and Perth take precedence over them. Embracing William the Wastrel must have been the only way they could think of to thwart the ambitions of the Mylne family that Schaw had unleashed via the Lodge of Scoon and Perth. But Schaw had left open the political loophole to show allegiance to the Laird of Roslin with the first sentence of his first statute, "that they observe and keep all the good ordinances set down before concerning the privileges of their Craft by their predecessors of good memory." The First St. Clair Charter follows this line exactly when it says:

> Be it known to all men by this letter that we Deacons, Masters and Freemen of the Masons of the realm of Scotland with the express consent and agreement of William Schaw, Master of Works to our Sovereign Lord, confirm that from age to age it has been observed amongst us that the Lairds of Roslin have ever been Patrons and Protectors of us and our privileges.

As Professor Stevenson noted, Schaw's attempt to obtain a Royal Charter and a Royal Grand Master for the Freemasons seems to have failed because some

Lodges insisted on adhering to an older tradition which linked them to the St. Clairs of Roslin. Yet, as he also notes, the outrageous character of the man they gave their loyalty to suggests that the tradition must have been important to them, otherwise they could have gone along with Schaw's plan and taken Bro. His Majesty King James VI as their new Royal Patron. Certainly the King joining the Craft encouraged many of his courtiers to join as well, among them Lord Alexander, Lord Hamilton, and David Ramsey (clockmaker to the King and gentleman of the Privy Chamber), who all joined the Lodge of Edinburgh.[398] Stevenson concludes that the hereditary wardenship of the St. Clairs must have been a genuine tradition. I suggest it was instead driven by a desire for Masonic precedence, which seems as old as Freemasonry itself.

Nevertheless James VI, through his Master of Works, William Schaw, developed the modern Lodge system of Freemasonry in Scotland before he moved to England. Once he had been "made a Mason," he realized what fun the ceremonies of Masonry can be, and for the rest of his life he was fascinated with the rituals of Solomon's Temple, which play such an important part in Freemasonry.

When James moved down to London, he continued to carry out ceremonies that involved acting out the role of King Solomon—the role taken by the Master of the Lodge during the opening and closing ceremonies. And he certainly does not seem to have been secretive about this interest. Sir John Harrington, who spent an evening at Court while the King was entertaining King Christian of Denmark in 1617, reported:

> After dinner the ladies and gentlemen of the Court enacted the Queen of Sheba coming to King Solomon's Temple. The lady who took the part of the Queen of Sheba was, however, too drunk to keep her balance on the steps and fell over onto King Christian's lap, covering him with wine, cream, jelly, beverages, cakes, spices and other good matters which she was carrying in her hands.[399]

Not quite the ritual we carry out in our Lodges today, but the spirit of King Solomon's festive board certainly inspired King James. Nor was this the only occasion on which James is reported to have carried out such. He became so obsessed with re-enacting the story of the events surrounding Solomon's Temple that his courtiers began to call him the British Solomon.[400] William Preston, one of the first historians of Freemasonry, claims in his 1746 work *Illustrations of Freemasonry* that the King also carried out regular Freemasonic ceremonies:

> In 1607, the foundation stone of this elegant structure [part of the Palace of Whitehall] was laid by king James, and his wardens who were attended by many brothers, clothed in form. The ceremony was conducted with the greatest pomp and splendor.[401]

So the politics of the two Schaw statutes and the First St. Clair Charter are now clear. Professor Stevenson sums it up:

Schaw was intending to get King James VI to give royal authority to the privileges of the masons, no doubt based on revision and amalgamation of the First and Second Statutes, and copies of such a royal grant would have been circulated to all lodges— had such a grant in fact ever been made. But Kilwinning Lodge . . . reacted to the First Statutes with such indignation that Schaw hastily compiled the Second Statutes, a provisional and temporary code intended to placate Kilwinning until a royal grant could be obtained which would greatly strengthen Schaw's hand in dealing with recalcitrant lodges.[402]

The combination of the two Schaw Statutes and the First St. Clair Charter gives a vivid picture of a strong system of Lodges, each highly opinionated and ready to fight for its own view of its importance in Masonic history. These Lodges are often dismissed by apologists for the much later United Grand Lodge of England as merely "operative" (i.e., functional groups of working stonemasons), drawing on the "great differences, social, cultural, political, religious and legal, that existed between Scotland and England."[403] But the fact of James VI of Scotland becoming James I of England tends to negate this view, for he brought his attitude to Freemasonry to England with him.

Certainly the idea that there was no ritual aspect to early Scottish Masonry is not shared by non-Mason Stevenson, who says:

There is one aspect to the emphasis of the Second Schaw Statutes on the traditions of the craft and the importance of preserving them that has previously been totally overlooked . . .

Statutes 6 and 10 refer to those masters most perfect and worthiest of memory testing others in their art, craft, science, and ancient memory, and to those wishing to become fellow crafts having to give proof of memory (among other necessary qualifications) . . . the bombshell which reveals conclusively the full significance of such references explodes in statute 13. The warden of Kilwinning Lodge was ordered to test every entered apprentice and fellow craft in "the art of memorie and science thairof." Those who have "lost ony point thairof" were to be punished according to the common use and practice of the common lodges of the realm. "Art of memory" was not merely a rather strange and clumsy term for what has been memorised (as has been assumed in the past). It was a technique for memorising things which had its roots in ancient Greece . . . The question of whether Schaw was introducing the art of memory to the masons for the first time, or whether he was continuing an existing practice is one of the many that cannot be answered with certainty . . . [But] the statutes speak of it as something long established.[404]

So why, some twenty-six years later, did a wider group of Scottish Masons combine with other craftsmen to publish a second St. Clair Charter in favor of the 16th Baron Roslin? Stevenson describes this Baron as a different type of man from his father:

[He] emerged as a solid citizen even while his father was still around to embarrass him . . . in 1609, [he] . . . took possession of the family barony of Pentland. By 1617 he was a knight . . . then his father went to Ireland, for the lands of Roslin were transferred to him in that year. He was appointed a justice of the peace in 1615 and repeatedly in later years, and took office as sheriff of the shire of Edinburgh in 1622.[405]

Here was a far more respectable patron for the Masons, but this alone does not give any motive for a wider group of craftsmen to publish the second St. Clair Charter in 1628. Professor Stevenson thinks that Roslin Chapel had created a special relationship between the St. Clairs of Roslin and Freemasonry, and this may have played a part in the Second Charter. He explains:

> The tradition of patronage of the mason craft by the Sinclairs of Roslin was connected . . . with the remarkable church of Rosslyn built by William Sinclair, earl of Caithness and Orkney, and his son in the mid fifteenth century . . . The amount and complication of the carving involved must have provided work for many masons for a prolonged period. These men must have been excited and had their skills challenged by working on such an outstanding project; and of course there was the hope of much similar work to come if the rest of the great church was built. In the circumstances it would have been understandable for the masons to have hailed their Sinclair employers as patrons and protectors of the craft—though it is more plausible to conceive of this as having been a local arrangement than a national one . . . the idea that the Sinclairs had some special relationship with the craft could have [emerged] around 1600—and come to be believed by the Sinclairs themselves— when interest in the craft was stirred up by the activities of William Schaw.[406]

The fact that William's grandfather, the 14th Baron and the grandson of the chapel-builder, had employed a considerable number of Masons to build what Stevenson describes as "a massive dwelling block" (wing) onto Roslin Castle could have helped revive the tradition by providing a solid and reliable source of income for many Masons.[407] And when the Masons of Lothian and Fife saw they were about to be sidelined by the Masons of Perth, they may well have decided to make use of such a verbal tradition to avoid yielding precedence to the Mylne family and their Lodge in Perth. Stevenson also takes this view, saying:

> It is possible that such professional contacts between masons (probably from Edinburgh, just 8 miles from Roslin) and the supposed traditional patron of their craft was in some way connected with the revival of the Sinclair claim to the position. But it is hardly surprising that the king failed to appoint as patron of the mason craft the fornicating, brawling Catholic laird of Roslin . . . The greatest mystery of the First St. Clair Charter is how on earth William Schaw and the masons thought the craft could possibly benefit from reviving the claims over it of such a man.[408]

I believe I have found the answer to this mystery in simple Masonic politics. The Lodges had already fought for their social and Masonic precedence with William Schaw. The second draft of his statutes established Edinburgh as the first Lodge of Scotland, Kilwinning as the second, and Stirling as the third. The only other possible contender, the Lodge of Aberdeen, had kept out of this battle for preferment. This had surprised Gould, who was not afraid of indulging in the politics of Masonic precedence and became a founder member of the *Quatuor Coronati* "research" Lodge as part of his personal quest for Masonic preferment.[409] He found it hard to understand a Lodge like Aberdeen that preferred to practice the brotherly love of Masonry rather than struggle to put its rivals down.

Having fought hard for their positions, the "premier" Lodges of southern Scotland were not going to let Perth overtake them by default, so they pressured William Schaw into accepting a verbal tradition about the St. Clairs of Roslin, and in the process were able to reject his idea of a Royal Charter. If Schaw had achieved that Charter, he would have secured the prestige of the office of Warden General of Masons[410]and avoided the next thirty years of squabbling by his successors.

The first round of the dispute between the St. Clairs and the Masters of Works ended with Schaw's death in 1602 and was forgotten for a while when the King moved down to London and lost interest in the project. But it was revived when a more ambitious man, Anthony Alexander, became Master of Works, at a time when Sir William St. Clair, 16th Baron Roslin, was also trying to consolidate his grip on the Mason Craft.

This Sir William St. Clair was as respectable as his father had been dissolute. Not only was he an upstanding member of the Protestant Kirk, he had married Anne, the daughter of Bishop John Spottiswood, who at the time was Bishop of Glasgow (he later became Archbishop of St. Andrews and Moderator of the Kirk in 1615). Bishop Spottiswood was a powerful force in Scottish politics under Charles I, becoming Chancellor of Scotland in 1635. He supported Charles's attempt to impose the Book of Common Prayer—although he came to regret that when the Edinburgh riots of 1637 were followed by the signing of the National Covenant in 1638 and began the process that would lead to the British Civil War. But before the war intervened, another dispute was brewing between the King's Master of Works and the Masons.

THE SECOND ST. CLAIR CHARTER

When William Schaw died in 1602, he was succeeded by David Cunnngham, who showed no interest in Schaw's mission to coordinate and organize the Mason Craft. He died in 1607, and his place was filled by James Murray. Murray was not a Mason, but prior to becoming Master of Works had been the King's Master Wright. (A Wright is someone who makes or repairs something, and is more a wood-worker than a stone-worker.) Murray's wider interest in the whole building trade encouraged him to try to set up companies or incorporations of building craftsmen that included other trades as well as Masons. The Masons saw this as an infringement of their ancient privileges and responded by appealing to the 16th Baron Roslin, the son of the man they had supported in the First St. Clair Charter.

Murray, as the King's Master of Works, assumed the right to control which individuals should be allowed to work on royal buildings, but he wanted to extend this right to give him control of all building-related craftsmen, including Masons.[411] The Edinburgh Masons responded by reiterating the claims of the First St. Clair Charter. They managed to get some support from a few Masons from the Kilwinning Lodge, and also persuaded the Ayrshire "Hammermen" (those building trades who used a hammer in their work, such as smiths and carpenters) to support them as well.

But why did Sir William St. Clair become involved? After the Second St. Clair Charter, he became active in support of his "rights" over the Masons, and took part in an extensive dispute with Murray and his successors. Early in 1628 rumors were abroad in Edinburgh that James Murray was seeking royal confirmation of his right to control all the building trades, Masons included. Officers of the Lodge of Edinburgh had a meeting with Sir William St. Clair. On May 1, 1628, a brief record of the Lodge says: "At Rosling. The quhilk day Sir Williame Sinkler." The Scots word "quhilk" means simply "which",[412] making the phrase "The which day", so the minute paraphrases into English as "At Roslin. That day—Sir William St. Clair." Stevenson says of this note:

> It indicates active links between the craft and Sir William in that year . . . the document itself contains evidence that a meeting of some sort took place, for a single notary signed for members of several lodges . . . The claim of the Second St. Clair Charter that there had been previous royal grants to the Sinclairs as patrons of the masons is not plausible . . . Having failed to obtain royal approval through the First Charter, it seems that the masons sought to strengthen their case in the second by inventing previous royal grants—which they may well have genuinely convinced themselves had once existed.[413]

This is what they said in that 1628 Charter. I have reproduced my paraphrase into modern English to make it easier to follow:

> Be it known to all men by this letter that we Deacons, Masters and Freemen of the Masons and Hammermen within the kingdom of Scotland have from age to age acknowledged the Lairds of Roslin as the Patrons and Protectors of us and our privileges. Likewise our predecessors have obeyed and acknowledged them as Patrons and Protectors as they held letters of authority and other documents granted to them by most noble progenitors of noble memory who were also Lairds of Roslin. These writings were destroyed by a fire within the Castle of Roslin. The destruction by fire of these letters is well known to us and our predecessor Deacons, Masters and Freemen of the Masons. Because of negligence and slothfulness, the protection of our privileges is likely to be lost and the Lairds of Roslin be deprived of their just rights and our Craft be deprived of any Patron Protector. The lack of an overseer will result in imperfection and corruptions and will cause many people to form a bad opinion of us and our Craft. Many and great enterprises will not be undertaken if this misbehavior is not corrected. To keep good order among us in the future, and

for the advancement of our Craft within his Highness's kingdom of Scotland, we in the name of all the brethren and craftsmen, and to further the polices of our predecessors made with the express consent of William Schaw, Master of Works to his Highness, and with one voice agree that William Sinclair of Roslin, father to Sir William Sinclair, now of Roslin, for himself and his heirs should purchase and obtain at the hands of his Majesty the liberty, freedom and jurisdiction over us and our predecessor Deacons, Masters and Freemen of the said vocation, as patrons and judges over the use of the whole profession within the said kingdom. We acknowledge him and his heirs as patrons and judges of our Craft, under our Sovereign Lord, without any limits to their ability to pass judgment, under the agreement subscribed by the said Master of Works and our predecessors. In this exercising this office of jurisdiction, over us and our vocation, the said William Sinclair of Roslin continued until he went to Ireland where he presently remains. But since his departure from this realm many corruptions and imperfections have arisen both among ourselves and in our said vocation for want of a Patron and Overseer and our Craft is likely to fall into decay. And now for the safety of our Craft and having full experience of the good skill and judgment which the said Sir William Sinclair of Roslin has shown to our Craft, and to repair the ruin and manifold corruption and damage being done by unskilled workers we are all of one voice in ratifying the previous letter of authority and freedoms granted by our brethren and his Highness's own Master of Works at the time to the said William Sinclair of Roslin, father to the said Sir William Sinclair whereby he and his heirs are acknowledged as our Patrons and Judges under our Sovereign Lord over us and all worthy practitioners of our Craft within this his Highness's kingdom of Scotland, without any limit on their judgments in any time hereafter. And further we all in one voice confirm that the said Sir William Sinclair, now of Roslin, and his heirs are our only Patrons, Protectors and Overseers under our Sovereign Lord. This applies to us and our successor Deacons, Masters and Freemen of our vocations of Masons and Hammermen, within the worthy kingdom of Scotland and we acknowledge that the Lairds of Roslin have held this office for many ages with full power granted to them to appoint Wardens and Deputies and to call meetings at places of their choosing for the purpose of keeping good order in the Craft. We say this so that it may be known to all Masons that they may be called to account for absences and be subject to fines if they fail to carry out the responsibilities of the Craft. The Lairds of Roslin have the right to make proper use of deputies, clerks, assistants and other such officers as are needed to ensure that all transgressors are brought to order. And the same [Lairds] have the power to enforce all the privileges, liberties and immunities of the said Craft and to exercise that power as their predecessors have done and freely, quietly and in peace against any revocation, obstacle or impediment whatsoever.

The Lodges of Edinburgh, Dunfermline, and St. Andrews signed the Second Charter, but some signatures of the First Charter (Aitcheson's Haven and Haddington) were missing. However, new supporters of the St. Clair claim had appeared, the Lodges of Stirling, Dundee, and Glasgow, and, for the first time, members of the Incorporation of Masons and Wrights of Ayr, the town which is home to Lodge Mother Kilwinning.

Why did the "Deacons, Masters and Freemen of the Masons and Hammermen within the kingdom of Scotland," as they described themselves, feel the need to seek the support and protection of the son-in-law of the Archbishop of St. Andrews? Perhaps because they were living under an absentee king and felt that the officials he had appointed were more interested in lining their own pockets than ruling in Scotland's best interests. In this view they may well have been correct, but by appealing to Sir William St. Clair to protect their ancient privileges against the absentee King's Masters of Works, they seemed to confirm the tradition of the St. Clairs as hereditary Grand Masters of the Masons of Scotland. I was now convinced that this belief had first emerged as a pawn in the game of Masonic precedence played by the southern Scottish Lodges at the beginning of the seventeenth century.

Did they have grounds to fear the King's Masters of Works? Certainly James Murray did well for himself out of being Master of Works. He was knighted, becoming Sir James Murray of Kilbaberton, and earned enough to build himself a fine mansion at Baberton, near Edinburgh. But he did not seem rapacious. He didn't need to: He could safely delegate greed to his assistant.

In 1625 Murray had taken as his assistant a man called Anthony Alexander, who would later succeed him as Master of Works. Alexander certainly had ambitions of bringing the Masons under his control. Just before Murray died in November, 1634, Alexander was initiated into the Lodge of Edinburgh. He also persuaded his elder brother, Lord Alexander, to join at the same July meeting. Stevenson says of this action:

> This looks like an attempt by Anthony Alexander to show an interest in things Masonic and flatter the masons by joining in the affairs of their lodge, in order to improve his standing with them and thus bring himself an advantage in the dispute with Sinclair. Sir James Murray died on Saturday 29 November 1634, and just two days later a draft grant confirming that Anthony Alexander was sole master of works was dispatched to London for signature by the king . . . He himself left for London two weeks later. The haste suggests that Alexander feared that Sinclair might seek to take advantage of the situation before the new grant was ratified, by renewing his own claims to jurisdiction over the masons and hammermen.[414]

Alexander was not a rich man when he became Master of Works, but he if he had succeeded in forcing through the changes he wanted, then he would soon have become one. He intended to set up a system where any Master of a building-related trade, Masons included, would be charged £30 to be accepted into his local company. Half the money would go to support the running of the company, and the other half into the pocket of the Lord Warden General, as Alexander was now calling himself. This scheme is outlined in a document called the Falkland Statutes, which he issued in October of 1636.[415] Alexander pushed to have the office of Warden General (which combined control of the Masons with the role of Master of Works) made a crown appointment, but the disputes between the King and Covenanters meant this did not happen until the Restoration of Charles II in 1660. The first holder of the combined post was William Moray of Dreghorn, a member of the Lodge of Edinburgh and the brother of Sir Robert Moray, perhaps the most famous Freemason at that time.

But how strong was the support of the other building trades for the patronage of Sir William St. Clair? Not as strong as an initial reading may suggest. The only non-Masons to sign the Second Charter were a glazier and wright from Kilwinning.[416] The problem with the Second St. Clair Charter is that it takes actions which do not fit with the idea that the St. Clair family were hereditary guardians of some secret Masonic rituals. It includes the "hammermen" and the "squaremen" as honorary Masons. This charter does not support the distinctive character of the esoteric rituals which Stevenson detects in the Second Schaw Statutes. Was the Second St. Clair Charter really suggesting that the hammermen should be initiated into the secrets of "the Mason Word"? (This is the secret word that is ritually whispered into the ear of the aspiring Fellowcraft at the moment when he is raised to what is now called the Third Degree of Freemasonry, or the sublime degree of Master Mason.) I would suggest not. I think that St. Clair was motivated by power and profit. He had been approached by the powerful Lodge of Edinburgh and offered a platform to challenge the lucrative monopoly of the King's Master of Works to control the building trade. Questions of ritual and tradition would not have entered into this political calculation. Stevenson, a non-Mason, says that from his reading the Portland Manuscript, he believes that: "The Sinclairs of Roslin were obliged to receive the Mason Word."[417] But he points out a strong political motive for such a choice when he adds:

> Perhaps the intention of the Second Charter was that Sir William Sinclair should be protector of all the building trades, but should have a special relationship with the Masons through being himself initiated to the secrets of the Mason Word.[418]

The motive of the officers of the Lodge of Edinburgh now becomes clear. If Sir William had managed to win a royal grant to control the building trades, the Masons, because they shared the ritual of the Mason Word with the St. Clairs, would become the elite and favored of the building trades in Scotland. It might have worked if the hammermen had accepted the invitation, and if King Charles I had supported St. Clair rather than his own Master of Works. But, as Stevenson points out, the King did not:

> [Charles I] was indignant at this interference, writing (27 February 1635) of Alexander's grant having been stopped by Sinclair "pretending ane heritable charge of the Maissones of our said kingdome, though we have nevir gevin warrant for strengthning of aney heritable right" . . . [claiming an inheritable control of the Masons of our kingdom, though we have never given any warrant for strengthening any inheritable right] Charles sought the ultimate abolition of all hereditary offices,

and this now counted strongly against the pretensions of the Sinclairs of Roslin . . .
Charles was determined that his master of works should have the full rights of his
predecessors unless there was some just reason for determining otherwise.[419]

As it was, the Second St. Clair Charter came to nothing. All it achieved was to
reinforce the legend of the St. Clairs as hereditary Grand Masters of Masons, who
would support the Craft in time of need. But this had a direct result on the formation of the Grand Lodge of Scotland, as I was soon to find out.

Conclusions

I now knew that William Schaw had created the modern Lodge system and begun
the Masonic tradition of writing down records of their meetings and decisions.
He had encouraged the ritual teaching of the skills of memory, which were associated with the Mason Word, and given the Masonic Lodges a sense of pride and
history, which had resulted in the battles of precedence of the early seventeenth
century. Sir Anthony Alexander, through his Falkland Statutes, had tried to build
on Schaw's foundations to create a system of companies to include all building
craftsmen who were not already part of an existing incorporation, and this was
the origin of the battle between Sir Anthony Alexander and Sir William Sinclair
that inspired the Second St. Clair Charter.

Perhaps Sir Anthony Alexander (a Mason initiated into the Lodge of
Edinburgh) and Sir William Sinclair (whom Stevenson believes had also received
the ritual of the Mason Word) were both simply trying to create an organization
that celebrated the ideal of the architect. But they may just have been trying to
ingratiate themselves with the Masons as a way of ensuring their right to tax all
building crafts. Either way, the myth of the Masonic Grand Mastership of the St.
Clairs of Roslin was now firmly lodged in the Scottish mindset, and it had tremendous implications in the Great Age of the formation of Grand Lodges. But this
love affair between the Freemasons of Scotland and the Sinclair family was far
from over, as I was soon to discover when my research took me back to 1736, to
snoop into the details of the election of a Grand Master Mason to rule over a
Grand Lodge of Scotland.

CHAPTER 10

THE GRAND BIRTH PANGS

THE ST. CLAIR HEREDITARY GRAND MASTERS

The role of the St. Clairs of Roslin in Freemasonry took on greater significance when yet another William St. Clair of Roslin, this time the 19th Baron, used his family's "hereditary Grand Mastership of Freemasonry" as a reason to become the Grand Master Mason of the newly formed Grand Lodge of Scotland in 1736. An election took place in Mary's Chapel on Tuesday, November 30, 1736, at half-past two in the afternoon. At that meeting, William St. Clair, 19th Baron Roslin, read out the following statement, which seems at first sight to settle the matter of his family's role in the beginnings of Freemasonry:

> I, William St. Clair of Rossline, Esquire, taking into my consideration that the Massons in Scotland did, by several deeds, constitute and appoint William and Sir William St. Clairs of Rossline, my ancestors and their heirs, to be their patrons, protectors, judges, or masters; and that my holding or claiming any such jurisdiction, right, or privilege, might be prejudiciall to the Craft and vocation of Massonrie, whereof I am a member and I, being desireous to advance and promote the good and utility of the said Craft of Massonrie to the utmost of my power, doe therefore hereby, for me and my heirs, renounce, quit, claim, overgive, and discharge all right, claim, or pretence that I, or my heirs, had, have, or any ways may have, pretend to, or claim, to be patron, protector, judge, or master of the Massons in Scotland, in virtue of any deed or deeds made and granted by the said Massons, or of any grant or charter made by any of the Kings of Scotland, to and in favours of the said William and Sir William St. Clairs of Rossline, or any others of my predecessors, or any other manner of way whatsomever, for now and ever: And I bind and oblige me and my heirs, to warrant this present renounciation and discharge at all hands; and I con-

sent to the registration hereof in the Books of Councill and Session, or any other judge's books competent, therein to remain for preservation; and thereto I constitute my procurators, &c. In witness whereof I have subscribed these presents (written by David Maul, Writer to the Signet), at Edinburgh, the twenty-fourth day of November one thousand seven hundred and thirty-six years, before these witnesses, George Fraser, Deputy Auditor of the Excise in Scotland, Master of the Canongate Lodge; and William Montgomerie, Merchant in Leith, Master of the Leith Lodge.

Sic Subscribitur
WM. ST. CLAIR
Geo. Fraser, Canongate Kilwinning, witness
Wm. Montgomerie, Leith Kilwinning, witness

But is there more to this story than a simple act of magnanimous self-sacrifice? I suspect that there is. As we saw in the last chapter, the whole backdrop to the St. Clair involvement in the development of Freemasonry had been as part of a struggle for precedence between some of the oldest and strongest Lodges of Freemasonry. This was a struggle that took place across the prosperous and more densely populated Lowlands and Midlands of Scotland. It mainly involved two Lodges, Mother Kilwinning and Edinburgh.

Gould, in *The History of Freemasonry*, says that the Brethren of Scotland were so fascinated with the "magnanimity, disinterestedness and zeal" displayed in William St. Clair's resignation that the Deed was unanimously accepted, and his abdication from an obsolete office in Masonry cleared the ground for St. Clair to fill the post of first Grand Master in the Scottish Grand Lodge of Speculative Masons.

The attempts of the Lodge of Scoon and Perth, led by the Mylne family, to take the top place had been thwarted by drawing up the first St. Clair Charter. Soon after this, the Mylne family had thrown in their lot with the Lodge of Edinburgh. The grandson of the John Mylne who initiated King James VI, also called John, joined the Lodge of Edinburgh in 1633 (soon after the second St. Clair Charter had put Edinburgh in front in the race with Kilwinning) and went on to initiate Sir Robert Moray, founder of the Royal Society, in Newcastle in 1641. His nephew Robert Mylne joined the Lodge of Edinburgh in 1653 and became Warden in 1663. His son William Mylne joined his Lodge in 1681, to be followed by his son Thomas Mylne in 1722. Thomas's sons Robert and William also joined the Lodge of Edinburgh, and this connection only ended in 1811 when Robert Mylne died. Gould points out that the Mylne family supported the Lodge of Edinburgh for five generations after their move from the Lodge of Scoon and Perth, which their previous three generations had supported.[420]

Not all the early Lodges were interested in this battle for status. Stirling Lodge, which had been named the third in Scotland in 1599, lost interest in this argument. Even the Lodge with the oldest written record of its existence, Aberdeen, took no part in these battles about who was the oldest and most worthy of respect. So now I needed to review the actions of the southern Scottish Lodges to see what was really going on.

STABLING, SACKING AND ABANDONMENT: THE SAGA OF ROSLIN CHAPEL

The St. Clairs of Roslin had fallen on hard times since the Second St. Clair Charter was written at the peak of their Masonic popularity in 1628. Their family chapel itself, Roslin Chapel (now Rosslyn), had not fared much better. In 1650, during the British Civil War, Cromwellian troops under General Monk attacked the castle, and their cavalry horses were stabled in the Chapel.[421] This would not have been much of a problem— the chapel had an earthen floor, and its windows were not glazed—but during the Glorious Revolution of 1688, when William of Orange drove James II into exile, a Protestant mob marched from Edinburgh to Roslin and were joined by local villagers in destroying the Chapel's furniture and ornaments, which they thought Popish and idolatrous.[422] Thereafter the Chapel was abandoned until 1736, when the windows were glazed for the first time, the roof repaired, the floor laid with flagstones, and a new boundary wall was built around the churchyard.[423]

The Sinclair (or St. Clair) empire, which had peaked under William the 12th Baron, who built the chapel, was now but a shadow of its former glory. As W.P.L. Thompson puts it in his *History of Orkney*:

> Ever since the death of Earl William [the chapel builder], the great Sinclair empire had been in a state of progressive disintegration, irrevocably fractured.[424]

The line of the Roslin St. Clairs had reached a low during the time of depraved 15th Baron, but the memory of the powerful Earl William and his massive injection of wealth into the Mason Craft during the building of the Chapel, had revived Masonic interest in the St. Clairs, and the dissolute, lewd, and Catholic 15th Baron was happy to support the local Masonic Lodge against Protestant King James VI and his intrusive Kirk.

His son had built on this claim in the second St. Clair Charter to try to take from absentee King Charles I's Master of Works a lucrative trade in initiation and settlement fees. He had seen his chance when the Lodge of Edinburgh had approached him to cooperate with them in producing the charter to challenge the reforms of Anthony Alexander. Then, six years after the publication of the second St. Clair Charter, Alexander joined the Lodge of Edinburgh, probably as a gesture of reconciliation, or to bring the Lodge back to his side in his ongoing battle with Sir William St. Clair. But both were overtaken by the events of the Civil War and the Restoration, as we have seen. Now, in the early eighteenth century, a group of supporters of Lodge Mother Kilwinning saw a chance to revisit the mythical role of the St. Clairs in order to win a tactical advantage over Edinburgh.

A Spreading of Grand Lodges

In 1717, the London Masons had formed themselves into a Grand Lodge, and had proved that by doing so they could greatly expand the movement. Because of the links between the Scots Lodges and the deposed Stuart line of kings, the London Masons had distanced themselves from their Stuart roots—probably a wise move in the years just after the 1715 Jacobite rebellion. In the first thirteen years of existence of the London Grand Lodge, I had noticed that four Scots lords had served as Grand Master of London Freemasonry and seemed to have enjoyed the pomp and glamour a Grand Lodge offered. They were:

1723 The Duke of Buccleugh
1725 Lord Paisley, Earl of Abercorn
1733 The Earl of Strathmore
1734 The Earl of Crawford (a member of Lodge Kilwinning Scots
       Arms, Edinburgh)

Gould had noticed this influx of Scottish noble Freemasons, and had commented:

> In proceeding with the history of the Grand Lodge of Scotland, the remark may be expressed, that if any surprise is permissible at the establishment of that body in 1736, it can only legitimately arise from the circumstance that the Masons of Edinburgh allowed the brethren in York, Munster, and Dublin to precede them in following the example set at London in 1717. If any one influence more than another conduced to the eventual erection of a governing Masonic body for Scotland, it will be found, I think, in the fact that within the comparatively short space of thirteen years, six prominent noblemen, all of whom were connected with the northern kingdom, had filled the chair of the Grand Lodge of England. One of these, the Earl of Crawford, would probably have been made the first Grand Master of Scotland.[425]

(I was unable to find two of these Scots-connected Grand Masters of London, and Gould does not name his six. But the four I did find are in themselves enough to support his argument.)

The spread of centrally organized London Freemasonry required secondary centers of administration as its new form of Grand Lodge Masonry diffused through the rest of the Britain. There was already an existing system of independent Masonic Lodges in Ireland, Scotland, and Wales, and the Irish noticed what was happening in London. The *Dublin Weekly Journal* of June 26, 1725, reports that on June 24 a Grand Lodge of Ireland was convened to install the first Grand

Master Mason of Ireland, the Earl of Rosse.[426] There was obviously a great interest among the Irish nobility in developing Freemasonry, as the next two Grand Masters of the Grand Lodge of London were Irish peers: the Earl of Inchiquin in 1726 and Lord Coleraine in 1727.

Grand Master Inchiquin, realizing that the Welsh Lodges were extremely disorganized, created an Office of Provincial Grand Master as a means of assisting the management of the larger and geographically ambitious London Craft. On May 10, 1727, this system was used to extend the reach of the Grand Lodge of London into Wales. Hugh Warburton was installed as the first Provincial Grand Master, and the province he was given was North Wales. On June 24, 1727, Sir Edward Mansell, Bart., was installed as Provincial Grand Master for South Wales.[427]

The idea was obvious: If the natives were unable to organize a Grand Lodge for themselves, then the London Masons could do it for them. Now this message was taken back to Scotland. For some eighteen years after the creation of the Grand Lodge of London, Scottish Masons had felt no need to be told what to do by Grand Masters, but in 1735 the politics of Freemasonry changed. Lord Crawford returned to his Masonic roots in Edinburgh, after serving a year as Grand Master of the London Masons, and a movement began among the Lodges of the city to create a Grand Lodge in Scotland.[428] The coincidence of timing is hard to ignore, particularly as Crawford's Scottish Lodge was involved in the initiative.

Scotland had no hierarchical structure above the Lodge and no formal way of marking out Lodge seniority since the statements of the Schaw Statutes. There is plenty of evidence from the sequence of conflicting statutes that Lodge seniority was a key issue for at least some southern Scottish Lodges. The new structure, unsurprisingly invented by the status-conscious London Masons, offered three benefits to Lodges and noble Masons concerned about the public perception of their status. First, it offered an additional level of preferment and the chance to develop and sport a superior range of titles and regalia. Second, it offered a system of Lodge numbering where a lower number conferred a higher status. And third, it offered an opportunity to break out of the ranking established by the second Schaw Statute, using the path which the Lodge of Scoon and Perth had tried before being thwarted by the first St. Clair Charter.

At first sight, I assumed these reasons might make it attractive to any noble lairds with a sense of their own superiority, and the Earl of Home, who was then Master of the Lodge Kilwinning Scots Arms, appeared eager to put himself forward as a candidate for Grand Master Mason of Scotland. It appeared that Lords Crawford and Home had tried to do a deal whereby Crawford, who also saw himself as a prime candidate, with his experience as Grand Master of London Grand Lodge, was persuaded to stand aside and give his support to Home.[429] Only when I looked more closely at the events did I realize there was a deeper layer of cunning at work, which would add to the growing myth of the St. Clairs of Roslin.

The preliminaries for the Grand Election for the first Grand Master Mason of Scotland were supposed to have been organized by the four main Lodges in and around Edinburgh. However, there were six Lodges in the metropolitan district at that time, and two were ignored. The ones left out were Lodges which had formed themselves without the authority or approval of the King or his Warden General—which, as we have seen, had become an understood principle of the Craft. The Lodge of Edinburgh refused to recognize them, although they still worked as independent units.[430]

Those promoting the formation of a Scottish Grand Lodge were the Lodges of Edinburgh (now also known as St. Mary's Chapel), Canongate Kilwinning, Kilwinning Scots Arms, and Leith Kilwinning. (These last three Lodges had been formed officially by what had become the alternative Grand Lodge of Mother Kilwinning.)

From the early part of the seventeenth century, it had been permitted for members of a Lodge to initiate Freemasons and to pass them as Fellowcrafts at times and places other than regular meetings of their Lodge. When this was done, the action would be reported at the next regular meeting of the Lodge and recorded in the minutes. Provided the fees were paid, the membership would be allowed. In 1677, this idea was extended by Lodge Kilwinning. Gould says:

> The Grand Lodge of Scotland was formed in 1736—nearly twenty years after the institution of the Grand Lodge in London—but in the north the functions of such a body were exercised by two "head lodges," Kilwinning having been the chief in that respect. Though these united with the other lodges in forming the Grand Lodge at Edinburgh, the Kilwinning members still continued to grant warrants after 1736, which was inconsistent, to say the least, with its profession of adhesion to the new regime. The brethren were also uneasy at accepting the second position on the roll, and soon fully resumed their independent career. Three lodges we know, and very probably several others, were constituted by "Mother Kilwinning" prior to 1736, viz., "Canongate Kilwinning" (No. 2), "Torphichen Kilwinning" (No. 13), and "Kilmarnock Kilwinning." In fact, there are numerous references in the Records and old papers, which testify that the "Kilwinningites" were very actively engaged in extending their influence by chartering lodges soon after 1670. As a lodge warranted for Paisley, by its authority bore the number 77, and later charters being 78 and 79 respectively for Eaglesham and East Kilbride, although in the lists of "Kilwinning" charters, only some thirty-three are recorded, it is clear that there are still more than forty lodges to be accounted for. These are more likely to have been constituted by Mother Kilwinning before 1736 than afterwards, and probably several were established during the latter part of the seventeenth century. This point of itself is sufficient to account for the number of old lodges which append the name Kilwinning to their own special titles.[431]

Mother Kilwinning had several members who lived in Edinburgh, and they did not wish, or were not allowed, to join the Lodge of Edinburgh. They wanted a Lodge of their own, which would mean that they did not have to travel completely across the country to attend a meeting. On December 20, 1677, Mother Kilwinning issued the first warrant to form a new Lodge. The fact that it was within the jurisdiction of their old rivals the Lodge of Edinburgh—who, according to the second Schaw Statutes, outranked them as the first and head Lodge of Scotland—did not seem to matter. Gould describes the warrant creating Lodge Canongate Kilwinning as the "Premier Scottish Warrant of Constitution."[432] It reads as follows:

> At the ludge [Lodge] of Killwining the twentie day of December 1677 yeares, deacons and wardanes and the rest of the brethren, considering the love and favour showne to us be the rest of the brethren of the Cannigate in Edinbroughe, anc part of our number being willing to be boked and inroled the qch day gives power and liberty to them to enter, receave, and pass any qualified persons that they think fitt, in name and behalf of the ludge of Killwinning, and to pay ther entry and booking moneys due to the sd ludge, as we do our selves, they sending on of ther number to us yearly, and we to do the lyke to them if need be. The qlk day ther names are insert into this book.[433]

Of the four Lodges involved in the initial discussions to form a Grand Lodge in Scotland, three were daughter Lodges of Mother Kilwinning. But Gould reported that one Lodge was to become the main instigator of the process, and that was Canongate Kilwinning.

> In the agitation for a Scottish Grand Lodge the initiative was taken by Canongate Kilwinning. On September 29, 1735, as appears from the minutes of that body, the duty of "framing proposals to be laid before the several Lodges in order to the choosing of a Grand Master for Scotland," was remitted to a committee, whilst there is no recorded meeting of the four (subsequently) associated Lodges, at which the same subject was considered, until October 15, 1736, when delegates . . . met, and agreed upon a form of circular to be sent to all the Scottish Lodges, inviting their attendance either in person or by proxy for the purpose of electing a Grand Master.[434]

The Earl of Home was the current Master and a founder member of another daughter Lodge, Kilwinning Scots Arms, and among his fellow founders was Lord Crawford, the ex-Grand Master Mason of the Grand Lodge of London. The gossip at the time, as I mentioned, was that these two had done a deal to sew up the Grand Mastership of the new Scottish Grand Lodge.[435] But could they be sure that the Lodges of Scotland, and Mother Kilwinning in particular, would accept an Edinburgh Grand Master Mason to rule over them?

In Scotland, unlike Ireland, there had been no rush to create a Grand Lodge, as each Lodge was convinced that it knew best how to manage itself. There were over a hundred Scottish Lodges, and only thirty-three were showing any interest in forming a Grand Lodge. Lords Crawford and Home might well have fancied the idea of one of them becoming Grand Master Mason of Scotland, but if they were seen to be pushing their own cases the fiercely independent Scottish Lodges could easily turn against the whole idea. Since the first Schaw Statute, there had been considerable disagreement about priority and rank. If either Mother Kilwinning or the Lodge of Edinburgh were seen to be pushing too hard, then other Lodges could take that as a move to rule the rest—and that could scupper the project.

If a Grand Lodge of Scotland was to be created, then a more subtle approach was needed. The process of persuading as many Lodges as possible to unite was delegated to Lodge Canongate Kilwinning. The process began with the decision to call a meeting to bring other Lodges on board.

> 15 October 1736 . . . delegates from the Lodges of Mary's Chapel, Canongate Kilwinning, Kilwinning Scots Arms and Leith Kilwinning met and agreed to send a circular to all the Scottish Lodges inviting their attendance, either in person or by proxy, for the purpose of electing a Grand Master. It was decided that the election should take place in Mary's Chapel on Tuesday 30 November 1736, at half-past two in the afternoon. At the appointed time representatives of 33 of the hundred or more Lodges that had been invited assembled. To obviate jealousies in the matter of precedency, each Lodge was placed on the roll in the Order in which it entered the hall.[436]

Naturally—as the meeting was held in St. Mary's Chapel, where the Lodge of Edinburgh met—they were there first, closely followed by the representatives of Mother Kilwinning and the stage manager of the meeting, Brother George Fraser, Master of Canongate Kilwinning. Most of the Masons attending the meeting expected Lord Home would put his case to become the first Grand Master Mason of Scotland, but they were about to get a surprise.

The order of business had been agreed before the meeting. First they voted to accept the draft constitutions, which had already been circulated. The next step was to agree to the provisional order in which the Lodges would be entered on the roll of the new Grand Lodge (which was of course a most important piece of business). The order of entry into the hall was accepted, with the provision that a final order would be agreed later on the basis of evidence of antiquity, and the matter was set aside for the moment. (It would resurface violently within twelve months, as I shall explain later.)

Finally, the meeting arrived at the point where they had to address the tricky question of who to elect as their first Grand Master Mason. At that point, William St. Clair, the nineteenth Baron Roslin, stood up and asked permission to speak. This was granted, and he read out the resignation statement which I quoted at the beginning of this chapter. From nowhere, a focus of Masonic loyalty, whom all the Lodges could agree to support without any loss of face, was sprung on the meeting. Gould describes what happened next:

Several at least, and possibly a majority of the representatives present [probably not though], had been instructed to vote for the Earl of Home, whilst none of the Lodges, with the exception of Canongate Kilwinning . . . up till the period of election, appear to have been aware upon what grounds the latter's [William St. Clair's] claims were to be urged. Nevertheless, the brethren were so fascinated with the apparent magnanimity, disinterestedness, and zeal displayed in his "Resignation," that [his candidature for the office of Grand Master Mason] was accepted with a unanimity that must have been very gratifying to the Lodge at whose instance it had been drawn, and the abdication of an obsolete office in Operative Masonry was made the ground of St. Clair being chosen to fill the post of first Grand Master in the Scottish Grand Lodge of Speculative Masons.[437]

The architects of the Grand Lodge of Scotland had learned the lesson of the St. Clair Charters well, and had used that knowledge to unite a disparate ragtag of separate Lodges behind a St. Clair Grand Master. This might well have been inspired by a romantic longing for a non-existent "golden age" of hereditary Grand Masters, but in the process they had avoided a clash between Edinburgh and Mother Kilwinning. Both Kilwinning and Edinburgh voted for "Sinclair of Rossland, Esquire."[438] (The spelling of the family name of the Barons of Roslin gradually changed over time from St. Clair to Sinclair, and I have used both versions, as appropriate.)

Lodge Canongate Kilwinning had managed to do what the Lodge of Scoon and Perth had tried to do and failed. They had become the first Grand Master's Lodge. And they could claim the "hereditary Grand Master Mason of Scotland" who had willingly resigned his ancient office to freely stand for election in the new Grand Lodge. Who could resist such a deal? Certainly not William St. Clair. One consequence of his action was that, after standing derelict for nearly fifty years, Roslin Chapel was glazed and restored, with a new flagstone floor laid.[439] It was about to become the foremost Masonic shrine in Scotland—perhaps not quite what William the 12th Baron had intended when he built it (but that is a different matter, and one I will return to). It seems to have been a satisfactory result for the St. Clairs of Roslin nevertheless.

What had been the role of Lords Crawford and Home in this? Whatever public statements they might have made later, the voting proxies (a voting proxy is a written instruction to the Lodge Secretary of how the members have instructed him to cast the Lodge's vote) show what they wanted. Crawford, as a past Grand Master of England, would probably not have been acceptable to the Scottish Lodges, and the Earl of Home, as Master of an Edinburgh Lodge, would have alienated as many Lodges as would have supported him. Gould, from his English perspective, missed the subtlety of the public statements, which look calculated to avoid the ignominy of rejection:

The Earl of Crawford would probably have been elected the first Grand Master of Scotland, but declined the honour, as he was leaving for England, and was sensible that nothing could be a greater loss to the first Grand Lodge than the absence of the Grand Master. The Earl of Home, Master of the Lodge of Kilwinning, at the Scots Arms, Edinburgh, appears after this to have stepped into the place of Lord Crawford as the candidate whose election would have been most acceptable to the Lodges.[440]

But all this posturing had been short-circuited by the prearranged drama of William Sinclair's electrifying resignation.

Canongate Kilwinning's Grand-Master Stroke

But just how did Canongate Kilwinning manage to pull off its coup? The Lodge had begun its planning over a year earlier, just about the time Lord Crawford returned to Edinburgh as Immediate Past Grand Master of the Grand Lodge of London. The minutes of the Lodge Canongate Kilwinning show that the matter of creating a Grand Lodge for Scotland was first discussed in October 1735.[441] First, it approached William St. Clair and invited him to join the Lodge. Perhaps they reminded him that his ancestors had accepted the Mason Word, and encouraged him to emulate them.[442] Eight months later, on May 18, 1736, the Lodge initiated William St. Clair. A month later, he was advanced to the degree of a Fellow Craft, "paying into the box as usual."[443]

But now the plot thickens. On August 4, 1735, Brother Dr. John Douglas, a surgeon from the Lodge of Kirkcaldy, became a joining member of Canongate Kilwinning, and was immediately given a key job. It was described in the Lodge minutes as "Secretary for the time, with power to appoint his own deputy, in order to his making out a scheme for bringing about a Grand Master for Scotland."[444] But the scheme was already well advanced when Dr. Douglas joined it.

Ten days before the crucial election meeting at St. Mary's Chapel, William St. Clair was advanced to "the degree of Master Mason." Two days later, he signed the resignation document that was the key to his becoming the first Grand Master. It was written by John Douglas and witnessed by George Fraser, the Master of Canongate Kilwinning, and William Montgomerie, Master of Lodge Leith Kilwinning.[445] The late preparation of this strategically important document, a matter of eight days before the meeting, suggests that whoever had brought Douglas on board did not want knowledge of it to leak out and so dilute its impact at the election meeting.

Gould said of these events:

> The circumstances connected with the affiliation of Dr. Douglas, render it probable that he had been introduced for the purpose of perfecting a previously concocted plan, whereby the election of a Grand Master might be made to contribute to the aggrandisement of the Lodge receiving him. His subsequent advancement and frequent re-election to the chair of Substitute Grand Master would indicate the possession of high Masonic qualifications, and to these the Craft may have been indebted

for the resuscitation of the St. Clair Charters, and the dramatic effect which their identification with the successful aspirant to the Grand Mastership gave to the institution of the Grand Lodge of Scotland. Whatever may have been the immediate motive of the originators of the scheme, the setting up a Grand Lodge ostensibly upon the ruins of an institution that had ceased to be of practical benefit, but which in former times had been closely allied to the Guilds of the Mason Craft, gave to the new organisation an air of antiquity as the lineal representative of the ancient courts of Operative Masonry; while the "opportune" resignation of St. Clair was, if not too closely criticised, calculated to give the whole affair a sort of legal aspect which was wanting at the institution of the Grand Lodge of England.[446]

The wisdom of using William St. Clair to bring about the formation of a Grand Lodge became clear over the next few years. At the end of his year of office, William was succeeded by the Earl of Cromarty. At this meeting, it was agreed that the Grand Master would be elected annually, but the Grand Secretary and his clerk would be permanent appointments, provided they practiced "good behaviour." It was also agreed that all Lodges subscribing to the Grand Lodge should be enrolled in order of their seniority, which "should be determined from the authentic documents they produced—those producing none to be put at the end of the roll, though the Lodges thus postponed were to have their precedency readjusted, on adducing subsequent proof of their being elder." A new Grand Master was elected each year, but in addition a Deputy Grand Master, Captain John Young of Kilwinning Scots Arms Lodge, and a Substitute Grand Master, our old friend Dr. John Douglas, were appointed and allowed to retain their appointments for the next sixteen years. This meant that the government of the Grand Lodge was effectively in the hands of permanent officials, the Deputy Grand Master, the Substitute Grand Master, and the Grand Secretary. This system had its advantages, as Gould pointed out:

> The brief occupancy of the Masonic throne by more persons of distinction than would have been possible under the . . . [system used by the Grand Lodge of London] greatly conduced to the general favour with which Masonry was regarded by people of every rank and position in the Scottish kingdom.[447]

William St. Clair, his function as central focus for Masonic loyalty fulfilled, now faded from the scene. He lived a further forty years after retiring from the Grand Mastership, dying at the age of seventy-two. His three sons and four daughters all died young, and he had passed the estate of Roslin over to James St. Clair (his cousin Henry, Lord St. Clair's son) soon after he became Grand Master Mason. James died in 1762 without issue, and the Roslin estate passed to the line of Sir James Sinclair-Erskine, who became the first Earl of Rosslyn and sired the later Earls of Rosslyn. William seems to have taken little part in the development of the Grand Lodge apart from his grand gesture of resignation from a post which had never really existed outside the battle for supremacy between Mother

Kilwinning and the Lodge of Edinburgh. But that battle was not concluded with the formation of the Grand Lodge.

Mother Kilwinning had been unable to produce any written evidence to show that it had existed before 1642, while the Lodge of Edinburgh had records going back to 1599:

> In accordance, with the principle laid down, by which the precedency of Lodges was to be determined, the first place on the roll was assigned to Mary's Chapel, and the second to Kilwinning. However unsatisfactory this decision may have appeared to the Lodge of Kilwinning its validity was not at first openly challenged by that body, which for several years afterwards continued to be represented (by proxy) at Edinburgh.[448]

But the preferment of Edinburgh produced tremendous discontent at Kilwinning. They complained that the Rules of the Grand Lodge called them second in order, and another Lodge was set above them. But nothing could be done, because they were unable to produce any document to prove their antiquity:

> Finding itself thus permanently placed in a secondary rank, the Lodge of Kilwinning, without entering upon any disputation or formal vindication of its claims, resumed its independence, which in the matter of granting Charters it had in reality never renounced, and for well nigh seventy years continued to exist as an independent Grand Body . . . In estimating the pretensions of the Lodge of Kilwinning, dates become material, and we must not lose sight of the fact, that in 1743, many influences were at work, e.g. Scots degrees, and Ramsey's Oration— which, without any stretch of the imagination, may have afforded the Ayrshire Masons, at least, a reasonable excuse in claiming a pre-eminence for the old court of Operative Masonry at Kilwinning[449]

Even the Lodge of Aberdeen, which had written evidence of its existence from 1483, at the time could only prove a claim to be No. 36 on the roll, as, although the Council Records spoke of it, the Lodge itself had no records to prove it held meetings, whereas other younger Lodges did. (It now shares the No. 1 with Edinburgh St. Mary's Chapel and the Lodge of Melrose).

In 1807 the Grand Master, Lord Moira, brought Mother Kilwinning back into the fold of the Grand Lodge. The pressure of the Secret Societies Act of 1799, discussed in Chapter 4, was the driving force here. Negotiations had begun the previous year, and the two sides met in Glasgow on October 14, 1807. The records of the Lodge of Kilwinning were produced, and also the Charter of the Lodge of Scoon and Perth, to support "the great antiquity" of Kilwinning.

Eventually, Mother Kilwinning was placed at the head of the roll without a number (i.e., No. 0), although at that point the Lodge of Edinburgh threatened to secede from the Grand Lodge. There followed a period of civil war in Scottish Freemasonry, only settled when those threatening to leave the Grand Lodge of

Scotland realized that they would fall foul of the Secret Societies Act as a result. After a period of intense legal challenges, a compromise was finally reached at a meeting held on March 31, 1813. But Mother Kilwinning had to pay a price for respectability: She had to give up working Templar Masonry degrees.

But not everyone did this. Indeed Templar Masonry was now becoming so popular that it was considered a threat to the Scottish Grand Lodge itself.

> On September 19, 1815, the foundation-stones of the Regent Bridge and the New Jail were laid with the usual Masonic solemnities, and certain "Knights Templars," headed by Alexander Deuchar, not only joined in the procession, but took precedence over the regular Lodges and brethren. The subject was brought before the Grand Lodge in the ensuing November, and after a committee had reported, resolutions were passed—August 4, 1817—that the Grand Lodge only recognised the three degrees of Apprentice, Fellow Craft, and Master Mason of St. John's Masonry; and that any Lodges admitting persons to their meetings or processions belonging to other Orders, with regalia, insignia, badges, or crosses other than those belonging to St. John's Masonry, would be proceeded against for infringement of the regulations.[450]

So once again my research had led me to Templar Masonry. The Templar myth continued to attach itself to the St. Clairs and to the Freemasonic bodies they supported. And it plays an important part in building up the modern myth of the St. Clairs' part in Masonic history. And I also kept returning to Roslin. The Templar myths drew on it. The St. Clair Charters all drew on the Roslin link with Freemasonry. The St. Clairs of Roslin were active in the formation of modern Freemasonry, and yet their links seemed to be by default and were often simply useful political tools during the two-hundred-year battle for supremacy between the Lodges of Edinburgh and Kilwinning. Roslin Chapel had been a derelict ruin when William St. Clair became Grand Master Mason of Scotland, but during his year of office, it was restored and elevated to the Masonic shrine it is today. What was it about Roslin which powered such long-term devotion? I now needed to understand why William, the 12th Baron Roslin, built the Chapel in the 1400s.

CONCLUSIONS

As we have seen, William St. Clair, the 19th Baron of Roslin, was used by the Lodge of Canongate Kilwinning as a tool in a battle for supremacy among the senior Scottish Lodges. He was useful, even though he lacked political power, because of the Masonic myths that had become attached to his family and its chapel at Roslin. He seems to have been bribed and then discarded once he had served his purpose.

But what of the creator of the chapel and its mysterious images? Who was this William St. Clair, and what had he been trying to do? It was time to revisit Roslin Chapel itself and find out. Turn the page and share what I discovered about this marvel of Templar Masonic imagery.

CHAPTER 11

WHY BUILD ROSLIN CHAPEL?

A FAR-SIGHTED BUILDING PLAN

The extensive building work at Roslin (now Rosslyn) Chapel, and the consequent need to employ lots of Masons, had been an important factor in the long-running involvement of the St. Clair family with Freemasonry. But the Chapel was built a hundred and fifty years before it played this role: Three generations of Barons had ruled Roslin before the Chapel was used as a tool in Masonic politics. It is stretching credulity a little far to believe that William, the 12th Baron of Roslin, decided to spend most of his fortune bribing Masons in order that their great-grandchildren would support a dissolute 15th Baron as a potential hereditary Grand Master Mason. So why *did* he spend so much money building the Chapel?

The website of the Chapel Trust offers this explanation:

> Rosslyn Chapel, or the Collegiate Chapel of St. Matthew as it was to have been, was founded in 1446 by Sir William St. Clair, third and last St. Clair Prince of Orkney. It is in fact only part of the choir of what was intended to be a larger cruciform building with a tower at its centre.
>
> More than thirty-seven collegiate churches were built in Scotland between the reigns of James I and James IV (1406–1513). They were secular foundations intended to spread intellectual and spiritual knowledge, and the extravagance of their construction depended on the wealth of their founder.
>
> After Sir William died in 1484 he was buried in the unfinished Chapel, and the larger building he had planned was never completed.
>
> What was built, however, is extraordinary enough. "This building, I believe, may be pronounced unique, and I am confident it will be found curious, elaborate

and singularly interesting, impossible to designate by any given or familiar term" wrote John Britton in his *Architectural Antiquities of Great Britain* (1812), adding somewhat despairingly that its "variety and eccentricity are not to be defined by any words of common acceptation."[451]

GOING TO THE CHAPEL

While researching my book *The Hiram Key*, I had visited Roslin Chapel many times, and I had experienced the power of the myths about the building first-hand. I have long kept a working journal where I record facts, feelings, and impressions when researching a topic. I have been filing these on my computer systems for decades, so I still had those I made during the research trip to Roslin, in the mid-1990s, when I first took my co-author Chris Knight with me to see the place.

I had noted down how I felt about the chapel and how I responded to showing Chris what was carved into the stonework. I had then used part of these notes in *The Hiram Key*.[452] I decided to trawl through them again, to recall what I thought while I was looking at Roslin for the first time. Had I noticed anything that I had not understood at the time? Was there anything that, with the benefit of the greater background knowledge I now had, might help me?

Here are some extracts from my journal notes, which set down how I felt about Roslin Chapel on those early visits. (This was long before the success of *The Hiram Key* made the place famous. It was not covered in scaffolding when I saw it, and it had few visitors.) When I first visited it, the chapel was a sleepy backwater without a visitor center. It had one small unisex toilet in an outbuilding in the bottom corner of the churchyard. It was run by a small group of chatty, jolly, friendly ladies. The two most important were Judy Fisken, who ran the little shop and sold the entrance tickets to try to promote the tourist aspects and earn some money to keep the building from falling into disrepair, and the Reverend Janet Dyer, who ran the Church affairs.

Here is what I wrote back then: It's a warm late summer day with broken cloud cover as I drive into the chapel car park. The sun's shooting out roving beams of light like a demented theatrical spotlight, and they rove over the hillside of Roslin Glen picking out many different shades of green. When the light hits all the many towers of Rosslyn Chapel, it's really dramatic. Coming back to this chapel is like meeting an old friend. It's familiar and inviting but also interesting and exciting at the same time.

Judy Fisken was on duty at the gate and she remembered me from my earlier visits. First she sold us some tickets to go in, then made us a cup of tea, plugging in an electric kettle behind the counter, after our long drive. She sat with us at one of three small tables in the little outbuilding, which had the look of an old converted barn. She sat in front of a photograph of Prince Charles visiting the place, and chatted about how the Friends of Rosslyn were trying to get more people interested in visiting it to earn some money, as the building needed so much work.

The chapel itself was deserted when I took Chris across the gravel walkway and through the arched northern doorway. I was pleased it was so quiet, as it gave him an opportunity to experience the powerful personality of this incredibly carved building without distraction. Ever since I first visited it I have felt that Rosslyn Chapel seems to exude a sort of living spirituality. It has a solid feeling of the "here and now" which seems to melt imperceptibly into a sense of an infinite past. I knew Chris shared my fondness for church buildings, and I hoped he would respond to Rosslyn as positively as I had. It makes almost every other church I know seem lifeless and empty when compared with it. It's hard to describe the warm feeling I get when I go inside this medieval structure without sounding a tad fanciful. Whatever causes it, it makes me feel that I would be quite happy to sleep the night alone in it.

I took Chris round the nave and just let the atmosphere of the place wash over us. Then I went to show Chris the carvings of the maize [corn] and the aloe cactus which I had seen on earlier trips. As we were studying the cactus lintel a friendly looking lady vicar came in through the side door (in the north). She gave me a warm smile, came over, and asked if we had noticed the Indian maize. I told her that we had and asked her what she could tell me about it. Her name was the Reverend Janet Dyer, and she had a degree in botany. She also said her husband was a professional botanist.

"It's remarkable, isn't it?" She said glancing up at the frieze with the aloe cactus. "It could be something else . . . but if it isn't aloe then I don't know what is." She had then turned and pointed to the Indian maize arch. "My husband says that maize image is accurate, and it's probably a slightly immature plant."

She told me that there was a lot of documented evidence that a Prince Henry Sinclair, who was the first St. Clair Jarl of the Orkneys, had, with the help of Templar money, commissioned a fleet of twelve ships for a voyage to the New World. This fleet which was commanded by an Antonio Zeno was reported to have landed in Nova Scotia and explored the eastern seaboard of what is now the United States of America prior to 1400. She said that that date could be fixed with some degree of certainty because Henry Sinclair was murdered in Orkney in 1400.

She also told me that some of the members of the expedition died in America and that a knight by the name of Sir James Gunn was buried there. An image of this medieval knight had been found in Westford, Massachusetts, and it was believed to be his tombstone.

The Chapel has a nice Hamilton pipe organ in a loft high in its western end. I asked permission to have a look at it and Janet lent me the key to the loft. I also asked permission to play it, explaining I was a church organist. She gave me permission, and so I fired it up and played "Cwm Rhondda" with all the stops out.

Great fun! The acoustics were excellent and the tracker action had a positive feel and seemed in good repair. It has a nice thumpy diapason.

There's a good view of the layout from the loft, but it's odd there is no altar. There is a table which has been set up in the centre of the building because there is no room in the east, where an altar should be placed in a Christian church. There are three pillars in the way. Was it really built as chapel? There are three stone pedestals set against the wall behind the pillars but these are not altars. The symbolism is not just Christian. It looks Jewish, Christian and Celtic all mixed together. There's a star-studded ceiling, and vegetation sprouts from the mouths of the Celtic Green Men, which gets all tangled round pyramids. Moses has a pair of devil's horns; the towers of a Heavenly Jerusalem sit alongside engrailed crosses and square and compass lozenge shapes. The main Christian symbols are Victorian furnishings and in the stained glass windows, which give a superficial gloss of Christianity to the interior when the morning sunlight highlights the free-standing Madonna and child. But the stonework is something else.

The range of images which have been carved into these walls look more like a chance to show off than symbols to inspire Christian awe. I don't reckon this was built as a place of worship![453]

When I stood beside Chris and gazed round the interior, we looked up at the solid stone, three-foot-thick vaulted roof that runs the length of the nave and marveled at the heavy decoration. I had easily found the maize [corn] cobs arched over a window in the south wall and the aloe cactus appearing across a nearby lintel. Elsewhere, I could see many other recognizable plants, and everywhere there were manifestations of the "green man"—the Celtic figure that represented fertility. Over a hundred "green men" have been counted on the chapel walls, but it is believed that there are even more subtly peeping out of the vegetation. The chapel is a remarkable and magical place, with an odd mix of symbolism. It links Christianity with ancient Celtic folklore, and the "Templar" gravestone of what was described as a "St. Clair hero of the battle of Bannockburn" (1314), links the doomed order of warrior monks with the later St. Clair Charters of Freemasonry. Symbols of all these myths are everywhere. It is a unique building.

In the light of what I now knew, I needed to revisit the stories of Roslin. It is a place which easily inspires compelling myths. The vast surge of interest which *The Hiram Key* generated showed the potential, and when Dan Brown used that book as a source of inspiration for his thriller *The Da Vinci Code*, the hordes of his fans following the Rosslyn trail shows that the Chapel's power is not diminishing with age. But surely Roslin had not been built just as a seed for myth-making? Or had it?

I had now accumulated far more information about the St. Clairs of Roslin, and it was clear that they had been growing in political power until the time of William the Chapel-builder, and thereafter had rapidly declined into nonentities. In a book a called *The Second Messiah*, I had speculated that William St. Clair had made a play for the Crown of Scotland. Now is the time to look more closely at the background to my claim. But, as a preliminary, we need to look at the temper of the times in which William, 12th Baron Roslin, the Chapel-builder, was operating.

TURBULENT TIMES

The 290-year period from 1446 until 1736, the maximum duration of the St. Clair family's involvement with Freemasonry, was a turbulent one. The Renaissance popes were notoriously worldly individuals, practicing open abuses of power, such as simony, nepotism, and carefree financial excess, and their church was riddled with venality and immorality. This aroused a feeling the church had to be reformed, and a widespread movement arose within Western Christendom to restore the doctrines and practices that the reformers believed fitted a Biblical model of the church. The loss of papal control that resulted is now called the Reformation.

The Reformation began in Germany on October 31st, 1517, when Martin Luther, an Augustinian monk, priest and university professor at Wittenberg, posted 95 theses inviting debate over the legitimacy of the sale of indulgences on the door of his local church. The papacy saw this as a political threat to their profitable international dictatorship and labeled the freethinker a heretic.

Luther's three famous treatises of 1520, *An Open Letter to the Christian Nobility of the German Nation Concerning the Reform of the Christian Estate*, *On the Babylonian Captivity of the Church*, and *On the Freedom of a Christian*, won him widespread popular support. He thought that salvation was a free gift to all people through the forgiveness of sins by God's grace alone, and therefore a Pope was unnecessary. Not surprisingly, the papacy did not welcome the notion, and he was excommunicated in 1521. But Luther was clever, and later that year at the Diet of Worms (a general assembly held in the town of Worms), he stood before Holy Roman Emperor Charles V and the German princes, and refused to recant unless they could prove him wrong by either Biblical text or reason. They couldn't.

England had its own religious reform movement, which was loosely based on the ideas of Luther, but it was not motivated by a puritanical desire to stem papal excesses. Instead, it was a direct result of King Henry VIII's efforts to divorce his first wife, Catherine of Aragon. Henry's breakaway from papal power was masterminded by Thomas Cromwell, who piloted the Act in Restraint of Appeals through Parliament in 1533. A year later the Act of Supremacy defined royal control of the English Church. The Archbishop of Canterbury, Thomas Cranmer, authorized a new translation of the Bible and commissioned a Book of Common Prayer in English, dispensing with the Latin of Rome and making the church a national one.

The Church of England replaced the Roman Catholic Church, apart from a brief reversal from 1553 to 1558 during the reign of Queen Mary I, remembered as Bloody Mary. (She was the daughter of Henry VIII by the Catholic wife he had ditched because she did not bear him a male heir.) When her father and brother died, Mary restored Catholicism, re-established the traditional Latin services, and accepted the authority of the Pope. When she married the future Philip II of Spain, a Catholic, in 1554, this set off several rebellions, resulting in over three hundred Protestants being burned at the stake for their beliefs. She died in 1558, and Queen Elizabeth I then turned England into the permanently Protestant nation it remains.

The St. Clair family's religious history mirrored their country's. William the 12th Baron Roslin—the Chapel-builder—was a Catholic, William of the First St. Clair Charter, the 15th Baron, was still Catholic, but from then on until William the 19th Baron and first Grand Master Mason of Scotland, the family was Protestant. The religious function of Rosslyn Chapel is currently run by the (Protestant) Church of Scotland. But these reforms were all far in the future when William St. Clair (the 12th) sought papal permission to build the collegiate church at Roslin.

Two Williams but One True Cross

The concept of building a church as a way of demonstrating power and influence was popular during the fifteenth century. Remember, the website of Rosslyn Chapel says of William's motive:

> More than thirty-seven collegiate churches were built in Scotland between the reigns of James I and James IV (1406–1513). They were secular foundations intended to spread intellectual and spiritual knowledge, and the extravagance of their construction depended on the wealth of their founder.[454]

All the same, I suspect that William's motive went beyond a desire to impress the simple folk living around Roslin Glen with how rich he was.

Churches are repositories of myths. In particular, just to the north of Roslin in the city of Edinburgh was a church that resonated with some of the most powerful myths of Christianity, the Abbey of the Holy Rood ("rood" is an archaic word for "cross"). The *New Advent Catholic Encyclopedia* sums up the founding myth of the Abbey of the Holy Rood:

> Located in Edinburgh, Scotland; founded in 1128 by King David I for the Canons Regular of St. Augustine, probably brought from St. Andrews. The foundation is said to have been an act of thanksgiving for the king's miraculous escape from the horns of a hart, whilst hunting near Edinburgh on Holy Cross day. In the church was preserved, in a golden reliquary, the fragment of the True Cross brought by David's mother, St. Margaret.[455]

During his miraculous escape David had a vision of the Holy Cross arising before him and diverting the charging antlers of the enraged stag. He was so overwhelmed by this Divine Sign that God was on his side, and wished to preserve him as King of Scotland, that he built a large and imposing Abbey church to house a chunk of the True Cross. (That is, an actual piece of the tree trunk which had been used by the Romans to crucify Jesus nearly 1,100 years before some 1,800 miles away.) His sainted mother, Margaret (you will recall from chapter 3, a saintly ancestor is always useful if you want to be a really powerful king), had provided this relic for him.

The cult of relics was a powerful political tool, and one which the Templars' nemesis Philip the Fair of France had made full and free use of when he set up a church to house the relics of his grandfather St. Louis, who had been canonized for destroying the French economy in overseas adventures on behalf of the papacy. Now, according to the Sinclair Clan website, the family experienced at first hand the power to impress that came from having a "holy relic" and a church to enshrine it in, as the St. Clairs became Barons of Roslin by acting as the guardian of St. Margaret and her splinter of "true" cross:

> Malcolm III of Scotland . . . lived between 1031–1093 becoming King of Scotland in 1053 . . . In 1057, after Macbeth was killed, he became King of all Scotland. His first wife, Ingeborg, was the widow of Thorfinn, Earl of Orkney. When she died, he married Margaret, the sister of Edgar "the Atheling" who had come to Scotland with William "the Seemly" St. Clair and others from Hungary . . . She made William "the Seemly" St. Clair her cup-bearer because he was "perfect in all his members." The king gave him Roslin in "life-rent" but this was changed to "in free heritage" when William's son, Henry, took over when his father had been killed whilst fighting against the forces of his "cousin" William, "the Conqueror".[456]

William, the first Baron of Roslin, may have had a set of perfect members, but he didn't have any holy relics or enough money to build a shrine to keep any in. But as a favorite of Queen Margaret, he would have been well placed to observe how such devices were used to support royal privilege.

Margaret must have been a barrel of laughs for Malcolm, who (don't forget) had previously enjoyed a full married life with a worldly-wise and previously widowed Viking princess who had given him a male heir (Duncan II). According to the official website of the British Monarchy:

> Margaret had a strong influence over her husband, who revered her piety and secretly had jewel-encrusted bindings made for her religious books, which he himself was unable to read, never having learned to do so. [She] corresponded with Lanfranc, Archbishop of Canterbury, brought Benedictine monks to Dunfermline and did away with local usages in the Scottish Church. Margaret also began building what was later to be known as St. Margaret's Chapel, situated on the highest part of Edinburgh Castle.[457]

How she found the time to conceive the three sons and daughter she bore Malcolm[458] is not clear. But she was obviously entering into the spirit of providing future kings of Scotland and putting aside her early ambitions to become a nun.[459] She settled for being the sainted wife of the illiterate and rumbustious Malcolm, who spent most of his reign fighting the English (he invaded England no less than five times) and finally died in battle against them in Northumberland.[460] But she was not above laying on the odd demonstration of her special relationship with God to impress her husband's subjects. For example, "her book of the Gospels, richly adorned with jewels," was carelessly dropped into a river, but God made sure it floated to the surface and was recovered totally unharmed. But who could expect anything less from a woman of whom the *New Advent Catholic Encyclopedia* says:

> Her private life was given up to constant prayer and practices of piety. She founded several churches, including the Abbey of Dunfermline, built to enshrine her greatest treasure, a relic of the true Cross. Her book of the Gospels, richly adorned with jewels, which one day dropped into a river and was miraculously recovered, is now in the Bodleian library at Oxford. She foretold the day of her death, which took place at Edinburgh on 16 Nov, 1093, her body being buried before the high altar at Dunfermline.[461]

She was made a saint in 1250 by Pope Innocent IV, and soon afterwards went into the relic business personally. Her bones were dug up and displayed in a new shrine, specially built to house them, alongside her famous chunk of the "True" Cross at Dunfermline. They kept her skull in a separate box and gave to Mary Queen of Scots as a coronation gift (who must have been delighted with such a unique present). Then, after Mary lost her own head, Margaret's was sold off to a bunch of Jesuits at Douai, and was not finally put out of its posthumous wandering misery until it was destroyed during the French Revolution.

The remainder of her bones were given to Philip II of Spain, during the period when Elizabeth I had imprisoned Mary Queen of Scots and Philip was supporting her as heir to Elizabeth's crown. The reason for giving him Margaret's bones, at a time when the relationship between Elizabeth and her brother-in-law was still reasonably cordial, was clearly political. If Margaret's relics had remained in Scotland, then their shrine would have been a focus for any underlying Catholic discontent at a time when many influential families—and even the dissolute 15th Baron Roslin, William of the First St. Clair Charter—could have used them as a rallying point. Philip placed Margaret's surviving bits in two urns in the Escorial, the mausoleum of the Spanish Monarchs, but diplomatically managed to lose them forever. When Bishop Gillies of Edinburgh asked Pope Pius IX to give them back in the nineteenth century, they could no longer be found. So if you have ambitions towards sainthood, remember this story and reflect that it's not restful being a dead sainted queen! The to-ing and fro-ing of relics and shrines does, however, show the importance of relics as a means of supporting the Divine Right of Kings to boss everybody else around because God gave them permission to do so.

David I, Margaret's eldest son, saw the advantage of capitalizing on the mythical power of the famous relic his mother had owned. The legend of the Holy Rood is summarized in the *Cambridge History of English and American Literature* thus:

> Adam being on the point of death, Eve and Seth go to Paradise to ask . . . for the healing oil . . . Seth . . . is denied entrance [but] the angel gives him three pips [seeds] of cedar, cypress and pine. When Seth returns . . . Adam [is] already dead; he places the three pips under Adam's tongue, [before he] is buried by the four archangels in Paradise. The pips fructify in the ground, and from them spring three rods, which remain green until the time of Moses. Moses . . . finds that three rods have sprung up, one at his head, and one at each side. With these rods he makes sweet the bitter waters . . . David . . . carries them to Jerusalem, where there is a pit of water so bitter that none can taste of it. The rods are placed in it, and they join together into a mighty tree, the growth of which is marked by silver rings. After the death of David, Solomon attempts to use the tree for the building of the Temple; but, owing to the fact that it continually alters in length, this proves impossible, and it remains untouched within the sanctuary. Finally, when the Jews seek for a tree on which to crucify Christ, they remember this rood, and use part of it for the cross.[462]

David I of Scotland knew that his namesake, King David of Jerusalem, was the first hereditary king instituted by God. And the wood of the "True" Cross was made from seeds given by God to the line of David, and then used to prove his love through the death of His own Son. This piece of wood was a powerful symbol to have on your side. Its essence had been touched, in chronological order, by God, Michael the Archangel, Seth, Eve, Adam, Moses, David, Solomon, Jesus, and David's soon-to-be-sainted Mother. That is some pedigree for a king's relic! But, the full power of the myth could only be harnessed if David was seen to be favored by the patriarchs and guardian angels who oversaw the relic. He needed a miracle of his own, and, sure enough, he got one when he survived a stag attack.

> David I founded the Palace [of Holyrood] as an Augustinian monastery in 1128. The king had a vision in which a cross, or "rood." belonging to his mother St. Margaret appeared between the antlers of an attacking stag. Hence the Abbey's symbol—a stag's head, with its horns framing a cross.[463]

The holy relic of his mother saved the life of her beloved son, so that he might continue to rule the people of Scotland. What better sign could a king want that he was destined by God to do exactly as he chose? All he needed was a shrine that focused his subjects' attention on his miracle, rather than on his mother's piety. So he built a new Abbey of the Holy Rood conveniently close to Edinburgh castle, and moved the miraculous splinter from Dunfermline to Holyrood.

In 1259, more than a hundred years later, the moldering bits of Margaret's bones were dug up from under the floor at Dunfermline and put on display to fill the gap in its magical powers which David's removal of the Black Rood (as her piece of the Cross was called) had created. It may only be coincidence, but this was about the time Margaret's great-great-grandson, Alexander III, was pressured to pay homage to Henry III of England. He had replied, "to homage for my kingdom of Scotland no one has right except God alone, nor do I hold it except of God alone."[464] Creating a new shrine for his sainted ancestor who had brought the Holy Rood of God to his kingdom certainly did no harm to the morale of his subjects. The lesson of these actions is that successful kings of Scotland knew how to harness religious myths to drive political ambitions.

THE RISE OF THE ST. CLAIRS

But what was happening to the St. Clairs during this period? They were an ambitious family, and they built upon the Barony of Roslin that William I received from King Malcolm.

William I's son Henri (it would be several generations before the name was Anglicized to Henry) was confirmed the second Baron Roslin, and the barony was made hereditary by King Malcolm. Henri also acquired the Norse Jarldom of Pentland from Harald Hardrada, the King of Norway, either because of his Norse heritage and descent from Jarl Rognwald or possibly as a bribe to support King Harald Hardrada's invasion of England, which was defeated by King Harold Godwinson at the battle of Stamford Bridge in 1066. Despite, or possibly because of, the defeat at Stamford Bridge, the St. Clairs retained the title until 1470, providing eleven Barons of Pentland.

Henri's son, another Henri (3rd of Roslin) did little in the way of empire-building, but his son William (4th of Roslin) was granted the Barony of Cousland in Fife by King William I of Scotland (the King whose coat of arms was a red lion on a yellow background, still a potent symbol of Scotland). King William had tried to reconquer Northumbria, but was beaten in battle and taken captive by King Henry II of England. When he was eventually released, he had problems with his feudal nobles rebelling in southwest Scotland, because he had failed to defend them against the English.

William St. Clair appears to have been bribed to support King William by being given the Barony of Cousland. This title and its lands in Fife and around Edinburgh remained with the St. Clair family until 1470, during which time the family provided nine Barons of Cousland. The St. Clairs were steadily building a power base in both Scotland's Norse areas of Orkney, Shetland, and Caithness and in its Scottish areas. The next three barons, Henri (5th of Roslin), Henri (6th), and William (7th), did nothing to increase the family's holdings. But Henry (8th) took advantage of a Scottish crown weakened by the tussle for the Scottish succession between John Balliol and Robert the Bruce, and built himself a formidable castle at Roslin.

> The Castle as we now know it dates back to c. 1304 with the construction of a peel tower (the Lamp-tower). From that time onwards, whilst the castle remained the

seat of the powerful St. Clair family, it was much altered, rebuilt, enlarged, etc. It is described as having been strongly fortified with walls 9ft thick, accessible by a drawbridge and built on 5 levels . . . It was built just after the Battle of Roslin, fought on the Plains of Roslin in 1303.[465]

In this battle:

8,000 Scots led by John Comyn faced an English army numbering 30,000. This Battle of Roslin still ended in victory for the Scots, and gave the country new hope for independence from England.[466]

The battle was provoked by Henry St. Clair's decision to marry Lady Margaret Ramsay, sister of Sir Edward Ramsay of Dalhousie. This offended Sir John Segrave, whom Edward I had appointed as Governor of Scotland and Commander of Edinburgh Castle, who wanted to marry the lady himself.

In 1302 Sir John Segrave, now stationed in Carlisle, learned that Lady Margaret had consented to marry Sir Henry St. Clair. He was furious, and sent to Edward I asking for permission to invade Scotland. . . . since he [Edward] was planning a Scottish campaign for 1303 anyhow, he gave Segrave his backing. Segrave took his force of 30,000 men and discreetly crossed the border into Scotland, avoiding detection until he reached Melrose in the middle of February 1303. There he divided his force into three. Sir Robert Neville was to lead one division in taking Borthwick Castle, which was held by St. Clair's ally, Sir Gilbert Hay. The second division, under Sir Ralph Confrey, was to "protect" Lady Margaret's residence at Dalhousie. The final division would advance upon Henry St. Clair's seat of Roslin, led by Segrave and Ralph de Manton.[467]

Sir Henry's entry in the *National Dictionary of Biography* reads: "Warrior; captured by Edward I at Dunbar, 1296; exchanged 1299. Sheriff of Lanark 1305; fought for Bruce at Bannockburn; received pension 1328."[468] Henry St. Clair's action at Bannockburn (the battle where King Robert the Bruce defeated the English near Stirling) in 1314 has duly become part of the St. Clair mythology. Here is a statement from the recent *Templars in America*, which rather extends the facts of history but adds to the romance with a Templar link. Unfortunately, it ascribes this famous victory to the father, rather than the son, but why let facts get in the way of a good story?

Yet another Sir William St. Clair, the newly wed Baron of Roslin, destroyed three British [*sic.* English?] armies on his wedding day in 1303, before returning to Roslin Castle to consummate his marriage. This triple victory is known as the Battle of Roslin Moor and is commemorated by a memorial erected in Roslin village a few years ago. Sir William and his son, Sir Henry St. Clair, are believed to have led the charge of the Templar cavalry at the Battle of Bannockburn in 1314. The grave marker of Sir William St. Clair, decorated with Templar symbolism, has been preserved and now rests in the sanctity of Rosslyn Chapel.[469]

In the light of their ongoing animosity with Edward Longshanks of England, it is small wonder that the St. Clairs took the opportunity to build a strong castle to defend themselves. In the process, they employed a lot of Masons for a long period of time and paid them well. Here is the beginning of the Masons' affection for the St. Clair family.

After Edward I died in 1307, Henry 7th of Roslin was among the eight earls and forty-five barons who signed the Declaration of Arbroath in 1320. This was an important document because it limited the power of the King of Scots. (At that time the King was Robert I, also known as the Bruce.) The Constitution Society says of this document:

> Firstly it set the will and the wishes of the people above the King. Though they were bound to him "both by law and by his merits" it was so that their freedom might be maintained. If he betrayed them he would be removed and replaced . . . Secondly, the manifesto affirmed the nation's independence in a way no battle could, and justified it with a truth that is beyond nation and race. Man has a right to freedom and a duty to defend it with his life.[470]

The declaration, coincidentally, provides a proxy variable to suggest a pecking order for the supporters of King Robert. The list makes interesting reading; they signed in order of superiority, so it shows how the nobility of Scotland ranked themselves, from greatest to least powerful. Of the 53 signatories, Henry St. Clair was the twentieth.

If Henry St. Clair was the twentieth most important laird in Scotland in 1320, four generations later, William the Chapel-builder, and 12th of Roslin, had added most of the lands and power of the first, fourth, and seventh signatories on the list to the St. Clair holdings, and formed an alliance by marriage with the sixth. His additional private purchase of extensive lands would soon make him the most powerful man in Scotland and the Northern Isles. With Orkney about to become part of Scotland, a child king on the throne, and the crown in the hands of an unpopular regent, the power to depose a King of Scots, an act which the Declaration of Arbroath legitimized, must have been seen as a serious threat from a man like William St. Clair, who could command the loyalty of so many subjects.

The next baron, Henry's son—William the 9th Baron Roslin, did little to distinguish himself; to be fair to him, though he died young. The *Dictionary of National Biography* says: "Son of Sir Henry Sinclair (d. 1330); accompanied Sir James Douglas to take the heart of Bruce to Palestine; slain with him by Saracens in Andalusia."[471] His romantic gesture contributed to the growing legend of the St. Clairs but did little to increase their political power. However, his son Henry (10th of Roslin) we have met already: He was the same Norse pirate king, "Prince" Henry St. Clair, who seized the Jarldoms of Orkney and Shetland, built the great castle at Kirkwall, and encouraged smuggling trips to Greenland in defiance of the King of Norway.

William 9th's son, Henry 10th of Roslin, was also the first St. Clair Earl of Orkney. He is described by Willie Thompson in his *History of Orkney*:

Henry I [of Orkney and 9th of Roslin] had received political backing from the Scots, but that support had come mainly from the rebel fringe. Henry II married Egidia Douglas, heiress to Lord William Douglas of Nithsdale and grand-daughter of King Robert II, so his involvement in the affairs of the Scottish establishment was close, if not noticeably successful . . . In contrast to Henry I's "Viking Jarl" image, Henry II [of Orkney and 10th of Roslin] was a purely Scottish nobleman.[472]

The *Dictionary of National Biography* adds this snippet about him: "second Earl of Orkney, admiral of Scotland; captured at Homildon Hill 1402; taken by James I on voyage to France 1406."[473]

By 1420, at the succession of William the Chapel-builder (12th of Roslin), the St. Clair family was politically powerful. The list of this William's achievements is long, as his entry on the British Peerage website shows:

In 1421 he was a hostage for King James I when he was allowed to return to Scotland. He succeeded to the title of 3rd Earl of Orkney circa 1 February 1420/21. He held the office of Admiral of Scotland in 1438, and conveyed the Princess Margaret of Scotland to France to marry the Dauphin (later King Louis XI). He was created 1st Lord St. Clair [Scotland] in 1449. In 1453 he founded the Collegiate Church of Roslin, Midlothian. He held the office of High Chancellor of Scotland between 1454 and 1456. He was created 1st Earl of Caithness [Scotland] on 28 August 1455, in settlement of a claim to the Lordship of Nithsdale through his mother.[474]

What William lacked was a family shrine and a powerful relic to keep in it. If he had wanted to replace the under-age James III as Monarch of Scotland, then he would have needed something to match the power of Holyrood to inspire respect and confer Divine approval. This gets me at last to a realistic motive for building the chapel at Roslin.

CONCLUSIONS

The Masonic myths of Roslin tapped into a deep-seated belief system about the power of holy relics, which had served the kings of Scotland well since the time of Malcolm Canmore and his wife Saint Margaret. William, the 12th Baron Roslin, may well have built his chapel as an alternative focus of spiritual power for the St. Clair family, and I was beginning to suspect that it formed part of a wider plan to try to create a St. Clair kingdom in Scotland. Although, as we will see, the kingdom William envisaged was stillborn when King James's Regent broke William's power and split up his holdings, the chapel did become just such a spiritual power center.

But how did William the Chapel-builder manage to produce such a powerful focus for mythical inspiration? Over half a millennium after its construction, it still grips the popular imagination. Books are still written repeating its myths and attempting to interpret its motifs. Crowds of fans still line up to marvel at its stone complexity and bask in its spiritual presence. That is no mean achievement. And it poses the question of how it was done? Where did William learn such skills? There was obviously more I needed to know about William and his Chapel.

Despite the plethora of myths and legends about William the Chapel-builder, I couldn't find any sort of complete biography. I decided that I needed to build up a better picture of him. So let us see if we can sample the turbulent world of William St. Clair, and find out the power of relics, saints, and martyrs—not to mention kings and king-makers.

CHAPTER 12

RELICS, SHRINES, AND CROWNS

WILLIAM ST. CLAIR'S CATHEDRAL OF CODES

As a present-day focus for mythical inspiration, the chapel at Roslin (now, as we have seen, called Rosslyn Chapel) is superb. Edward Black, writing in *The Scotsman* on July 27, 2005, said:

> The 15th-century chapel, six miles south of Edinburgh at Roslin, has seen visitor numbers almost double from 38,000 in 2003 to over 68,000 in 2004 thanks to its portrayal . . . as the Cathedral of Codes . . . Last month it emerged the chapel is to get a new entrance as well as recruit more staff to cope with extra visitors . . . Stuart Beattie, the chapel's director . . . said: "The chapel has been a popular destination for hundreds of years. There are many stories in Rosslyn's long history and I'm sure the chapel will make a superb backdrop for this particular one."

Roslin/Rosslyn may be a long-term success story now, but it didn't always look as if it would turn out that way. The Chapel went into a steep decline after the death of William, the 12th Baron of Roslin and its builder. As a place used for Catholic worship and burial, it suffered during the Reformation. The chapel website says:

> The Chapel was generously endowed by the founder, with provision for a provost, six prebendaries [a type of priest] and two choristers, and in 1523 by his grandson, also Sir William, with land for dwelling houses and gardens. On February 26th, 1571, however, just forty-eight years after his last endowment, there is a record of the provost and prebendaries resigning because of the endowments being taken by "force and violence" into secular hands as the effects of the Reformation took hold.[475]

And this was only the beginning of a long decline. At the time of William 15th of Roslin, in 1589, it was described as a "house and monument of idolatrie, and not ane place appointit for teiching the word and ministratioun of ye sacramentis." In 1592 it ceased to be used as a house of prayer and fell into disrepair. But even this neglect did not stop further abuse, as we've seen: In 1650, during the British Civil War, Oliver Cromwell's troops under General Monk attacked Roslin castle and stabled their horses in the Chapel. Then, in 1688, it was sacked and vandalized by a mob from Edinburgh who thought it Popish and idolatrous.[476]

THE IMPORTANCE OF A GOOD BURIAL GROUND

William's motive for building Roslin Chapel, as given on its own website, can be summed up as saying that he built Roslin Chapel as a way of displaying ostentatious wealth.[477] But that is not how the myth tells it. So let's look a few other possibilities. Willie Thompson, in his *History of Orkney*, observes:

> The affairs of Roslin also prospered with the founding of an elaborate collegiate church in 1446 and the town's erection as a burgh of barony in 1456.[478]

Thompson thinks William built the chapel to raise the political value of his Scottish holdings and enhance his reputation at the Court of James II. David Stevenson, the non-Masonic historian interested in the history of the Craft, agrees it was built as to demonstrate wealth, but notes that the work of creating it had an unexpected Masonic consequence:

> The tradition of patronage of the mason craft by the Sinclairs of Roslin was connected somehow with the remarkable church of Rosslyn built by William Sinclair . . . Only the choir was ever built, but this fragment contains an elaboration of carved decoration unique in Scotland. The building of the choir and the amount and complication of the carving involved must have provided work for many masons for a prolonged period . . . and of course there was the hope of much similar work to come if the rest of the great church was built. In the circumstances it would have been understandable for the masons to have hailed their Sinclair employers as patrons and protectors of the craft . . . succeeding generations of masons must have been awed by it and struck by its uniqueness. In trying to account for this, the idea that the Sinclairs had some special relationship with the craft could have arisen.[479]

And Gould, although he does not mention the Chapel, picked up on the legend:

> It deserves to be remarked that in both these deeds [the two St. Clair Charters] the appointment of William Sinclair, Earl of Orkney and Caithness, to the office of Grand Master by James II of Scotland, is spoken of as a fact well known and universally admitted.[480]

By the late nineteenth century, the Masonic establishment in Scotland was accepting the link between the St. Clairs and Masonry, which Stevenson thinks arose as an accidental side effect of spending so much money on stone-carvers for the building work. Frederick Pohl thought the chapel was a mausoleum, and described it as:

> The St. Clair family's burial chapel . . . [a] fifteenth-century architectural masterpiece [with] a unique style of sculptural decoration.[481]

Pohl goes on to link the Chapel to Henry, the first Earl of Orkney, and while discussing William the Chapel-builder (12th Baron of Roslin) he notes.

> In Roslin, where he dwelt in luxury, he kept an almost regal court, with three hundred riding gentlemen continually in his house, and fifty-five gentlewomen, of whom thirty-five were noble ladies. He had a greater number of retainers than any feudal baron of his times. He built the chapel at Roslin, which became famous for its unique architectural features. It was intended to be a great collegiate church to take the place of the old Church of St. Matthew, which was in decay. It became the burial chapel of the Sinclairs. When the old church at Roslin was torn down, Henry's [First Earl of Orkney] armoured skeleton was laid to final rest in the chapel . . . The Norse tradition of tomb-fire and fire-boat burial haunts the chapel; for that building is said to appear to be on fire just before the death of any of Henry's descendants.[482]

The romantic idea of the armor-clad body of "Prince" Henry being translated, in the manner of a saint, to provide a focus for veneration within the new shrine to the St. Clairs makes mythical sense. Pohl instinctively realized that something about Roslin Chapel was able to grip the hearts and minds of the St. Clair supporters, and he seeks to explain it. This is because he believes William's reason for building the chapel was as a grander replacement for the decaying old church of St. Matthew, where generations of a much-loved and respected family had been interred since the time of William the Seemly, the first Baron Roslin. But Pohl was simply letting his writer's nose for a good story take him further than the facts allow.

Roslin did not replace a decaying old church, and the armor-clad bones of the eleven previous St. Clair barons were not reverently transferred into the crypt of the new building. The first Baron Roslin to be buried in Roslin Chapel was William the Chapel-builder. One of his motives does seem to have been to create a high-status burial vault for his family's future use, and he was so successful in this that the myth of the St. Clair burial ground seeped backwards to include his predecessors, many of whom have no known grave. (For instance, Willie Thompson notes that "Prince" Henry was killed in Orkney around the year 1400, but the exact circumstances of his death and the fate of his body are unknown.[483])

Pohl seems to have been influenced by Sir Walter Scott's poem "Rosabelle:"

> Seem'd all on fire that chapel proud,
> Where Roslin's chiefs uncoffin'd lie,
> Each Baron, for a sable shroud,

Sheathed in his iron panoply . . . .
Blazed battlement and pinnet high,
Blazed every rose-carved buttress fair—
So still they blaze, when fate is nigh
The lordly line of high Saint Clair.

As a burial ground with built-in pyrotechnic advertising for new occupants, Roslin seems to have captured the market. William the Chapel-builder certainly knew the trusted adage that all rulers need a good burial ground, and was following the precedent set by the MacAlpin kings of Scotland when they covered over the burial ground of the Norse kings on Iona and made the *Reilig Odhrain* their own, as we saw earlier.

THE PROS AND CONS OF PORTABLE RELICS

The focus of power provided by the grave of St. Columba dispersed when his moldering bones were dug up and shared out as good-luck tokens between the Irish and Scottish kings.[484] The Scottish kings realized that a more powerful, portable relic was needed to channel the support of St. Columba from this remote island to where they fought and ruled.

Their solution was simple and practical. Taking inspiration from the story of Moses, who created the Ark of the Covenant to contain the Ten Commandments, they fabricated a small chest in the shape of Columba's monastic cell, and placed inside it a text copied by Columba's own hand. This miniature ark (about four and a half inches long), called the Brecbennoch, was carried by its guardian monks before the Scots army in the way the Israelites had carried the Ark of the Covenant. Columba's biographer Ian Finlay tells us: "If it were carried thrice, sunwise, around the army . . . victory must follow."[485]

In this way, the House of Alpin drew down the heavenly support of St. Columba via his most important relic, which is now known as the Monymusk reliquary. An Abbey was built at Arbroath to house the ark or reliquary. (Control of this important national relic explains in part why the Abbot of Arbroath was chosen to draft the famous Declaration of Arbroath, which I discussed in Chapter 11.) After the battle of Bannockburn, where the Abbot had been delegated to carry the reliquary as part of Robert the Bruce's battle plan, and had clearly not enjoyed this military duty, he passed responsibility for it to the Monymusk Priory:

> In 1314, after having been at the battle of Bannockburn, Bernard, Abbot of Arbroath, with consent of his chapter, no doubt to avoid further military service, granted the Brecbennoch [the reliquary] and its lands to Malcolm the Prior of Monymusk, on condition that he should perform in their name the military service connected with it.[486]

The National Museum of Scotland, which now houses it, says of the reliquary:

This shrine is believed to be linked to St. Columba, who brought Christianity to much of Scotland. Made around the 8th century AD, it shows how finely crafted objects were important to the Church. Although distinctively Irish in shape the ornament is characteristically Pictish. Some believe that the shrine is the famed Brecbennoch, carried before Robert the Bruce's army at the Battle of Bannockburn in 1314.[487]

Historian Robert Hale confirms that "Robert Bruce . . . was the last king of Scots to carry Columba's relics into battle. The reliquary called the Brecbennoch, now in the Museum of Antiquities Edinburgh, was trooped through the Scottish ranks on the morning of the epic victory of Bannockburn."[488]

The way in which King Malcolm Canmore drew upon Columba and Iona shows that he realized the power of traditional sacred sites where you could bury your noble ancestors for the peasants to visit. But once he married Margaret, he quickly realized that a fragment of the "True" Cross was potentially far more powerful than one of Columba's old scribblings, which he didn't control and had to get the Abbot of Arbroath's permission to use.

The history of inspirational buildings and sites in Scotland is littered with similar examples of ways in which they have been used as political tools. In particular, the Abbey of the Holy Rood (and its relic, St. Margaret's Black Rood of Scotland), have a very checkered history. In 1072 King Malcolm invited some Benedictine monks from Canterbury to come to Scotland to build a Priory Church at Dunfermline to house his wife's religious treasure. (In due course Malcolm planned also that he and his descendants would be buried there and have a community of monks on hand to pray for their souls.)

As a direct result Dunfermline was a place of pilgrimage for two hundred years. (The complex was extended into an Abbey in 1150 and rededicated to the Holy Trinity.) Scots came to marvel at a heaven-sent relic that had demonstrated God's personal support for the dynasty that sprang from the union of King Malcolm Canmore and his sainted second wife, Margaret: the Royal House of Atholl.

I noted in chapter 2 the importance of relics in general and to the Templars in particular, and their potent political power. (Perhaps the most unscrupulous act of the trade in politically powerful relics occurred when the "Crown of Thorns"—yes, the one Jesus wore during his crucifixion—was sold by King Baldwin II of Jerusalem to King Louis IX of France, who then built a shrine to house it.) The "True Cross," from which all later fragments came, was said to have been found in the year 326 by the mother of Constantine I, the Empress Helena, who, naturally, was made a saint for her efforts.

During the crusades, many fragments of the "True Cross," including the one known as the Black Rood of Scotland, had made their way to Europe. It had been an astute political move by David I to link the goodwill of this relic to his own Divine

Right to rule. And his mother, Margaret, when she became a saint, gave her descendants a hotline to God. With such support, who would question their right to rule?

But this then raises another question: Why, knowing the successful history of the Black Rood, should Robert Bruce revert to using the Brecbennoch at Bannockburn in 1314? The answer is simple. The Bruce had lost control of the Black Rood (and Scotland's other portable dynastic relic, the Stone of Destiny), and so this was the only mobile relic he had left to use.

Here is an outline of the vicissitudes of the Black Rood. After Margaret brought it to Scotland, it lived in Dunfermline Abbey until David I built Holyrood to house it. During the troubled times after the death of Alexander III in 1286 it was stored in Edinburgh Castle. Edward I took the Castle from John Balliol in 1296 and seized the Rood as part of the spoils of war (along with the Stone of Destiny—now better known as the Stone of Scoon). He hauled it around with his cortège for while, using it to scare feudal lords who made oaths holding it, revealing who they thought should be the next King of Scots. These were recorded in the Ragman Roll, a copy of which can be seen on the web.[489]

When he had finished browbeating Scottish nobles with it, Edward sent the Black Rood to Westminster for safe-keeping. In 1328 it was returned to Scotland under the Treaty of Northampton, drawn up between Robert Bruce (Robert I) and Edward III of England, which guaranteed Scotland's independence and finally put an end to the ambitious plans for English domination started by Edward I.[490] So Bruce brought the Black Rood home to Holyrood, but England kept the Stone of Scoon (as it was then known) until the twentieth century. Then, when King David II set out to invade England in 1346, he took the Black Rood with him. He thought that carrying such a powerful relic would guarantee his victory. It didn't. Just outside Durham, he was defeated,[491] and the Black Rood was carried off in triumph to Durham Cathedral.[492] (Later, unfortunately, it was looted and mislaid when the Cathedral was sacked during the Reformation.)

As I will show, William the Chapel-builder (12th of Roslin) was politically astute. He was prepared to use each and every political tool at his disposal, and I believe he was aware that relics and sacred shrines have a political dimension. But the Black Rood was no help to the St. Clairs, so if William wanted a similar political tool he needed something at least as emotive. He took his inspiration from a building, St. Magnus's Cathedral in Orkney, and built something equally powerful.

The Effectiveness of Political Relics

All this highlights the problems of the different classes of relics as political tools. Buildings cannot be stolen, but they can be destroyed. The English managed to sack Holyrood Abbey with monotonous regularity. Edward II plundered it in 1322 and Richard II burned it in 1385, but it was soon restored by the Scots' kings.

During the Reformation, much of the Abbey outbuildings were destroyed, and the church itself was finished off by followers of John Knox in 1567. James VII tried to rebuild it in 1685, but made a poor job of it, and the roof fell in soon afterwards, leaving it the romantic ruin it is today.

Sacred isles are a safer bet. Nobody has ever managed to steal or demolish Iona, even though its Abbey has been ravaged more than once.

The tug of war over the Black Rood shows the vulnerability of a portable relic. The Stone of Destiny gives another good example of the problem. This was also a relic of St. Columba, but was linked by legend back to the Patriarch Jacob and through him to the Archangel Michael, who wrestled with him before Jacob slept on the stone, using it as a pillow, and had his vision of ladders reaching to Heaven. I had researched its legendary provenance in a previous book, *Uriel's Machine*:

> According to legend, Teamhair was an Israelite princess of the royal line of David, who came to Ireland and married Eochaid, to form the first royal family of Ireland. A few miles to the south of the Boyne Valley complex of megalithic sites is the Hill of Tara, where the ancient High Kings of Ireland were acclaimed by placing their foot on the Lia Fail, the Stone of Destiny. This magical stone was said to have been brought from Jerusalem by the Prophet Jeremiah when he took Teamhair the daughter of King Zedekiah to the safety of Ireland to escape the wrath of the invading Babylonian King, Nebuchadnezzar. According to Jewish legends, Hezekiah's daughters escaped because they were taken by Jeremiah to an island in the far north. The Stone of Destiny was said to have belonged to Jacob, the founder of the land of Israel . . . It is said that this stone was taken to Scotland by Columba where it became the king-making Stone of Scone, upon which all kings and queens of England since Edward I (including Queen Elizabeth II) have had to sit when they are crowned.[493]

When linked to an ancient mound, this stone was a key part of the ritual of making a King or Queen of Scots, and I had researched this aspect also in a different book, *Freemasonry and the Birth of Modern Science*:

> The traditional crowning place of the King of the Scots, since the times of King Malcolm MacAlpin, had been at Scoon, just outside Perth. The traditional coronation stone which had once been used in the ceremonies at Moot Hill had been removed to Westminster Abbey in 1296 by Edward I of England . . . To this day the kings and queens of England have to be crowned while sitting above the stone of Scoon . . . the power of this stone created a legitimate king: The jewel-studded regalia takes second place to that piece of rough and apparently valueless stone on which the sovereign sits for the actual crowning. No doubt a desire to perpetuate an ancient custom could account for the continued use of this Coronation Stone, but this does not explain the origin of this custom; why this particular stone was chosen or the veneration in which it has always been held by people of the British race. According to tradition . . . for nearly a thousand years, the kings of Ireland were crowned while seated on it. It was then taken to Scotland and used for the same purpose until Edward I took it to Westminster.[494]

The link with St. Columba was strong, as he was reputed to have made a prophecy about the stone:

> Except old seers do feign and wizard wits be blind. The Scots in place must reign, where they this stone do find.[495]

And Columba was considered a powerful saint to have on your side, hence the popularity of his relics.

Roslin—The New Relic

William St. Clair had no relics to use as political tools, and he did not have a building or a sacred isle. Notwithstanding that, though, he created a focus which has lasted as long as the Stone of Destiny. Michael Baigent and Richard Leigh, in *The Temple and the Lodge*, describe Rosslyn Chapel as:

> A cathedral in miniature . . . overload, dripping with Gothic carvings and floridly intricate embellishments . . . like a fragment of Chartres, transplanted to the top of a Scottish hill . . . a focus for secrets and for legends.[496]

As a focus for legends, it remains an enormous success. Some modern writers, like Tim Wallace-Murphy and Marilyn Hopkins, link it specifically to the Knights Templar:

> Rosslyn Chapel is a temple to the spirituality and mysticism that transcends all of the great religions and yet pervades each on of them . . . [it] . . . is a memorial to the heretical order of the Knights Templar . . . an enigmatic, arcane library of secrets, sculpted in stone and shrouded in mystery. What gives Rosslyn Chapel its reputation today as a unique shrine is the variety, candour, and exuberance of its carvings which certainly have no equal anywhere else in Britain.[497]

Each successive book or writer seeks to outdo previous attempts to capture the mystery that is Roslin, witness this passage from *Templars in America*:

> The carvings within Rosslyn Chapel represent, with powerful symbolism, nearly every known spiritual pathway that had impinged upon European consciousness prior to the date of its foundation. There is a chaotic mixture of spiritual symbols from the Celtic worlds of Western Europe, Norse and Saxon pagan beliefs, the initiatory practice of Zoroastrianism, the worship of Ishtar and Tammuz from Babylonia, the Mithraic mysteries, Judaic traditions, and, scattered here and there, occasional references to esoteric aspects of Christianity. The all pervading theme that unites these disparate spiritual streams is that of a hymn to nature in all its bounty so beloved of the medieval Christian mystics.[498]

Thriller writer Dan Brown summed up the wilder aspects of speculation when he wrote this about the Chapel in his blockbuster novel *The Da Vinci Code:*

Rosslyn Chapel—often called the Cathedral of Codes—stands seven miles south of Edinburgh, on the site of an ancient Mithraic temple. Built by the Knights Templar in 1446, the chapel is engraved with a mind-boggling array of symbols from the Jewish, Christian, Egyptian, Masonic and pagan traditions . . . For centuries, this stone chapel had echoed with whispers of the Holy Grail's presence. The whispers had turned to shouts when ground-penetrating radar revealed the presence of an astonishing structure beneath the chapel—a massive subterranean chamber. Not only did this deep vault dwarf the chapel atop it, but it appeared to have no entrance or exit. Archaeologists petitioned to begin blasting through the bedrock to reach the mysterious chamber, but the Rosslyn Trust expressly forbade any excavation of the sacred site. Of course, this only fueled the fires of speculation. What was the Rosslyn Trust trying to hide?[499]

My own view on the nature of Roslin Chapel, expressed in *The Hiram Key* some ten years earlier, is that:

Rosslyn is a spiritual interpretation of Herod's Temple . . . but not a free interpretation of the ruins in Jerusalem; as far as the foundation plan is concerned, it is a very carefully executed copy. The unfinished sections of the great western wall are there, the main walls and the pillar arrangements fit like a glove and the pillars of Boaz and Jachin stand precisely at the eastern end of what would be the inner Temple.[500]

But to understand the inspiration of the chapel was not to fathom why William had spent so much time and money building what might have been just a rich man's folly. However, now that I had looked far more closely into the political significance of the cult of relics—particularly as developed to support the Scottish crown, via the myth of the Black Rood and St. Margaret—it was starting to make more sense. I remembered something Willie Thompson had said about the early days of William's rule as third Earl of Orkney:

Evidence of continuity is to be found in the whole technology of rural life . . . old habits of thought, superstition, and story formed a continuing basis for the Orcadian's mental world . . . [And] Earl William's first entry into public life had been in Orkney where he had skilfully out-manoeuvred his ex-guardian, David Menzies of Weem, seized control of the islands and forced Denmark to recognise him as earl.[501]

What had William learned about relics during his battle to take Orkney from David Menzies?

WILLIAM ST. CLAIR, POLITICAL PRAGMATIST

William recognized that living out a good story was a means to achieve political power. In Orkney, he drew on the almost legendary status of his grandfather, "Prince" Henry, as an Orkney Jarl in the traditions of the Sagas. His father Henry II had never visited Scandinavia. But when William, 12th of Roslin and 3rd of

Orkney, was faced with displacing his uncle David—an unpopular regent of Orkney during Henry's reign and William's minority—he did it in the traditional Norse way: first presenting himself to the people of Orkney as their new Earl and receiving their acclamation, and then sailing to Copenhagen to demand the benefit of installation from the king. He was turned down, but still managed to outmaneuver his Uncle David in a swashbuckling move worthy of the *Orkneyinga Saga*, as we shall see.[502]

William had also seen how holy relics could reinforce the will of a ruler in the way that St. Margaret's chunk of waste timber—once "miraculously" transformed by its vendor into a piece of the True Cross—had become a force powerful enough to create the great abbeys and palaces at Dunfermline and Holyrood, which in turn could show subjects that God was on the side of their temporal Lords. The continuous streams of pilgrims coming to venerate the holy relics were a self-reinforcing system of support which had great political value. And William had already proved he knew how to harness folk myths to aid his cause.

In medieval times, the central focus of the spiritual world was the Temple in Jerusalem. Its central role in the Old Testament, and its importance as a symbol of God granting a Divine Right to Rule to ordained kings, ensured the all western rulers took its meaning seriously. Its loss to the Muslims, who also venerated the site for their own religious reasons, formed one of the motives for the Crusades. Maps of the time show it as the center of the world. A portable relic such as the Black Rood could be removed and used against its owner, as Edward I had demonstrated by carrying it off to Westminster in the early 1300s. But a temple could not be moved, and was a well-proved way of creating a focus for spiritual inspiration and support. Was William St. Clair's decision to build a spiritual interpretation of the ruins of Temple Mount in Roslin a move of inspired political cunning? It was beginning to look that way.

William was a busy man with limitless political ambitions, as his entry in the *Dictionary of National Biography* shows:

> SINCLAIR, Sir WILLIAM, third earl of Orkney and first earl of Caithness (1404?–1480), chancellor of Scotland; son of Henry Sinclair, second earl of Orkney; hostage for James I, 1421; acknowledged Norwegian jurisdiction on investiture with earldom, 1434; as high admiral of Scotland conveyed Princess Margaret to France, 1436; summoned to Norway, 1446; there probably received diploma setting forth pedigree; began foundation of Roslin, 1446; assisted in repelling English invasion, 1448; created Lord Sinclair, 1449, and Earl of Caithness, 1455; chancellor of Scotland, 1454–6; active against the Douglases; one of the regents and ambassador to England, 1461; resigned Orkney to Scottish crown, 1471, receiving lands in Fife and a pension in exchange; envoy to England, 1472–3.[503]

Despite studying the St. Clair family for many years, I realized I really knew surprisingly little about William the 12th Baron of Roslin. His ancestors William the Seemly, the romantic cup-bearer for the Sainted Queen Margaret, who founded the Roslin dynasty, and Henry, his grandfather, who became a pirate king in true Norse-saga fashion, both emerged as fully rounded characters whose motivations I could understand. Among his descendants, the William of the First St. Clair Charter looks like an eccentric rogue with a taste for the ladies, and his son, of the Second St. Clair Charter, appears as a strait-laced political opportunist. Even William the first Grand Master of Freemasons emerged from the pages of Masonic history as a schemer down on his luck and prepared to cooperate in all sorts of political skullduggery to earn a few bucks. But William the Chapel-builder was still a shadowy figure whose image seemed to be made up from the smoke and mirrors of the legend that clings to his great creation.

I had already created a timeline of the Barons of Roslin, and had added to it the various other titles they had acquired and the dates on which they acquired them. This made one thing clear: It was on the Chapel-builder's watch that the St. Clairs of Roslin peaked in terms of the titles and lands they held. For a while I have suspected that William became the most powerful noble in Scotland at a time when the succession to the Scottish Crown was wobbly, but I had not yet checked the full facts. Now, as I mapped out the timeline of events and the accumulation of titles, I saw just what threats and opportunities the politics of the time presented. It was also clear that after William the 12th, the power of the St. Clair family was never again so strong or so centralized under the hand of one man.

In 1437 King James I of Scotland, who had been held captive in England during his early life, along with some formal hostages (including at various times both William the 12th and his father Henry the 9th of Roslin), returned to have a protracted battle with his corrupt and out-of-control parliament, and ended up being murdered in Perth. His son James II was crowned at the age of six and spent his childhood and adolescence being used, or rather abused, by a series of self-seeking guardians. When he took power in 1449, he found that many of the noble families, in particular the Lords of the Isles and the Douglases, were close to open revolt. By 1460 James II was at war with the English, and he died during the siege of Roxburgh Castle at the age of twenty-nine. His son James III was crowned King of Scots at the age of nine, and another series of regents fought over Scotland until James took control after his marriage to Margaret of Denmark in 1469. William lived through this period and prospered, reaching some of the highest state offices of Scotland. He would have been a remarkable man if he had not felt some ambitions for the crown once he had consolidated his holdings by 1465.

I decided that, if I was to understand William and his chapel, then I would need to do a little data-mining for as many datable facts as I could find, to build up a profile of his actions. I collected dates on his appearances at court, his awards, and the births, marriages, and deaths that mattered to him, and from these facts, a driven man emerged. Previously my impressions of him had been colored by some of the more popular writers who held him in mystical respect. This description from Tim Wallace-Murphy and Marilyn Hopkins is typical:

> The fascinating and complex character of Earl William St. Clair has a strong bearing on any analysis of the meaning of the spiritual and artistic content of the carvings with the chapel . . . had Earl William St. Clair gained the spiritual ability to look backwards and forwards through time and foresee the dramatic change in human consciousness when human thinking would gain a new objective to gain mastery over nature itself?[504]

He is portrayed as some kind of intellectual giant, sensitive and with great artistic talent. But the facts tell a different story.

THE HIDDEN POLITICAL LIFE OF THE REAL WILLIAM ST. CLAIR

William was born in 1404, so he never knew his grandfather Jarl Henry, who had died four years before. He spent his early years at Roslin or in Edinburgh, as his father never traveled to Orkney.

William's father Henry is described by Willie Thompson as "a purely Scottish nobleman" (that is, interested in his affairs in Scotland, not in his Norwegian Jarldom of Orkney) and an "absentee" Earl who took "little part in part in the government of Orkney."[505] During Henry's tenure and William's minority, Orkney was run on behalf of the St. Clairs, as we have seen, by Henry's brother-in-law, David Menzies of Weem. Henry's lack of attention to Orkney, combined with David Menzies' poor management of the local people, gave Thomas Sinclair, Henry's cousin, a chance to appeal to the King of Denmark (Denmark, Norway, and Sweden had become one kingdom by this time) to be appointed a Warden to look after the King's interests. This happened in 1419, the year before Henry died, and put his continued tenure of the Earldom at risk.

When William became Earl designate in 1420, his Uncle David was appointed his guardian, and returned to Orkney to act in William's name as Earl-regent. As his mistreatment of the Orcadians had started the problems that Thomas Sinclair was complaining about to the King of Denmark, this cast still more doubt on the continued St. Clair tenure of the Earldom. It began to look as if young William could lose control of Orkney and its revenue streams.

And there were other factors in play too. His father Henry had been a well-known figure at the Scottish Court of Robert III, which was riven with internal battles for supremacy between the Scots-speaking Lowlands and the Gaelic-speaking Highlands. Soon after King Robert III's coronation in 1390 his brother Robert, Earl of Fife, made a statement claiming King Robert was not capable of ruling the kingdom. The other nobles made him Governor of the Realm. Robert III's royal income was greatly reduced, and lawlessness grew in Scotland. The Earl of Fife then persuaded Robert's queen, Annabelle, to make him Duke of Albany and seemed set to oust his brother and take the throne for himself.

In 1406 Henry St. Clair, as High Admiral of Scotland, was given the job of taking King Robert's heir, James I, to safe exile in France. Unfortunately, he was captured en route by the English and imprisoned with James in the Tower of London. King Robert was said to be so upset at the news that he took no further food and died within a few days. This left the new King of Scots an English hostage, and the Duke of Albany Regent of Scotland until he died in 1420. Given that Henry St. Clair had spent much of his tenure as Earl of Orkney, acting as a hostage with King James of Scots in the Tower of London, it is not surprising that he was an absentee Earl.

These events left William in a precarious position. His father's flight to France with James I and their subsequent capture by the English did not win him any favors from Robert of Albany, so he was unlikely to have been able to capitalize on his father's rank at the Court of Robert III. In addition, his father's enforced neglect of his northern holdings, Orkney and Pentland (both feudal Earldoms from the combined crowns of Norway, Denmark, and Sweden), put the political future of the St. Clairs at risk of collapse. Only the strength of his castle at Roslin, its closeness to Edinburgh, and the fact his father Henry was held captive alongside King James I protected William during this period of political meltdown in Scotland.

As I previously noted, the *Dictionary of National Biography* reports that William became an English hostage for James I in 1421, but the official Treaty of London, which freed James in return for twenty-one noble hostages to be imprisoned in his place, was not signed until December 1423, coming into force the following year. The most likely explanation of this mismatch of dates is that William traveled south around the time of the death of his father—he may possibly have been called to Henry's deathbed. Certainly he did not stay in England, as the following year he went to Orkney.

William's trip to Orkney was not motivated by a nostalgia to see the marine vistas of his grandfather's Jarldom, but a necessary measure to preserve his family's political power. King Eric of Denmark had just given control of the St. Clair stronghold, Kirkwall Castle (built by Jarl Henry I in defiance of an agreement with Norway), to Bishop Tulloch of Orkney. The St. Clairs' grip on Orkney was slipping fast, and all the ill-will that William's uncle David had sown over the years was turning on the family. And the situation for William was desperate, for David was not going to relinquish Orkney to him easily.

At this point, William capitalized on the local reputation of his grandfather Jarl Henry. By 1422, William, now aged eighteen, arrived in Orkney to ask his uncle to hand over the Earl's seal. David refused. William resorted to the tradition of St. Olaf's Law and called a convention of Orcadian gentry to support his claim to take over the Earldom, but his uncle had a tight enough grip to make sure that no one of any consequence supported William. William's next move was to take his petition to Copenhagen, where the Scandinavian Royal Court sat, and present his case to the King; he was supported by his cousin Thomas St. Clair and the Archdeacon of Shetland.[506] The King decided not to install young William as Earl of Orkney. But when his uncle David rushed to Copenhagen and made a counter-claim, he was also turned down.

William solved this impasse with a neat political trick. During his 1421 visit to England, he must have met James I and seems to have won his confidence. By 1423 the Treaty of London was in the process of negotiation, and William sug-gested that David Menzies would be a suitably powerful noble to have the honor of becoming an English hostage to allow King James I to return to Scotland. How could David refuse? In his *History of Orkney*, Willie Thompson comments:

> It seems not improbable that David Menzies selection as one of the Scottish hostages was deliberately engineered by William to remove his obstructive guardian from Orkney.[507]

In 1424 William took physical control of Orkney, and David went into English confinement. The Danish Court, hearing of the problems, summoned William to Copenhagen. But with the support of the gentry of Orkney, who seemed to admire his daring coup (which harked back to the great times of Jarl Henry), he was able to produce a petition from the Orcadians assuring Denmark that all was well. William declined to attend in person to deliver the letter, as he said he was "preoccupied with his Scottish affairs."[508] And he probably was, as James I had now returned to Edinburgh and was in the process of carrying out a vast bloodletting with his uncle's family.

Murdoch, James I's cousin, who had succeeded as Duke of Albany during James's absence in England, had the honor of starring in the first public execution in Scotland for a hundred years. The establishment of Scotland was about to undergo a massive shake-up, and William, now aged twenty, was placed to benefit from it, as his influence over James's choice of hostages demonstrates. At this time Elizabeth, the woman who would eventually become his first wife, married John Stewart, Third Earl of Buchan and son of Robert Stewart, Duke of Albany and son of King Robert II. She was the daughter of Archibald the Fourth Earl of Douglas, Lord Warden of the Marches, and his wife Margaret Stewart, who was the daughter of King Robert III. If she had had sons, they would have been serious contenders for the Scottish Crown, but she only had one daughter by her first husband, a girl called Margaret.

Meanwhile, William was showing the beginnings of political skill in his han-dling of the Danish Court. He managed to sucker Queen Philippa into investigat-ing what became known as "The Complaint of the People of Orkney" into the regentship of David Menzies. As Willie Thompson comments, "It suited William to encourage such investigations. He had seized power illegally from Menzies who held Orkney by royal grant, so allegations of misrule by Menzies could be used to justify, or at least excuse his actions."[509] The matter dragged on through 1426, with Bishop Thomas Tulloch of Orkney summoned to give evidence in Copenhagen and to discuss the renewal of the Treaty of Perth, which gave sovereignty of the Western Isles to Scotland in return for an annual rent that had not been revised for years. The Scots had in the same treaty confirmed Norway's right to grant the Earldoms of Orkney and Shetland.

The negotiations dragged on for years. Meanwhile, William was refining his political skills. In 1434 he persuaded James I to suggest to King Eric that as part of the deal, William, now thirty, was confirmed by Denmark as Earl of Orkney and Shetland. Eric did so, but inserted a clause in the deal that committed William to get James I to affix his seal to the documents which installed William as the Third Earl of Orkney. This would have confirmed that the King of Scots accepted Denmark's right to assign the Earldom. It never happened, because James was murdered before William was officially installed as Earl.

James had not been a popular king. His strong views on the role of kings and their Divine right to rule are perhaps best expressed in one of the poems he wrote:

> God gives not Kings the style of Gods in vain,
> For on his Throne his Sceptre do they sway:
> And as their subjects ought them to obey,
> So Kings should fear and serve their God again
> If then ye would enjoy a happy reign,
> Observe the Statutes of your heavenly King,
> And from his Law, make all your Laws to spring:
> Since his Lieutenant here ye should remain,
> Reward the just, be steadfast, true, and plain,
> Repress the proud, maintaining aye the right,
> Walk always so, as ever in his sight,
> Who guards the godly, plaguing the profane:
> And so ye shall in Princely virtues shine,
> Resembling right your mighty King Divine.[510]

His first act as King was to reintroduce public executions at Stirling Castle, having Murdoch, Duke of Albany and both his sons beheaded along with the Earl of Lennox. He followed this up by arresting Alexander, Lord of the Isles, and decided to renew the "Auld Alliance" with France by offering his daughter in marriage to the Dauphin. He ran a totalitarian regime, played favorites (an example being his active support for William St. Clair's illegal seizure of Orkney from the guardianship imposed by Denmark), and taxed the church when it exported gold bullion to Rome. He showed little interest in the noble establishment of Scotland, and began to act like a total despot, passing laws which restricted the traditional rights of his nobles. He was murdered at Blackfriars in Perth by Sir Robert Graham, with the eager support of the Earl of Athol.

Prior to this, in 1436, James had made William St. Clair High Admiral of Scotland, the office his father had filled during James's minority and imprisonment. William had only just returned to Scotland when James died. He had sailed to France with James's daughter Margaret to deliver her for her marriage. He attended that marriage as the personal representative of King James I. When James was murdered, the new King was a child of six, and so the government of Scotland was again up for grabs. The Earl of Douglas seized the regency and began a period of political skullduggery that would last until 1449.

How to Become a Norse Saint

William now needed to consolidate his position with his Norse holdings, as there was no certainty that he would be able to maintain his position in Scotland. By now, he was becoming more attractive to the Danish Court, as he was a known quantity in an uncertain relationship with Scotland. When a country's nobles murder its King, it engenders distrust in the monarchs of its neighbors. In such a circumstance, William was perceived as loyal to his murdered King by the Danish Court, because of James's letter of support.

In 1446, he was invited to Copenhagen to be installed as Earl of Orkney and Shetland. This time, he went. The *Dictionary of National Biography* says that he "there probably received diploma setting forth pedigree." This was the lineage which linked him, via his grandfather "Prince" Henry, to the semi-mythical Earls of Orkney, names which echo through the Norse sagas: Rognwald of Moray, Sigurd the Mighty, Thorfinn Skull-Splitter, and Magnus the Saint.

It might be no coincidence that in the same year that his continuation of the traditions of the larger-than-life Norse heroes who had preceded him as Jarls of Orkney were celebrated at his public installation, he lodged a petition with Pope Eugenius IV for permission to build a collegiate church beside his stronghold of Roslin. He had seen how the Scots line of MacAlpin had used the sanctuary of Iona to add *gravitas* (weight) to their position, building Dunfermline and Holyrood abbeys to celebrate their lineage. During the recitation of his predecessors as Jarls of Orkney, William would have realized that he, too, had inherited the underused asset of an impressive mausoleum church. It had been built in 1137 as a home for St. Magnus, Jarl of Orkney, with his reliquary in a shrine at the east end of the Cathedral. Magnus was a contemporary of Malcolm Canmore, and was reputed to have been a good friend to St. Margaret.[511]

St. Magnus Erlendsson is a major figure in the *Orkneyinga Saga*. It says he was a pacifist who was drafted by the King Magnus of Norway to fight against the Welsh in the Battle of Menai Straits.

[When] King Magnus arrived in Orkney he seized the Earls, Paul and Erlend, sent them east to Norway, and made his own son Sigurd overlord of the islands with regents to govern the earldom. Magnus went on to the Hebrides and with him the Earls' sons, Hakon Paulsson and the Erlendssons, Magnus [St. Magnus] and Erling. As soon as King Magnus landed in the Hebrides he attacked and took control of Lewis. In the course of the expedition he took over the whole of the Hebrides and captured Logmann, the son of Godrod, King of the Western Isles.

From there he sailed south to the coast of Wales and fought a fierce battle in the Menai Strait against two Welsh earls, Hugh the Stout and Hugh the Proud. When the troops were getting their weapons ready for battle, Magnus Erlendsson settled down in the main cabin and refused to arm himself. The King asked him why he was sitting around and his answer was that he had no quarrel with anyone there.

"That's why I've no intention of fighting," he said. . . . [he] took out his psalter and chanted psalms throughout the battle, but refused to take cover.

The Welsh lost a great many troops and in the end they had to run. . . . After this King Magnus took possession of Anglesey, which lies as far south as any region ever ruled by the former Kings of Norway and comprises a third part of Wales.[512]

St. Magnus defied the King and escaped into exile, spending some time at the abbey of St. Asaph in North Wales. When the King died, St. Magnus returned to Orkney and reclaimed the Earldom, but his half-brother Hakon, who had seized the Earldom, would not give it up. The new King of Norway, King Eystien, made the two half-brothers joint Earls. The story proceeds rather like that of Snow White and her Wicked Stepmother. The saga portrays Earl Hakon as the personification of evil. He refused to abide by King Eystien's ruling, and amassed a fleet of Viking marauders to attack the good Magnus, whom the saga describes thus:

St. Magnus, Earl of Orkney, was a man of extraordinary distinction, tall, with a fine, intelligent look about him. He was a man of strict virtue, successful in war, wise, eloquent, generous and magnanimous, open-handed with money, sound with advice, and altogether the most popular of men. He was gentle and agreeable when talking to men of wisdom and goodwill, but severe and uncompromising towards thieves and Vikings, putting to death most of the men who plundered the farms and other parts of the earldom. He had murderers and robbers arrested, and punished the rich no less than the poor for their robberies, raids and other transgressions. His judgments were never biased, for he believed divine justice to be more important than social distinctions. While he was the most generous of men to chieftains and others in powerful positions, he always gave the greatest comfort to the poor. He lived according to God's commandments, mortifying the flesh through an exemplary life in many ways which, though revealed to God, remained hidden from the sight of men.[513]

Such a paragon of virtue sounds almost too good to be true, and this is exactly how the story proceeds. The evil Earl Hakon called a meeting, saying that he wanted to make peace with Magnus. All Magnus's advisors warned him to not trust Hakon, but Magnus insisted it was his duty to attend the meeting. Then as he set off for the meeting, God sent an omen, to improve the suspense of Magnus's story:

[Magnus] had two ships, with the agreed number of men and, when he was ready, off he went to Egilsay. As they were rowing away upon a calm, smooth sea, a breaker suddenly rose high over the ship he was steering and crashed down upon the spot where he was sitting. His men were astonished to see such a breaker rise up from a calm sea: no one had seen anything like it before, and there was deep water beneath them.

"It's not surprising that you should be worried by this," said the Earl, "for I think it forebodes of my death. It may be what was prophesied about Earl Hakon will turn out now to be true. We'd better reckon with the possibility that cousin Hakon isn't going to be entirely honest with us at this meeting."

The Earl's men were disturbed by what he had said, to hear him predict his own imminent death, and they asked him not to place his trust in Earl Hakon but to watch out for his own safety.

"On with the journey," the Earl replied, "let it turn out as God wills."[514]

Of course, the evil Hakon had planned an ambush, and with an overwhelming force of Vikings who took Magnus prisoner on Egilsay, an island in Orkney, and summoned all the local Orkney chieftains. Hakon said that he was not prepared to share power with Magnus and only one of them could rule Orkney. The chieftains backed Hakon. So Magnus first offered to leave Orkney and go on a pilgrimage to the Holy Land and never return. This was refused. Next he offered to be exiled to Scotland. This too was refused. Then he offered to let Hakon mutilate him in any way he chose and imprison him, rather than have Hakon's soul suffer the sin of murder by killing him. Hakon at first accepted this, but the chieftains would not accept this compromise. They wanted an end to civil war and one Earl to rule them. At this point, Magnus volunteered to be killed for the good of the community. But no one would execute Magnus. Each man who was given the job refused until only Lifolf, the cook, was left. Hakon ordered the hapless cook to kill Magnus. This is how the saga continues:

> Lifolf started to weep out loud. "This is nothing to weep over," said Magnus. "A deed like this can only bring fame to the man who carries it out. Show yourself a man of spirit and you can have my clothes according to the old laws and customs. Don't be afraid, you're doing this against your will, and the man who gives you the order is a greater sinner than you are."
>
> At this, Earl Magnus took off his tunic and gave it to Lifolf, then asked for leave to pray. This was granted, and he prostrated himself on the ground, committing his soul to God and offering himself as a sacrifice. He prayed not only for himself and his friends but for his enemies and murderers, forgiving them with all his heart for their crimes against him. He confessed his own sins before God, praying that his soul might be washed clean by the spilling of his own blood, then placed it in God's hands. He asked that he might be greeted by God's angels and carried by them into the peace of Paradise . . . As this friend of God was being led to his execution, he spoke to Lifolf.

"Stand in front of me and strike me hard on the head," said Magnus, "it's not fitting for a chieftain to be beheaded like a thief. Take heart, poor fellow, I've prayed that God grant you his mercy."

With that he crossed himself and stooped to receive the blow. So his soul passed away to Heaven.[515]

As soon as Magnus was dead, he began to perform miracles. His grave at Birsay became a place of pilgrimage, and mystical lights appeared around it when pilgrims prayed to him. The saga tells us that "people in peril prayed to him, and no sooner did they pray than their troubles came to an end." Pilgrims came from all over Orkney and Shetland to visit his grave and to be healed of their ills.[516]

Magnus became such a popular Norse saint that in 1137, Rognwald, then Earl of Orkney, built a magnificent cathedral at Kirkwall to house his bones and give more space for all the pilgrims who wanted to pray to him. It is said that he brought in Masons from Durham to do the stonework. And Magnus's relics managed to survive the Reformation, though the Black Rood of Scotland was lost. Iain Macdonald, in his life of St. Magnus, tells us:

> In 1919, human remains were uncovered in the stonework of the pier on the south side of the cathedral choir, the skull bearing marks corresponding to the death-wound received by Magnus at Egilsay. The relics were restored to the same resting place where they are today.[517]

When he was reminded of this heritage of the Earls of Orkney, it must have struck William how useful it would have been if Magnus had been a Scot and St. Magnus's cathedral had been a focal point for pilgrimage that he controlled in Midlothian. Such a place would have been an alternative political rallying point during the period of political uncertainty in Scotland. Iain MacDonald says the cult of St. Magnus represented a sea change in attitude in the northern lands:

> Magnus' refusal to pursue aggression for its own sake . . . [and] the distinctive quality of the Viking lifestyle, which produced his own death . . . [created his] reputation as a saint. In his resistance to war and bloodlust, Magnus' martyrdom represents a choice of path which was all too vital and relevant for his time. The new way of Christianity, with its civilizing implications, still had an uncertain hold, and even in Magnus' time, efforts were being made "to root out the evils which had long attended heathenism." These affected the very fabric of society, its customs and arrangements, quite apart from the old ways of piracy and plunder which continued to beckon strongly, upheld in the songs and traditions guarding the reputations of the pagan gods and heroes. Magnus' death was therefore the assertion of a new kind of power, a power that was to heal and bind in order to rule.[518]

Magnus had been entertained and even venerated at the Scottish Court of King Edgar, the son of Malcolm Canmore and St. Margaret. But Willie Thompson thinks this link was more than social:

Magnus's usefulness to the King of Scots was political, not religious. Magnus was one of a long line of claimants to a divided earldom whom the Scots kings manipulated, with the object of making trouble for the Norse and increasing their own influence. As a preliminary step, Magnus became earl in Caithness where he seems to have gained general acceptance.[519]

William had proved himself a political opportunist in the way he took back Orkney from his uncle David. During his installation as the Earl of Orkney, he must have discussed the history and future of the Earldom and realized that he now held a key position between Denmark and Scotland at a time when both crowns were weak. He would also have realized how the use of relics and shrines had served the Crown of Scotland in the past, and would also have recognized the growing trend to create collegiate churches in Scotland, with no less than twelve being newly founded within his own lifetime.[520]

As a political tool, a family shrine could be very useful, especially if it had a powerful legend of a strong line of rulers attached to it. Dunfermline and Holyrood showed this only too clearly. But the circumstances in which William found himself in 1446, as a mature man of forty-two at the height of his political power, presented an enormous opportunity for him. Scotland had a king who was a minor and a series of infighting, unpopular regents. And Denmark was nearly bankrupt. William, however, was going from strength to strength.

He took official possession of the shrine of Magnus at his installation in Denmark, when the Bishop of Orkney, whose palace stood alongside St. Magnus's Cathedral in Kirkwall, paid homage to him. William acted quickly on the insight, and taking advantage of his role as patron of St. Magnus's, applied to the Pope for permission to build a similar structure to celebrate his Scottish roots in Roslin.

The political possibilities of two impressive spiritual focal points for loyalty, one in the North and one in the South of Scotland, seemed as obvious to me now as they must have seemed to William at the time. So my detailed study of his actions in the context of the history of the times had suggested a different motive for wanting to build Roslin Chapel from those that are usually offered. Would further study of William's actions reveal more?

A Crown, A Crown, My Earldom for a Crown!

Soon after William was installed as Earl of Orkney, the Earl of Douglas seized power in Scotland, as regent for the young James II, and reopened hostilities with Henry VI of England. In 1448, William got involved in the defense of Scotland, as we saw in his entry in the *Dictionary of National Biography*. The English were driven out. When James II came of age in 1460 he started to take more control. That year, William was made Lord St. Clair and given estates in Fife by the new king; this suggests that James saw him as a supporter of the crown against the Earl of Douglas.[521]

William was by now forty-five years old, and had extensive lands but no direct heir. In light of this, it is hardly surprising that he decided to take a wife. What is surprising is that he took as wife Elizabeth, the twice-widowed Dowager Countess of Buchan, who was a woman in her forties. William married her in 1450, quickly had two children by her—a daughter, Elizabeth, and a son, Henry—but she died while giving birth to Henry. I have already mentioned that Elizabeth was the sister of Archibald, Fifth Earl of Douglas, who had been regent of Scotland until 1439, and was a granddaughter of King Robert III of Scotland. So it appears that William's motive for marrying her was no romantic infatuation, but the intention of having children by her, so as to give his heirs a claim to the crown of Scotland and to establish a link with the powerful Douglas family.

William continued to consolidate his position by cultivating James II, who was a second cousin to his late wife. In 1445 he was made Earl of Caithness. By 1454 he was Chancellor of Scotland, a post he held until 1458. James needed to gather more supporters around him, since he had started a major civil war with the Douglas family by personally murdering William Douglas, the Eighth Earl of Douglas, during a dinner at Stirling Castle in 1452. William was linked to both sides by his marriage to Elizabeth, and so was well placed to side with the winners, whoever they might be.

Only in 1456, when William had control of large swaths of Scotland and a son with a claim to the crown, did he begin his building work at Roslin chapel. He was now fifty-two years old, yet he remarried. This time, he chose a woman in her early twenties. Perhaps this was a romantic attachment, for his second wife was an attractive young lady from Dunbeath by the name of Marjory Sutherland. Over the next twenty years, she gave William four more children (making his total heir-count six: three sons and three daughters) before dying in childbirth in 1476, by which time William was seventy-two years old. His children by Marjory were Eleanor, Catherine, Oliver, and William (Henry became the Second Lord Sinclair, and was twenty-five years older than his younger brother William, who became the Second Earl of Caithness).

The relationship between James II and King Christopher of Denmark over the payment of rent for the Hebrides, known as the Annual of Norway, was deteriorating. A peace conference was arranged by the King of France between the Kings of Denmark and Scotland, to be held in Paris in 1457, but before it could take place, William managed to create a diplomatic incident. Willie Thompson believes it was a deliberate attempt to increase tension between the two states:

> Bjarn Thorleifsson, Governor of Iceland, on the homeward voyage to Denmark accompanied by his wife and family and transporting the royal and ecclesiastical rents, was imprisoned in Orkney where his ship was forced to take shelter from a storm. The incident has been interpreted as deliberate mischief-making by Earl William with a view to souring relations between Scotland and Denmark.[522]

William had not just been awarded estates and titles by King James II of Scotland and by King Christopher of Denmark, he had also been buying land in his own right, and had inherited extensive lands from his first wife, Elizabeth, which included the Earldoms of Buchan, Mar, and Nithsdale, as well as the Wardenship of the Marches. By 1451 William controlled more land in Scotland, Orkney, and Shetland than the King of Scots did. So why would he want to cause mischief between the young King Christian of Denmark and the King of Scots? It would appear that he suspected James II of wanting to annex Orkney and Shetland to the crown of Scotland. And in taking this view he was correct, although James II didn't live to do it (he died at the siege of Roxburgh in 1460, killed by an exploding cannon). His son, James III, was eight at the time, and so once more, Scotland was plunged into uncertainty while its King lived through his minority.

At first things went well for William. His collegiate Church was coming on well, he was rich and powerful, and he was in favor with the Bishop of St. Andrew's, whose jurisdiction covered Roslin, where William was building his magnificent church. Bishop Kennedy of St. Andrew's was co-regent of Scotland along with Queen Marie of Guelders, James II's widow. William became a close political adviser to Bishop Kennedy, and was given the delicate job of Scottish Ambassador to England the year after James II died.[523] It was not an easy job, as England was nearing the climax of the Wars of the Roses, and Edward IV was about to become King of England. Soon after this, Edward IV did a deal with the Douglas family and John MacDonald, Earl of Ross, also known as the Lord of Isles, to carve up Scotland and oust young James III.

The timing of William's visit, following so closely on his attempts to embarrass the Crown of Scotland with Denmark, suggests to me that he may have had a hand in it. I suspect his purpose would have been to destroy the Scottish Crown, sacrifice the Scottish Lowlands to England and the Hebrides to the Douglases, and create for himself a new independent kingdom stretching from Kirkwall to Roslin.

Exploiting his position of influence with Bishop Kennedy, William was able to press for harsh terms in any settlement with Denmark. A marriage had been suggested between James III and Margaret of Denmark as a way of resolving the issue of the Annual of Norway. After James II's death, William continued to push for conditions which included the cancellation of all arrears of the Annual, transfer of Orkney and Shetland to Scotland, and a dowry of 100,000 crowns to accompany Margaret in her marriage. Willie Thompson makes clear that it was obvious that these conditions were going to result in the deal being refused, or deferred, which is exactly what William wanted.[524] Thompson reports that William was active and living in Orkney during 1461, as he was summoned from there to Denmark by King Christian, but refused to go, claiming he was busy defending Orkney from the Earl of Ross and in the midst of delicate negotiations with him.

As this followed immediately after his delicate negotiations in England, I couldn't help wondering if rather than arguing with John, Earl of Ross, was William attempting to do a deal to partition the kingdom of Scotland with Ross and Edward IV of England? The Earl of Ross had already organized one revolt against James II and almost succeeded. His Earldom of the Western Isles had remained stubbornly independent of the Scottish Crown. It presented an ongoing threat to the security of the Crown of Scotland. If Ross and the King of England could have been encouraged to snip off the Lowlands and the Western Isles at the same time, William would have been well placed to create a new kingdom in eastern Scotland around his own holdings, with himself as king.

THE FINAL BATTLE

Things were looking good for William. He had gotten himself into a political position where he could take the crown of a reduced Scottish kingdom and meld it into his holdings in Nithsdale, Caithness, Orkney, and Shetland, and then try to split Orkney and Shetland away from Denmark. But it was not to work out for him. In 1463, before William managed to put his ideas into action, Queen Marie died. Bishop Kennedy was soon replaced by Robert, Lord Boyd, who became Great Chamberlain of Scotland (and had his own designs on the throne of Scotland, which did not involve carving up the kingdom). At this point, things began to unravel for William. William's eldest son had a far better claim to the throne of Scotland, and William owned more land than either James III or Robert Boyd. But the Boyd Clan website makes no secret of Robert's ambitions:

> Lord Boyd held the office of Great Chamberlain between 1466 and 1469, his brother, Sir Alexander Boyd of Drumcol, was appointed instructor of knightly exercises to the young King, and Robert's son, Thomas Boyd, married the King's sister, Mary and received the title "Earl of Arran." In 1469 Thomas arranged the marriage of the eighteen-year-old king and the ten-year-old Margaret, princess of Denmark and Norway. The Orkney and Shetland Islands passed to Scotland as part of the dowry.

The Boyds had become one of the most powerful and influential families in all of Scotland. The rise to power also made them some powerful and envious enemies amongst the Scottish nobility.[525]

William was undoubtedly among these "powerful and envious enemies," but events overtook him. James III was almost old enough to take control of his own kingdom, and the threatening ambitions of the Boyd family forced him to act. The Boyd Clan website tells what happened from their point of view:

> As James III grew older the Boyd's enemies conspired against them, eventually persuading the young King that the Boyds' ambitions lay with the throne of Scotland itself. In 1469 all three were summoned to appear before the King and parliament in

Edinburgh on charges of treason. Alexander answered the charges, was found guilty and beheaded. Robert fled to England and was sentenced to death in his absence, his peerage and lands were forfeited; Thomas who was in Europe at the time of the summons, stayed in exile. His marriage to the King's sister was annulled by James III.[526]

James was now firmly in control of Scotland, and in the process of the battle between James and Robert Boyd, William was forced to resign the Earldoms of Orkney and Shetland to James in 1471. At the age of sixty-seven, William St. Clair saw his dreams of becoming king of a new Northern kingdom of Scotland destroyed. Orkney and Shetland had finally been taken from Denmark, but by the stealth of Robert Boyd—who had agreed that they be mortgaged to James III as part of Princess Margaret's dowry that the impoverished King Christian could not afford to pay.

The threats of Edward of England and John Macdonald, the Lord of the Isles, to annex large parts of Scotland came to nothing. James discovered the Treaty of Westminster-Ardtornish, which John Macdonald had signed in 1462 (it obliged John to pay homage to Edward of England for the Lordship of the Isles in return for help to oust James III), and denounced him as a traitor. Most of MacDonald's lands were seized by James, and the title Lord of the Isles was taken back to the Scottish Crown. John Macdonald fled to exile in the outer Hebrides. William was now stripped of his potential allies and his most important Northern titles by a revitalized King of Scots.

All the events of William's life show him to have been a political realist. His chance of a crown was gone, and the James III was now fully in control of what had been a disordered rabble of potential threats to his control. William took a pragmatic course, and reverted to becoming a loyal subject of James. He took on the job of Scottish Envoy to England to sort out the ongoing problems with Edward (who by now had executed Richard of York to become undisputed King of England). This was William's last major official action as an officer of the Scottish Crown.

When he returned from England, William was seventy years old. He retired to Roslin, where he devoted his final years to breeding more heirs. He had a second son, Oliver, in 1475 at the age of seventy-one, and a third son a year later whom he called William, despite having an older son with that name already. (When I first realized this dual naming, I couldn't help wondering if he was getting forgetful in his old age, but it seems that the practice giving the same name to more than one child in the family was a common medieval custom, provided they had different titles, I suspect this custom arose because so many children died young.

The political pressure that William was under from James III (who was systematically removing all the entrenched threats to his crown) resulted in his resigning the Earldom of Caithness to his newborn son, resigning the Barony of

Roslin to Oliver, and surrendering his Fife title of Lord St. Clair to his eldest son. He died with his empire broken into such small pieces that it would never again be a threat to the Crown of Scotland. In his *History of Orkney*, Willie Thompson sums up the position in which William left the St. Clair empire:

> The death of Earl William . . . [left] the great Sinclair empire in a state of progressive disintegration, irrevocably fractured into the three main families [founded by his three sons] of Ravenscraig, Roslin and Caithness, . . . [with] over a dozen lesser lines emerging as Orkney landed gentry in their own right.[527]

In 1544 Henry VIII of England burned Roslin Castle, and by 1611 the other major symbol of St. Clair supremacy, Kirkwall Castle, was razed to the ground. The chapel of Roslin fell into steady disrepair, and was only restored in 1736. But at least in death, William turned his creation of Roslin chapel into a famous mausoleum church, when he became the first, and potentially the most legendary, St. Clair to be buried in it.

However, my analysis of William's political career, with the detail of actions and potential motives it uncovered, had left me with another puzzle. Whatever else William St. Clair might have been, a visionary dreamer, capable of creating out of his own mind the plans to realize a vision of a rebuilt Temple of Solomon on a remote Scottish hillside, seemed unlikely. (And yet I knew from my previous research that Roslin was *just* such a building.) And the more recent myth that the foundations of a much larger cruciform church were discovered in the ground of the chapel do not bear close scrutiny. There certainly are foundations in the grounds of Rosslyn, but as long ago as 1877 *Proceedings of the Edinburgh Society of Antiquaries*, described their origin:

> It will be observed that St. Matthew's Church, being then the only church in Rosslyn, must therefore have been the one in which the earl's first marriage was solemnised. Its foundations are occasionally exposed by the grave-digger [at Rosslyn], and several ancient slabs with incised crosses and swords have been found, one of which, inscribed "William de Saincler," is preserved above the entrance to the chapel grounds, another in the adjoining garden, and a third was dug up about two years ago, but it is now much defaced and used as a gravestone. The foundations of the old church are not far below the surface, but there is no record of the area having been carefully examined.[528]

Despite its external appearance, it turns out that Rosslyn Chapel is not the unfinished remnants of a much larger project, as many other writers have suggested. It is a St. Clair shrine, designed as a political tool to complement and enhance the shrine of St. Magnus and to draw to its owner all the temporal power that comes from being associated with a building of popular acclaim. When Dr. Jack Millar, a geologist from Cambridge University, examined the chapel in 1996, he said:

"This debate about whether the west wall is a replica of a ruin or an unfinished section of an intended bigger building," Jack said pointing to the Northwest aspect. "Well, there is only one possibility—and I can tell you . . . that west wall is a folly."[529]

I believe William conceived the idea of a shrine as a spiritual focus for his leadership, and he had certainly made enough money to be able to afford to pay for its building. But who had actually designed the chapel and overseen the work to such a high standard of embedded symbolism?

That remained a puzzle. The task seemed well beyond William's capabilities.

CONCLUSIONS

William St. Clair, twelfth Baron of Roslin, devoted his life to the pursuit of power and influence. He became a skillful politician and diplomat, able to play off the interests of Norway, Scotland, and England. He learned the importance of holy relics from Scotland's loss of the Stone of Destiny, the political use of Holyrood Abbey, and the focus on the cult of St. Magnus during his successful attempt to regain the Earldom of Orkney from his uncle David.

William decided to build his own family shrine in Roslin to bolster his family's claims to be Scottish royalty. Unable to see his way clear to the Scottish throne, he still wanted his own kingdom, and tried to set up a partition of Scotland between Edward IV of England, who would take over the Lowlands, John Macdonald, Earl of Ross and Lord of the Isles, who would take over the Western Isles, and himself, who would take the remainder of Scotland from Lothian to Caithness, with Orkney and Shetland thrown in for good measure. Roslin (now Rosslyn) Chapel was largely built before this plan fell apart.

All the same, it remains an inspirational shrine, seemingly well beyond William's skills to create. So the question remains, who did such a good job of designing and building Roslin? To find out, I now had to dig out the real story of Roslin Chapel and its many mysteries. Turn the page, and join me for a flavor of this spiritual mystery.

CHAPTER 13

THE TEMPLE AND THE SPIN DOCTOR

A MEDIEVAL SOLOMON

Roslin, now known as Rosslyn, Chapel is one of the most intriguing buildings ever created. It is a powerful focus for mythical inspiration. But how did William the Chapel Builder create such an inspirational structure? Over half a millennium after its construction, it still grips the popular imagination. Books are still written repeating its myths and attempting to interpret its motifs; crowds of fans still line up to marvel at its stone complexity and bask in its spiritual presence. That is no mean achievement, and poses the question of how was it done? Where did William learn such skills? I needed to know more about William and his chapel.

I already had an opinion about the Chapel, which I had expressed in *The Hiram Key*.

> Roslin is a spiritual interpretation of Solomon's Temple [The temple which Herod rebuilt at the time of Jesus] . . . but not a free interpretation of the ruins in Jerusalem; as far as the foundation plan is concerned, it is a very carefully executed copy. The unfinished sections of the great western wall are there, the main walls and the pillar arrangements fit like a glove, and the pillars of Boaz and Jachin stand precisely at the eastern end of what would be the inner Temple.[530]

But now I had the problem that my detailed study of William St. Clair's life provided no evidence that he had the depth of knowledge to create such an inspirational shrine. Roslin draws on a wealth of symbolism that speaks to people today as clearly and as powerfully as it did when it was first carved. If William had set out to commission an inspirational mausoleum shrine to showcase the best features of the St. Clair heritage, and to inspire new layers of legend to enhance the mythical reputation of his family, then the building works had succeeded. But who designed and built it for him?

MACHIAVELLI'S APPRENTICE

We have seen that, writing around 1700, the historian Father Hay reported Earl St. Clair had wooden patterns made by his masons, which he then personally approved before the designs were cut into stone.[531] This suggests a detailed knowledge of both the symbolism of the work and the ability to judge the skill of the workmen. I decided that I needed to see if I had overlooked an artistic side to William's well-developed political nature. Willie Thompson was my first port of call, as I remembered that he had noted in his *History of Orkney* that William had commissioned translations of some French works on chivalry into the Scots language while acting as the personal representative of the King of Scots to the Court of France:

During the lifetime of James I, Earl William was an important figure. As Admiral of Scotland (a post becoming hereditary in his family) he accompanied the king's daughter to France for her marriage to the dauphin and he represented the Scots' king at the ceremony. Thereafter regarded as an expert on those fashionable occasions, he acted as steward at the marriage of James II and Mary of Guelders. His keen interest in chivalry was typical of the age and he commissioned translations of French treatises which were rendered into Scots as *The Buke of the Law of Armys* and *The Buke of the Ordre of Knychthede*.[532]

The Scottish Text Society is in the process of reprinting these books in a three-volume edition edited by Jonathan Glenn. This is how the series is introduced:

In 1456, at Roslin Castle, Sir Gilbert Hay translated three European best-sellers for the then Chancellor of Scotland, William St. Clair, earl of Orkney and Caithness. Hay's excellent prose style and his recastings of his originals make these translations intriguing works in their own right.[533]

The first volume (not yet published at the time of writing) will provide a commentary on Sir Gilbert, his sources and use of language, plus a glossary and index. The second volume (published in 2005) contains the text of *The Buke of the Law of Armys* [*The Book of the Law of Arms*], "a treatise on the principles of warfare, renowned throughout Europe. It provided a conspectus of instruction and lore that any self-respecting nobleman would have wished to have in his library." (That seemed to fit in well with the picture of William that I had built up as an ambitious noble with an eye on the crown.) The third volume includes not just *The Buke of the Ordre of Knychthede* [*The Book of the Order of Knighthood*] but also *The Buke of the Gouernaunce of Princis* [*The Book of the Governance of Princes*].

The former is Gilbert Hay's translation from the French of a chivalric manual originally written in Catalan by the mystic philosopher Ramon Lull, while the latter is a translation from the French of a version of the *Secreta Secretorum* [*Secret of Secrets*], one of the key works in the "advice to princes" tradition.[534] The *Secreta Secretorum* is a book about the science of government, supposedly written by Aristotle as a guide for Alexander the Great during his campaign in Persia—its full content of this book is available on the Internet.[535] If you read it, you will find that it is a manual on how to become a king and retain control of a kingdom. Perhaps William's interest in artistic French texts was driven more by a yearning to understand the nature of political control than by the love of chivalry that Willie Thompson attributes to him.

The prologue of *The Buke of the Law of Armys* provides us with a significant piece of information. It describes Gilbert Hay as "chaumerlayn umquhyle to the maist worthy King Charles of France" [sometime chamberlain of the most worthy King Charles of France], who at that time, in 1456, was living in Scotland and working for its Chancellor, William, Earl of Orkney and Caithness, "in his castell of Rosselyn."[536]

At the time when he commissioned Hay to translate these textbooks on how to take over a kingdom, William St. Clair was, as we saw in the previous chapter, the strongest noble in Scotland. He had used his marriage to a daughter of the Douglas family to position himself high up in the Scottish pecking order. He had control of Orkney, Shetland, and Caithness, was Chancellor of Scotland, and his main power base of Roslin had just been made a burgh. (The effect of this local freedom was to enhance William's political status, as he could now appoint and control the burghers who in turn would rule the township.) Although James II, who had recently grown old enough to take the throne of Scotland, was beginning to react against the Douglas family, this was working in William's favor, as Willie Thompson points out:

> The death of his first wife enabled Earl William to extricate himself from the potentially dangerous Douglas connection before James II set about his relentless destruction of a family which had been over-mighty during his minority. By cutting his ties at the right moment, William emerged strengthened rather than weakened by the fall of the Douglases. He was entrusted with escorting the "great bombard" (possibly Mons Meg) to lay siege to the Douglas stronghold of Threave. In the next few years he and Bishop Kennedy were recognised as the young king's principal counsellors, and in 1453 Earl William was appointed Chancellor of Scotland.[537]

At this time, too, William had obtained papal permission to create a focal collegiate church at Roslin, but had not yet begun to build. He needed a Master of Works who understood how to utilize the power of myth and relics within the fabric of a building and use it to bolster political power. At this exact moment, William decided to employ the ex-chamberlain of King Charles VII of France to translate three of the most important books on the political theory of seizing and holding kingdoms.

Gilbert Hay had been present at Reims, in July 1430, at the coronation of Charles VII.[538] He had witnessed the success with which Charles of France had turned the popular support for Joan of Arc to account in seizing the crown from which his father excluded him via the Treaty of Troyes. William St. Clair, meanwhile, had spent some time at the court of France in 1436, when he had escorted Princess Margaret Stuart to marry the Dauphin (later Louis XI). Andrew Kerr, in his essay "Rosslyn Castle: Its Buildings Past and Present," had commented on the influence of the French culture on William at this time:

> Sir William St. Clair resided for some time in France, under circumstances which led to him being intimately associated with the court and nobility of that country. He thus had ample opportunity for observation, and doubtless acquired a taste which originated much that was afterwards done at Rosslyn, both as regards his domestic arrangements and the buildings erected during his lifetime.[539]

So who was this ex-French chamberlain that William took on to translate those revolutionary French self-help manuals for would-be kings? The *Encyclopædia Britannica* says that Sir Gilbert Hay was a "Scottish poet and translator of works from the French, whose prose translations are the earliest extant examples of literary Scots prose."[540] He was born in 1403, making him about the same age as William, but he was a scholar who took a degree at St. Andrew's University between 1418 and 1419. Apart from the translations of French works he did for William, Sir Gilbert also wrote a political biography of Alexander the Great *The Buke of Alexander the Conquerour*.[541]

Hay was a scholar of the political manipulation of power, with practical experience (from the Joan of Arc period) of creating new relic myths to support political positions and win control of kingdoms. He came from a court steeped in the myths of the Holy Grail and the ideas of Chrétien de Troyes, and personally translated the classic work of chivalry, *The Buke of the Ordre of Knychthede*. With Gilbert Hay working for William, the mystery of how he originated the ornate and complex symbolism of the building becomes clear. It wasn't William St. Clair who conceived the enduring design of Roslin, it was Gilbert Hay. But what did he do, what myths did he draw on, and what symbols did he exploit?

Unraveling the Myth and Symbolism of Roslin

The novelist and literary critic David Lodge made a telling comment about the process of storytelling when he said:

> It is only because an artifact works that we infer the intention of the artificer . . . Literary texts are obviously intentional objects—they do not come into existence by

An early illustration of Roslin Chapel

accident . . . A poem can only *be* through its meaning—since its medium is words—yet it simply *is*, in the sense that we have no excuse for inquiring what part is intended or meant . . . [it] is a feat of style by which means a complex of meaning is handled all at once.[542]

He goes on to expound on the idea that a work of art can have an independent existence in the public mind in a way that is "unconditioned either by its creative origins or by its individual readers."[543] In other words, some artistic artifacts are much greater than the sum of their parts or even the imagination of their creator.

When I read these comments, I thought that this concept offered a way for me to understand the enormous impact that Roslin has had on the public mind over the last five hundred years. By now, I was convinced that William's intention in building Roslin was to build a mausoleum collegiate church to provide a public focus for the St. Clair family, and so establish them as a potential line of kings for a partitioned Scotland—a ploy which had almost succeeded. But the coup by Lord Boyd in 1469, and the later actions of James II when he took control of his kingdom, broke up William's empire and so fragmented the St. Clair family that it would never again be strong enough to aspire to the throne of Scotland.

During these heady years of maneuvering for kingship, though, William employed the scholar, poet, and political theorist Sir Gilbert Hay to oversee the construction of the St. Clair Royal Shrine at Roslin. Hay created a heroic poem in stone with a political purpose—but, once completed, this artifact took on an independent existence in the collective mind. The craftsmanship that went into its constriction has stood the test of time, despite the chapel's many ups and downs. Roslin initially prospered, then was sacked during the Reformation, fell into ruin and disrepair; was restored as a Masonic shrine during the Masonic battles of the St. Clair Charters; only to decay once more until Queen Victoria sponsored another restoration, which had in turn decayed until the surge of interest in the late twentieth century again pushed the chapel to prominence. Whatever William St. Clair and Gilbert Hay had in mind when they cooperated in the design of the stonework, I am quite sure that they did not expect to achieve over half a millennium of success as a source of mythical inspiration.

But why was it that their design was so successful? I decided to begin addressing this by reviewing what present enthusiasts see in the structure.

The Stories in the Stones

John Ritchie, editor of the Edinburghguide.com website, has lived in Roslin all his life, and the study of the chapel has become his personal obsession. In May 2006, he coauthored an article in *The Scotsman* in which he discussed how Sir Gilbert Hay supervised the building of Roslin. This article began:

> Great stonemasons settled next to the wooded glen to construct the library in stone, a building alive with symbolism and bursting with imagery. Rosslyn Castle already housed one of the finest collections of books in Europe—so what did St. Clair and Hay hope to achieve by preserving their knowledge in stone? . . . Some believe that it conceals hidden buried treasure, tells a great biblical secret or is a temple for a pre-Christian mystery tradition. Conspiracy theorists find evidence of a global cover-up while others believe it celebrates the eternal feminine . . . Everyone who comes to Rosslyn finds their own interpretation—and perhaps that is the real point of the chapel. [544]

Ritchie goes on to list the main themes of the chapel:

The Legend of King Arthur and the Holy Grail. Ritchie points to a pillar beside the west entrance showing two dragons fighting. These, he says, represent the red and white dragons of the local Merlin legend, which figured in Merlin's dream. He adds that Merlin died at Stobo in Scotland, and fought magical battles in the woods of Caledon, of which Rosslyn Glen is a remaining fragment.

The Merovingian French Kings. Ritchie describes them as guardians of Templar treasure and the descendants of Mary Magdalene. They are symbolized by bees (A hive of bees lived in the chapel from the time it was built in 1460 until recently, when the hive and its Roslin strain of bees were destroyed, being deemed a Health and Safety risk to the visiting public. They had lived in the beehive carved into the roof of the chapel, flying in through a specially carved entrance in the heart of a flower.) Ritchie tells us that bees were a symbol of the Merovingian dynasty, and that three hundred golden bees were found in the grave of the Merovingian ruler Childeric.

The Temple of Jerusalem. Ritchie tells us the Temple is indicated in an inscription which reads: "*Forte est vinu[m], Fortior est rex, Fortiores sunt mulieres: sup[er] om[nia] vincit veritas.*" This means: "Wine is strong. The king is stronger. Women are stronger still: but truth conquers all." The lines are from the Book of Ezra, and answer a riddle set by the Persian King Darius to Zerubbabel, who rebuilt the Temple of Jerusalem.

The Knights Templar. Ritchie draws attention to the carvings of Masonic initiation ceremonies (which I discussed in Chapter 6), including men kneeling with ropes twisted round their necks, and says that Earl William St. Clair who built Rosslyn was a descendant of a member of the Knights Templar, who guarded Jerusalem after the first crusade and discovered a fabulous treasure or great secret among the ruins of the Temple in Jerusalem. He adds that the eight-pointed star on the grave-stone of the 9th Baron of Roslin reveals him as a member of the Knights Templar. He also draws attention to the Apprentice Pillar in Rosslyn Chapel and the myth attached to it. This says that a Master Mason was asked to carve it and set off to tour the great sites of Rome and Greece to study how pillars could be made. While he was away his apprentice carved the wonderful pillar now known as the Apprentice's Pillar. The Master was so enraged at this that he struck his apprentice on the forehead with a heavy setting maul and killed him; afterwards he was so remorseful that he carved the Master's pillar as an act of penance. Ritchie believes this story is a myth mirroring the tale of Hiram Abif, the Masonic builder of the Temple of Jerusalem, who was also killed by Masons jealous of his skill and craftsmanship.

Symbols of the Great Goddess. Ritchie says Martha, the Virgin Mary, and Mary Magdalene are prominent in Bible scenes carved around the chapel, and the roses and lilies carved in the roof are symbols of the female wisdom tradition. He says that by the south door of the chapel, which was traditionally used as the women's entrance, is a carving showing the veil of Veronica, a famous medieval relic.

The Green Man. Ritchie has documented more than a hundred Green Men in Rosslyn Chapel, which he links to the Celtic pre-Christian and Druidic traditions. Each window has a Green Man at the center of the lower sill, recognizable by the tendrils of plants coming from their mouths. The degree of growth of the vegetation coming from their mouths varies in the east, south, west and north, reflecting the cycle of the seasons and the death and rebirth of plants. This is also reflected in the heraldic symbol of the Lamb of God, the *Agnus Dei*, which can be found beneath a window on the north side. Ritchie adds that the Lamb of God was one of the symbols of the Knights Templar, and appears in many Templar chapels.

The Bruce's Crusade. The last major theme Ritchie identifies in the chapel is the final crusade of Robert the Bruce. He explains that William St. Clair, whose gravestone lies at the rear of the chapel, died while taking the heart of Robert the Bruce to the Holy Land. It was the Bruce's last wish to go on a crusade, but the nearest he—or rather, his heart, the part of him that actually went on the posthumous journey—got was Teba in Spain. There 25 Scottish knights, led by Sir James Douglas, attacked the Moors and split the Muslim army. Most of the Scots were killed, including two St. Clair brothers, in what amounted to a suicidal action. Ritchie tells how the charging Douglas hurled the heart of the Bruce at the enemy, saying: "Go brave heart, and we lesser mortals will follow." This story is symbolized by an angel, carved in a window on the south side of the chapel, holding the cross of the St. Clairs and clutching a heart. He also notes that in one of the windows in the Lady Chapel, there is an eerie flattened face, which is carved from the death mask of Robert the Bruce.[545]

Ritchie says there are messages written in symbols throughout the chapel, and its roof is covered with a star pattern, thought to be an astrological map with symbols of Jesus, angels and a dove of peace hidden among the stars.

John Ritchie has since published a book, *Rosslyn Revealed, A Library in Stone*, describing in detail the stories, myths, and symbols he sees carved in the chapel building. He believes the main theme of the chapel is based on the myth of St. Mathew's staff, which is why the chapel was dedicated to St. Matthew. This myth tells how the apostle is given a magical staff by a manifestation of the resurrected Jesus and told to take it to Myrna and plant it at the gate of the church there, where the membership is being persecuted by King Fulvanus. Matthew plants the staff, and it immediately grows into tree "great and lofty and with many branches." It gives fruit, food, and shade to the land, and becomes a sign to both believers and nonbelievers of the power of Jesus and his support for Matthew and the church of Myrna. King Fulvanus tries to kill Matthew, but is unable to, because Matthew is protected by the Divine Tree of Life, which has grown from his staff. Eventually, after many miracles and signs from God, Matthew is taken into Paradise and Fulvanus surrenders his crown to the Church, takes the name Matthew, and becomes a bishop of the Church of Myrna. Ritchie comments:

> Fanciful though this tale may seem in the 21st Century, there is little doubt that the majority of believers in the 15th Century would have accepted it as being a true account of events surrounding the last days and death of St. Matthew. The story

would have been well known, especially to ecclesiastics and Earl William could quite convincingly have suggested that the whole Chapel was merely a representation in stone of the events detailed in the story of St. Matthew.[546]

This main myth would have been an ideal motif to use as the central symbol of spiritual focus for St. Clair political power to rival the Abbey of the Holy Rood—which, you recall, was the symbol of the Stuart kings, as it held St. Margaret's famous piece of the True Cross, the Black Rood. Gilbert Hay was skilled in the art of religious spin, though, and as Ritchie has pointed out, he built into the walls of the Roslin Chapel other stories, which in their turn supported the contention that the St. Clairs were natural rulers, supported by God in their quest to win back the land from a weak and evil king.

At least seven different motifs underpinning the central myth of St. Matthew's staff were listed in Ritchie's newspaper article, and looking through them, I was impressed by the knowledge of the basic principles of storytelling that the chapel displayed. As David Lodge had said, "[it is] . . . because an artifact works that we infer the intention of the artificer," and from the themes in Roslin's stones that impress modern commentators, I could see a pattern in the choice of themes which was thousands of years old. I now knew that I would have to look at the theory of story-telling and the idea that there are only a limited number of different types of story. The currently accepted number is seven, and Roslin Chapel makes use of most of them. Was this accidental or deliberate?

Just Seven Simple Stories

As part of my day job, I teach postgraduate students how to write dissertations, and I share with some colleagues an idea that helping students understand how a myth works can help them present their own research findings in a logical and readable manner. For a number of years now, I have been assigning an odd piece of homework to postgraduates wanting to learn how to present a detailed technical argument: I have sent them away to read fairy tales. My reason is simple. As children we all listen to fairy tales, and as a result we develop an expectation of how a story will proceed. When you hear "Once upon a time . . . " or perhaps "In a certain kingdom . . . ," then you enter a different world, with its own internal rules. When we are told a new story, we bring all the baggage of the previous stories we have heard with us as we listen. As children, we quickly develop expectations of what is going to happen, and when we hear stories as an adult, initially we will revise our expectations along the lines of our childhood conditioning as the story unfolds. As long as the story fits one of the early templates that were burned into our childhood minds, then we are comfortable with how it develops, even if we are surprised by the new detail it contains. But if none of our templates fits the developing story, then we start to become disappointed, and may even begin to distrust the account we are given, thinking to ourselves, "That doesn't seem right!" without really knowing why. ("What?" We think. "No "happily ever after"?!)

I teach my students to use the traditional fairy tales they learned as children as scaffolding to erect a reasonable narrative thread for telling the business stories which their dissertations have researched. As part of the process, I always ask them which is the first story they remember being told and which is their favorite story. I also ask them to state the question they have posed for their research and the answer they have discovered. Then I explore with them how to tell the story of the journey from the question to their answer. Once they have established the roles and sequences of a storyboard, they can dispense with the fairy story and concentrate on telling a compelling business story, making sure they support the narrative with suitable business theory.

The method has been so successful that the external examiner who conducts the Viva examinations (a Viva is a formal interview, where the student has to explain and justify the written thesis) asked me what I did to my students to enable so many of them to write extremely readable dissertations. I told him the trick, and he asked if I would run through a presentation he was making using the methodology I had developed for teaching my postgrads. He now uses the method himself and reports that the feedback he gets suggests that his storytelling has greatly improved.

I believe that one of the major spurs towards the evolution of the human mind is the ability to tell stories, and along with this goes the use of metaphor to explain complex things we do not understand in terms of simpler things we can visualize. In this way, we pass on knowledge to the next generation, without their having to learn everything for themselves. This human ability lies at the heart of the advance of civilization. Steven Pinker says in *The Language Instinct*:

> You and I belong to a species with a remarkable ability: We can shape events in each other's brains with exquisite precision. I am not referring to telepathy or mind control or the other obsessions of fringe science; even in the depictions of believers these are blunt instruments compared to an ability that is uncontroversially present in every one of us. That ability is language. Simply by making noises with our mouths, we can reliably cause precise new combinations of ideas to arise in each other's minds. The ability comes so naturally that we are apt to forget what a miracle it is.[547]

To be sure, scientists since the time of Newton have used mathematical reasoning to help them understand the universe. According to Richard Feynman, Nobel Prize winner in physics:

> If you are interested in the ultimate character of the physical world . . . our only way to understand that is through a mathematical type of reasoning . . . I don't think a

person can fully appreciate . . . these particular aspects of the world . . . without an understanding of mathematics . . . there are many, many aspects of the world that mathematics is unnecessary for, such as love . . . [but to] not know mathematics is a severe limitation in understanding the world.[548]

But even this eminent scientist uses the power of myth and the insight of metaphor to help him visualize the way forward. The mathematics come after the insight and justify it.

Feynman explained where he developed his way of using stories to teach and to help himself understand the world:

I got a kick, when I was a boy, out of my father telling me things, so I tried to tell my son things that were interesting about the world. When he was very small we used to rock him to bed, you know, and tell him stories, and I'd make up a story about little people that were about so high who would walk along and they would go on picnics and so on and they lived in the ventilator; and they'd go through these woods which had great big long tall blue things like trees, but without leaves and only one stalk, and they had to walk between them and so on; and he'd gradually catch on that that was the rug, the nap of the rug, the blue rug, and he loved this game because I would describe all these things from an odd point of view and he liked to hear the stories and we got all kinds of wonderful things—he even went to a moist cave where the wind kept going in and out—it was coming in cool and went out warm and so on. It was inside the dog's nose that they went, and then of course I could tell him all about physiology by this way and so on. He loved that and so I told him lots of stuff, and I enjoyed it because I was telling him stuff that I liked, and we had fun when he would guess what it was and so on.[549]

But although he saw stories as a good way of teaching, he went on to say:

It is probable that the human mind evolved from that of an animal; and it evolved in a certain way such that it is like any new tool, in that it has its diseases and difficulties . . . one of the troubles is that it gets polluted by its own superstitions, it confuses itself.[550]

The power of a story can take hold of person's mind and be so convincing that it sounds as if it simply *must* be correct. For many years, the Church believed, and taught, the myth that the sun went round the earth, because it was such a convincing story. When Galileo invented the telescope and found that it wasn't true, the myth was stronger than the science, and Galileo was forced to state his public belief in the myth he had just disproved to avoid execution. In this case, the story was stronger than the truth, and it served the Church's political purposes better.

But sometimes thinking in terms of myth and metaphor can bring about change. One such instance was Albert Einstein's first encounter with Aaron Bernstein's *Popular Books on Natural Science*. Einstein recorded that this was "a work which I read with breathless attention," and one which inspired him.

This book would have a fateful impact on [Einstein], because the author included a discussion on the mysteries of electricity. Bernstein asked the reader to take a fanciful ride inside a telegraph wire, racing alongside an electric signal at fantastic speeds.

At the age of sixteen, Einstein had a daydream that led him to an insight which would later change the course of human history. Perhaps remembering the fanciful ride taken in Bernstein's book, Einstein imagined himself running alongside a light beam and asked himself a fateful question: What would the light beam look like? Like Newton visualizing throwing a rock until it orbited the earth like the moon, Einstein's attempt to imagine such a light beam would yield deep and surprising results.[551]

This fanciful daydream enabled Einstein to formulate his Theory of Relativity: He used myth and fancy to understand the reality of the world. In a similar way there is a substantial body of current research literature looking at the use of myth as a tool for understanding business, and this type of analysis of how stories work has a long history. In 350 BCE Aristotle wrote in the introduction to his *Poetics*:

> I propose to treat of Poetry in itself and of its various kinds, noting the essential quality of each, to inquire into the structure of the plot as requisite to a good poem; into the number and nature of the parts of which a poem is composed; and similarly into whatever else falls within the same inquiry. Following, then, the order of nature, let us begin with the principles which come first.[552]

In this first real study of how structure is essential to successful storytelling, Aristotle analyses the craft of the poet as that of a teller of stories which inspire the human spirit and are of universal and timeless interest:

> It is not the function of the poet to relate what has happened, but what may happen—what is possible according to the law of probability or necessity. The poet and the historian differ not by writing in verse or in prose. The work of Herodotus might be put into verse, and it would still be a species of history, with meter no less than without it. The true difference is that one relates what has happened, the other what may happen. Poetry, therefore, is a more philosophical and a higher thing than history: for poetry tends to express the universal, history the particular. By the universal I mean how a person of a certain type on occasion can speak or act, according to the law of probability or necessity; and it is this universality at which poetry aims.[553]

When anybody writes a story or retells myth, there are a limited number of logical alternatives; some are generally interesting, others are not. Conflict between strangers is of little interest, because it is a natural part of human nature, he observes. But conflict between people who we feel should love each other intrigues us. A mother who thanks God that it is her son rather then her lover who has been killed is a deep subject for a story, as Henry James showed. The drama of the situation forces us to turn the next page to see what will happen next. This led Aristotle to develop a basic algorithm of dramatic relations, which he used to produce a taxonomy of story lines that exploit all the logical possibilities of a good story. He had noticed that there are deep themes which fascinate all humans. These are the ingredients of our social life which make us human.

In 2004 literary critic Christopher Booker, who was also a founding editor of *Private Eye*, wrote an analysis of the seven main themes in fiction called *The Seven Basic Plots: Why We Tell Stories*. In reviewing it, Denis Dutton, Editor of *Philosophy and Literature*, remarked:

> The basic situations of fiction are a product of fundamental, hard-wired interests human beings have in love, death, adventure, family, justice, and adversity. These values counted as much in the Pleistocene as today, which is why they are so intensively studied by evolutionary psychologists. Our fictions are populated with character-types relevant to these themes: beautiful young women, handsome strong men, courageous leaders, children needing protection, wise old people. Add to this the threats and obstacles to the fulfillment of love and fortune, including both bad luck and villains, and you have the makings of literature. Story plots are not unconscious archetypes, but follow, as Aristotle realized, from human interests and the logic of what is possible. [554]

I found that Booker's analysis articulated the main fairy-tale motifs that had been making regular appearances in my students' listing of their favorites. Here are the seven basic stories that Booker lists; the examples come from the more popular entries on my students' lists of favorite or best-known stories:

1. Killing the Monster (Jack and Beanstalk)
2. The Quest (King Arthur and Search for the Holy Grail)
3. Voyage and Return (Robinson Crusoe)
4. Rags to Riches (Cinderella)
5. Death and Resurrection (Snow White)
6. Comedy (Jeeves and Wooster)
7. Tragedy (Hamlet)

Every successful story ever told uses combinations and blends of these basic stories. Booker makes this point in the introduction to his detailed analysis of storytelling:

> We spend a phenomenal amount of our lives following stories: telling them; listening to them; reading them; watching them being acted out on the television screen or in films or on a stage. They are far and away one of the most important features of our everyday existence . . . Not only do fictional stories play such a significant role in our lives, as novels or plays, films or operas, comic strips or TV soaps. Through newspapers or television, our news is presented to us in the form of stories. Our history books are largely made up of stories. Even much of our conversation is taken up with recounting the events of everyday life in the form of stories. These structured sequences of imagery are in fact the most natural way we know to describe almost everything which happens in our lives.[555]

The interesting implication of the existence of these basic plots, which Booker has shown are endemic throughout human society, is that everybody identifies with the mythical structure as these stories unfold:

> These patterns serve a far deeper and more significant purpose in our lives than we have realised . . . wherever men and women have told stories, all over the world, the stories emerging to their imaginations have tended to take shape in remarkably similar ways.[556]

From the research I had carried out for *Turning the Hiram Key*, I was already aware of the importance of storytelling in forming a sense of self-identity. I commented then:

> Human beings like stories. When you offer to tell a young child a story she will clap her hands in anticipation of the joy it will bring her. She expects pleasure, she hopes for an experience to excite her imagination and transport her to emotional places she will enjoy visiting. And this love of a good story stays with us humans throughout our lives. In fact, if I were asked to say how humans differ from other primate species I might try suggesting we are the only species to tell each other stories . . . The myths that groups of people create define their society's values and beliefs. And those myths can long outlast the people who first tell them.[557]

Since writing that comment, I have become even more convinced that myths speak to people at a level that takes no account of reality. Storytelling seems to be a way of codifying memories as a means to develop the self-awareness that makes us human.

In many ways it works in our favor, helping the species to share knowledge over generations and conditioning the young to listen their elders. Richard Dawkins, professor of the Public Understanding of Science at Oxford University, notes this effect:

> More than any other species, we survive by the accumulated experience of previous generations, and that experience needs to be passed on to children for their protection and well-being. Theoretically, children might learn from personal experience . . . but there will be a selective advantage to child brains that possess the rule of thumb: believe, without question, whatever your grown-ups tell you.[558]

Dawkins goes on to recount a story that made at great impression on him as a child. The tale he tells uses one of the classic plots, following the rules of tragedy. It begins with a dream of perfection, and ends with the inevitable death that all the listeners foresee as inevitable. Dawkins tells how this story struck his childish mind and became so indelibly imprinted that he still finds it horrifying almost half a century after hearing it:

> I have never forgotten a horrifying sermon, preached in my school chapel when I was little. Horrifying in retrospect, that is: at the time, my child brain accepted it in the

spirit intended by the preacher. He told us a story of a squad of soldiers, drilling beside a railway line. At a critical moment the drill sergeant's attention was distracted, and he failed to give the order to halt. The soldiers were so well schooled to obey orders without question that they carried on marching, right into the path of an oncoming train. Now, of course, I don't believe the story and I hope the preacher didn't either. But I believed it when I was nine, because I heard it from an adult in authority over me. And whether he believed it or not, the preacher wished us children to admire and model ourselves on the soldiers' slavish and unquestioning obedience to an order, however preposterous, from an authority figure. Speaking for myself, I think we did admire it. As an adult I find it almost impossible to credit that my childhood self wondered whether I would have had the courage to do my duty by marching under the train. But that, for what it is worth, is how I remember my feelings. The sermon obviously made a deep impression on me, for I have remembered it and passed it on to you.[559]

This anecdote shows the lingering power that a story has even on the adult mind of a man who is noted for his rational and scientific thinking. Just imagine what impact powerful myths can have on a superstitious population! Daniel C. Dennett, the philosopher of Consciousness, puts forward this disturbing view on the power of stories in academic disciplines:

> One of the few serious differences between the natural sciences and the humanities is that all too many thinkers in the humanities have decided that . . . it's all just stories, and all truth is relative . . . End of story.[560]

He goes on to say:

> For example, right now I am typing on my keyboard with the intention of creating a coherent story about the logic of postmodernism. Were someone to study me, they might look beyond that surface level intention I just offered and infer instead that what I really am doing is inventing a story from my personal experiences for the purposes of advancing my academic career. To accomplish this, they might argue, I am constructing a discourse that sets me apart from other people and thus increases my value as a writer. (The more I confuse you, the smarter I appear!) Why do I do this? Because I am a self interested white heterosexual privileged Protestant male who uses knowledge for power (a strategy not of savvy but of manipulation and exploitation). For postmodernists, that which gets presented as truth (e.g., this book) is an invention, just a take on reality, that masks what I am really doing—tricking everyone in order to acquire and maintain power.[561]

This take on storytelling echoed my own thoughts. Had William St. Clair noticed this effect way back in the fifteenth century and hired a well-read spin doctor to implement this technique in the building of Roslin Chapel? The knowledge of the basic plots has been known since the time of Aristotle, so Gilbert Hay, who specialized in translating classic texts, could easily have known about these ideas. But the structure of Roslin also showed a powerful grasp of the use of symbols to encapsulate myths.

Manipulation by Symbol

Daniel Dennett explains what a powerful motivating force a symbol can be:

> Since September 11, 2001, I have often thought that perhaps it was fortunate for the world that the attackers targeted the World Trade Center instead of the Statue of Liberty, for if they had destroyed our sacred symbol of democracy I fear that we Americans would have been unable to keep ourselves from indulging in paroxysms of revenge of a sort the world has never seen before . . . it would have befouled the meaning of the Statue of Liberty beyond any hope of subsequent redemption . . . the World Trade Center was a much more appropriate symbol of Al-Qaeda's wrath than the Statue of Liberty would have been, but for that very reason it didn't mean as much, as a symbol, to us. It was Mammon and Plutocrats and Globalization, not Lady Liberty. I do suspect that the fury with which many Americans would have responded to the unspeakable defilement of our cherished national symbol, the purest image of our aspirations as a democracy, would have made a sane and measured response extraordinarily difficult. This is the great danger of symbols—they can become too "sacred."[562]

I have come to believe that William St. Clair set out to create just such a sacred symbol for his own political purposes, and—even though those purposes have long since become irrelevant—the power of the myth and the symbolism used in Roslin have continued to resonate with people's feelings. It is that strength of emotional response that has made Roslin figure so large in the myths of Freemasonry and of Templar Masonry. It was designed using the best available tools of political spin in an age that embraced and relished superstitious beliefs. And the symbols retain their power even today, as any New Age Pilgrim doing the Dan Brown tour of Europe can testify. The myths are part of this appeal, but the images cut into the stonework also work a dark magic which is more powerful than we realize.

While researching *Turning the Hiram Key*, I had discovered that some academics had studied a longstanding European tradition of sacred symbols. Such a scholar was the late Professor Marija Gimbutas of UCLA, who commented in her book *The Language of the Goddess*:

> The old European sacred images and symbols were never totally uprooted; these most persistent features in human history are too deeply implanted in the psyche to be uprooted.[563]

I had also looked at the work of Betty Edwards, a Professor of Art at California State University, who had found that her students could see meaning in drawings. She explained it thus:

> Students . . . suddenly see that drawings (and other works of art) have meaning. I am not, of course, referring only to drawings of things—portraits, landscapes, still-life subjects. That kind of meaning . . . can be summed up in a few words. But

meaning is also expressed in the parallel visual language of a drawing, whether it represents recognizable objects or is completely non-objective. This different kind of meaning requires a different kind of comprehension. A drawing, to be comprehended for meaning, must be read by means of the language used by the artist, and that meaning, once comprehended, may be beyond the power of words to express. Yet in its parts and as a whole, it can be read.[564]

Dr. Edwards is saying that symbols can be read like a language, that abstract shapes can reveal to the viewer what emotions and thoughts are going on in the mind of the mark-maker.[565] In *Turning the Hiram Key*, I noted:

> Betty Edwards . . . is convinced that drawing allows people to express ideas or feelings that are too complicated or imprecise to fit into the straitjacket of words. She says "drawings can show relationships that are grasped immediately as a single image, where words are necessarily locked into a sequential order." Words have to be processed in single file, while the ideas in symbols can march into your mind in line abreast.

She makes the point that words, and the sequential thinking that goes with them, have dominated human life since our species invented writing. So now it is difficult for us to imagine that there might once have been a visual language for translating experience, one which did not use words. And yet this language of symbols is open to everybody. Mathematics and science require at least minimal levels of training; even nature, if her secrets are to be penetrated, demands the use of advanced techniques of science, meditation, or philosophy—but symbols can speak directly to our emotions.[566]

I had also conducted a series of GSR (Galvanic Skin Response) tests. These measure the degree of cold sweat generated on the palms of our hands when we are emotionally aroused: a subconscious reaction that reveals when we are excited or afraid of something. I showed my students pictures of ancient Neolithic symbols, and noted which ones excited their subconscious responses. I had found that certain symbols, particularly lozenges and spirals either alone or in combinations, were extremely emotionally attractive to a whole range of individuals. I had tested individuals brought up in British, Asian, and Chinese cultures, and taught to read in different writing systems, using different methods of recording words. And I tested equal numbers of females and males in each culture/alphabet group.[567] Over the last couple of years, I have repeated this test with a further 500 or so students, and the results remain consistent with the explanation I proposed in 2005:

> Symbols enter our visual system via the optic nerve and, when processed directly by the limbic system of the brain, can have a subconscious emotional impact . . . this hidden process can be more flexible than concrete concepts.[568]

These sorts of symbols are used in Roslin, and I was reminded of the unanswered questions I had left dangling in the first book of this present trilogy, when I said:

Do these symbols survive because they were instinctively appealing? Or were they shapes which some evolutionary force had shaped our brains to like? And if human brains are hard-wired to like particular symbols, what is the evolutionary pay-off?[569]

My next step had to be to trace the evolution of these appealing shapes and myths that continue to make Roslin so popular. Where had they really come from?

Conclusions

William St. Clair had met and recruited Gilbert Hay, a scholar of literature from the French Court and employed him to oversee the work of designing and building the new St. Clair inspirational shrine that was to be Roslin Chapel. The evidence of the long-term success of the chapel shows that Gilbert Hay was a master of storytelling and the use of symbolism. He used a myth of St. Matthew's staff as the tree of life to incorporate a whole raft of highly emotive symbols into the chapel walls.

To understand how he did this, I investigated the basic structure of storytelling and the basis of successful myths. I found that there are only seven basic plots, but that these are extremely powerful, and humans seem to be programmed to respond to them. Roslin Chapel made use of these powerful storytelling devices and linked them to well-established symbols, which I had found from my own research to hold a deep emotional attachment for all humans, no matter what their culture or mother tongue. It is the use of these primeval myths and symbols that gives Roslin its ongoing power to fascinate. I already knew that these symbols and myths had been adopted by Freemasonry, but now I wanted to find out where such powerful stories began. To do so, I had to travel back over eleven thousand years to an ancient lost city of Goddess-worshippers. So now let's look at the symbols they used, what they used them for, how these symbols influenced the creation of Roslin Chapel—and how they still influence us today.

CHAPTER 14

EDEN WAS A CITY

SECRET SYMBOLS OF THE DEAD

Tracking the development of symbols through human history is made more difficult because of a longstanding tradition of secrecy in the archaeological profession. Professor Colin Renfrew commented in 1996 that 60 percent of all modern excavations remain unpublished after 10 years, and only 27 percent of digs funded by the American Science Foundation since 1950 have been published in any form at all.[570] He went on to note that, of excavations carried out in Israel, 39 percent in the 1960s, 75 percent in the 1970s, and 87 percent of those in the 1980s have not even produced a draft site report of the digging.[571]

As archaeological excavation tends to involves the total destruction of the site and all on-site evidence, this poor rate of publication of findings is unacceptable. In every other realm of publicly funded activity, practitioners are forced to produce interim reports accounting for their use of public money. Why should archaeologists be exempt?

They destroy much of the evidence they investigate, so logic suggests it should be part of the conditions of their permission to excavate that they report their findings as they go along. Failure to report annually on progress, just as a business has to have its accounts audited each year, should become grounds for refusing permission to dig further.

In *Archaeology: Theories, Methods, and Practice*, Renfrew and his co-author Paul Bahn deplore this attitude of secrecy:

> Whatever the reason, deliberate non-publication is a form of theft—in fact a double theft, involving the misuse of other people's money and the withholding of unique

information. Some archaeologists compound the felony by hoarding finds, which they consider to be their scientific property, deliberately preventing colleagues from gaining access to the material or from publishing research connected with the site.[572]

And when archaeologist Ian Richmond, who excavated a considerable number of Romano-British sites, died, Sir Mortimer Wheeler said of Richmond's publication record: "Not more than a quarter of his productive work fieldwork can now ever see the light of day . . . in spite of constant entreaties. He obstinately declined to keep pace with his digging by the normal method of interim reports."[573] As a physical scientist, I have little sympathy with the attitude that "the professional archaeologist knows best" and can decide for himself when and what to publish. Archaeologists who evade publication destroy valuable sites for nothing more than their own gratification, and in the present climate of academic accountability, it is a practice that should not be allowed to continue.

Fortunately, not all archaeologists are cast in this unscientific mold, and while researching this book, I have met many enthusiasts who are eager to share their findings, and even their speculations, with the public. But even the normally tolerant Renfrew can sometimes set his professional archaeologist's face against writers who attempt to apply new ideas to understanding our past, as when he said: "It is necessary to set our faces against the lunatics and fringe archaeologists who seek to confuse or corrupt our view of the past."[574] But he redeems himself by adding a scientific rider to his remark: "The real antidote is a kind of healthy skepticism: to ask where is the evidence?"[575]

However, the sad fact is that often what evidence there might be is hidden in the unrecorded secret excavations of archaeologists who treat their finds about the past as confidential knowledge, not to be shared with the public who pay their salaries. One of the most public examples of this abuse is the investigation of the Dead Sea Scrolls, which remained an archaeologists' secret for 44 years, until academic outrage by an American university finally forced their contents into the public domain.

Dr. Caroline Wickham Jones, whom I have had the good fortune to meet at various Orkney Science Festivals over the years, made some telling comments about the problems of any systematic investigation of early Neolithic material:

> Most sites are revealed when the ground is disturbed, for example, when ploughing pulls chips and flakes of flint to the surface of field, or when a ditch cuts through a concentration of charcoal and burnt stone . . . current knowledge of early settlement is constrained more by the modern factors that lead to discovery of sites than by the ancient factors that reflect the use of the countryside in the past.[576]

DARK CORNERS AND LOST SECRETS

The random discovery of sites combined with a similar random publication of excavation reports about those sites leads to a patchy spread of evidence for the evolution of symbols, and that evidence can be difficult to analyze. Under these circumstances, it seems appropriate to apply philosopher Karl Popper's view that science throws new light on observations, not only profiting from observations but leading the way to new ones via the tattered jigsaw of published evidence.[577] Some archaeologists are quick to draw on other disciplines when it suits them, yet they will just as quickly decry such methods when they do not understand the professional application of particular techniques. But archaeologists' failure to understand "the scientific myths" of other disciplines in no way invalidates the application of these methodologies to unsolved archaeological problems. Renfrew gives a clear example of this lack of understanding when he discusses the work of Oxford Professor of Engineering Alexander Thom. Thom used measurement and statistical analysis to reveal a standard unit of length in use in the British Isles 5,000 years ago.

Renfrew dismissed Thom's findings about the origin of this unit of length, commenting:

> The alternative suggestion has been put forward that the regularity is no more precise than would be expected from the use of a human dimension such as the pace in the layout of the circles.[578]

When I read this comment, I was surprised that Renfrew felt able to put this idea forward so dogmatically, without any attempt to test the hypothesis by observation. Thom's analysis of his data shows a low standard deviation in the variability of the measurement over a wide range of sites, 480 in all. (For a full analysis of Thom's work by physicist Dr. Robin Heath, see *Alexander Thom—Cracking the Stone Age Code.* [579])

Renfrew's objection to Thom's findings led me to assign the problem of looking at the frequency distribution of a human pace by measurement to a group of my undergraduate students who were studying statistics. Using a first-year group of around 200 students, my class measured their average length of pace and calculated the distribution before measuring its standard deviation. The standard deviation was over three orders of magnitude greater than that measured by Thom (that is a thousand times too big). The height of modern students may well be greater, on average, than that of an equivalent group of Neolithic people, giving a longer stride length, but the degree of variability in average length of stride is a property of the different gaits of the individuals. This factor can be measured for any population, and if the assumption so confidently made by Professor Renfrew were correct, then the standard deviation would be of the same order as that measured by Thom. Clearly, it is not.

But let's return to the question of the evolution of the symbols, which my own observational research had shown to be attractive to most humans. Faced with the difficulties of patchy observations, often inadequately recorded, the task looked close to impossible. But then, while browsing in the university library, I had the good fortune to happen on the work of the late Marija Gimbutas, former professor of European archaeology at the University of California. I later found Renfrew describing her as "a pioneer in the emphasis of the importance of women in prehistory."[580] But what I realized as I browsed through her work was that she had documented and contextualized a whole range of ancient symbols that spanned the last 30,000 years. She said in *The Language of the Goddess*:

> Symbols . . . constitute a complex system in which every unit is interlocked with every other in what appears to be specific categories. No symbol can be treated in isolation; understanding the parts leads to understanding the whole. I do not believe that we shall never know the meaning of prehistoric art and religion. Yes, the scarcity of sources makes reconstruction difficult in most instances, but the religion of the early agricultural period of Europe and Anatolia is very richly documented. Tombs, temples, frescoes, reliefs, sculptures, figurines, pictorial paintings, and other sources need to be analyzed.[581]

I knew this from my own work, but I didn't know the history of the shapes that my students found so appealing. Perhaps a careful study of the images Marija Gimbutas had so painstakingly collected and cataloged might help me understand more.

The Spiral and Lozenge

One depiction of symbols has proved particularly attractive to my students and has been the consistent favorite among all the images I have tested. Shown at figure 1, it combines both the lozenge and the spiral. Gimbutas says it originated in Eastern Yugoslavia about 7,000 years ago, and she describes it as a loaf-shaped clay object that is probably a model of sacred bread which was an offering to the Pregnant Goddess.[582]

In 2005 I traced the history of this image in a paper, "A Three-ring Circus for Orkney," given to the Orkney Science Festival. The symbol is well known in Orkney, as it was found on a ceramic pendant excavated at the Neolithic village of Skara Brae (c. 3000 BCE), where it took the form shown in figure 2. The pendant was found by Gordon Childe during his excavations between 1925 and 1930.

The Skara Brae version is the most recent of the Neolithic forms of this symbol that had I had found, but I had noticed patterns in the earlier versions of it. The next one (figure 3) comes from a large curbstone to the rear of the great mound of Newgrange in the Boyne Valley in Ireland and dates from 3200 BCE, slightly earlier than the Skara Brae symbol.

Another version, on a corn or grain storage jar dated to about 6,000 years ago, incorporates a figure to form the lozenge symbol (figure 4). Gimbutas recorded it as from north-eastern Romania, and said this about it:

The hour-glass Goddess in Cucuteni vase painting . . . flanked by snake spirals and surmounted by large meanders. The hourglass form symbolizes the subterranean or subaqueous life force of the Goddess and imminent rebirth. Note: her hands are bird's claws. Painted white, red, and dark brown. Cucuteni. NE Romania; *c.* 4000 B.C.[583]

Two versions of the symbol also appear carved on the walls of temples in Malta about 6,000 years ago. The one shown in figure 5 Gimbutas recorded at the entrance to a temple at Tarxien, and that in figure 6 came from a temple at Hagar Qim.

The version shown in figure 7 is earlier, about 8,000 years old, and comes from Southern Italy. Gimbutas describes it as a clay stamp used to impress an image onto bread, which would then be baked to form a votive offering for the Mother Goddess.[584]

But the oldest version of the combined symbol that Gimbutas recorded is that in figure 8. It is 9,500 years old, is cut into hardened ceramic clay and comes from Anatolia, in modern Turkey. Gimbutas noted that it was found it inside a shrine at a place called Çatalhöyük, where it was used to stamp its embossed image onto loaves of sacred bread.

The stamp was found alongside a clay model of such a sacred loaf.[585] This model, impressed with the sacred symbols to create a votive offering, was also around 9,500 years old:

The Rise of Farming

Plotting these symbols in order of appearance reveals that the first recorded use of the combined symbol of lozenge and spiral was in the eastern plateau of Anatolia, and that it spread from the East to the western islands of Britain over a period of about 6,000 years. This was a significant period in human prehistory, because around 10,000 years ago, farming began in Anatolia, and over the next 6,000 years spread westward from there as part of a period and a process known as the Neolithic Revolution. This was the time when humans changed their mode of living from hunter/gatherers to farmers. This was the engine of change which drove the beginnings of civilization as we know it today. As Renfrew says:

> In the Near East, we can recognize the origins of this transition [from hunting and gathering to food production] . . . for the process may have been gradual, but the consequence was the restructuring of the social organization of human societies . . . well-established farming, dependent on wheat and barley as well as sheep and goats (and later cattle), was under way there by about 8000 BC. Farming had spread to Europe by 6500 BC.[586]

Renfrew plotted this spread of farming practice on a map, as shown in figure 10, which shows the wave of farming villages spreading like a ripple on a pond

Figure 1

Figure 2

Figure 3

Figure 4

Figure 5

Figure 6

Figure 7

Figure 8

Figure 9

from its beginnings in Anatolia.[587] I have overlaid on this map the time and place of the appearance of the combined lozenge and spiral symbols, and it closely follows Renfrew's recorded sequence of the spread of farming. Did the symbols travel with the farmers? Did they have anything to do with the decision to switch from hunting/gathering to farming? They certainly occurred at the same times and in the same places, but what was their significance? Were there any more clues in Gimbutas's collection of images?

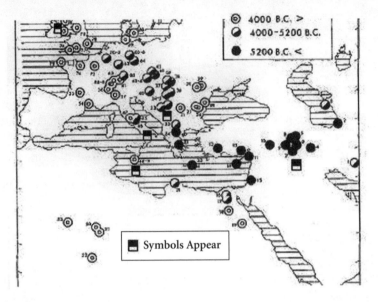

Figure 10

We have seen that the earliest example she recorded appeared at Çatalhöyük, a site first excavated by James Mellaart in the 1960s. It was a Neolithic city over 9,000 years old, which covered 32 acres, housed a population of about 7,000 people, and prospered for over a thousand years. The site also shows evidence of the development of modern farming techniques over this period. This Neolithic city was right at the center of the region where the farming civilization of Europe began, and Mellaart writes of it in *Earliest Civilizations of the Near East*:

> Anatolia . . . has now been established as the most advanced centre of neolithic culture in the Near East. The neolithic civilization revealed at Çatalhöyük shines like a supernova among the rather dim galaxy of contemporary peasant cultures. The comparison is apt for Çatalhöyük with its successors, Hacilar, Çatalhöyük West and Can Hasan, burnt itself out and left no permanent mark on the cultural development of Anatolia after *circa* 5000 BC . . . Its most lasting effect was not felt in the Near East, but in Europe, for it was to this new continent that the neolithic cultures of Anatolia introduced the first beginnings of agriculture and stockbreeding and a cult of the Mother Goddess, the basis of our civilization.[588]

And Mellaart had no doubt about the importance of farming to its economy:

> The economy of Çatalhöyük was based on extensive agriculture, on stock breeding (sheep and cattle) and on hunting wild cattle, Red deer, wild ass, boar, and leopards . . . The standard of agriculture is amazing: emmer, einkorn, bread wheat, naked barley, pea, vetch and bitter vetch, were widely grown. Vegetable oil was obtained from crucifers and from almonds, acorn and pistachio. Hackberry seeds occur in great

quantities suggesting the production of hackberry wine, praised by Pliny, and it may certainly be assumed that beer was also known.[589]

MOTHER GODDESS OF THE GRAIN

Mellaart had linked the rise of farming to a cult of the Mother Goddess. I now knew that the Skara Brae symbol was linked to the spread of farming. So was it also linked to the Mother Goddess? I returned to Gimbutas to see what she had said about the religion of Çatalhöyük:

> In the early Neolithic, peoples constructed special rooms where birth took place. We may conceive of those rooms as birthing shrines. At Çatalhöyük . . . excavations revealed a room where inhabitants apparently performed rituals connected with birthing. They painted the room red, reminding us that red, the color of blood, was the color of life. Stylized figures on the walls illustrate women giving birth, while *circular forms and wavy lines* painted nearby may symbolize the cervix, umbilical cord and amniotic fluid. A low plaster platform could have been used for actual birthing. The color and symbolism in the room suggest that people regarded [what happened in it] as a religious event and that they accompanied it with ritual.[590]

The circular forms and wavy lines were similar to the shapes shown in figure 8, and they had been found on a stamp for embossing patterns into bread which was made into sacred offerings. It seemed that the Goddess of Çatalhöyük was linked to farming, because Gimbutas reported that the symbols of this pregnant Earth Mother were:

> frequently unearthed near bread ovens. She personified the analogy between human and animal pregnancy and the annual cycle of plant germination, growth, and harvest.[591]

In Çatalhöyük, Mellaart had reported excavating altars within these Goddess birthing shrines where he found offerings consisting of small deposits of grain preserved between layers of red clay on what he described as ceremonial hearths.[592] Similar "votive deposits," including carbonized barley seeds placed in the post cavity and covered over, have been reported by other researchers.[593] Gimbutas notes that the practice of adding grain seeds into clay figures spread along with the practice of farming:

> The early Cucuteni (Tripolye) culture, which dated from circa 4800–3500 BC, provides us with the clearest insight into Neolithic rituals honoring the pregnant vegetation goddess . . . figurines showed traces of grain, and some sixty figurines bore evidence of grain impressions on the surface . . . When technicians X-rayed these very porous clay figurines, they found three grain types (wheat, barley, and millet) stuffed inside . . . Here we have powerful evidence for a ritual associating grain, flour, and baking with the goddess performed in order to assure abundant bread.[594]

This insight into the ritual planting of seeds within the clay layers of ritual goddess figures inspired me to take a closer look at the symbols carved onto these figures and into a group of female torsos in particular. One (figure 11) came from the Cucuteni culture in central Bulgaria and dated from around 5,000 BCE. Now I could see a context.[595]

If I unwrapped the symbols from around the torso of the figure and drew them out on a flat plane, then a familiar symbol was revealed. Gimbutas explains these figures as graphically demonstrating the connection between the double-egg buttocks and lozenges. The egg-shaped buttocks were decorated with energy symbols, whorls and concentric circles, which I had noted in a previous book, *Uriel's Machine*, are shapes that are formed by the shadow of the noonday sun over the changing seasons of the year.[596]

Figure 12 is the sketch I drew of how the symbol would unfold. The symbolism is clear. So not only has Gimbutas provided evidence of extremely early use of the lozenge and spiral symbols that continue to fascinate my undergraduates, she has also succeeded in placing them in a religious context. She links them to a belief in a Great Earth Mother Goddess, and, by studying the context of their discovery, has linked them to particular features of the Goddess:

> The innumerable Neolithic figurines preserved in their original settings intimate the richness of Old European spirituality . . . Their makers often incised them with symbols, such as two or three lines, spirals or meanders, a chevron or a lozenge . . . artisans could create schematic figurines easily, and, like the Christian cross, in religious practice these figures communicated the same symbolic concepts as the more representational art. These simplified images . . . express a sacred message.[597]

Gimbutas had already studied the symbolic significance of the Goddess's body parts. She noted that the downward-pointing triangle was well-established as symbol of the vulva and womb of the Goddess. She said the symbol stood for the "cosmic womb of the Goddess as the source of the waters of life, the sprouting of life and the giving of birth."[598]

The upward-pointing triangle in figures 11 and 12, formed by the spread of the Goddess's legs, symbolize death and the womb as tomb, as seen in the structures of

Figure 11   Figure 12

so-called "horn-mouthed tombs."[599] Gimbutas says that "the caves, crevices and caverns of the earth are natural manifestations of the primordial womb of the Mother. Burial in the womb is analogous to a seed being planted in the earth, and it was therefore natural to expect new life to emerge from the old."[600] The large protruding buttocks, as shown in figure 11, are, according to Gimbutas, a metaphor for "a double egg or pregnant belly," [601] and are a symbol of intense fertility. In this context, a meaning for the combined symbols becomes clear. The upward-pointing triangle represents death and the act of planting a seed in the womb of the Goddess. The downward-pointing triangle represents the new life that will come in the spring. Their points meet at the vulva of the Goddess and the intersection of the double emblem of fertility represented by the exaggerated buttocks.

Marija Gimbutas believes that the Neolithic farmers of Europe developed a sacred script out of their religious symbols and signs.[602] As she explains:

> The observation that certain signs appear only on specific figurines and associated cult objects led me to decipher Old European deity types and functions. The results of this study first appeared in *The Language of the Goddess* (1989). For instance, in Old European art, bird goddess figures show X and V signs, chevrons, meanders, and parallel lines similar to those from the Upper Paleolithic. The longevity is amazing: The signs endure for about 15,000 years, from the Upper Paleolithic through the Neolithic. V signs and chevrons mark vases and other ritual objects through time, serving the same divinity . . . The Starcevo-Vinca culture manifested the most examples . . . Some thirty abstract signs build a core set. It is important to observe that these signs indeed represent writing: Instead of individual or random occurrence in pottery panels, the script signs appear in rows or clusters, with several different signs following one another . . . Abstract, not pictorial, signs comprised the script.[603]

Ever since my own first inkling that these signs did represent a formal script, I had continued to look for a context. I had already noticed that the V or chevron, when topped off to form a lozenge or diamond shape, was a pattern that occurs in the shadows cast on the land by the rising and setting sun as it moves through the seasons. The lozenge when plotted out in this way encodes the latitude of the observation and so can contain information about the place it was observed. This mechanism is shown in figure 13: The farther north the latitude, the taller and thinner the lozenge shape becomes. In latitudes nearer to the Equator, it becomes short and fat.[604] I have used this observation to check the shape of many lozenges, including the earliest ones ever discovered (70,000 BCE at Blombos Cave, South Africa, which I will discuss more fully later), and found the technique to be consistent in locating the latitude of the site where the lozenges had been inscribed.[605]

Likewise the shape of the two spirals, which was superimposed on the buttocks of the Goddess in figure 11, could also be derived from the observation of the path of the sun's shadow during the seasons, with each spiral being traced out over a quarter of the year.[606] This observational mechanism, which is carried out

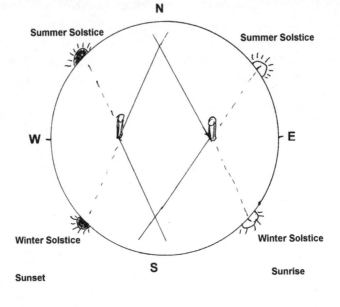

Figure 13

by plotting the fall of the tip of the shadow of the freestanding pole at midday, as described in *Uriel's Machine*, traces out the pattern observed on the buttocks of the Goddess in figure 11.

I could now add this practical insight of the observational basis of the symbols of the Goddess to Gimbutas's symbolic interpretation, and read the latest form of the symbol, which I had observed at Newgrange in Ireland (figure 3, which I've repeated here to show the comparison).

The two lozenge shapes represent the extreme latitudes of the British Isles, and they intersect, in the form of a downward-pointing triangle with an upward-pointing triangle, at the place where the spring spiral of the sun's path moves across to begin tracing out the spiral of summer. This point is known as the vernal equinox, and is the time to plant your seeds for an autumn harvest. So the symbol says "plant your dead seed in the womb of Mother Earth at the vernal equinox, and by the end of summer it will be reborn as abundant grain to give you

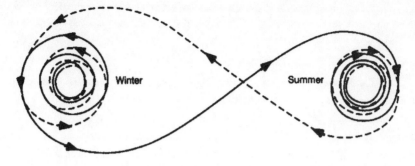

Figure 14

bread through the winter." It is a powerful symbol, and in its final form is virtually a textbook on how and where to grow grain.

This interpretation posed a further question, though: How did this knowledge, coded so wonderfully into this complex but widespread symbol, arise? If Gimbutas is correct and these symbols arise from sacred rituals, did this mean that farming originally began as a religion?

Most of the evidence that gave me my first clues as to how farming began came from Palestine and Anatolia and from two archaeologists who did trouble to write up their findings, Kathleen Kenyon and James Mellaart. Kenyon excavated Jericho, and Mellaart excavated Çatalhöyük—both of them cities that were founded before farming began and were established as trading centers.

It would be nearly thirty years after Mellaart completed his investigation before anybody else followed up his remarkable findings, but, fortunately, the archaeologist who took over Mellaart's work believes in sharing his findings by means of a frequently updated website. Dr. Ian Hodder, now a Professor at Stanford University, is head of the Çatalhöyük Research Trust based at Cambridge University. He works under the auspices of the British Institute of Archaeology at Ankara, and since 1993 has been excavating this important site. The excavation will take until 2018 to complete, but in a move which is a magnificent example to all archaeologists, Professor Hodder's team runs the website http://catal.arch.cam.ac.uk/, which gives accurate and up-to-date information on the progress of their work.

Ian Hodder's attitude is refreshingly open. He is aware that the excavation for which he is responsible was the site of Neolithic Goddess worship, and that some New Age groups have formed themselves into a Goddess community. He has taken on board the need to provide facts and not to color them with preconceived ideas. This is his message to the Goddess community:

> Some of the Goddess groups that have visited the site . . . have said "but we are not interested in YOUR interpretations; they are already biased; we want to make our own interpretations." This is an important challenge to archaeologists. WE cannot

assume that the provision of "raw data" is enough. This is because the data are never "raw." The data are immediately interpreted by the archaeologist. And it is quite possible that someone from the Goddess community would interpret the "primary, raw data" differently.[607]

Hodder's research group is to be commended for making their raw finds available online and separating facts from speculation. This is a world away from the secretiveness and selectivity of some old-fashioned archaeologists. This detailed information about artifacts and buildings, when combined with newly published DNA analysis of Neolithic Anatolian women, gives a remarkable new perspective on the beginnings of farming, as I will demonstrate.

Çatalhöyük might well provide vital clues to help answer the question of why the human race became farmers. The central issue is the improbable change of lifestyle from hunting/gathering to farming. How do you start farming? What do you eat while you are sitting around hoping that you can grow enough crops to feed yourself, your family, and your tame animals? If nobody has ever done such a thing before, you are gambling with your very existence. And, as a general rule, the foolhardy do not live to pass on their genes to future generations.

If you look at the matter impartially, it is such an unlikely thing to happen that some writers often feel the need to suggest that there must have been some earlier lost civilization, or race of space men, which discovered farming and then passed on its secrets to the newly evolved *Homo sapiens*. To me, this is simply begging the question. If there was such a lost civilization or alien influx, how did *it* manage the same highly unlikely transition from hunting and gathering to farming?

Understanding the Origins of Farming

How did the traditions of farming and living in cities first begin? Why have they persisted down to the present day? John W Hodges' excellent statistical study of comparative life-spans of Neolithic farmers and the hunters who lived alongside them shows that hunter-gatherers had an easier lifestyle, lived longer, and worked less than early farmers.[608] Why opt for the hard slog of subsistence farming? Why, after some three and a half million years of living a very successful nomadic lifestyle, did humans give up the idyll of hunting and gathering and opt for the hard work, susceptibility to pests, and uncertain harvests of the farmer? Why did they give up the space and openness of nomadic wandering for the cramped, enclosed hovel of the city dweller?

Current theories arise from different fields. Anthropology, history, archaeology, and economics all have their own views, but they all seem to agree that cities are bolt-on additions to a pre-existing rural farming economy. But as I looked at the history of the sacred symbols of farming, I was beginning to feel uncomfortable with this dogma of agricultural primacy and the city as necessary evil. It was beginning to have the feeling of just another "good story," one of our race's childhood "truths" that is not really true. By now, I was beginning to realize that the beliefs humans like most are those which have the best story attached to them.

The accepted belief can be simply stated: When *Homo sapiens* first appeared, these hunting people lived in small, economically self-sufficient family-based groups. They found their own food and made their own weapons, tools, and anything else they wanted. Only when some of these primitive groups settled down and learned how to grow crops, raise livestock, and build houses, did villages emerge. And from these villages emerged the new disciplines of division of labor, large economic building projects, and intricate social organization, which in turn laid down the foundations of civilization.

Once this new technique of food production called farming began, then it is assumed, in the archaeological literature, that it spread by one of three possible methods. The first is known as the model of diffusion, which says that hunter-gatherer bands came into contact with farming villages and decided to copy their way of life. The second says that there was a wave of colonization, when a group of established farmers decide to migrate to new lands to set up new farming villages. The third maintains that there was a wave of advance where, as the families of successful farmers increased, some of their children stayed on the parental farm, while others moved off a few miles to seek convenient land for themselves.

All these theories assume that cities only appeared once farming was well established. All three create a story of how farming spreads out and replaces hunters with farms, the farms begin to support villages, and from the villages grow the city-cultures that we call civilization.[609] The only problem with all three of these models is that they do not fit the latest known facts. The earliest known cities are Jericho[610] and Çatalhöyük,[611] and neither was based on a farming economy.

THE SECRET AGENDA OF ADAM SMITH

Startling as it sounds, the present accepted theories of how farming began are based not on archaeological evidence but on the work of Scottish economist Adam Smith (1723–1790). As I will discuss later, it appears that many twentieth-century archaeologists indirectly base their assumptions about the beginnings of farming on Smith's seminal work on economy, *The Wealth of Nations*, without their even realizing it. Perhaps in our present age of specialization, many archaeologists may not even know who Smith was, so let me explain. Although he was an inspired economist and the founder of the discipline, he was a man of his time. He lived in the strictly regulated religious atmosphere of eighteenth-century Glasgow and was a committed creationist.

Smith knew that Adam, his Biblical namesake, was a dispossessed gardener, and his virtuous son, Abel, was a farmer, while it was the murderous outcast Cain who went on to build the first city. Obviously, from Smith's point of view, man had been created in a garden. Archbishop James Ussher had even published an exact year for the event. Another enthusiast refined this down to a day and time, so Adam Smith could well have believed that the Earth was created at God's whim at 9:00 a.m. in the morning of Sunday, October 23, 4004 BCE. His Bible confirmed that the fruits of the field and animal husbandry were gifts from God, first given to mankind during the seven days that it took to make everything in the known universe. The sequence of prehistorical construction was clear: first the stars, next the Earth, then day and night, sea and land, animals, and finally mankind. It was obvious, a matter of holy writ, for Dr. Smith that hunting/gathering and farming came before cities and civilization. This was a simple and easy-to-understand story that didn't even need to be mentioned in his study of economics, as it was so obviously true.

But the facts say it is wrong. Because Adam Smith believed the Biblical myth, he got the sequence of causes wrong. A careful reading of his seminal book on economics shows him struggling with data which goes against this sequence, but never becoming confident enough to question Biblical truth.[612] The archaeological evidence shows that cities came before farming. As I will also demonstrate, the facts can only be explained if cities became centers of trade before farming started.

In the early twentieth century, archaeologists had, to their own satisfaction at least, solved the question of the prehistoric origins of civilization. A major contributor to this solution, Professor Gordon Childe, wrote in *The Dawn of European Civilisation* that the theme of European prehistory was "the irradiation of European barbarism by Oriental civilization."[613] Childe's assumption was that the chief advance in the prehistory of Europe was the result of the influence of the Near East carried west by migrations of whole peoples.

Childe's school of belief, which accepted that all civilization spread from a starting point between the rivers Tigris and Euphrates, was known as Diffusionism. In some ways it was right, but in others quite wrong. Childe saw the ancient cities of Sumer and Egypt as the source of all civilized innovations, and archaeologists became concerned with studying the waves of "diffusion" of people, which spread these ideas from the enlightened East to the barbarian West. But farming, as we have seen (figure 10), was already well established in the west before the cities of Sumer and Egypt began.

Childe's view remained unchallenged until the 1960s. In 1957 Childe described the function of prehistoric archaeology as:

> distilling from archaeological remains a preliterate substitute for the conventional politico-military history, with cultures instead of statesmen as actors and migrations in place of battles.[614]

Childe summed up his basic idea under five headings:

1. Civilization in the Orient is extremely ancient.
2. Civilization can be diffused.
3. Elements of civilization were in fact diffused from the Orient to Europe.
4. The diffusion of historically dated Oriental types provides a basis for bringing prehistoric Europe within the framework of historical chronology.
5. Prehistoric European cultures are poorer than contemporary European cultures, i.e. civilization is later in European cultures than in the East.[615]

He was wrong on a number of counts. The belief of the archaeologists was that the Neolithic period in Britain began in 2,000 BCE. But the developing science of radiocarbon dating was pushing this back nearly 750 years, and some members of the archaeological establishment, such as Professor Stuart Piggott, author of the standard work *Neolithic Cultures in the British Isles* found the radiocarbon findings "archaeologically unacceptable."[616] The radiocarbon dates showed that farming had already developed in Anatolia, the Levant, and western Iran long before it started in Egypt.

But the worst was yet to come.

There were problems with the accuracy of early carbon dating, and the problems lay in the assumption that the creation rate of radiocarbon in the upper atmosphere was constant. When the technique was first applied, it was assumed that the rate of creation of radiocarbon in the upper atmosphere had been constant for all time. But careful analysis of the radiocarbon content of ancient trees, which could be independently dated by counting the growth rings, showed that the rate of conversion of nitrogen into radiocarbon varied over the centuries, as a function of the flux of radiation from the sun and the degree of ionization of the ionosphere.[617]

In 1970, an accurate calibration chart was published by Professor H. E. Suess of the University of La Jolla, in California, which took account of the variation in radiocarbon production. It showed that radiocarbon dates before 2,000 BCE were tremendously underestimated.[618] Now it was clear that the Neolithic buildings of Western Europe long predated anything in Sumer or Egypt. This finding provoked a total crisis in the complacent world of archaeological certainty.

Colin Renfrew said of this:

Suddenly and decisively the impressive megalithic tombs of western Europe are set earlier than any comparable monuments in the world. There are no stone-built monuments anywhere approaching them in antiquity. Perhaps even more remarkable, some of these underground burial chambers, with their roofs of stone, are preserved entire, so that we can enter them and stand inside a stone chamber which looks today just as it did more than 5,000 years ago . . . Now the paradox is with us again: that such impressive monuments were created many centuries before the Pyramids by barbarians who lacked even the use of metal. The urgent task confronting us is to explain just how these monuments did come to be built, if it was not by colonists from the early civilizations of the Near East.[619]

My own discipline of physics had made its unique contribution to upsetting the archaeologists' grip on the understanding of the past, but other academic disciplines also had ideas to add to the debate. And foremost among these is that practiced by many of my colleagues at Bradford School of Management, the discipline of economics.

Hunting for Early Cities

The word "city" seems to be a controversial word to use about prehistoric concentrations of people. Archaeologists in general accept the view that cities can only develop after the beginning of agriculture. Economist Jane Jacobs, an outsider to archaeology, dared to look at the mechanism behind the formation of cities in prehistory, and she came to very different conclusions.

Jacobs based her hypothesis on her interpretation of the excavation evidence from Çatalhöyük and summarized her findings in *The Economy of Cities*.

> The logical inference is that in prehistoric times agriculture and animal husbandry arose in cities. But if this is so, then cities must have preceded agriculture. [620]

She demonstrates that the city's total food supply would be made up of its own hunting territory's yield of wild animals and plants, its imports of wild animals and seeds, and its own homegrown meats and grains. As the city grows, its total need for food increases, but it also creates conditions for the more efficient creation of new internal sources of food, so its need for imports decreases. As an increased range of products starts to be made in the city, so it is able to trade in other items.

Çatalhöyük was a real city that extended to over 100 acres; James Mellaart estimated that it supported a population of over 7,000 people. It was a sophisticated city, consisting of cube-shaped terraced houses that had timber-supported flat roofs with access holes in them, so they could be used as rooftop verandas. Carved into the wall of one of the buildings was a detailed map of the city showing its terraced housing, and behind it a picture of a twin-peaked active volcano, now long since extinct.[621] This volcano was a source of obsidian, a variety of black volcanic glass, which was highly prized for making stone tools and mirrors. this was the specialist product that, Jacob said, explained how the city was born.

Mellaart found that the city had been an important trading center for obsidian and artifacts made from the volcanic glass. The city also had an agricultural infrastructure based on the farming of barley, wheat, and cattle. It was clear from a detailed study of its rubbish heaps that the people of Çatalhöyük also ate the meat of wild animals.[622]

The level of workmanship demonstrated in the artifacts Mellaart dug up—jewelry, tools, pottery, and obsidian mirrors—was extremely high. The craftsmen of the city had developed high levels of skill in their various professions, and this implies specialization. But mirror grinders still have to eat, and so they must have been able to trade their mirrors for food. This specialization also suggests that the society they were living in was a peaceful one. Societies that have to fight to survive cannot afford the luxury of artists and craftsmen working on non-essential items such as jewelry and mirrors. But what is most surprising about this site is its date: It was already well developed by 6,500 BCE.[623] In addition, from the shrines and statues that he found, Mellaart concluded that the inhabitants of the city worshiped a Great Goddess.

The archaeologist's dogma says: agriculture first, cities later. At first I thought this idea might have been inspired by a romantic belief, probably influenced by Rousseau's idea of the noble savage, that in pre-Neolithic times hunters lived only in small, self-sufficient groups which found their own food and made their own tools, weapons, and other manufactured goods, such clothes and pottery. The unspoken assumption is that only the chance discovery of grain crops and animal husbandry first led to the development of fortified villages, which in turn lead to the division of labor, social organization, and the development of building skills.

The problem with this idea is that it makes little economic sense. As Hedges demonstrated in his detailed statistical study[624], life is actually harder for farmers than for hunter/gathers. Hunting and gathering for their own needs involves the latter in less work per individual than farming of either crops or animals. So why should anybody voluntarily adopt a harder way of life? Why choose to work harder simply to keep somebody else in food—unless that extra mouth could offer something useful in return?

Dr. N.J. Berrill, a biologist at the University of Leeds, was another archaeological outsider who was puzzled by the sudden change that the discovery of farming brought about. In *Man's Emerging Mind* he said:

> In terms of more significant time, probably no more than fifty human generations and possibly less were responsible for the greatest transformation and the greatest inventions in the whole of human history. Following any trail is a relatively easy matter, but doing something that no one has ever thought of doing before is not only difficult, it is nearly impossible. Just as new ideas dawn slowly for an individual, so I am sure that in the case of a collective change of such magnitude the clarity of understanding we seem to see from here is an illusion gained from hindsight, and the whole process of thought and action responsible for the cultivation and breeding of plants and animals which took the place of the old gathering and hunting was in reality a prolonged and heart-breaking effort of the human mind. [625]

He goes on to comment that on the plains of Anatolia, where farming began,

> The rivers are still full of sturgeon. Wild fruit of many kinds we now enjoy in cultivated form are abundant—peaches, pears, plums, almonds, apricots, apples and grape; while pheasants, grouse, ducks and geese abound in the swamps and among

the highlands wild sheep, boar, goats and deer are still plentiful and at one time so were wild cattle.[626]

He is pointing out that there was no need for farming when food was so abundant, but that all the raw materials were present for its development if something happened to trigger the change.

Berrill makes the point that the most likely candidate for the ancestor of the domesticated goat is a wild species that originated in Turkestan and Afghanistan, and the prototype wild sheep is found to the south of the Caspian Sea.

> The pig in its earliest western form undoubtedly came from the wild boar that ranges from Africa and Europe to Siberia. Yet the first domesticated ox was a dwarf. Either the neolithic men bred a small race from the great unmanageable beast of the plains or they found and took advantage of a dwarf race that lived in the forests. The last seems to be the case, for where man has taken a wild animal and subsequently dwarfed it, as in the bulldog, the teeth remain too large for the jaws, whereas in natural dwarfs everything is in proportion.[627]

Berrill's specialist knowledge of plant biology puts the development of cereal crops in perspective too.

> Cereals, the first and foremost of domesticated plants, were originally wild mountain grasses. Two wild grasses ancestral to wheat are known, dinkel and wild emmer, the first growing throughout the whole of the Caspian and Black Sea region, the second farther south in Palestine and parts of Persia. Dinkel is the parent of a small, unsatisfying wheat cultivated in Asia Minor, while emmer seems to have been the oldest kind grown in Egypt, Asia Minor and western Europe. Most modern bread wheats, however, appear to be a cross between emmer and an unknown grass, and it is this hybrid which is the oldest type found in Persia, Turkestan, Mesopotamia and India. Barley ancestors also appear to have belonged to the general region of mountainous country around the Caspian Basin. Cereal grasses undoubtedly were gathered head by head before they were cultivated, and no tool needed for the purpose, but this process of cultivation produced remarkable discoveries or inventions. Strains of wheat, barley and rye were discovered that grew heads which did not shatter and scatter their grain, a suicidal type for a wild grass to be but ideal for the human cultivator who could bide his time and reap his crop all at once. And flint sickles were made for cutting the hard stemmed grasses. Neither non-shattering cereals nor the sickles they inspired were acquired in a hurry.[628]

But they were acquired in Çatalhöyük, as James Mellaart points out:

> The presence of sickle blades lends substance to the theory of early agriculture, that is, reaping rather than sowing, but the main form of economy was evidently still the hunt.[629]

As Mellaart notes, though, this opportunistic reaping was not the main source of food. That remained hunting. Jane Jacobs shows that, without large groups of people living in proto-cities, the conditions necessary to develop the type of cereal farming that Berrill describes just do not occur. She sets out three economic rules that describe the conditions under which new and useful varieties of seed suitable for farming might develop:

1. Seeds that normally do not grow together must come together, frequently and consistently over considerable periods of time.
2. In the same place variants must consistently be under an informed and close observation of people able to act relevantly in response to what they see.
3. That same place must also be well secured against food shortages, so that in time the seed grain can become sacrosanct, otherwise the whole process of selective breeding will be repeatedly aborted before it can amount to anything. In short, property is a prerequisite. Although time is necessary, time in itself does not bestow cultivated grains on the settlement.[630]

Jacobs shows that a city grows by trading, and the important point to understand about early trade is that it developed from individuals going out in search of goods, not from the sudden birth of bag-carrying traveling salesmen. She explains this using as an example the trade in obsidian, the volcanic glass rock that makes extremely sharp knives and that was a specialist product of Çatalhöyük:[631]

> The initiative is taken by the people who want to buy something. The traders regard themselves as traveling purchasing agents. They take trade goods of their own to the place of purchase, but this is used like money to buy whatever it is they came for. Thus, the traders who come to the city from greater and greater distances come there purposely to get obsidian. For the most part, the barter goods they bring consist of the ordinary produce of their hunting territories. When the people of the city want special treasures like copper, shells or pigments that they themselves do not find in their territory, parties of their own traders go forth to get these things from other settlements. With them they take obsidian, as if it were money.[632]

Only non-perishable food is traded, because it stands the trip to the settlement best and it can be stored by the settlement. The major types of non-perishable food will be live animals and hard seeds. With a successful settlement, large quantities of live animals and seeds accumulate in what has now become a small city. The settlement quickly develops specialized individuals whose job is to look after the stores of food. Those who herd and look after wild animals will slaughter the most dangerous animals first, and the more docile species that can eat grass will be kept until they are needed for food, and will probably end up breeding. As Jacobs says, "the stewards were intelligent men and fully capable of solving problems and catching insights from experience. But they were not trying to domesticate animals; they were simply trying to manage the city's wild food imports to the best of their abilities." In this way they would naturally keep alive only the most docile animals, even if they had no intention of domesticating them.. As Jacobs explains:

> The only reason that second or third generation captives live long enough to breed yet another generation is that they happen to be the easiest to keep during times of plenty.[633]

The conclusions of Jane Jacobs about the economics of cities are that they were born directly out of social groups of hunter-gatherer societies and grew by trade. Without the density of population that proto-cities provided, civilization could not spontaneously appear.

However, her conclusions about the importance of Çatalhöyük have been largely ignored by the archaeological establishment, which continues to espouse old-established theories of prehistory. But why should this be? Why should the origins of farming give rise to so much confusion?

The Creationist Agenda

Around 6000 BCE, a revolution in human behavior took place, a change which founded the modern technology we take so much for granted. Archaeologists refer to it as the Neolithic Revolution, while ordinary mortals know it as the beginning of farming.

As I pointed out, archaeology offers three possible models to explain the spread of farming. Colin Renfrew explains them in *Archaeology and Language*:

> On the one hand, there is the model of diffusion, where the existing, rather sparse population of hunter-gathers comes into contact with communities in neighbouring territories which already practice farming. From these they acquire the necessary domesticated plants, and the livestock, as well as knowledge of farming practices, and so they come to take up farming. On the other hand there is the deliberate colonization model where a well-defined group of people deliberately set off for a distant land, to set up a new community.
>
> The wave of advance model differs significantly from both these. Movements of people are involved but only over very short distances. It notes that a marked increase in population follows the adoption of farming in a new territory. The authors argue that in a particular area the increase follows what is termed the logistic growth pattern, which starts off very rapidly and then slows down as the maximum population density, the saturation point for that particular area with that kind of farming, is reached . . . local farmers will sometimes shift the position of their farms by a few kilometres, perhaps as the soil in their fields becomes temporarily exhausted. Or it may be that in each new generation, some of the offspring stay on the parental farm, while others move off a few kilometres to seek convenient land elsewhere.[634]

The originators of this "wave of advance" model add this:

> If such a phenomenon of increase in population numbers coincides with a model of local migratory activity, random in direction, a wave of population expansion will

set in and progress at a constant radial rate . . . the wave of advance model would be one involving slow continuous expansion with movements usually being over short distances.[635]

This model says that farming spontaneously arose in various areas, then spread remorselessly throughout the world at a rate of a kilometer (about two-thirds of a mile) a year. Renfrew says of it:

It is an explicit mathematical model, drawn from the statistics of genetics. Given the underlying assumptions, the conclusions follow with mathematical rigour. That does not mean to say that the model has to be right: but if it isn't, there has to be something wrong with the assumptions.[636]

There does indeed. The problem with the model's assumptions are that it is entirely based on the idea that agriculture arose spontaneously at a particular point in human history, and, once that had happened, then its acceptance was automatic. It fails to ask the question: Why would anybody ever want to begin to farm? As I've noted, the farmer's life is harder than that of a hunter-gatherer, and it leads to a shorter life expectancy. This implies that farmers work harder to scrape by on a less healthy diet. They also become susceptible to diseases from living near their own wastes and in close proximity to their animals. And that is assuming that they know what they are doing in the first place. It can be a short-cut to extinction if they have no idea when or what to plant and when to harvest.

There is an implicit assumption that underlies all thinking about the origins of farming. Let us return to Renfrew's definitive and much respected *Archaeology: Theories, Methods and Practice* and see what he says about the beginnings of farming:

Following the development of farming . . . the economy underwent a process of intensification where more productive farming methods were accompanied by an increase in population. In such cases there was usually increased contact between different areas, associated with developing exchange . . . The urban revolution, the next major transformation that we recognize widely, is not simply a change in settlement type: it reflects profound social changes.[637]

The sequence set out here is this: First we have hunter-gathers, in the form of *Homo habilis*, who emerged about 2.5 million years ago. These proto-humans hunted and gathered their way along an evolutionary track through *Homo erectus*, via *Homo neanderthalensis*, to arrive eventually at the beginnings of our species of *Homo sapiens sapiens*, or modern man, about 200,000 years ago. For the next 190,000 years, we sat around on our naked butts, picking the fruit from the trees and barbecuing an occasional mammoth or antelope; then, about 10,000 years ago, a dozen or so oddballs scattered around the world decided to start farming. They were so successful at domesticating animals and growing grain that over the course of the next half-percent of our racial history, they transformed the world.

I find this story hard to believe; and the most difficult thing to accept is the spontaneous world-wide decision to begin farming that lies at the root of the assumptions driving the detailed mathematical models of the spread of agriculture. Hunter-gatherers lived on average four or five years longer than early farmers, were less prone to disease and famine, and didn't need to work as hard.[638] So why change?

The problem lies in the sequence of events which underlies Renfrew's statement of the theory of modern archaeology. It can be stated thus: "The four stages of society are hunting, pasturage, farming and commerce—a quote taken from Adam Smith's seminal work on the method of economics, *The Wealth of Nations*.[639] Most archaeologists accept this sequence without question. Indeed Renfrew reinforces this view when commenting on the refinement of radiocarbon dating in *Before Civilisation*: "The first revelation was the extreme antiquity of farming, and *even* of urban settlement, in the Near East."[640] [emphasis mine].

The first wave of uncalibrated radiocarbon dates for the city of Jericho gave dates of circa 6000 BCE (calibrated dates pushed it even further back). Dr. Kathryn Kenyon, who excavated the site, said of the finding:

> the pre-pottery Neolithic city of Jericho is not only the oldest city in the world but the oldest Neolithic settlement so far known.[641]

Her statement provoked a response from Colin Renfrew that shows how the possibility of organized economic units existing at such an early date was not a concept the archaeological establishment was happy about. At first reading, Renfrew seems to be retreating into unimportant semantics when he says of Dr. Kenyon's choice of words:

> The use [by Dr. Kenyon] of the word "city" is not a happy one, for pre-pottery Neolithic Jericho was not really a city, with the internal organization which that implies, but simply a large fortified village.[642]

His response suggests an academic need to be careful about use of the word "city." But why should such a word be dangerous to the *status quo*? It is only controversial if you accept, as a given, that cities have to develop out of farming, as Adam Smith so much wants to believe. Renfrew reveals his deep attachment to Smith's historical sequence when he adds this comment about the city of Jericho:

> The real surprise was that this early *farming* site should be dated so fantastically early.[643] [emphasis mine]

He reinforces this idea later in his discussion, saying:

> These dates are not of interest solely because they are early. What matters is that they allow the development of *farming centres, and of civilisations*, arising quite independently in different parts of the world, to be studied and dated in their own right

and compared to each other . . . The main force of the radiocarbon revolution in the Old World was to transform the dating of the early farming cultures. The origins of farming in the Near East had been set by guesswork . . . Now at last there was a way of determining dates before the periods of the great civilisations.[644] [emphasis mine]

ADAM SMITH AND GOD'S DIVINE PLAN

I have already hinted at why Adam Smith originally proposed this hallowed sequence when he published *The Wealth of Nations* in 1766. But to understand his mindset, I needed to look more closely at the times he lived in.

When Adam Smith was born in 1723, the science of geology did not exist. James Hutton, the man who founded modern geology, did not present his groundbreaking paper about the age of the Earth to the Royal Society of Edinburgh until 1785. By this time Adam Smith was nearing retirement and basking in the glow of the success of the third edition of his *Wealth of Nations*. Smith lived in a world of religious certainty which Hutton was challenging with little success. As a later Professor of Geology from Edinburgh University, Dr. A. Holmes, explains:

> Hutton's genius received scant recognition in his lifetime, mainly because of the prevalent belief that the world had been created in the year 4004 B.C. Far from being welcomed, Hutton's discoveries [about the true age of the Earth] were generally regarded with righteous horror . . . Christians no longer had any incentive to study the ways of Nature because men had a complete theory as to why things happen.[645]

The man responsible for the belief that the world was 6,000 years old was the Archbishop of Armagh, James Ussher. He is now quoted as being responsible for the calculation that determined that the moment of creation occurred at nine o'clock in the morning on October 23, 4004 BCE. Ussher was one of the greatest scholars and theologians of his time. He traveled widely, building up a large collection of books that came to form the nucleus of the major library of Trinity College Dublin, and his chronology of the world became the accepted standard dating used in the Authorized edition of the Bible. It was that same official Bible that Adam Smith used in his daily worship.

Smith knew that farming came before commerce because God created Adam, and Adam was a gardener. And Adam Smith was privy to the mind of God, as Professor Andrew Skinner, Smith's biographer, points out:

> Adam Smith's *The Theory of Moral Sentiments* . . . [belongs to] a distinctive School of Scottish Philosophy. This School generally adopted the position that certain characteristics are implanted in man by the Author of Nature, thus providing the means by which a Rational or Divine Plan, whose purposes are not always known to man, is unfolded.[646]

Smith confirms this in *The Theory of Moral Sentiments* (1759):

> But by acting according to the dictates of our moral faculties, we necessarily pursue the most effectual means for promoting the happiness of mankind, and may therefore be said, in some sense, to co-operate with the Deity, and to advance as far as in our power the plan of Providence. By acting other ways, on the contrary, we seem to obstruct, in some measure, the scheme which the Author of nature has established for the happiness and perfection of the world, and to declare ourselves, if I may say so, in some measure the enemies of God. Hence we are naturally encouraged to hope for his extraordinary favour and reward in the one case, and to dread his vengeance and punishment in the other. [647]

This statement illustrates one of Smith's characteristic ideas, the view that man is led as if by an "invisible hand" to promote ends that were not part of his original intention.[648] Smith's strongly held belief in a Divine Plan for the development of a world that was only 6,000 years old prevented him from ever questioning the order of events portrayed in the Bible. And here we find the basis of his assumption that cities arose out of agriculture when he says:

> According to the natural course of things, therefore, the greater part of the capital of every growing society is, first, directed to agriculture, afterwards to manufacture, and last of all to foreign commerce.[649]

When Smith first published his analysis of economic theory, he was breaking new ground. Much of his work on the division of labor and the theory of value has become integral to modern economics. The famous twentieth-century economist J. A. Schumpeter said of Smith's work:

> Though the *Wealth of Nations* contained no really novel ideas and though it cannot rank with Newton's *Principia* or Darwin's *Origins of Species* as an intellectual achievement, it is a great performance all the same and deserved its success.[650]

When world-famous economists pay this sort of respect to Adam Smith's system of economic analysis, it is hardly surprising that mere archaeologists take his reasoning for granted and fail to notice the enormous blind spot his creationist view of the world imposes on him. Smith asserts not only that the four stages of society—hunting, pasturage, farming, and commerce—exist and have existed, but that each society will tend to pass through them in sequence.[651] Skinner, in his analytical introduction to *The Wealth of Nations*, points out that this sequence, which Smith supported, became a key concept in the thinking of an influential group of scholars known as The Scottish Historians. It included not just Adam Smith, but Adam Ferguson, Lord Kames (Henry Horne), Dugald Stewart, and John Millar.[652]

But Smith's own evidence in the case of the city of Pisa, as quoted by Skinner, shows that:

Pisa was to some extent independent of the development of the agricultural hinterland, meaning that it represented an enclave of prosperity based largely on foreign trade.[653]

But because he "knew" that farming had to exist before trading cities could begin, Smith does not explore this idea any further, although he draws attention to the fact that the most highly developed agricultural nations of his time were precisely the nations in which industry and commerce were most highly developed. (And he saw and reported that the countries that had the least well-developed manufacturing centers also had the poorest agriculture.) Smith also observed that it is not agriculture that leads the way for the development of industry and commerce, when he commented on the fact that the superiority of English industry and commerce over that of other nations was more marked than the superiority of English agriculture. In short, he reported that the really big difference in the superior English economic development of his time was the greater development of industry and commerce, not the greater development of its rural agriculture. He also noticed that the most productive, prosperous and up-to-date agriculture was to be found near cities, and the poorest agriculture was distant from them. However, he did not go on to make the logical deduction that city industry and commerce came before agriculture.

In the pre-Darwinian world that Adam Smith inhabited, everybody knew that agriculture and animal husbandry were givens: The Bible said this was the original way in which men earned their daily bread. So the only valid question left for him to ask was how could commerce and industry arise from agriculture? It left him with the need to propose a very special chain of economic causes and effects unlike any which have been observable since, but which he presumed must have been in place at the beginning, when God made the world and placed man in it.

The end result was that Adam Smith converted Biblical history into economic doctrine, and his assertions are faithfully repeated to this day by the archaeologists who continue to accept his Biblical sequence of hunting, pasturage, farming, and commerce, when all the evidence says the real economic sequence is hunting, commerce, cities, farming, and pasturage.

But who made the leap from commerce to farming? And why did they do it? The work of Marija Gimbutas suggested a possible explanation to me. In *The Living Goddess* she had said:

> In Neolithic Europe and Asia Minor (ancient Anatolia)—in the era between 7000 B.C. and 3000 B.C.—religion focused on the wheel of life and its cyclical turning . . . the focus of religion encompassed birth, nurturing, growth, death, and regeneration, as well as crop cultivation and the raising of animals. The people of this era pondered untamed natural forces, as well as wild plant and animal cycles, and they worshiped goddesses, or a goddess, in many forms . . . She revealed herself in multiple ways through the myriad facets of life, and she is depicted in a very complex symbolism.[654]

Was she right? Did farming begin as a religious practice? That would certainly explain the proliferation of irrational acts that were involved in the foolhardy step of committing a family's whole future to the success or failure of a handful of seeds.

Conclusions

The work of Marija Gimbutas traces the evolution of symbols from the earliest days of farming in Çatalhöyük, the first city, across Europe to the Neolithic farming communities of north-western Britain. These symbols form the earliest type of writing, which led eventually to the invention of Sanskrit. We no longer speak the language which these symbols encoded, but it is possible to deduce the meaning of certain symbols from the context of their use. I have traced the development of one particular symbol made of lozenges and spirals, which encapsulates basic instructions about when and where to plant seeds to ensure a successful harvest.

The evidence of the symbols, and supporting economic analysis by Jane Jacobs, shows that farming was a byproduct of the first cities: not something that developed spontaneously as a lifestyle choice. The present archaeological theories of how farming arose are based on the work of the eighteenth-century Scottish economist Adam Smith, who was a committed creationist and incorporated his religious views into his economic analysis. His assumptions did not fit the emerging archaeological facts, but they are not usually called into question.

The lozenge and spiral symbols, which appear in such profusion in the decoration of Roslin Chapel, had all developed alongside farming, and I was now beginning to wonder if the development of farming was also the source of the seven basic stories which underpinned its mythical success. So who was it who introduced farming as a lifestyle, and what motivated them to do it? Were these stories part of a religious motive for the introduction of farming? In the next chapter, we'll find out how it was possible for a small group of irrational female religious fanatics to inflict farming on their lazy and easygoing menfolk.

.

CHAPTER 15

A History of Irrational Acts

Caught Wearing Your Mother's Genes!

Studying the building blocks of the cells that make up all living bodies has become a fashionable subject in recent years. Since the discovery of the basic structure of deoxyribonucleic acid (DNA), the chemical language that allows a living cell to make replicas of itself, biologists have been studying the genetic codes that are contained in the long spiral-wound chains of molecules that form the smallest units of our bodies. In 1953 Francis Crick and James Watson were working on the process of cell replication at Cambridge University, and that year they published a paper that in 1962 would win them the Nobel Prize for Physiology or Medicine. They showed how the molecules in the nucleus of a living cell contained instructions to build all the different cells that make up the body of any living animal, including humans.

The science of genetics was well established in terms of the rules that animal breeders used to selectively improve the bloodlines of domesticated animals. But the discovery of molecular biology opened up a new understanding of the potential of DNA. It is an immensely complicated area of study, as the average human being has between 60,000 and 80,000 genes—and each gene is made up of thousands of differently intertwined strands of DNA, all of which interact in order to produce a particular individual. It took fifty years from the discovery of the code to mapping out the complete sequence of all the genes that make up a human being. This human genome is a vast blueprint of the DNA interactions that make us what we are, and understanding it offers the possibility of understanding, and eventually curing, many of the common diseases inherent in the human condition. But, as this great research project was unfolding, interesting applications of DNA mapping techniques were also being developed.

The strands of DNA in the cells of mammals, including mankind, group into sets called chromosomes. Unless you are one of a pair of identical twins, the particular set of chromosomes in your cells is unique. This means it is possible to create a "DNA fingerprint" by breaking up the individual strands using special chemicals called enzymes before drawing out their patterns to be photographed. The picture they form can be translated into a coding sequence, which can be matched to other samples from the same individual.

This method of identifying individuals was first developed in 1985, and it has become a popular tool for forensic scientists, who can use it to show if a particular individual was present at a crime scene. But some scientists soon realized that this technique can do much more. It stores the history of human interactions over thousands of years.

The technological advance that made this possible was the invention of DNA amplification: a form of cloning technique that can be used to multiply very small samples of DNA until there is enough identical material to produce a DNA fingerprint. This made it possible to extract DNA sequences from extremely old samples. For example, in 1977 DNA was successfully extracted from the first Neanderthal bones which had been found, over a hundred and twenty years earlier in the Neander Valley near Düsseldorf in Germany. Comparison of the DNA sequence of this Neanderthal showed that modern *Homo sapiens* is not descended from this now-extinct race of early humanoids, disproving a widely held belief at that time.[655]

The technique used to uncover the disjointed family tree of *Homo sapiens* and *Homo neanderthalensis* was the study of a small fragment of DNA code that is only inherited down the female line. This is called mitochondrial DNA, and is the genetic code that controls the formation of a symbiotic parasite that enables all humans to convert oxygen into energy. But all the mitochondria in your cells came from your mother, and she got them from her mother before her.

The study of the sequences of mitochondrial DNA (mDNA) can tell the matriarchal history of humanity. And it turns out that we have a surprisingly small number of maternal ancestors.

The Tribes of Woman

There has long been a debate about why humanity evolved into the most successful species on the planet. In 1993 Dr. Christopher Stringer, a researcher into modern human origins based at the Natural History Museum in London, and Dr. Clive Gamble, Reader in Archaeology at Southampton University, wrote in *In Search of the Neanderthals*:

The geographical origins of anatomically modern humans lie somewhere in Africa . . . [But] . . . the source of modern behaviour will remain conjectural until we have a better understanding of which evolutionary forces and mechanisms actually shaped modern behaviour. What is quite clear, however, is that wherever new developments took place they did so rapidly (the flick of a switch), adapting to the anatomy of modern humans that had been around for perhaps 70,000 years. Such behaviour, based on the structural principles of symbolically organized culture, spread rather like a virus among the host population, and then spread further as the host itself now expanded. The rapidity of the process, which took place so many thousands of years ago, makes it difficult for archaeologists to study.[656]

By now I was convinced that the development of symbols was a key factor in the spread of Neolithic culture, which in turn was the beginning basis of modern cultural behavior. And Dr. Marija Gimbutas has shown that the symbols that appeared at the heart of the Neolithic Revolution were intrinsically linked to women. The relatively new technique of mitochondrial DNA sequencing seemed to offer the best insight into the history of women's involvement in prehistory.

The person who has done most to develop and explain the research methods in this area is Bryan Sykes, Professor of Human Genetics at Oxford University. In *The Seven Daughters of Eve* he tells us:

Each of us carries a message from our ancestors in every cell of our body . . . Within the DNA is written not only our histories as individuals but the whole history of the human race. With the aid of recent advances in genetic technology, this history is now being revealed. We are at last able to begin to decipher the messages from the past. Our DNA does not fade like an ancient parchment; it does not rust in the ground like the sword of a warrior long dead. It is not eroded by wind or rain, nor reduced to ruin by fire and earthquake. It is the traveler from an antique land who lives within us all.[657]

Sykes has made the study of mitochondrial DNA (mDNA) his own. The mDNA, which each organism receives with its mother's egg, is the particular part of the cell that enables it to process oxygen into energy. It is a vital component of human life, but appears to be the result of an ancient accidental bacterial infection. The first life forms on Earth were simple, single-celled creatures too biologically inefficient to develop into the complex communities of cells that make up modern life forms, such as primates. However, when these simple cells were invaded by another simple bacterium, the combined inner chemistry of the two organisms allowed them to extract energy from oxygen. Newly evolved, oxygen-using, "proto-breathing" single-cell entities now had access to enough energy to grow into more efficient organisms made up of communities of specialized cells. It's strange to think that human life as we know it started out as a microscopic blob that caught a cold.

Mitochondria are rather like the chlorophyll that enables plants to turn sunlight into chemical energy, a class of objects known as prokaryotes. These structures started out in life as parasitic bacteria, but over many millions of years have become an integrated part of living cells. The role of mitochondria is to process nutrients and turn them into energy. This combination of cell and parasite has proved immensely efficient. Every multicellular plant and animal on the planet today has mitochondria that can be traced back to those original infected host cells, and both the human egg and sperm cells contain mitochondria. The role of the sperms' mitochondria is to provide the power source that drives the sperms' tails. Once the sperm head penetrates the egg cell wall, it abandons its tail, and so loses touch with its father's mDNA. With the sacrifice of its tail, the mitochondria of the sperm are not incorporated into the fertilized egg, and consequently the only mitochondrial genes transmitted to offspring are those of its mother. A newly fertilized human egg contains about 200,000 molecules of mDNA.

Over time, mutations occur, so that the mitochondrial chromosomes of various human families gradually diverge, and differences become more distinct over thousands of years. Because mDNA does not recombine, every human female retains an inbuilt coded record of her evolutionary history back to the dawn of our species, and beyond. This mDNA sequence is the "traveler from an antique land" in Professor Sykes's quotation above.

Geneticist Wesley Brown, of the Howard Goodman Laboratory of the University of California, was the first to realize that it was theoretically possible to use mDNA to trace back all the linkages in the human species to the great-grand-mother of mitochondrial chromosomes from which all others descend. (It also occurred to him that in the process, he might reach so far back in time that the creature carrying the ancestral chromosome would not be human at all.) But when this mitochondrial family tree was traced, it revealed a quite recent common female ancestor for all living humans. Every human alive today evolved from a single mitochondrial donor who lived somewhere between 180,000 and 360,000 years ago: just one female from which all mankind descends. Naturally, the Press called her "Mitochondrial Eve."[658]

This was a stunning find. Human evolution is known to have taken many millions of years, yet between one or two hundred thousand years ago, there was one woman from whom all six thousand million people today have sprung. Bryan Sykes describes her:

> Incredibly, even though the African clans [of women] are easily the most ancient in the world, we are still able to reconstruct the genetic relationships among them. Thus we probe the ancestors of the ancestors . . . One by one the clans converge until there is only one ancestor, the mother of all of Africa and of the rest of the world. Her existence was predicted in the original scientific paper on mitochondrial DNA and human evolution in 1987. Immediately she was dubbed "Mitochondrial Eve," hardly a convincing African name. She lies at the root of all the maternal ancestries of every one of the six billion people in the world. We are all her direct maternal descendants.[659]

(The paper he refers to was published by a team at the University of California who first coined the name Mitochondrial Eve.[660])

So our extended human family is much more closely related than most people realize, and our genes are about 98 percent identical to those of an African ape. Yet *Homo sapiens* is different. But we are different only in as much as we are surprisingly prolific. How did we become such successful reproducers? If the cause is not genetic, how did this difference evolve?

Our species did not evolve culture for over 120,000 years, and this began in the northern hemisphere no more than 30,000 years ago, according to almost all the evidence—with the exception of a single item dug out of a cave in Africa. Here is how *The Times* of London reported that find:

> A pair of decorated ornaments unearthed in a South African cave have been dated at more than 70,000 years old, proving that human beings could think abstractly and appreciate beauty much earlier than is generally accepted.

The engraved pieces of ochre, a type of iron ore, are by far the oldest examples of symbolic art—a standard benchmark for recognisably modern thought and behaviour. The earliest similar objects, from Europe, were made less than 35,000 years ago, and subtle intelligence is usually held to have begun at this time.

The find at Blombos Cave, 180 miles from Cape Town in the Western Cape, will therefore completely revise one of the first chapters of human history.

It indicates that not only did the first human beings evolve in Africa and spread throughout the world, but that they became mentally sophisticated by the time they did so.

This helps to explain the ease with which *Homo sapiens* supplanted other human relatives, such as the Neanderthals in Europe, and thus to explain the development of the modern human race.

All the anatomical features of *Homo sapiens* are known to have evolved in Africa between 150,000 and 130,000 years ago, but the question of when the species began to behave in a modern fashion has remained more elusive . . .

Some scientists, such as Professor Chris Stringer, head of human origins at the Natural History Museum have argued that "behavioural modernity" actually evolved much earlier in Africa, citing evidence such as bone tools found at Katanda in the Democratic Republic of the Congo, but their claims have been widely disputed.

The Blombos Cave, discovered by Professor Chris Henshilwood of the Iziko South African Museum in Cape Town, resolves the debate decisively.

The pieces of ochre, one 2 in. long and another 3 in. long have no practical function and were clearly intended for decorative or ritual use. This proves that the people who made them must have been capable of subtle thought, and probably indicates that they spoke a language of syntax and tenses, Professor Henshilwood said.[661]

Author's sketch of the 70,000-year-old symbols from the Blombos Cave

One of the most striking features of the article, for me, was the symbols these long-dead *Homo sapiens* had chosen to carve on one of these pieces of ochre. If I had been shown the symbols without a context, I would have said that they could have been symbols of the Great Goddess of Çatalhöyük. See for yourself, from my sketch.

I couldn't help but wonder if our species draws these symbols so often because our perception systems have evolved to find them attractive in a way that gives us some sort of reproductive advantage. I shall try to find out by adding this image into the regular test samples I investigate each year with my undergraduate classes.

Meet Eve's Seven Daughters

By tracing the mDNA from our original African Mother down to modern times, Bryan Sykes showed that seven matriarchal clans make up the people of northern Europe. He gave names to the female founders of these clans, to fit the letters his computer analysis program assigned them as identifiers, so they became his "Seven Daughters of Mitochondrial Eve." They are:

Ursula: Her clan left Africa about 45,000 years ago and settled where modern-day Greece is. They were the first modern humans to appear in Europe. They were a successful group who spread rapidly across the whole of Europe. Sykes says that they make up around 11 percent of modern Europeans, and there are large con-centrations of this tribe in the west of the British Isles and in Scandinavia.[662]

Xenia: Her clan arrived on the plains of what was then the great tundra of Europe about 20,000 years ago. This tundra stretched from southern Britain (which then was still joined to mainland Europe) to Kazakhstan. The people descended from her moved east across the steppes of Asia and even spread as far as the Americas. Sykes has determined that about 1 percent of Native Americans are her direct descendants. In Europe, her tribe split into three groups, one centered in Eastern Europe and the other two living farther west in France and Britain.[663]

Helena: She also arrived in Europe about 20,000 years ago, but her daughters settled along the Mediterranean coast of what is now the South of France. Her tribe were the most successful early colonists of Europe, and Sykes has shown that around 47 percent of modern Europeans have her as a direct maternal ancestor.[664]

Velda: Arrived some 3,000 years later to found her maternal dynasty in northern Spain. Sykes found that around 5 percent of present-day Europeans descend from her, but her daughters traveled widely, establishing family groups as far north as Finland and Norway.[665]

Tara: Founded her clan about the same time in Tuscany, in north-western Italy. She has left about 9 percent of modern Europeans carrying her mDNA. They live mainly along the coasts of Europe, from the Mediterranean round to the western coasts of the British Isles.[666]

Katrine: She lived along the edge of the lagoon that is now Venice, although it was miles inland when she lived there. She founded her dynasty about 15,000 years ago. Today it extends to about 6 percent of native Europeans, and is spread throughout the continent.[667]

Jasmine: Was the founder of the last of the maternal clans which make up modern Europe, and, as far as my research is concerned, she is the most interesting. She was born in Mesopotamia about 10,000 years ago, and is the maternal great-grandmother of about 17 percent of the modern Europeans. Her clan is not evenly distributed. This is how Bryan Sykes described it:[668]

> The descendants of Jasmine are not found evenly distributed throughout Europe. One distinctive branch follows the Mediterranean coast to Spain and Portugal, whence it has found its way to the west of Britain where it is particularly common in Cornwall, Wales and the west of Scotland. The other branch shadows the route through central Europe taken by the farmers who first cultivated the fertile river valleys and then the plains of northern Europe. Both branches live, even now, close to the routes mapped out by their farming ancestors as they made their way gradually into Europe from the Near East.[669]

Jasmine and her daughters arrived with farming. Were they the original farmer's wives, or were they something more? I was puzzled by what triggered their move from hunting/gathering to farming. As I have said, I do not accept the eighteenth-century Scottish economist Adam Smith's explanation:

> According to the natural course of things, therefore, the greater part of the capital of every growing society is, first, directed to agriculture, afterwards to manufactures, and last of all to foreign commerce. This order of things is so very natural that in

every society that had any territory it has always, I believe, been in some degree observed. Some of their lands must have been cultivated before any considerable towns could be established, and some sort of coarse industry of the manufacturing kind must have been carried on in those towns, before they could well think of employing themselves in foreign commerce.[670]

This does not fit what has been discovered about Çatalhöyük. There had been no farming when this trading city developed. The farming appeared to have to begun in the city for sound economic reasons, but not with any special plan. It is certainly true that farming can produce food surpluses, but it does so at the price of exploiting some sections of the population. Why did these farm laborers take the risk of trying to farm food for somebody else's benefit? It seems an irrational thing to do. Smith was aware of this paradox. The choice involved in developing cities, supported by farming, must lead to exploitation, although Smith tried to put a positive spin on this:

> Among civilized and thriving nations, though a great number of people do not labour at all, many consume the produce of ten times, frequently of a hundred times more labour than the greater part of those who work; yet the produce of the whole labour of the society is so great that all are often abundantly supplied, and a work-man, even of the lowest and poorest order, if he is frugal and industrious, may enjoy a greater share of the necessaries and conveniences of life than it is possible for any savage to acquire.[671]

Smith's answer was that it was all part of God's purpose, and it was quite all right to be exploited as long as you knew your place, and your betters made sure you were well fed. This idea went right back to his belief in the Garden of Eden. As he put it:

> to cultivate the ground was the original destination of man, so in every stage of his existence he seems to retain a predilection for this primitive employment.[672]

But a study of the DNA of the population of Orkney, where farming was established over 5,000 years ago, told a different story. What attracted my attention to this problem was the occurrence of a symbol which, as I showed in Chapter 14, summarizes the essence of farming in the sophisticated village of Skara Brae.

The Bloodlines of Orkney

Geneticist Jim Wilson carried out a detailed study of the DNA profiles of the native Orcadian population, and I was lucky enough to hear him deliver this at the 2003 Orkney International Science Festival. The hall was packed to hear the young Orcadian geneticist describe his research, which traced the ancestors, both male and female, of the islands of Orkney. Afterwards, I asked Jim for a copy of the full results and he kindly forwarded me the paper, which I quote here.

The abstract from his paper makes an important point about the Neolithic Revolution:

Human history is punctuated by periods of rapid cultural change. Although archaeologists have developed a range of models to describe cultural transitions, in most real examples we do not know whether the processes involved the movement of people or the movement of culture only. With a series of relatively well defined cultural transitions, the British Isles present an ideal opportunity to assess the demographic context of cultural change. Important transitions after the first Paleolithic settlements include the Neolithic, the development of Iron Age cultures, and various historical invasions from continental Europe. Here we show that patterns of Y-chromosome variation indicate that the Neolithic and Iron Age transitions in the British Isles occurred *without large scale male movements*. [673] [emphasis mine]

So farming was linked to the migration of women! As Jim Wilson *et al.* go on to explain:

We have utilized a number of genetic marker systems to determine the genetic legacy of cultural change . . . we contrast the pattern observed on the Y chromosome [found only in males] with that observed by using multiple genetic systems influenced by female migration (mDNA and unlinked X-chromosome systems) to evaluate whether cultural changes in the British Isles have involved different demographic roles for males and females . . . we have focused mainly on two, the pre-Anglo-Saxon British and the Scandinavians. We have achieved this by concentrating on the Celtic-speaking populations and on Orkney, a Northern Scottish archipelago with Viking and pre-Anglo-Saxon British heritage.[674]

His findings, which I first heard in his soft Orcadian brogue echoing through the amplification system of the Pickaquoy Cinema complex at Kirkwall, made me realize that there was far more to the story of farming and the myths it evokes than had been previously believed. Wilson drew the conclusion that:

at least one of the Neolithic or Iron Age cultural transitions in the British Isles involved some female immigration . . . [and] had a major effect on the maternal genetic heritage of the Celtic-speaking populations.[675]

But what was really striking about Jim Wilson's presentation was that the maternal heritage he had identified as having a major effect on the Neolithic population of northern Britain had come from the area we now call Turkey. Anatolia—where the city of Çatalhöyük thrived at the beginning of the farming revolution—is on the Turkish plateau. The implication of Wilson's analysis was that farming had to have been spread by women.

This is a disturbing idea for the archaeological establishment, which had long espoused Adam Smith's Biblically-inspired idea that men were God's natural gardeners and had developed and spread farming. The facts, however, are different, and they need explanation. Three facts in particular do not fit the Adam Smith view of the development and spread of farming:

1. The DNA audit trails of Brian Sykes show that modern *Homo sapiens* arose in equatorial Africa about 180,000 years ago. Both mDNA and Y-chromosome analysis give similar estimates for the date of the genesis of our species. Earlier species of human, such as Neanderthal and *Homo erectus*, used tools and moved out of Africa into Eurasia, but did not become farmers or city builders. *Homo sapiens* did. Why?

2. A steady stream of archaeological finds, and the detailed economic analysis of them by Jane Jacobs, show that cities began before farming. Sites of hunter-gatherer cities date back at least 11,000 years, millennia before the domestication of plants or the widespread systematic husbandry of animals. How could this be?

3. Jim Wilson's mDNA and Y-chromosome analysis shows that a group of humans who became farmers diffused westwards from Turkey some 10,000 years ago. They reached western Europe about 6,000 years ago. The DNA which drove this migration was female—there is no trace of male DNA in the resultant western populations. The implication is profound: Women spread farming. The question is, how did they do it and why?

FARMER'S WIVES OR THE MIDWIVES OF FARMING?

When Jim Wilson published his findings, they immediately provoked a response in the same issue of the peer-reviewed journal that accepted his findings. This came from no less a member of the archaeological establishment than Lord Renfrew, eager to defend the male-centered "wave of advance" theory of the spread of farming. His opening remarks accepted that genetics could shed light on archaeological subjects:

> Applying molecular genetics to questions of early human population history, and hence to major issues in prehistoric archaeology, is becoming so fruitful an enterprise that a new discipline—archaeogenetics—has recently come into being. That many of its applications have so far related to prehistoric Europe is due in part to the detailed archaeological attention devoted to Europe by a series of nineteenth and twentieth century scholars. It is also due in part to the early application of a specific demographic model, the "wave of advance," to explain the chronological patterning that emerged as farming spread across Europe at the onset of the neolithic period and to elucidate the structuring resulting from an early principal components analysis of the classical genetic markers for Europe. The application of DNA sequencing, permitting female lineages to be investigated through mDNA and male lineages through the Y chromosome, has already brought a series of new questions into perspective, generating lively debate. The time is ripe, therefore, for more closely

focused regional studies, devoted to specific historical problems. The paper by Wilson *et al.* in this issue of *PNAS* breaks new ground.[676]

But then he moved to a more critical position:

Although the question that they pose is an entirely valid one, there would clearly be need of a more ambitious sampling strategy to begin to formulate a definitive answer. The matter is underlined, so far as the neolithic is concerned, by the circumstance that the Orkney Islands may well have lacked any permanent population until the arrival of neolithic settlers. This, like the inception of the neolithic period in Crete, is one instance where the movement of females as well as males seems an indispensable assumption![677]

This is true, as far as it goes, but disingenuous in respect of the differences Jim Wilson had found. The men were local, coming from western Europe and the British mainland, while the women were of the tribe of Jasmine. They were the daughters of the women of Çatalhöyük who began the farming revolution. The reason for their migration from the plains of Anatolia to the windswept lowlands of Orkney is a puzzle, which, if answered, could tell the human race where its civilization came from.

I left that Science Conference inspired to try to find better answers than Renfrew's defensive response to the questions Jim had posed. And I began by looking for a motive to explain why women may have wanted to begin farming. Jane Jacobs had ruled out any economic motives as irrational.

I have previously mentioned that Marija Gimbutas had said that those women had developed a religious belief system which involved religious rituals that increased the chances of women giving birth successfully. Increased success in surviving the birthing process has a strong evolutionary advantage. Hedges had shown that one of the factors which helped early farmers was that their women had children more frequently than hunter-gathers did.[678] (He deduced this from statistical study of the age profiles of bones in tribal tombs.) A farming women could give birth to, and nurse, a new child every year, while hunter-gather women could only successfully rear a new child when the older child could walk alongside the mother, something that happens around the age of four or five. This meant that farmers were able to outbreed the hunter-gatherers in a ratio of about five to one.

Now a religious system which fosters interest in the welfare of birthing women does not in itself give any motive to begin farming. Nonetheless, this birthing preoccupation was long-lived among the early farming communities. As Dr. Gimbutas pointed out, it was still around when the symbols in figures 5 and 6 in Chapter 14 (see page 284) were carved:

On the island of Malta in the central Mediterranean, the Tarxien and Mnajdra temple artifacts indicate similar practices; these artifacts include a model of a low couch that could have served birth-giving, and a birth-giving figurine with nine lines across her back.[679]

We have seen Dr. Jacobs made the point that it was trade that provided the motive for creating the city of Çatalhöyük, and farming grew out of the trading. She concludes:

It was not agriculture then, for all its importance, that was the salient invention, or occurrence if you will, of the Neolithic Age. Rather it was the fact of sustained, inter-dependent, creative city economies that made possible many new kinds of work, agriculture among them.[680]

James Mellaart agreed with the importance of trade in obsidian (a hard volcanic glass used for making stone blades) to Çatalhöyük:

Trade was . . . the most important source of income for the inhabitants of Çatalhöyük . . . the city . . . held the monopoly of the obsidian trade with the west of Anatolia, Cyprus and the Levant . . . . Obsidian spearheads in prime condition are frequently found in groups of up to twenty-three specimens buried in a bag below the floor, where they were evidently stored as capital.[681]

He had also made observations of the religious practices of the women of Çatalhöyük, in whose shrines:

Statues allow us to recognize the main deities worshipped by neolithic people at Çatalhöyük. The principal deity was a goddess who is shown in her three aspects, as a young woman, a mother giving birth or as an old woman.[682]

Dr. Gimbutas believed this threefold Goddess concept was already a well-established image before the invention of farming. She says:

The birth goddess appears for more than twenty thousand years, from the Upper Paleolithic through the Neolithic. She may appear in threes.[683]

And this early manifestation of a Divine Trinity was also linked by the Skara Brae symbol to religious rituals involving grain (as I have already mentioned in the symbol shown in figures 12 and 13 on page 278 and 280, respectively). As we have seen, Gimbutas found evidence for a ritual associating grain, flour, and baking with the Goddess, in order to assure abundant bread.[684]

This link between rituals of the grain harvest and birthing platforms seemed to persist, as Gimbutas points out:

At Achilleion in southern Thessaly, Greece, my colleagues and I found altars and special stone platforms with offering pits near ovens, perhaps associated with harvest rituals.[685]

Was this the answer? That planting grain at the vernal equinox was a religious duty imposed by the Goddess, not a rational act at all? And was it carried out by a tribe of women who had a sacred duty to help their daughters give birth safely? These two ideas, if they had been brought together as a religious belief, would provide both a motive and an evolutionary advantage to any group who adopted them. But how could I test this in practice?

PLAYING GODDESS

The obvious course was to test the notion via a computer simulation. So I took my computer and created a great empty land, made up of mile-squares of tundra, with an aspect ratio approximately similar to that of the pan-continent of Eurasia, and made it fit a wide-screen monitor: i.e. a rectangle, wider east–west than north–south. Next, I created herds of wandering animals to graze on the grass of my empty land. My virtual herds wandered randomly from square to square as they exhausted the grazing. I set up rules for rate of grass growth, and stopped my creatures from returning to already-grazed squares. I felt quite goddess-like as I watched the herds meandering about the land I had built on my computer screen.

Encouraged by this initial success, I decreed there should be winter and summer so that the herds migrated north in the summer and south in the winter. Again, I felt a warm glow as the onset of winter showed the herds moving southwards to warmer climes. Now was the time to introduce death into my land. I set up rules to control the grass consumption per animal, and made each female breed when it reached an age of two seasons. The young were born in late winter, and then migrated with the herd. All animals died after ten seasons, and females had a single calf each spring, the sex being chosen randomly. Herds that grew too big had to move more frequently, and if they moved too quickly (more than a couple of miles a day), I set up a rule to make half their calves die. This reduced the size of the herd, allowing it to move more slowly and reducing the attrition rate to its young. I ran the simulation a number of times and watched as the herds stabilized at an equilibrium size that was determined by the grass replenishment rate.

When I was satisfied with the seasonal migration of my herds, I decided to introduce Adam into my Garden of Eden, but (unlike Adam Smith's namesake) my Adam was not a gardener, he was a hunter. Adam and his tribe fed on the meat of the animals, and this meant they had to camp within a reasonable distance of a grazing herd—but not too close, or it would spook them. I decided that they would camp no closer than a mile and no more than six miles from a herd. They would take only enough animals for their needs, and I decided to allow them to kill one animal per ten people of their tribe per week.

I also decided that they would be intelligent enough to recognize a comfortable campsite (it probably would have shelter and fresh water), and would only move their campsite if the herd moved too far away for them to hunt. I kept a database of the addresses of the squares they had used for their campsites, and if they returned to a region that was within range of where they had previously camped, I made them return to the same site. (I made this assumption about returning on the basis that they would naturally seek out the best campsites in an area; I let my tribes choose where these were and simply noted them for possible future use.) I ran the program, watched the hunting camps follow the herds randomly around the continent, and noted how they moved with the seasons.

I was quite certain, from Kathleen Kenyon's comments about the siting of Jericho by a group of hunter-gatherers over 10,000 years ago, that even nomads had favored sites that they would return to if possible. She said:

> The importance of Jericho stretches far back beyond this time when rich civilisations in the Crescent and hungry nomads in the interior met in the age-long struggle of the Desert and the Sown. It has long been recognised that the very origins of civilisation are to be sought in the Fertile Crescent. These origins lie in the first steps towards settled life which is the characteristic of the Neolithic Period. For hundreds of thousands of years, primitive man had lived on wild foods, as a hunter and food-gatherer. As such, he was a nomad, following the supplies of wild food, with the seasonal growth of wild fruits and the movements of wild animals. Any one area could hold only a limited population, so settled life of groups of men was impossible. The revolutionary step forward was the discovery that wild grains could be cultivated and made more productive, and wild animals herded and their products made constantly available. With this discovery, the growth of fixed settlements became possible.[686]

But even the early city of Jericho A (which is now dated at about 500 years after Çatalhöyük[687]) was based on a farming economy, quite different from the hunter/gatherer/trader economy of Çatalhöyük. Kathleen Kenyon describes what she found in *Digging up Jericho*:

> Their tools and weapons were mainly made of flint, but occasionally of obsidian . . . Arrowheads showed that hunting still supplemented food production, though the numbers are not very great in proportion to the other implements. Some of the most attractive flints are the sickle blades, which are very numerous. The edges are very finely serrated, and the making of these teeth shows high technical skill. The use of these toothed blades for cutting grain is shown by the high gloss which is produced by the silica in the stalks they have cut, and the number of the sickle blades shows the extent to which grain was a staple diet . . . Further evidence of the use of grain comes from the frequent find of querns . . . They consist of a roughly oblong block of conglomerate stone, with a grinding hollow which always runs out to one edge of the block, while at the other end is a flat ledge on which perhaps the operator sat, and there is a narrower flat ledge along the two sides.[688]

Before it had become a Neolithic walled city, Jericho must have been a strategically favored campsite. By now, I was convinced by the evidence of Mellaart and Jacobs that farming had begun by accident as a spin-off from the trading economy of Çatalhöyük. If this was so, and if it had been spread in some way by the women of Çatalhöyük, then there should be more early farming villages dotted about. I checked on a more recent survey by Professor Steven Mithen of Reading University, and I found this is exactly the state of affairs. In *After the Ice* he writes:

> Jericho was the first of the early Neolithic villages to be discovered and remains the most renowned. But its long-held pre-eminent position, as constituting the origin of the Neolithic and a farming way of life, has become severely challenged in recent years by new discoveries in the Jordan valley and in the northern reaches of the Fertile Crescent. These have also provided new and quite astonishing insights into Neolithic religion.[689]

Mithen also confirms what I had assumed about the re-use of favored campsites:

> In the 1980s, as director of the British Institute in Amman, Jordan, Garrard undertook a major programme of excavations in the Azraq basin, documenting the presence of . . . hunter-gatherers . . . Garrard's work exposed . . . sites . . . that some had been used repeatedly for many thousands of years, resulting in huge scatters of artifacts. The attraction of Azraq would have been the herds of gazelle which came to drink and graze on the lakeside vegetation; they most likely did so in great numbers and at predictable times of year and day. The hunter-gatherers would have known those times and arrived in large numbers to capture the vulnerable prey, probably returning to the campsite they had used the year before.[690]

As I was keeping a record of the campsites in my computer simulation, I was also able to work out how often, on average, a tribe would leave a campsite in the spring, as the herds migrated north, and then return to the same campsite in autumn. I ran a large number of cycles, using many different starting configurations for tribes and herds, and was surprised to find that on average, there was a 25 percent chance of a tribe returning in the autumn to a campsite that had been used in the spring either by themselves or another hunting tribe. This result was unexpectedly high. I expected something under 1 percent from purely random selection. It seemed that allowing the tribes a choice of campsites led to the selection of favored sites. So I made my land wider, to see if that would reduce the re-use rate. Once again, I was surprised to discover that over the long term it stayed around the same level of 25 percent. There was considerable variation in the short term, but I found that even if I increased the number of hunting tribes (I did not allow tribes to share a campsite), then it did not increase the re-use rate beyond the 25 percent limit, as tribes would use alternative campsites.

Next, I played the role of serpent, and introduced human sex and death into my pristine world. I drew up an algorithm for reproduction that used the Neolithic attrition rates calculated by John Hedges in *Tomb of the Eagles*.[691] This gave a life expectancy of 9 years for a woman of reproductive age (i.e., a total life expectancy of 24 years, with each female becoming fertile at 15. Males had a life expectancy of 29 years. I set the birth rate at Hedges' figure for hunter-gatherers, as a child every four to five years. (I chose either four or five with a random-number generator, so some women had two children, while others only had one). Children's sex was also chosen by a random-number generator, setting an equal probability of male or female, and a female had her first child nine months after she reached the age of 15. All females died when they reached the age of 24, and all males at the age of 29. (I realized that a small percentage would live longer, but for the sake of this simulation they were insufficient to make it worthwhile modeling them.)

I set my initial tribe size at 40, with an initial mix of one-third adult male, one-third female (with all the males and females aged 15, which made the males old enough to hunt and the females old enough to breed), and one third mixed children, their sex chosen randomly with a fifty-fifty chance for either sex. I used this starting condition as a figure towards the top end of Neolithic group size that would be sustainable over the longer term, again taken from Hedges.[692] I kept the hunting limits I had already set, but added an additional rule which made sure that all children under the age of 15 died if the tribe did not kill sufficient food to feed them all. I ran my groups over a number of generations and found that they did stabilize, although the range of tribe sizes varied from around 20 up to about 50. If a tribe fell below 20, it usually died out. None of the tribes grew much larger than 50. If they had too low a proportion of hunters, they starved, and the size stabilized.

Now, as I was ready to test my theory of a female religion of farming, I was amused to read this comment, written in 1955 by Dr. N.J. Berrill of Leeds University:

> We are inclined to think of men as the inventive sex, as though inventiveness were theirs exclusively. I think the idea itself is undoubtedly a male invention which tends to keep females in their place both by suggestion and to a great extent by denying opportunity, yet the two sexes are equally human and, given sufficient motive, women can invent and create just as well as men. It stands to reason that a woman who has her heart set on producing and rearing children has little interest in tampering with an expanding universe or making atoms pop. Yet apparently women and not men started humanity upon its era of technology. Men, being primarily opportunists, took things over only after women had laid the creative foundation. There are some in fact who would assign to female inspiration and effort not only technology but agriculture and the domestication of animals as well, suggesting that the men were always out hunting and fishing. I feel this goes too far, although I suspect it is my own pride of sex that makes me feel so, for there are few males, old or young, even in these sophisticated days who would not prefer to hunt or fish than sit down and tend to business.[693]

My wife agrees with him, and pointed out to me that it is always the women who do the practical things to keep a home running. But I was worried by the problem that raising a farm crop for the very first time is not a practical thing to do: It is highly risky, and could easily result in the death of the children that Neolithic women valued just as much as today's women value theirs. What could possibly make such a practical sex take such a risk? I had no problem in explaining why men wouldn't voluntarily switch to farming—not only was it risky, it also involved unnecessary hard work. I needed an irrational motive that would be strong enough to convince a rational woman to act in an irrational way.

THE SEVEN COMMANDMENTS OF THE GODDESS

I decided it was time to introduce into my virtual world a woman who believed in a religion of farming. First I thought about what form this religion would take, and I built it using the information I had gleaned from studying the symbols of farming and the reports of shrines from James Mellaart and Marija Gimbutas. I was not too concerned about the theology of belief my worshipers would follow, but I did intend to draw up a rigid set of commandments which must be followed if my worshipers wanted to earn the favor of the Great Goddess. Here are the seven commandments of the religion I invented for Farmer Eve:

1. You must observe the movements of the sun over the seasons and use this knowledge to create the lozenge symbol of the Goddess. If it is the same shape as the talisman you have been given, then the Goddess will smile on you at that place and allow you to create new life.
2. When day and night become the same length—when the shadow of the sunrise falls on the sunset marker and the shadow of the sunset falls on the sunrise marker—you must take your holy seed and lay it in furrows which you scrape in the body of Mother Earth. Before the sun sets, you must cover the seed with the Earth body of the Goddess and smooth Her skin to cover the wound you have inflicted on Her body. In this way, you will ensure that the Great Mother will look kindly on you and make you fertile.
3. When your sister or daughter becomes pregnant, you must take care of her. When her belly grows big, you must carry out the birthing rituals and provide a couch for her to lie on while she allows the new life to flow from her womb.
4. You will care for the mother and baby as you would for the Goddess Herself, as the mother and child are the true symbol of the love of the Great Mother. You will feed them and give them shelter in the shrine until the mother is recovered enough to nurse the child.
5. When you find grain and make bread with it, you should set aside a portion of the bread, mark it with the Holy Symbol of the Goddess, and give it to the sisters whose bellies swell with child or who have a child at the breast. In this way, the love of the Goddess will nurture your and your sisters' children.
6. When a sister dies, you will expose her body for the Goddess to devour. The Goddess will take the form a bird and remove the flesh of your sister to expose the whiteness of her seed essence.

7. When the Goddess in her bird shape has eaten of your dead sister's flesh, you will take the white seeds of her being and will return them to the womb of the Goddess, which you will dig as a hole in the body of Mother Earth, where they will grow and return to make the bellies of your pregnant sisters swell. You may keep her head and decorate it with colored clays and mark her eyes with cowrie shells so that her spirit will help you in times of trouble.

These are an irrational set of rules, but are consistent with all the messages of the symbolism and the artifacts dug up in the ancient shrines.

My next job was to program them into actions for a single woman. I assumed that this woman had come from the city culture of Çatalhöyük, and I introduced her to one of my hunting tribes. All that made her different from the other women of the tribe is that she followed the rules of the religion I have outlined above, and that she had been given a bag of sacred seeds by her mother. I decided that her bag would contain early forms of wheat, barley, and pea seeds. She had wheat to make bread, peas to make a pottage stew, and barley to make beer or porridge. I chose these plant species because, as Jared Diamond points out in *Guns, Germs and Steel*:

> The earliest Fertile Crescent crops, such as wheat and barley and peas domesticated around 10,000 years ago, arose from wild ancestors offering many advantages. They were already edible and gave high yields in the wild. They were easily grown, merely by being sown or planted. They grew quickly and could be harvested within a few months of sowing, a big advantage for incipient farmers still on the borderline between nomadic hunters and settled villagers. They could be readily stored . . . They were mostly self-pollinating . . . and passed on their own desirable genes unchanged . . . Finally, their wild ancestors required very little genetic change to be converted into crops: for instance, in wheat, just the mutations for non-shattering stalks and uniform quick germination.[694]

I will also add that the seeds in Farmer Eve's bag have been selected for just these mutations. Not by the advice of a plant scientist, or even by a whim of mine to help my simulation work, but by an inadvertent process of economic selection after being traded for obsidian products at Çatalhöyük. In *The Economy of Cities* Jane Jacobs describes what happened to these sacred seeds before they formed the dowry of Farmer Eve:

> Seeds that have never before been juxtaposed are tumbled into baskets and bins. Husked, pounded and cooked, they are often further jumbled with peas, lentils and nut meats . . . When seeds remain after the winter, they are used for wild patch sowing, a practice not productive of much food; it just makes gathering wild seeds more convenient. In and around the barter space, around the storage bins within the city, and in the yards where women husk and pound and carry seed to and from the household bins, some seeds spill. Whether spill sown, patch sown, or sown by little predators—rats, mice and birds—these plants cross in unprecedented combinations. It is no problem to get grain crosses . . . Quite the contrary; crosses cannot be

avoided . . . The crosses and hybrids do not go unobserved. They are seen, in fact, by people who are experts at recognizing the varieties and estimating the worth of barter seeds, and who are well aware that some of these city seeds are new. Mutations occur no more commonly than they would in the wild, but they are not unnoticed either, as they most likely would be in the wild; nor do occasional batches of mutant seeds brought in barter go unnoticed. But crosses, hybrids and the rare mutants are not deliberately put to use in selective breeding.[695]

Perhaps the best, most fertile, seeds had been selected by the vulture-feather-cloaked priestesses of Çatalhöyük to be ritually planted in the layers of clay on the altars of the Goddess and on the spare ground around the seed bins at the vernal equinox, and the fruit of this ritual harvested for future use. The result is that the seeds in Farmer Eve's bag are mutants, but they have mutated in a way which will work in her favor.

Many plants have specialized mechanisms that scatter seeds (and thereby prevent humans from gathering them efficiently). Only mutant seeds lacking those mechanisms would have been harvested and would thus have become the progenitors of crops.[696]

Farmer Eve—The Happy Wanderer

Although I call my woman Farmer Eve, she is not an agriculturalist. She is not looking for a borderline advantage to aid a deliberate choice of lifestyle. She had joined a tribe of hunter-gatherers. Perhaps she has joined as a wife for love of a tall, dark hunter, perhaps as a slave being dragged by her hair, caveman-fashion (if you want a more macho image), or perhaps she had been accepted as a willing partial payment in a trading deal.

But it does not matter for my simulation why she joined the tribe. It does not matter what she believes about the Goddess. What matters is how she behaves. If she wants to be fed, she has to stay with the hunters. But she is also a devotee of the cult of the Great Mother Goddess, and I have assumed that she will meet her irrational religious duties at whatever cost. And her most important religious duty is to plant the sacred seeds in a cleft cut into the body of Mother Earth for that express purpose. And she must do it at the vernal equinox.

I programmed this action into my model and added Farmer Eve to a typical tribe, one I had allowed to stabilize over twenty years in my simulation. Eve was fifteen when she joined this roving band, and under the algorithm which ruled the tribe she was immediately impregnated. Come the vernal equinox, she planted her seeds where the tribe happened to be camping, and as the herds migrated, her tribe followed them, leaving her sacred seeds to the mercy of the Goddess. I ran this startup scenario a large number of times, and on a significant number of occasions her hunting band returned to the seeded campsite in the autumn, with Eve by then heavily pregnant.

The implication of this result was that there is no need to make a decision to switch from hunting to farming. When Eve's hunting band followed the migrating herds back to the seeded campsite, then there was a crop of edible seeds ready to be harvested. If Eve was close to giving birth at that time, then her religious duty was to prepare a birthing shrine and persuade her tribal sisters to help her with the birthing ritual (which would of course ensure that she gave birth with the maximum support and safety). She could argue that the Goddess had provided food to sustain them while they remained at the campsite for the birth, and if Eve had been generous and diligent in her religious observances, it would feed them through the winter. The need to create a birthing shrine would encourage Eve to remain in place, and the gift of winter food provided by the bountiful mercy of the Goddess would be a strong token to help convert her tribal sisters to this new-fangled city-based religion.

My simulated world had provided a simple motive for Farmer Eve and any chosen female assistants to remain behind while the rest of the band followed the herds. Perhaps her impregnator stayed with her, or perhaps he left her to follow the prey animals, only returning with the following seasonal migration. (That detail does not matter, as long Eve and her children stayed, survived and replanted the ground the following spring.) Now I could see how the first villages that Andy Garrard had found could have been founded for a compelling, even if irrational, reason.

Perhaps no male hunters did stay with the women and newborn children that first winter, but, given time, if a growing proportion of women of a hunting band decided to settle with their children and follow the religion of the Harvest Goddess, as the work of Dr. Gimbutas says they did, then in time the men would return, unable to resist the attraction of women who could feed them without their having to run the risk of injury offered by the hunt, and who had a permanent bed to welcome them into.

Next, I adjusted my code to allow my settled campsites to grow, and I changed the breeding rules for women who stayed there. Their life expectancy did not increase, because of the hard work involved in farming, but because they stayed in one place, they were able to breed a child each year. Their fertility rate increased by 77 percent. If I allowed the surplus girl children to go off with the hunting bands that now visited the site to trade meat for the bread, pease pottage, and beer which the daughters of Farmer Eve produced, then I soon found that the campsites became villages, and the religion of farming that they supported diffused outwards from their founding village.

Once Eve's village has a sufficient surplus to trade seeds, bread, or even beer, for meat, then animal husbandry is economically inevitable. If Farmer Eve wants to feed her children meat, then she will need to trade her farmed foodstuff for living animals. Let us assume for a moment that she is a successful farmer. The

Goddess smiles on her handiwork, and her crops prosper. Her storage problem is not too difficult, she just has to keep any traded animals alive until she is ready to slaughter and feed them to her children.

Jane Jacobs explains what happens next:

> The first animals chosen for slaughter are those that are either the hardest to feed or the most troublesome to manage, or both. Most carnivores fall into one or both of these categories and they are eaten very soon after their arrival . . . Animals that can live on grass are removed last from the natural refrigerator of life. And among the grass-eating animals, the females, being the less rambunctious, are kept longest. Sometimes they give birth to young before their time of slaughter comes; and when this happens there is, of course, extra wild meat and extra pelts. [Eve has] no conception of animal domestication, nor of categories of animals that can or cannot be domesticated.[697]

But she keeps second-, third- or fourth-generation captives alive long enough to breed because they happen to be the easiest to keep during times of plenty. She will kill her animals without hesitation if her children need food, but live animals represent fresh meat. So she comes to possess, and to protect, what we call breeding stock. And, if she does, her only choice is to keep the most docile alive and eat the troublesome.

Here at last I had found a motive and a mechanism for understanding the irrational act of abandoning the easy lifestyle of a hunter-gatherer for the hard work and long hours of a subsistence farmer. And this mechanism has the advantage that it explains how the spread of farming carries with it the mDNA of Çatalhöyük to the western fringe of Europe.

What is clear from this rather simple simulation is that the idea that women began farming as an irrational religious act is quite capable of explaining all the archaeological facts as well as the mDNA evidence.

NEOLITHIC FARMING HANDBOOKS

Now that I could propose a mechanism for the spread of farming, it was obvious that, if it were to work, the religious compulsion to carry out the rituals would have to be strong. And my previous research has pointed to the power of myth and stories to motivate people to carry out ritual acts. What were the stories Farmer Eve shared with her sisters and children? I would ask her if I could, but she is long dead and her language with her. I have struggled to decode even the simple symbol that explains the basics of farming. But I have learned from the work of Marija Gimbutas that the symbol of the lozenge, triangle, and spiral (which attracted me because forms of it are still used in Masonic ceremonies) had formed part of a language that we can no longer read. This is how she described it:

Around 5500–5000 BC, intriguing combinations of signs appear in the archaeological record . . . [They] represent a true writing system similar to Chinese, Sumerian, Indus, and pre-Columbian "nuclear" (logographic) writing systems.[698]

James Mellaart, too, had noticed how the images of the farmers had become increasingly more stylized:

Naturalistic art survived until the middle of the fifty-eighth century BC, but it is no longer found in the later cultures . . . where its place is taken by geometrically painted pottery, itself derived from the symbolic and geometric art which accompanied the naturalistic.[699]

He adds:

Other paintings seem to consist entirely of symbols, most of which remain unintelligible to us.[700]

These symbols became pictographs, which in turn became abstract symbols and the basis of the earliest form of writing. Many years before, while researching an earlier book, I had come across this early form of writing under the name of Vinca script, and noticed:

The story [of the origins of writing] gets more complicated once stone carvings from Tartaria, near Turdas in Transylvania are taken into account. These carved clay tablets date from 4,000 BC . . . and have been the subject of a great deal of archaeological debate, as they were found before carbon dating had been fully perfected. In 1961 they were thought to date from about 2,900–2,600 BC. Archaeologist Sinclair Hood, Director of the British School of Archaeology in Athens wrote in 1962 in the journal *Antiquity*: "The signs on the Tartaria tablets, especially those on the roundel No. 2 are so comparable with those on the early tablets from Uruk as to make it virtually certain that they are somehow connected with them. Several of the signs appear to be derived from Mesopotamian signs for numerals. The only difference is that on the Mesopotamian tablets the whole shape of the sign in the case of numerals was sunk in the clay with a round-ended stylus, while at Tartaria the equivalent signs were incised in outline." . . . Understandably, Sinclair Hood assumed that the Tartaria tablets had to post-date the Elamite script from Sumer . . . [but] when reliable carbon dating tests were eventually carried out, on the strata surrounding the artifacts, it revealed that the Tartaria tablets were much older than the earliest use of the symbols in Sumer. Since that bombshell the whole matter appears to have been ignored . . . But . . . it is inescapable that if there was a connection between these two writing methods, it must have been the Sumerians who learnt from the Transylvanians [or that] . . . both peoples were heir to a different common tradition.[701]

It didn't matter to me what the common tradition was: I knew that the Sumerian script had evolved from the Vinca script of the Goddess worshippers. And the longest work recorded in Elamite is an epic tale. It was not too late to hear again the stories Farmer Eve's daughters told each other when they felt in need of religious inspiration.

Conclusions

The study of mitochondrial DNA has shown that farming was spread by the physical migration of women from the region of the Neolithic trading city of Çatalhöyük in Anatolia, Turkey, not by a wave of advancing males. This inconvenient fact clashes with the traditional view, represented by Adam Smith's Biblically inspired idea that men were God's natural gardeners and had developed and spread farming, and only later got around to building cities.

By using what is known about the actions of early farmers and the religious practices associated with them, I proposed a model for the origins of farming which is based on a series of irrational religious-inspired actions, which can be shown to be consistent with what is known of the Neolithic religion of the women of Çatalhöyük. I modeled this scenario using a computer simulation, and found the hypothesis of a religion of farming explains all the known data in a logical manner, providing both motive and evolutionary mechanism.

In the process of doing context research to test the hypothesis, I found that the farming worshippers of the Harvest Goddess had developed a very early form of writing. We can no longer translate this writing, but it developed into a script called Elamite, which was used in Mesopotamia, and that is the oldest writing we can still read. One of the major surviving works written in Elamite is an epic story, so now I planned to see what stories the early farmers had used to inspire themselves. My next move must be to look at the literature of the ancient city of Uruk, to metaphorically sit at the feet of our great-great-great grandmothers and listen again to their stories of their Mother, the Great Goddess, and Her heroic sons.

CHAPTER 16

THE GREATEST STORY
EVER TOLD

READ ME A SACRED TABLET

The first story ever to be written down was etched into tablets of clay in the Elamite language, and then hardened in the sunlight that shone between the twin rivers of the Tigris and Euphrates. The *Epic of Gilgamesh* was first written down in the ancient land of Sumer—the land which became Mesopotamia, then Babylon, and is now Iraq.

Vinca script, which had so puzzled me when I was researching *Uriel's Machine*, had evolved into a primitive Sumerian script called Elamite. Now I understood that I would have to revisit the story of Gilgamesh, which had been part of a vibrant living tradition when the symbol of Skara Brae was still being worn as pendant by a living, working inhabitant of that Neolithic village. This story, believed to have been first written down around 2150 BCE but capturing events that occurred some many hundreds of years earlier, was already the world's most widespread work of literature when Neolithic builders were carving the symbol of the Harvest Goddess on the rear curbstone of Newgrange.

Marija Gimbutas had said that the Vinca script, which she prefers to call Old European Script, had been first uncovered by the archaeologist Zsófia Torma, while excavating the Turdas (Tordos) mound near Cluj in Transylvania (northwest Romania) in 1874. She had given it the name I knew—Vinca script. Dr. Gimbutas had pointed out in her book *The Living Goddess* that this form of writing was created to record sacred information:

> Whereas commerce and trade mainly inspired the Sumerian invention of cuneiform writing, the Old European script, developed two thousand years earlier, may have developed to communicate with the divine forces.[702]

This script was a special language that the Daughters of the Neolithic Revolution had invented to record their beliefs. As far as my computer simulation had been concerned, I did not need to understand what these daughters of Farmer Eve believed about the world they lived in, I only needed to be able to write down rules for them to follow. But if I was ever to understand their motivation, I needed to hear their stories. I chose to revisit some of the key elements of the Gilgamesh story and see how they related to the evolution of ritual and myth, using my favorite translation of Gilgamesh, the translation by my good friend Robert Temple, *He Who Saw Everything*.

Two Faces of Ritual Performance: Gilgamesh and Freemasonry

It is worth remembering that the epic has been in popular circulation for more than four thousand years—twice as long as the New Testament. During its two thousand years of existence the New Testament has moved from being recorded in Aramaic scrolls, via the Latin Vulgate and the poetic English of the King James Bible, down to the colloquial prose of the New English Bible, and each retelling has changed the mood and nuances of the story. Robert Temple was of course aware of such issues, and, where versions of the *Epic of Gilgamesh* are noticeably different, he has translated both and added notes to explain where, when, and in what language each version was popular. He also notes that what he calls "the underlying layer of Gilgamesh lore" underpins much of the later Greek and Hebrew traditional myths,[703] adding that the oldest account of the story of the Great Flood and Noah's Ark is 1,500 years older than Judaism and has been "borrowed" wholesale from Gilgamesh.

I had last looked closely at the epic while researching the stories of the deluge for *Uriel's Machine*.[704] Now, I as returned to it, I found I had amassed a great deal of additional information about the structure and power of myths, and about the background and actions of the Neolithic people who first recorded it. I also had a much greater understanding of the purpose and evolution of "Old European Script," which I had first met under the name Vinca script.[705]

Robert Temple's introductory notes say that while working with the original tablets he came to feel that the work was written to be performed as a ritual drama.

> The Epic was more than a work of literature, however; it was also a drama. Indeed, we now have the archaeological proof of this.[706]

He adds that the archaeological evidence for the Elamites using the epic as a ritual drama comes from an article about Urartu (the ancient name of Armenia),[707] which recounts how an Elamite princess traveled to Urartu to marry the king of that country. For her marriage ceremony, she took with her an entourage who performed the *Epic of Gilgamesh* in her own language.[708]

I believe that much of the power of Masonic ritual comes from the impact it has as on its performers and the observers who interact with it, like a vocal chorus. In *Turning the Hiram Key* I noted how I felt as I first played a part in a ritual drama of the Craft:

> The ritual of Freemasonry works by involving its students in a spiritual experience. When you do it, reflect on what you have done, and on what you felt while you were doing it . . . then you may begin to understand.[709]

Robert Temple had felt the same about the text of Gilgamesh as I had felt about Masonic ritual. He traces performance texts for Gilgamesh back to at least 2500 BCE. He also produces evidence that Gilgamesh prompted key developments in Hittite, Canaanite, and Egyptian religious dramas,[710] and he believes that much of the religious ritual drama in the early versions of Gilgamesh has elements in common with Egyptian religious ritual.[711]

Toads, Frogs and Bulls—A Sacred Zoo

Robert's feeling that there was a link between the ritual drama of Gilgamesh and of Egypt did not surprise me, as by now I knew that Marija Gimbutas had detected a similar link and traced it back to a period contemporary with the active use of the Skara Brae farming symbol, but she had found it via a toad and the symbol known as a sheela-na-gig.

> The frog and toad image, along with the frog-shaped woman displaying her vulva, appears across a wide time span, not only during the European and Anatolian Neolithic . . . Several closely related frog deity images in Egypt and the Near East help explain the function of this goddess. Egyptians revered the frog as Heket, primordial mother of all existence. In the early predynastic period (around 3100 BC), she was portrayed as a woman with a frog head, or as a frog or toad impersonating the goddess. "Frog" was her hieroglyphic sign. Heket controlled fecundity and regeneration after death. Heket has been connected with the Greek Baubo, probably a wet nurse, and with the Sumerian Bau, also called Baba. Bau is the goddess who displays her vulva, sometimes raising her skirt in a ritual that possibly dates to the Neolithic. Skirt-raising rituals are known from Egypt; the Greek historian Herodotus describes them in his histories, recorded in 445 BC . . . Diodorus, writing in 60 BC, mentioned that he saw women enacting a skirt-raising ritual before the sacred bull, Apis, in the Serapeum temple at Memphis.[712]

As I was checking out this quote from Dr. Gimbutas, I was struck by her comment that this vulva display was taking place before a symbol of a sacred bull. The birthing shrines of Çatalhöyük, where women must by necessity have displayed their vulvas while giving birth, were also decorated with the heads of horned cattle. I decided to check out what James Mellaart had to say about the use of the bull symbol in Çatalhöyük.

There are groups or even rows of bull's horncores [the skull of a bull with its horns attached] set in benches or bull-pillars, stylized bull's heads incorporating the horns, set on the edges of platforms in shrines and houses alike.[713]

When the reader first meets Gilgamesh in the prologue to the Epic, the tablet says "He the hero, he is of Uruk, he is the butting bull,"[714] and a few lines further it adds he is "The son of the revered Cow." Now, Mellaart had mentioned finding evidence that the Goddess of the Çatalhöyük birth shrines was sometimes shown with a son:

> The statues allow us to recognize the main deities worshipped by neolithic people at Çatalhöyük. The principal deity was a goddess who is shown in her three aspects, as a young woman, a mother giving birth or as an old woman, in one case accompanied by a bird of prey, probably a vulture A male deity also appears frequently in two aspects, as a boy or adolescent, the son or paramour of the goddess, or as an older god with a beard, frequently portrayed on a bull, the sacred animal.[715]

Sometime the Goddess appears with her child suckling her breast. The mother with a child at her breast is an extremely ancient symbol of a Deity, as Gimbutas points out:

> The mother and child sculptural tradition so venerated during Christian times actually began millennia ago, and Neolithic art provides numerous examples. Just as their historical equivalents, the figurines show a mother nursing or holding her child, but the representations are distinctly Neolithic.[716]

It was looking as if the myth of Gilgamesh, the son who had suckled at the teat of the sacred cow goddess and who was two-thirds god and one-third man,[717] would be able to help me understand the belief that drove the Daughters of the Neolithic Revolution to spread farming and create modern civilization.

The Story of Gilgamesh

In the beginning, Gilgamesh is driven by his lusts, so that "all young girls are made women" and "no virgin is left to her lover." He is "strong as a wild bull" and "none can survive fighting him."[718] But his behavior becomes so outrageous that the "Goddess of Creation" makes Herself a new and powerful son, Enkidu. She does this in way that was to become standard practice for later gods: She did it by pinching off "a little clay" and fashioning the form of a perfect man, with hair "like the hair of the corn Goddess, Nisaba."[719]

Enkidu is as strong as Gilgamesh, but lives with the wild creatures and does not know the ways of the city, being "innocent of the ways of mankind." He is described as "a star in heaven in his strength."[720] Hearing of his fame, Gilgamesh sends a trained harlot, who normally serves in Ishtar's Temple of Love, to teach Enkidu the ways of women and to seduce him away from the wild things, which are the source of his strength.

The holy temple harlot found Enkidu and went to him and "made herself naked." She "welcomed his eagerness, incited him to love, taught him the woman's art" so that Enkidu forgot his home, and the wild beasts "saw him and ran."[721] When the wild beasts shunned him, Enkidu decided to go to the city of Uruk to live. But he only became human when the priestess of the Goddess Ishtar fed him a ritual meal of bread and strong beer.

> The girl then spoke.
> She said to Enkidu:
> "Enkidu, eat that food.
> It is our due in life.
> Drink this strong drink;
> It is what is done here."
> So Enkidu ate the food,
> Ate until he was full.
> He drank that strong drink,
> Seven cups of it![722]

The Gilgamesh epic has a tendency to repeat things in slightly different ways, similar to the fashion in which Masonic ritual repeats everything in three slightly different ways when it has a point to make. Fortunately, when the epic repeats the motif of the sacred meal, it is expanded so its meaning becomes clearer:

> The harlot said to him,
> Said to Enkidu:
> "Eat the bread, Enkidu,
> That you will be worthy of godliness!
> Drink the fine beer,
> That you will be worthy of kingship!"
> Enkidu ate the bread,
> He drank the fine beer,
> And indeed seven jugs of it![723]

The ritual practice of eating a meal of bread and an alcoholic drink in order to become closer to a deity has a long history. The wheat that made the bread and the barley that made the beer were the fruits of the body of the Harvest Goddess. By eating them, you took into yourself Her body and Her blood. This idea carried through into Judaism, where it became a meal of good fellowship, such as the Passover meal eaten by Jesus and his disciples at the Last Supper, but since the rise of Christianity it has returned to its ancient roots. Once again, to a Christian, the bread and the wine are the body and blood of God. But looking at this ancient pre-Jewish myth, it seems that God was a woman, before She changed Her mind.

(While reading about Enkidu's meal, I couldn't help reflecting also that the ritual eating of bread and drinking of wine is still part of the Initiation of a Masonic Templar. And, drawing an even closer parallel to the original myth, the ritual meal is offered after the would-be Knight has completed a pilgrimage around a sacred delta, the triangle which, in the Old European Script, is the symbol of the Mother Goddess.)

But let us return to the epic. Once Enkidu is made human by eating the body and blood of the Goddess, the harlot-priestess brings him to Uruk to confront Gilgamesh with a clone of himself. Enkidu meets and fights with Gilgamesh. In this way, the Goddess sets out to teach Gilgamesh how destructive his emotional outbursts are, and makes him realize his responsibilities as a king. The two fight long and hard, but each being a holy child, neither can kill the other. After the long, hard battle, Gilgamesh's anger evaporates, and the two "Sons of the Goddess" become the best of friends. As Temple's translation of the epic says, "they kissed one another and formed a friendship."[724]

So this myth tells how Gilgamesh is confronted by, and fights to overcome, his emotional nature. Only then is he ready to develop his mind. He goes to his mother, the wise Cow Goddess Ninsun, who is described as "Ninsun, Custodian of Knowledge," and asks to learn wisdom from her.[725] She teaches him how the stars "assembled themselves in the heavens," [726] and how the "star-essence of the Great God Anu" could be used to give him great strength.[727]

Gilgamesh's studies are interrupted by news that an evil monster, Huwawa, who lives in the Cedar Forest, is threatening the lives of the people of Uruk. Gilgamesh and Enkidu set off to kill the monster, and his Mother, "who knows all, raises her hands to Shamash the Sun god,"[728] asking him to aid Gilgamesh as he sets out on his quest to follow "the wheel-rim" of the sun's path.[729] Before he leaves, Gilgamesh raises his arms to the rising sun, saying. "I go, O Shamash, my hands raised in prayer. Bless the future well-being of my soul."[730] And throughout the rest of his quest, the rays of the rising sun show him the route and "open the unopened path for him."[731]

Gilgamesh takes with him portions of sacred bread, and at regular intervals throughout his journeys, he stops to break off morsel to eat.[732] This seems to be a ritual action, rather like a Catholic priest saying Mass each day and blessing and eating the Host. But Gilgamesh does real work as well as carrying out symbolic meals. He regularly stops and digs a well with Enkidu at places indicated to them by the sun-god: "Before Shamash the Sun they dug a well."[733]

While reflecting on why he should want to do this, I recalled what Marija Gimbutas said about the importance of sacred wells and springs in the religion of the Goddess:

> The belief in the sacredness of life-giving water at the sources of rivers, springs, and wells extends from prehistory to this century. There is much in these early designs and images that witnesses a long-lasting belief in the magical potency of streams and wells.[734]

Now the function of the myth became clear. By digging a well at a place favored by the sun, Gilgamesh was not only paying homage to both the Goddess and the sun-god, he was creating future shrines to act a focus for further religious devotion. Surely a trick worthy of the respect and admiration of any modern spin-doctor!

After many adventures and famous battles, the two companions finally kill the monster, cut off his head, wrap it in a cloth, and take it as an offering to the god Enlil and his wife, the goddess Ninlil. Enlil becomes angry with Gilgamesh for killing Huwawa, but Ninlil, which is another name of the Corn Goddess (i.e. the fertile aspect of the Trinity of Goddesses), is so impressed with Gilgamesh's prowess that She comes to him in Her form as Ishtar, Goddess of Love, and tries to seduce him.

Robert Temple translates the story of Her attempt at seduction. She is quite open about what She wants, and does not hide Her desires:

"Oh, Gilgamesh, will you not be my lover? Give me that fruit the tree of man yields to woman. I will give you myself as wife. You shall be my husband."[735]

But Gilgamesh is suspicious of the Goddess's motives. He points out that Her favor is always fleeting and She is fickle with Her lovers. He complains that "in the cold seasons you will surely fail me."[736] He must have already learned that there is no such thing a free lunch as far as Harvest Goddesses are concerned. Perhaps he already knew that to grow the wheat and malt the barley, somebody has to work long hours in the spring and summer in order to store enough food to live through the winter.

This is how Robert Temple translates his reply:

Gilgamesh spoke, said to glorious Ishtar: "But what must I give? What give, to take you in marriage?

Must it be oil for the body? And clothing? Bread, and other foods? You would need food fit for the gods, You would need drink fit for kings."[737]

So Gilgamesh rejects Her advances and refuses to amuse Her as Her lover.

Now a woman scorned is said to be full of fury, so imagine what it's like to be on the receiving end of the bad temper of a rejected Goddess! Gilgamesh had not simply rejected Her offer of love, he had accused Her of being incapable of a full-time commitment. He reminds Her how She has deserted Her other lovers in the winter months, even those who have partaken of Her body and blood.

She is outraged that Gilgamesh dares to call Her motives into question. The drama is intense. What is She going to do to this young upstart? Naturally, the myth structure demands that She take a supernatural revenge that is appropriate for a son of Her other aspect, the Cow Goddess. So she borrows the "Bull of Heaven" from her Mother, Antum, Goddess of the Firmament, and sends it round to rough Gilgamesh up at bit and teach him a lesson.[738]

Of course, after a magnificent fight, Gilgamesh and Enkidu manage to kill the Bull of Heaven. They cut out its living heart and offer it up to Shamash, the sun god, and Enkidu rips out its right thigh bone and throws it up into the sky, where it shines to this very day as the constellation we know as The Great Bear or The Plough. This last act of defiance really upsets Ishtar, and She calls a wailing lamentation over the right thigh of the Bull of Heaven."[739]

The gods of the sky, including Shamash, meet in council and decide to punish Gilgamesh. Only Shamash, the sun god, speaks in his favor. The gods decide that Enkidu must die, and Gilgamesh must be forced to endure the lost of his "dear brother."[740] Gilgamesh is distraught at the idea of Enkidu dying, and tries to argue with the gods that it should not happen. Many times, as the "first intimations of dawn appear on the horizon," Gilgamesh stands and prays to the Gods of the Firmament that they spare Enkidu.[741]

Finally Shamash, the sun god, convinces him that there is nothing he can do to prevent what has been decreed and Enkidu must die, which he duly does. At first Gilgamesh will not accept his death, and he refuses to be separated from Enkidu's body until a "worm fell out of his nose."[742] Then he has a golden statue made of his dead friend.[743]

Faced with the grim reality of Enkidu's death, Gilgamesh becomes filled with dread and fear of his own demise. His worry drives him mad, and he rips off his fine clothes and wanders the steppes in search of the secret of eternal life.

He learns that this secret is held by a character called Ziusudra, who was the captain of an Ark which carried a human family, its animals and seeds safely through a Great Flood, instigated by the Gods, with the intention of destroying the whole world. (You may already know this story, with Ziusudra known as Noah, so I won't repeat it here.) Ziusudra is known as "the Survivor of the Flood," but Gilgamesh does not know where to find him.

He meets Scorpion-Man, the first of three "helpers," who advise him on his quest for immortality. Scorpion-Man guards the secret of the movements of the sun-god and reveals to Gilgamesh that he must cross the "Celestial Sea" of Death to find Ziusudra.[744] So Gilgamesh sets off to look for the Sea of Death, but he cannot find it, and continues to wander aimlessly over the steppes. At last, worn out and weary, he has a vision of Shamash as a bright light that overwhelms him while he prays at dawn. He shouts this prayer at the rising sun:

> Let me see the Sun! See the Sun and be sated with light. If there is light enough, then the darkness shrinks away. May the light of Shamash the Sun be seen even by he who is dead![745]

Finally, he discovers the house of the second "helper," a woman called Siduri the Refresher. She lives by the side of the Sea of Death, and is known as the Refresher because she brews strong beer, using vessels and a recipe supplied by the

Goddess. At first, she is so frightened by Gilgamesh's deranged appearance that she locks her door. He persuades her to let him in, and she counsels him, saying "You shall not find the life you seek. For at the creation of mankind the gods allotted death to men. They retained life in their own hands." She advises him to eat till his belly is full, to feast and rejoice in the pleasure of his children holding his hand, and then says "Take your wife to you and let her rejoice in you. For this is the lot of mankind to enjoy. But immortal life is not for men."[746]

Gilgamesh is convinced that the strong drink that Siduri produces is what makes the Gods immortal, and demands to know its secret. But Siduri, in a long ritual exchange, argues that Gilgamesh should not try to understand this mystery, but enjoy the fruits of the earth and the joys of marriage "for the sake of the Goddesses." Gilgamesh replies that "for the sake of the Gods, he wants to know the secret of life eternal."[747] Finally Siduri tells him that no man can cross the Sea of Death and return, only Shamash, the sun-god, can make a crossing of the Waters of Death. Then she introduces him to a third "helper." This is Urshanabi, who is a rather surly boatman in the employ of Ziusudra, the Survivor of the Flood.

After setting Gilgamesh various tasks, Urshanabi finally takes Gilgamesh to meet Ziusudra. In a separate, self-contained episode, Ziusudra tells the story of how he survived the Great Flood by building an Ark to save his family, animals, and seeds, after being warned by the gods that they were planning to destroy the world with a Deluge. Apparently, they did it to make it clear that all human life was mortal and must die when the Gods willed it. Once Ziusudra has told his story, Gilgamesh asks him for the secret of his eternal life, but Ziusudra says that it is the fate of all fine young men and fine young women to die. He says:

> From the days of yore there has been no permanence. The sleeping and the dead—how alike they are! Do the sleeping not compose a very picture of death? . . . As for life, its days are revealed. But as for death, Its day is never revealed.[748]

But Gilgamesh is not satisfied with this answer, and presses Ziusudra for the secret of life. Ziusudra sets Gilgamesh the task of staying awake for six days and seven nights.[749] But Gilgamesh falls asleep, and each day as he sleeps, Ziusudra has his wife bake a fresh loaf of bread and place it by his side. When Ziusudra wakes Gilgamesh, he protests he has only closed his eyes for a moment, but Ziusudra shows him the seven loaves, in varying states of decay, and proves to him that he has slept for seven days, when he should have been keeping watch. (I wonder if the Gospel writers knew this myth when they wrote the story of the disciples' vigil in the Garden of Gethsemane?) Because Gilgamesh has failed the task of staying awake, Ziusudra instructs his boatman to take Gilgamesh back across the Sea of Death and return him to his own land. But before Gilgamesh leaves, he tells him of a plant to be found at the bottom of a sacred river which, if eaten, will make a man immortal. The plant is called "Man-Becomes-Young-in-Old-Age."[750]

On his return to the land of the living, Gilgamesh seeks out the sacred river, and tying heavy stones to his feet dives into its depths. After a great struggle he brings the plant to the surface, even through it pricks and tears his hand. He decides to take the plant back to Uruk and stand on the city walls to eat it and become young forever. So he sets off on the journey back to his city kingdom.

It is a long journey, and he decides to rest by a sacred well, to bathe, to eat a morsel of sacred bread in honor of his Mother Goddess. Then he falls asleep. While he sleeps, a serpent rises from the depths of the well and seizes the magic plant and carries it back beneath the waters of the well. Gilgamesh sits down and weeps, because now he understands that it is his fate to die and he must accept it. He journeys back to Uruk and becomes reconciled to his fate.

The story closes with a moral. The Epic began with Gilgamesh, young, lustful, and willful, standing on the ramparts of Uruk and saying:

> See the foundation terrace, touch, then, the masonry—Is not this of burnt brick and good? I say; The seven sages laid its foundations. One third is city, one third is orchards, one third is clay pits, unbuilt-on land of the Ishtar Temple.[751]

By the end of the story Gilgamesh has learned that death is an essential part of life, and the quest for human immortality is meaningless. He returns to the same spot on the walls of his city of Uruk where his adventures began, but the myth shows how he has been transformed.

Now he sees his city in a different way. He has changed, and the temple of the eternal Deity at the center of Uruk provides a meaning for his existence. The epic closes with Gilgamesh saying: "These three parts and the precinct comprise Uruk."[752]

In these words, Gilgamesh reconciles the wild lusts of the wilderness, represented by the orchards, with the god-given knowledge and intellectual life of the city and the fear of death, which Goddesses do not experience but which he must. Gilgamesh, who was two-thirds god (the city and the temple) and one-third man (the wilderness),[753] has learned to bring into balance the Divine and the Profane; the urges of his body; the inquisitiveness of his mind; and the hunger for meaning of his spirit

The Meaning of Gilgamesh

This vast three-part story addresses the deepest questions of human consciousness: Why am I here, and what will happen to me when I die? By telling them as a story, it enables us to make sense of that which is unknown and unknowable.

The epic shows that the women who created the religion of farming had a basic human need for a narrative that explained their lives. The myth has been a fundamental human tool for making sense of experience. And the seven basic plots, which I investigated in Chapter 13, all make an appearance in Gilgamesh. It seems that stories have been forming our human world view, and inspiring us to irrational acts for tens of thousands of years.

We humans are the only species in the evolutionary history of the planet to discover that we are mortal. And we responded to the knowledge of our mortality by making up stories to explain how we came to be in such a dreadful fix, destined to die and unable to do anything about it. We invented myths and religions to explain the cause and give us hope for the future. We bury the bones of our dead in the womb of the Mother Goddess in the hope that they will be reborn in the spring, as the dead seeds we plant at the vernal equinox sprout and form the living grain by the end of summer. And if things do not go well for us, we explain the catastrophes as the revenge of powerful beings whom we have offended. And it's all in the *Epic of Gilgamesh*!

I decided to see what Christopher Booker, literary critic and the author of *The Seven Basic Plots*, had to say about the meaning of Gilgamesh.

As we have seen, the story ends when Gilgamesh returns to his city of Uruk, without the plant of eternal life and reconciles himself to doing good for his city until he dies of old age. Booker notes that this ending is unusual, saying:

> But Gilgamesh had to return home empty-handed. He was hailed as the king who had been on a long journey, "who was wise, who knew mysteries and secret things." But now he was "worn out with labour," and so he died, the greatest of heroes . . . In showing how its hero eventually dies a natural death of old age, the *Epic of Gilgamesh* was in fact to remain highly unusual in the history of storytelling. The riddle of how humankind was to cope with this new realisation that each individual centre of consciousness must die was one to which it would continue to come up with differing answers.[754]

Booker recognizes that the ending of the *Epic of Gilgamesh* is different from the way later epic stories were told. But this form of ending is one with which all Freemasons are familiar. (The happy ending portrayed in the triumph of the "rags to riches" hero over the force of death is a later Christian invention.) Gilgamesh becomes reconciled to the need to die, and concentrates on passing on his culture to the next generation. He has had a vision of a great light, which he only saw at the period of his greatest despair. He knows that nothing worse can happen to him, and he is content with his lot, not seeking a reward in some imaginary afterlife. He has learned the lesson that Freemasonry sets out to teach: He has finally learned how to die.

THE MASONIC MYTH OF INITIATION

In an essay I wrote for my own Lodge, I described how the three episodes in the story of Masonic Initiation take the Craftsman to the point of being reconciled with the fact of his own mortality. This is how I tell the story of the adventure of the three degrees of Freemasonry:

The First Degree equips us to develop a rational mind and bring our intellect into balance with the irrational urges of the flesh. To aid us in this we are equipped with postures, a Lodge structure to focus our thinking, and a set of symbols and spiritual tools. Only when we have balanced our rational mind against our bodily urges, learned how to use posture, and how to comprehend symbolism, and gained proficiency in the use of spiritual tools to control our irrational urges are we ready to move on to the Second Degree.

The Second Degree helps us to balance our intellect and our emotions, so that we learn how to recognize truth and discriminate between irrational urges, arising from the flesh, and the truth which we perceive with our spirit. We are given further postures, tools and symbols to help us strengthen our rational mind and learn to handle our emotions, so that we are prepared for the discovery of the blazing star of truth, which is as yet only visible as darkness at our center. Here we meet the spiral symbol, which can teach us how to approach this mysterious center. The postures affect our body and feed back hormonal responses into our rational minds, helping us learn how to subdue unruly emotion. But before we can proceed to the Third Degree, we must be prepared to let go of our ego and self-regard. We must face up to our own personal appointment with death.

In the Third Degree we allow our ego and rational mind to die, so that our spirit may be reborn as the keystone of our being and be supported in its quest to attain the vision of light that emanates from the center. The ritual of death and rebirth stills the urges of our body, our intellect, and our emotion, and brings forth the suppressed spirit. In this degree, the circle of our being is rendered complete and perfect by acquiring mastery over its four component parts. When this is fully achieved, you are a Master of the Craft and have undergone a radical transformation of your mind and a regeneration of your entire nature. Now are you ready to allow the light of the center to flow through fresh channels in your brain, so that the true secret of the Craft may be internalized into your consciousness.

In the ritual of the Third Degree, the various paths to the center are symbolized as three gates. These are the Gate of Will, The Gate of Intellect, and The Gate of Feelings. At each entrance stands an aspect of our lower self, each a traitor, seeking to use the secrets of the spirit for selfish ends. An intuition of right conduct arises in the Initiate's spirit; it attempts to escape through the southern *Gate of Will*. Our lower self, afraid that it must reform its bad habits and prune its excesses, refuses to let our spirit rise free.

Now our inner wisdom tries to escape through the northern *Gate of Intellect*. Here another aspect of the lower self resents the need to seek out the center, the lower self is afraid of the need to make fresh mental adjustments. Once more, our spirit is struck down.

Finally, this higher self staggers to the eastern *Gate of Feeling*, where all inspiration of spiritual vitality is stifled by our lower sensual nature. Our spirit, finding that its retreat is cut off at all the three gates it knows from the outer life of the world, is slain, and must await the predawn rising of the Bright Morning Star to revive it. We learn to discipline those three ruffians—will, intellect, and feeling—by enlisting those parts of our mind which act as the principal officers in our personal Lodge, that is, our own consciousness. Then, like Hiram Abif, we are raised in the cold light of the predawn sky, to become a balanced and harmonious personality, with the Blazing Star at our center enabling us to balance all the conflicting aspects of our life.

This is the great myth which is the driving force of Masonic ritual. And it has the same plot and sequence and conclusion as the *Epic of Gilgamesh*. Perhaps it is because this myth is inherently appealing that the Craftsmen who created that old Masonic Lodge in Aberdeen were drawn to use it in their explanations of their purpose in life, or perhaps they learned the stories while carving the stones of Roslin and naturally told and retold them. Whatever the route, Freemasonry has inherited a powerful motivational myth, a myth that powered the sweeping world change of the Neolithic Revolution. And Freemasonry has refined this myth until it has become a force for bringing about similar improvements in the mindset of individuals. Now, armed with this new knowledge, I needed to look again at Masonic ritual and symbolism. The earliest forms of the Epic had been written using the symbols of Vinca script. When reviewing them I was surprised at how many of the shapes of that Old European Script are still used as symbols to illuminate the lessons taught in a Freemasons' Lodge.

Gilgamesh Comes to Roslin

In *The Seven Basic Plots* Christopher Booker sums up the *Epic of Gilgamesh* thus:

> This great Sumerian epic brilliantly reflected how far mankind had travelled since it began the long process of emerging from unconscious dependence on instinct and nature. It tells the story of a man who begins at the mercy of his egocentric physical appetites, without any controlling discipline or self-understanding. To reach maturity and self-awareness it is first necessary for him to begin an inner dialogue, which is what is represented by the arrival of his shadowy alter-ego Enkidu. Just as Enkidu has emerged from the state of nature, so the two-in-one hero now overcomes Huwawa further representing the unconscious state of nature which has to be subdued to make the self-advancement of mankind possible. This is repeated in their victory over Ishtar. But all these victories for ego-consciousness, marking an ever greater emancipation from unity with nature, also bring with them an awareness of the inevitability of death. Gilgamesh then has to set out on his lonely quest . . . in search of that lost connection with the totality of life. Although, as he grows physically old and weary, he at least seems to come near to grasping the elusive secret he is seeking, then it slips

away from him. At last, full of years, he is forced to accept that which he has dreaded so long: the extinction of his separate conscious existence.[757]

As well as being a summary of Gilgamesh, this is also an excellent summary of the purpose and progression of the degrees of the Craft of Freemasonry.

Gilbert Hay did a magnificent job when he selected the myths he embedded in the fabric of Roslin Chapel, to engender interest, curiosity, and loyalty to the Patrons of that chapel. He could not have known of the *Epic of Gilgamesh* directly, and so could not have used it consciously, as it was not then known. It was discovered in 1854 and not published in English until 1872, as Wallace Budge reported in *The Annals of the Kings of Assyria.*

> The mass of tablets which had been discovered by Layard and Rassam at Nineveh came to the British Museum in 1854–5. The general meaning of the texts was quite clear, but there were many gaps in them, and it was not until December, 1872, that George Smith published his description of the Legend of Gilgamesh, and a translation of the "Chaldean Account of the Deluge." [758]

The symbols and myths of the Daughters of the Neolithic Revolution are so powerful that they have been incorporated into the myths of all the world's great religions, and have continued to be told and retold. Gilbert Hay probably selected a set of myths that he thought would work well as political motivators for the St. Clair cause. His choice was inspired, and the myths he worked into the stones of Roslin have been changed and adapted throughout the millennia, but have continued to exercise enormous influence on the human imagination.

Conclusions

When I modeled the spread of farming across Europe using the hypothesis that it was a religious act, I simply drew up some rules of behavior without making any attempt to understand the motives of the women involved. Studying *The Epic of Gilgamesh* had given me an insight into the beliefs that could have motivated the switch from hunting/gathering to farming.

What did surprise me about the epic, which had been in circulation for thousands of years before Genesis was thought of, let alone written down, was how many of the myths and motivating stories of modern religion were already in place.

There is the story of a Deity making a man from a pinch of clay. This man is a simple child of nature, until a woman seduces him and feeds him bread and alcoholic drink to make him fully human and capable of sin. Once he has eaten the body and drunk the blood of the Deity, he is exiled from his natural state, loses his ability to communicate with animals, and is forced to live in the city. The story of Adam and Eve has deep roots.

The story of a Deity deciding to destroy all life on Earth with a great flood is also here. As in the story of Noah, the survivor, Ziusudra, is warned by the Deity in time for him to make an Ark. Into this Ark he takes his family, breeding pairs of all the animals, and seeds for all the plants. After seven days of drifting on the endless seas, he releases a birds to find land: in this case a dove and a swallow, which have to return because they find no land, and finally a raven, which does find land. The Ark makes landfall on top of a mountain (Mount Nisar), and Ziusudra makes a sacrifice to the Deity and is granted the gift of eternal life.

And there is the story of an innocent, and holy, figure being sacrificed to atone for the sins of another. (Enkidu dies as a penalty for the sins of Gilgamesh.) There is, too, the element of the use of a ritual meal of bread and wine as a way of worshipping the Deity. There is even the story of bright stars appearing in the East, in the predawn sky, to guide Gilgamesh on his quest to eternal life. There is the concept of a threefold Deity, represented by a Trinity of different aspects of the whole.

All these motifs also appear in the Old and New Testaments. But there is a major difference between the climax of the Christian story of the New Testament and the resolution of the story of Gilgamesh. For Gilgamesh, death is an essential part of the natural cycle of life, and he becomes reconciled to its inevitability. Nature finally teaches him how to die. The idea of being reborn into an eternal afterlife is a Christian invention, which was not developed until thousands of years later. Christopher Booker had commented that this philosophical ending was unusual in the history of storytelling (a "voyage-and-return" plot, rather than a "death-and-resurrection" story). But it resonates with the main myth of Freemasonry, which says:

> It is my duty first to call your attention to a retrospect of the degrees of
> Freemasonry through which you have already passed, that you may be the better
> enabled to distinguish and appreciate the general excellence of our whole system
> and the relative dependence of its several branches.

Your admission into Freemasonry, in a state of helpless indigence, was an emblematical representation of the entrance of all mankind into this, their mortal term of existence. It inculcated the striking lessons of natural equality and mutual dependence; it taught you in the active principles of universal beneficence and charity to seek the solace of your own distress, by extending relief and consolation to your suffering fellow creatures; but above all, it taught you to bend with humility and resignation to the will of the Great Architect of the Universe and to dedicate your heart. Thus you were purified from every baneful and malignant passion and fitted only for the reception of moral truth and virtue, as well to His glory and to the welfare of your fellow creatures.

Proceeding onwards, still guided in your progress by the principles of moral truth and virtue, you were passed to the Second Degree, wherein you were enabled to contemplate the intellectual faculties, and to trace them, from their development, through the paths of heavenly science, even to the throne of God Himself. The Secrets of nature and the principles of intellectual truth were then unveiled before you, and to the man whose mind has thus been modeled by virtue and science, nature presents one grand and useful lesson more: the knowledge of himself.

She [nature] teaches you, by contemplation, to prepare for the closing hours of your existence; and when, by means of such contemplation, she has led you through the intricate windings of this, your mortal life, she finally teaches you how to die.

Such, my dear Brother are the peculiar objects of this, the 3rd Degree in Freemasonry. They invite you to reflect upon that awful subject and teach you to feel that, to the just and upright man, death has no terror equal to that of the stain of falsehood and dishonor.

Now my quest to understand how the myth of the Templars had become a part of the greater myth of Freemasonry is almost resolved. I have found the origins of both myths in a religion of farming, a religion which created modern civilization. And at its heart was the most important lesson of both Freemasonry and Templar Masonry, the practice of learning about yourself in order to be able to face up to your fear of dying.

My quest is nearing its end, but the journey offers one great and final trial before I can rest. I must face up to the problem of human death. In the final chapter we will see what Freemasonry and Masonic Templarism can teach us about our own mortality.

CHAPTER 17

FREEMASONRY, PHYSICS, AND THE TRIUMPH OF TEMPLARISM

THE LAST GREAT ADVENTURE

I began this book by asking, "Are the Knights Templar alive and well and meeting at a secret temple somewhere near you?" After a considerable amount of research, I have to answer, "No, they are not."

I then went on to ask,. "Could the Masonic Knights Templar really be the legitimate successors of the original Order of the Knights Templar? If so, how is it possible to explain the 480-year hiatus in their history?" Again, I have to answer, "No, they are not."

I haven't found any evidence that the Templar Masons are a direct continuation of the fourteenth-century Order whose members were arrested at dawn on October 13, 1307, but I have found a plethora of myths and legends whose intention seems to be to suggest they might be. Rumors that Freemasons are heirs to the secrets of the Templars form a persistent stream that regularly surfaces within the living rumor-mill which is Freemasonry.

The suggestion of knowledge of Templar secrets has been repeated over hundreds of years by various members of the Order of Freemasonry and their fellow travelers. In attempting to find out why this should be, I had to follow a trail of smoke and mirrors back to a fifteenth-century spin doctor who was a key player in a political plot to take over the crown of Scotland. It wasn't the answer I was expecting to find—but what I did find highlighted the political force of myth and the impact that certain stories have on the collective mind of the human race. The search led me back to the beginnings of civilization and an answer to the fundamental question of human existence, "Why do we have to die?"

The ancient answer that emerged from my researches is totally different from the concept of an immortal soul that after death will be rewarded in heaven for actions on Earth. The belief in an afterlife powered the drive for martyrdom that made the Order of the Templars such a powerful force in the Crusades. But the older belief system that I uncovered helped to explain one of the major puzzles of prehistory: Why did the human race suddenly switch from its long-established lifestyle of hunting and gathering in small wandering tribes to farming and living in cities? But what was even more surprising is that this alternative answer to the question of "Why do we have to die?" is still taught within the Third Degree of Craft Freemasonry.

After a long and interesting journey, I have now arrived at a surprising conclusion. I believe that Freemasonry has preserved one of the oldest religious stories, which early humans used to inspire themselves as they spread the practice of farming. It is a myth that dramatizes the idea that death is a part of life, and is something that humans have to learn to accept. Existentialist dread must have dogged humans since they first developed self-awareness, and Christianity developed a particular way of dealing with this worry by postulating an afterlife for a part of the human, called a soul, in another place, called heaven. But the belief expressed in these ancient myths shows a different approach to the question of how a self-aware entity should deal with the issue of its own extinction.

It may surprise many people to learn that neither the belief in the necessity of death as a way of progress, nor that in an immortal soul that will receive a supernatural reward after death, have existed forever. Their earliest appearances can be traced in myths and in the archaeological record. As the philosopher of science Daniel C. Dennett explains in *Breaking the Spell*:

> There was a time before religious beliefs and practices had occurred to anyone. There was a time, after all, before there were any believers on the planet, before there were any beliefs about anything. Some religious beliefs are truly ancient (by historical standards), and the advent of others can be read about in newspaper archives. How did they all arise? Sometimes the answer seems obvious enough, especially when we have reliable historical records.[759]

THE CHANGING NATURE OF DEATH

A key fact had stood out as I was studying the origins of storytelling. The religion of farming, which I had deduced to exist from Jim Wilson's DNA evidence and Jane Jacobs's economic evidence, had held a particular belief about the nature and importance of death. I had tested the type of behavior patterns that were necessary to spread farming by a female vector, and deduced seven commandments for a Religion of Farming. The *Epic of Gilgamesh* made a lot of sense when looked at in the light of these behavior patterns. I seemed to have found a theology to

1. Deduce- to infer by reasoning from known facts.

underpin the audit trail of irrational actions that I had modeled so successfully with my computer.

This belief said that humans must accept death as a necessary part of the great natural cycle of the world. A seed is dead during the winter months, but if it is placed within the womb of the Earth Goddess in the spring, new life will emerge from it and grow. In the autumn, that new life will die and leave behind it more dead seeds, which, if placed in the womb of the Goddess the following spring, will once more bring forth new life. There is no trace of any idea of human afterlife in this belief system.

✻ Gilgamesh had to learn how to die well, though he fought death and wanted to live forever. But, even when he managed to steal the secret of eternal life from the depths of a sacred stream, the Goddess emerged from one of her holy wells, after shifting her shape to that of a serpent, and took it back from him. The message of the myth is clear: Each generation must die to make room for the next. As part of this belief system, the fruit of the Goddess's body, in the form of sacred loaves of bread are ritually eaten, and beer (brewed from the seeds of Her barley) is drunk. This ritual probably is intended to take the regenerative power of Her seed into the worshiper's own body so that when it dies and is buried in the Earth (which is the womb of the Goddess), a new crop of children will be born to replace the dead.

✻ This problem of how to react to the inevitability of death is an ancient one, as Daniel Dennett points out:

✻ When somebody we love . . . dies, we suddenly are confronted with a major task of cognitive updating: revising all our habits of thought to fit a world with one less familiar intentional system in it. "I wonder if she'd like . . . ," "Does she know I'm . . . ," "Oh, look, this is something she always wanted . . ." A considerable portion of the pain and confusion we suffer when confronting a death is caused by the frequent, even obsessive, reminders that our intentional-stance habits throw up at us like annoying pop-up ads but much, much worse . . . we dwell on them, drawn to them like a moth to a candle. We preserve relics and other reminders of the deceased persons, and make images of them, and tell stories about them, to prolong these habits of mind even as they start to fade. But . . . a corpse is a potent source of disease, and we have evolved a strong compensatory innate disgust mechanism to make us keep our distance. Pulled by longing and pushed back by disgust, we are in turmoil when we confront the corpse of a loved one. Small wonder that this crisis should play so central a role in the birth of religions everywhere.[760]

This problem of death and its solution is a key plot element in the *Epic of Gilgamesh*, appearing in the sub-story of Enkidu's death. Even though Enkidu is dead, and his body has rotted so that worms and maggots fall from his nose, Gilgamesh will not be parted from his corpse. At last, when he is forced to admit that the body of his friend must be disposed of, his first response is to make a statue to preserve a relic of him. This practice of preserving relics of the dead to remind the living of their memory dates back to the beginning of cities. It is at the root of the cult of relics that was so powerful a political force at the time of the building of Roslin Chapel. There is evidence of early mausoleum shrines from Çatalhöyük, the first city. In *Earliest Civilisations of the Near East*, James Mellaart notes:

> The people of Çatalhöyük buried their dead below the platforms of their houses and shrines only after the flesh had been removed, probably for the sake of hygiene. The primary process of excarnation may have taken place in light structures, built of bundles of reeds and matting as depicted on a wall of a shrine, or by means of vultures. The fleshless corpses were then collected, wrapped up in cloth, skins or matting and intra-murally buried previous to the annual redecoration of houses and shrines. Sometimes the remains were coated or painted with red ochre, cinnabar, or blue or green paint was applied to the neck or forehead.[761]

In the slightly later city of Jericho, even though the bones of the dead were buried beneath the floors of the houses, their skulls were decorated with clay, paint, and cowrie shells, and put on display in the living areas of the houses. In *Digging up Jericho* Kathleen Kenyon describes one such collection she excavated:

> Each head has a strongly marked individual character, though the features and method of manufacture is similar. The interior of the head was packed solidly with clay, and a clay filling put into the eye-sockets as setting for the shell eyes. The lower part of the skull was then enveloped in plaster from the level of the temples, the crown of the skull being left bare. In one specimen there are bands of brown paint on the skull, perhaps indicating a head-dress. In all the intact specimens, the base of the skull was completely covered, with a flat finish to the plaster, so there is no question that they could ever have formed part of complete figures. The features, nose, mouth, ears, and eyebrows, are moulded with extraordinary delicacy. The plaster of one head is coloured to represent a fine ruddy flesh-colour; others show some colouring, but not so pronounced.[762]

This was the religion, as my computer model showed, which drove some fanatical women to create a civilization of cities and farms from a rabble of disparate hunters and gatherers. And it had no concept of heaven or an afterlife. Indeed, the myth specifically warns against such an idea. When Gilgamesh is seeking the secret of eternal life, Ziusudra—who should know, having himself been granted immortality—tells him that he is wrong to search for such a thing, because nothing should be forever. He says "Do we build a house to stand forever? Are contracts sealed for ever? Does the stream which has risen in spate bring torrents for ever?"[763] Siduri the Refresher also tells Gilgamesh that he should not waste his time searching for eternal life, but should take pleasure in what he has. "Attend to the baby who holds you by the hand. Take your wife to you and let her rejoice in you. For this is the lot of mankind to enjoy—but immortal life is not for men."[764]

To Freemasons, this sentiment is familiar. The ritual of Freemasonry transmits this idea when it stands a would-be Master Mason on the edge of an open grave containing a human skull and a pair of thigh bones. They are illuminated by the faint rays of the Bright Morning Star rising in the pre-dawn light of the East of the Lodge.[765] As he points to the preserved skull, the Worshipful Master says to the candidate:

 By this glimmering ray you will perceive that you stand on the very brink of the grave into which you have just figuratively descended, and which, when this transitory life shall have passed away, will again receive you into its cold bosom.

Let those emblems of mortality which now lie before you, lead you to contemplate your inevitable destiny and guide your reflections into that most interesting and useful of all human studies, the knowledge of yourself.

Be careful to perform your allotted task while it is yet day; listen to the voice of nature which bears witness that, even in this perishable frame, there resides a vital and immortal principle, which inspires a holy confidence.

Within this part of the ritual of the Third Degree of the Craft, we Freemasons have inherited elements of a myth which goes back nearly 9,000 years before Christianity. A sobering thought!

Our Search for Love and the Invention of the Soul

Why did this concept of a soul having a life eternal in a place called heaven arise? Professor Nicholas Humphrey, a research fellow in Social Research at Darwin College, Cambridge, suggests a reason in *Soul Searching*:

"With passion," Russell wrote, "I have sought knowledge." But with equal passion "I have sought love . . . I have sought it because it relieves loneliness—that terrible loneliness in which one's shivering consciousness looks over the rim into the cold unfathomable lifeless abyss. I have sought it . . . because in the union of love I have seen, in a mystic miniature, the prefiguring vision of the heaven that saints and poets have imagined." But . . . these two human passions—for knowledge and for love—cannot be expected to operate with equal strength. In the ideal world pictured by traditional religions—where the more you know, the more you can feel sure of being loved—the two passions complement each other.[766]

The solution to the problem of being loved, as far as the Daughters of the Neolithic Revolution were concerned, was expressed by Siduri the Refresher in the *Epic of Gilgamesh*. It is the love of a child, the love of a husband, and the love of family and tribe. Siduri calls it "The ten figs of marriage, the figs to be held by the bride. It is for Woman to bear and for man to engender."[767]

But as cities grew larger, and empires such as Rome expanded the scope of drudgery and the impersonal nature of city life, another solution was put forward. St. Paul suggested that the function of a Deity was to provide love for everyone. He suggested the definition that "God is Love," and he explains why in 1 Corinthians 13:

Read

If I speak in the tongues of men and of angels, but have not love, I am a noisy gong or a clanging cymbal. And if I have prophetic powers, and understand all mysteries and all knowledge, and if I have all faith, so as to remove mountains, but have not love, I am nothing. If I give away all I have, and if I deliver up my body to be burned, but have not love, I gain nothing. Love is patient and kind; love does not envy or boast; it is not arrogant or rude. It does not insist on its own way; it is not irritable or resentful; it does not rejoice at wrongdoing, but rejoices with the truth. Love bears all things, believes all things, hopes all things, endures all things. Love never ends. As for prophecies, they will pass away; as for tongues, they will cease; as for knowledge, it will pass away. For we know in part and we prophesy in part, but when the perfect comes, the partial will pass away. When I was a child, I spoke like a child, I thought like a child, I reasoned like a child. When I became a man, I gave up childish ways. For now we see in a mirror dimly, but then face to face. Now I know in part; then I shall know fully, even as I have been fully known.

St. Paul's God has replaced Gilgamesh's wife and children as his main supplier of love. Yet when Gilgamesh was offered the love of a Deity he refused, saying that an eternal being was fickle and would eventually desert him and leave him to die in the cold of winter. St. Paul has no such doubts, and discounts the warning that Ziusudra gives to Gilgamesh that "eternal life is a secret of the gods" and it is not for a man, whose role in the world is to be born, to live, and to die.

Indeed, Paul expands this idea of love and the reward of eternal life in Colossians 3:2, when he says: "Set your minds on things that are above, not on things that are on earth." He clearly believes that an imaginary heaven where he can enjoy eternal life is to be preferred to his present existence. This new concept caught on and became popular as the religion of Christianity spread. The earthly paradise that Gilgamesh—and Adam and Eve—had enjoyed had been replaced by the tyranny (not to mention poverty, sickness, and overcrowding) of the city, exemplified by Rome, with its slavery, cruelty, and class disparity. With the good life no longer achievable for the majority of people, and of questionable duration even for those who could command it, little wonder that belief in a better life after the misery of this one held appeal. As we have already seen from the history of the Knights Templar, Christianity grew into a system that encouraged people to make great sacrifices, even to the extent of laying down their lives, in order to store up rewards in heaven. Cambridge Psychologist of Religion Robert Thouless says:

The use of the language of human love as a symbol for religious love is found in the acceptance of such a work as the Song of Solomon as expressing the love of Christ for his Church, and in the Hindu religion of the loves of Krishna and the milkmaids as symbols of divine love . . . The religious man may indeed recognise the connection between human sexual love and religious love, and regard the love of God as the final purpose for which human love exists . . . [and see] human love as the precursor and explanation of and initiation into the divine . . . The fact of death is, of course, universal amongst living organisms; it is reasonable to suppose that man alone can formulate this expectation in words and finds it desirable to adopt an attitude to it which renders it tolerable. The obvious way of achieving this end in our own culture is to accept the belief that human life continues beyond the grave . . . Belief in survival is not, however, a necessary part of the religious adjustment to the fact of death; it is generally stated not to have been adopted by early Judaism.[768]

But neurotheologists Andrew Newberg, Eugene d'Aquili, and Vince Rause are convinced that the question of death is always occurring to each new generation of humans, and each generation answers the question using their preferred myth.

Death was not the only existential worry that early humans had to face. But by comprehending their own mortality, they stumbled onto a new dimension of metaphysical worries, and their questioning minds must have presented them with difficult and unanswerable questions at every turn: Why were we born only eventually to die? What happens to us when we die? What is our place in the universe? Why is there suffering? What sustains and animates the universe? How was the universe made? How long will the universe last? And, most pressingly: How can we live in this bafflingly uncertain world and not be afraid? These are confounding questions, but . . . for thousands of years in cultures around the globe, their resolution has been found in the form of myth.[769]

Does Religion Make Us Moral?

The myth that death is an essential part of progress for the tribe drove the Daughters of the Neolithic Revolution, while the Templars were motivated by the Martyr's Reward in Heaven. Daniel Dennett has pointed out the risks in the idea of heavenly reward and eternal life, while posing the question "Does religion make us moral?" He quotes the following statement by a young *mujaheed* from Pakistan:

Non-Muslims love their life too much, they can't fight, and they are cowards. They don't understand that there will be life after death. You cannot live forever, you will die. Life after death is forever. If life after death were an ocean, the life you live is only a drop in the ocean. So it's very important that you live your life for Allah, so you are rewarded after death.[770]

Those words could have been written by St. Bernard or any Grand Master of the Knights Templar. Their attitude to holy violence and death in battle against those they view as the enemies of their religion is identical. Compare the young Muslim's comments with the words of St. Bernard, written in the early twelfth century, to inspire the early Knights Templar. St. Bernard praises them in a document called *Liber ad milites Templi: De laude novae militae* (The Military Order of the Temple: In Praise of the New Knighthood):

> This is, I say, a new kind of knighthood and one unknown to the ages gone by. It ceaselessly wages a twofold war both against flesh and blood and against a spiritual army of evil in the heavens. When someone strongly resists a foe in the flesh, relying solely on the strength of the flesh, I would hardly remark it, since this is common enough. And when war is waged by spiritual strength against vices or demons, this, too, is nothing remarkable, praiseworthy as it is, for the world is full of monks. But when one sees a man powerfully girding himself with both swords and nobly marking his belt, who would not consider it worthy of all wonder, the more so since it has been hitherto unknown? He is truly a fearless knight and secure on every side, for his soul is protected by the armor of faith just as his body is protected by armor of steel. He is thus doubly armed and need fear neither demons nor men. Not that he fears death—no, he desires it. Why should he fear to live or fear to die when for him to live is Christ, and to die is gain? Gladly and faithfully he stands for Christ, but he would prefer to be dissolved and to be with Christ, by far the better thing.
>
> Go forth confidently then, you knights, and repel the foes of the cross of Christ with a stalwart heart. Know that neither death nor life can separate you from the love of God which is in Jesus Christ, and in every peril repeat, "Whether we live or whether we die, we are the Lord's." What a glory to return in victory from such a battle! How blessed to die there as a martyr! Rejoice, brave athlete, if you live and conquer in the Lord; but glory and exult even more if you die and join your Lord. Life indeed is a fruitful thing and victory is glorious, but a holy death is more important than either. If they are blessed who die in the Lord, how much more are they who die for the Lord![771]

Dennett finds the sort of ideas expressed in both St. Bernard's and the *muja-heed*'s statements chilling:

Without the divine carrot and stick . . . people would loll about aimlessly or indulge their basest desires, break their promises, cheat on their spouses, neglect their duties, and so on. There are two well-known problems with this reasoning: (1) it doesn't seem to be true, which is good news, since (2) it is such a demeaning view of human nature.[772]

From Knight Templar to Masonic Templar

In *Turning the Hiram Key*, the first book in this trilogy, I put forward the argument that:

Over the ages, the Craft has evolved and refined its ritual forms to help its followers find answers to such questions. [The questions of how should we react to the knowledge of our own inevitable death and what is the purpose of life?] It may be that the absolute truth about ourselves cannot be expressed in language, and can only be revealed through symbols [and, I would now add, through myths].[773]

But how does this theory explain the radically different form that the myth of the Templars assumed as it was assimilated into the Initiatory myth of Freemasonry? In Chapter 2, I summed up the Knights Templar as "an order of violent, death-dealing martyrs." But Templar Masonry has evolved to remember them within a much more tolerant philosophical system. Part of the ritual of one of the degrees of Templar Masonry says.

> No man truly obeys the Masonic law who merely tolerates those whose religious opinions are opposed to his own. Every man's opinions are his own private property, and the rights of all men to maintain each his own are perfectly equal. Merely to tolerate, to bear with an opposing opinion, is to assume it to be heretical, and assert the right to persecute, if we would, and claim our toleration as a merit.
>
> ✳ The Mason's creed goes further than that; no man, it holds, has any right, in any way, to interfere with the religious belief of another. It holds that each man is absolutely sovereign as to his own belief, and that belief is a matter absolutely foreign to all who do not entertain the same belief; and that if there were any right of persecution at all, it would in all cases be a mutual right, because one party has the same right as the other to sit as judge in his own case—and God is the only magistrate that can rightfully decide between them.[774]

This is a world away from St. Bernard's statement, which is not tolerant of anybody's religious views except those of Bernard himself. The violent hostility to non-Christians there is a long way from the sentiments in the next ritual, taken from another degree in the Templar Masonry series, which points out that the motives of the original Templars were much more intolerant than those of their Masonic successors:

> Masonry is the handmaid of religion. The Brahmin, the Jew, the Mahometan, the Catholic, the Protestant—each professing his peculiar religion, sanctioned by the laws, by time, and by climate—may retain their faith, and yet may be Masons.
>
> Masonry teaches, and has preserved in their purity, the cardinal tenets of the old primitive faith, which underlie and are the foundation of all religions. Masonry is the universal morality which is suitable to the inhabitants of every clime—to the man of every creed. It has taught no doctrines except those truths that tend directly to the well-being of man; *and those who have attempted to direct it toward useless vengeance, political ends, the Kabala, Hermeticism, Alchemy, Templarism, and Jesuitism, have merely perverted it to purposes foreign to its pure spirit and real nature.*
>
> The best, and, indeed, the only good Mason, is he who, with the power of labour, does the work of life the upright mechanic, merchant, or farmer—the man who exercises the power of thought, of justice, or of love—whose whole life is one great act of performance of Masonic duty. The natural work of Masonry is practical life: the use of all the faculties in their proper spheres and for their natural functions.[775] [emphasis mine]

So when did this change from fanaticism to toleration take place? Well, it certainly couldn't have taken place within Freemasonry before Templar Masonry began to be practiced (or its rituals "worked," as Masons would put it) in Masonic Lodges. I knew when this happened. But could I now understand what caused this evolution to the tolerant ritual of today?

I have traced the beginnings of the Masonic Initiation myth and a basic Templar legend to Roslin in 1453, when the design of Roslin Chapel was finalized. I have traced the recorded beginnings of Freemasonry to Aberdeen, Scotland, on June 27, 1483. And I have traced the recorded beginnings of Templar Masonry to 1696 in London. Why is there such a gap between the beginnings of Freemasonry, thirty years after the start of building Roslin Chapel, and the beginnings of Templar Masonry some 200 years later? Once more, the answer is political.

THE KING OF SCOTS: GRAND MASTER OF TEMPLAR MASONS

In 1696 Britain was ruled by William and Mary, who had deposed James II in 1688.

The earliest form of Templar Masonry to appear was that of the Royal Order of Scotland. The Royal Order is different from all the other Masonic Templar Orders, because it makes a special claim about the King of Scots, which is highlighted in this extract from the description of how to lay out a Reception Chamber for an aspiring knight:

> At the extreme east there is a dais, on the centre of which the chair of the Tirshatha is placed, with a chair on either side. The chair on the right (north) remains always vacant. It is retained for the King of Scots who is Hereditary Grand Master of the Order, A Royal robe and crown or other emblems of sovereignty should be placed on this chair.[776]

Many Scots had not really been happy about the Union of the Crowns in 1603. Why else would they have crowned the future Charles II King of Scots in 1650, after England had exiled him? Likewise, a considerable number of Scots did not support the Glorious Revolution of 1688. Scotland had played no part in the overthrow of James VII (James II of England), but the Lowlands, which dominated the Scottish Parliament, had immediately recognized the new king, William III, as William II of Scotland. They had apparently made a deal with him to abolish the Scottish episcopate, which he did in 1690. This made him popular among the Lowland Scots, but strengthened Highland support for the exiled King James as the true King of Scots. These Highlanders rose in support of James VII's son, Bonnie Prince Charlie, in the Jacobite rebellions of 1708, 1715, and 1745–46. But following the defeat of the 1745 Rebellion, the government forced the breakup of the clan system in the Highlands, and destroyed their military power forever.

So the Royal Order of Scotland appeared at exactly the time when the Highland Scots were fomenting rebellion against William and Mary, and planning to return the true King of Scots to the throne of Britain. This is what the empty chair in the Royal Order Chapter symbolizes. It was ready for James VII to occupy. Now it would have been dangerous to state this intent openly, so a symbolic myth was needed to explain this loyalty to the King of Scots. The traditional history of the Order provides it, saying:

> After the dissolution of the Templars, many of the Knights repaired to Scotland and placed themselves under the protection of Robert Bruce and that, after the battle of Bannockburn, which took place on St. John the Baptist's day (in summer), 1314, this monarch instituted the Royal Order and established the chief seat at Kilwinning . . . King Robert conferred on them the civil rank of Knighthood, with permission to them to accord it in their Grand Lodge to those faithful and patriotic Brethren who might succeed them, so that the Degree is, strictly speaking, a civil Order granted to Scottish Masons. Originally none were entitled to it but Scotsmen.[777]

Templar Masonry first appeared as a cover for Scottish Jacobite sympathizers to meet and plot rebellion against the English king in London. The myth of the Templars intervening at Bannockburn (the battle which became the symbol of Scotland's winning its freedom from England) was an ideal explanation for the empty chair of James VII/II. But the Jacobite issue, and the sympathy of many Scottish Masons for the Jacobite cause, distorted the history of Freemasonry in England and resulted in much confusion because of the need to avoid mentioning it. As I explained in *Freemasonry and the Birth of Modern Science*, the formation of the Grand Lodge of London (1717) was a direct result of the need for London Freemasons to distance themselves from the Jacobites after the 1715 rebellion.[778] The formation of the London Grand Lodge, in turn, forced the creation of Grand Lodges in Ireland (1725) and Scotland (1736), and provided fertile ground for the Templar myth to flourish.

The Jacobite cover story of the Royal Order had given the romantic myth of the Templars a foothold within the Craft. The Royal Order prospered, but it was an Order for Scotsmen and retained a naughty whiff of Jacobitism, particularly after the Declaration of Arras in 1747, when Prince Charles Edward Stuart (aka Bonnie Prince Charlie) publicly proclaimed himself the true hereditary Grand Master of the Royal Order.

Roslin Chapel and the Grand Lodge of Scotland

The battle for supremacy on the roll of the new Grand Lodge of Scotland opened up a new route for the Templar myth to grow within Freemasonry. The unscrupulous exploitation of William St. Clair, the 19th Baron Roslin, by Lodge Canongate Kilwinning to take control of the Grand Mastership of Scottish Freemasonry (which we uncovered in Chapter 10) had brought Roslin Chapel into play. The political and mythical groundwork of William St. Clair, the 12th Baron Roslin—

the Chapel-builder—now kicked in. He had created Roslin not with the intention of making it a Masonic and Templar shrine, but as a political tool to aid his ambitions to create a kingdom for himself by breaking up Stuart Scotland. His chief architect and his primary spin-doctor Sir Gilbert Hay had used as many fundamental religious myths as he could find, so long as they supported the idea that true Kings were created by God (hence the deliberate intent to copy the floor plan of Solomon's Temple,[779] because Solomon was the heir to King David, the first king appointed by God, and was so perfect that God made sure he replaced the flawed King Saul).

Roslin Chapel had been lying derelict since 1688, when it had been ransacked by an Edinburgh mob for being too idolatrous. Now, with the revival of his fortunes as First Grand Master Mason of Scotland, William the 19th Baron Roslin was able to reglaze and restore the building. The following year, in Paris, Scotsman Andrew Michael Ramsay issued his famous oration, claiming that Freemasonry was descended from the Knights Templar (see Chapter 5 for more on this). Now Roslin's place in Masonic legend was assured. All William the 12th's effort in having these ancient myths and symbols hewn into stone now paid off in spades, and the chapel remains a potent myth-generator that attracts hordes of visitors for the present owners.

But there still remains the question, "Why did Templar Masonry grow so rapidly in the late eighteenth century?"

I believe it did so because it satisfied a need among Masons to reconcile the philosophy about death, inherited from the traditions of the *Epic of Gilgamesh*, via Judaism and the myth of Solomon, with St. Paul's views on eternal life, heavenly rewards, and the mystery of the Trinity. Templar Masonry is an evolved philosophical system within Freemasonry whose rituals and myths explain the concept of the Trinity in the context of the Christian "death and resurrection" motif while retaining the tolerance of other religious views that justify the view of death taught in the Craft Initiatory legend.

So now I have my final task. I must explain how the evolved ritual of Templar Masonry, with its veneration of the Trinity, fits into the overall teachings of Masonic ritual, which accepts all views of Supreme Being as equal.

A Defense of Intellectual High Treason

In *Turning the Hiram Key* I explained how Freemasonry had evolved, by continually rehearsing and modifying its rituals to maximize spiritual satisfaction, from a collection of religious myths into "a tolerant, inclusive, spiritual banquet for the inner spiritual hunger we all feel which tries to function without fostering superstitious intolerance or persecuting the diversity of human belief."[780] Through its use of ritual, metaphor, and symbolism, Freemasonry can draw on a set of extremely potent symbols to provide a language to discuss deep spiritual matters that are difficult to put into words. Each individual Mason defines the meaning of the Craft's symbols by analogy. I explained how this means that people of different backgrounds can use its conventions to share ideas without having to make use of any particular religious dogma. The scientist can talk to the Christian, the Muslim to the Jew, and all can use a common language of spiritual symbolism. At its best, Freemasonry has evolved to become a calculus of the spirit.[781]

I am a physicist, and hence my belief in the concept of a Supreme Being is closer to that expressed by Einstein than by St. Paul. In *Turning the Hiram Key* I set down my personal definitions of Supreme Being, taken from quotes by my scientific heroes, and followed with what I have come to call my Physicist's Creed. I'll repeat them here.

First, the Definitions of Supreme Being I prefer, which are taken from the words of Einstein and Newton:

Einstein: The harmony of natural law, which reveals an intelligence of such superiority that, compared with it, all the systematic thinking and acting of human beings is an utterly insignificant reflection.

Newton: The most wise and excellent contrivance of things and final causes.[782]

My Physicist's Creed: I believe in a number of immutable laws that apply throughout the whole of creation. These relate to the way matter behaves and are often called the Laws of Physics. They include such well-known relationships as the conservation of energy and mass and their interchangeability, the Heisenberg Uncertainty Principle, Fermi-Dirac statistics and the laws of thermodynamics. I believe that matter is made up of twelve fundamental particles, six quarks and six leptons. There are four forces, strong, weak, electromagnetic and gravitational. I also believe that forces are mediated by the exchange of particles. I accept the existence of twelve force-carrying particles and think there might also be a thirteenth, the graviton, but I'm not sure about that.

This world view is the standard model of physics. To accept it is to believe in a supreme order throughout the universe. Why there should be six varieties of quark and six varieties of lepton is not a matter of discussion. It is derived from experiments, and its acceptance leads to the type of universe which makes possible the evolution of an intelligent life form capable of asking "Is there a supreme being within the structure of the universe?"[783]

To some of the reviewers of *Turning the Hiram Key* my position posed difficulties in understanding. Greg Clark, reviewing the book on *The Daily Grail* website found it difficult to understand why I, as a physicist, could be interested in discovering spiritual fulfillment through the practice of Masonic ritual.

I was quite puzzled at Lomas' quest. Throughout the book, he makes it quite clear that he is a materialist, and does not have a belief in spiritual realms . . .

[He quotes a passage from *Turning the Hiram Key*] "Wilmshurst believed he had found a direct telephone line to god. And, although as a scientist I find this unlikely, it is an issue about which I have no quarrel with him. There is no objective way to say which of us is right."

It's gratifying to see that Lomas leaves others to their own beliefs. However, I'm not sure of the attraction of Masonry to Lomas' eyes in this case—if Wilmshurst saw it as "spiritual arousal," is it then just "arousal" for Lomas? In this case, why spend 17 years of practicing Masonic ritual, when five grams of Psilocybin mushrooms from the local cow field would lead him to cosmic consciousness? Certainly, I must admit to not being a materialist, and so I find it difficult to identify with Lomas here—so this may be a result of my own biases, and in the same spirit exhibited by Robert Lomas I can only say "I have no quarrel with him." Perhaps further explanation of how Masonry contributes to the growth of the materialist human being may have been worthwhile in this concluding section though, for all the non-materialists out there.[784]

Greg's comments generated a great deal of interactive response via my website and seemed to have struck a chord. I must admit that I didn't really see what the difficulty was, but then I have already accepted that Masonic ritual offers me an emotional reward, which I interpret as spiritually satisfying. But it can do no harm to try to explain why this is so for the benefit of "non-materialists."

RECONCILING GOD AND SCIENCE

"Non-materialists," however, are not the only people puzzled by the attraction that spiritual and religious metaphor and myth hold for some physicists. Richard Dawkins, a writer and biologist I greatly admire, and whom I have often quoted, believes such a method of thinking is dangerous. In *The God Delusion* he says:

Einsteinisms like "God is subtle but he is not malicious" or "He does not play dice" . . . are pantheistic, not deistic, and certainly not theistic. "God does not play dice" should be translated as "Randomness does not lie at the heart of all things." "Did God have a choice in creating the Universe?" means "Could the universe have begun in any other way?" Einstein was using "God" in a purely metaphorical, poetic sense. So is Stephen Hawking, and so are most of those physicists who occasionally slip into the language of religious metaphor . . . Carl Sagan [said] . . . "if by 'God' one means the set of physical laws that govern the universe, then clearly there is such a God. This God is emotionally unsatisfying . . . it does not make much sense to pray to the law of gravity." . . . Nevertheless, I wish that physicists would refrain from using the word God in their special metaphorical sense. The metaphorical or pantheistic God of the physicists is light years away from the interventionist, miracle-wreaking, thought-reading, sin-punishing, prayer-answering God of the Bible, of priests, mullahs and rabbis, and of ordinary language. Deliberately to confuse the two is, in my opinion, an act of intellectual high treason.[785]

I do tend to agree with Dawkins that the word "God" carries a lot of emotional baggage that limits its usefulness as a thinking, or explaining, tool, which is why I prefer the neutral terms used by Masonry, such as the Great Architect of the Universe, the Grand Geometrician of the Universe, or even the Masonic Templar form of The Most Holy and Ever Blessed Trinity.

The fact that I am comfortable expressing a belief in a "Most Holy and Ever Blessed Trinity" requires explanation, as at first sight it might seem that I am committing a triple act of "intellectual high treason." But in my belief in a Trinity, I differ from Professor Dawkins, who is trained in, and practices at a high level, a form of science that does not see the big picture of life. Dawkins is an exponent of the theory of evolution. It is a theory that explains how complex life forms have developed from simple strings of DNA, but, for its results, it relies on the certainty of outcome that only occurs within a Newtonian frame of reference. The physicist sees both a bigger and a smaller picture, while the biologist works in the billiard-ball certainty of a Newtonian Universe.

I think that after the time of Newton, science and Freemasonry drifted apart. Newton's concept of a clockwork universe, set in an invisible framework of absolute time and space, left no role for the human spirit. Not until Einstein and Bohr showed that Newton's ideas failed on the very large and very small scales was there space in science for studying the self-conscious awareness which is the secret at the center of Freemasonry.

Although neither Einstein nor Bohr were Freemasons, their thoughts on the nature of the world have greatly influenced my personal definition of the Great Architect of the Universe (GAOTU). If I was asked to sum up the GAOTU in three equations to fit on a T-shirt, they would be $E=mc^2$, $P=mf$, and $\nabla^2\Psi=0$. And I would probably arrange those three equations in the symbolic shape of the Masonic Templar's symbol of the Most Holy and Ever Blessed Trinity—the Delta or equilateral triangle (the ancient symbol of the threefold Goddess of Farming). Should we physicists ever manage to combine these macro, micro, and Newtonian approximations of how the world works, we should surely know the mind of God.

At a quantum level, the certainty of Darwinian evolution does not hold, and that is why physicists lack the certainty of belief that biologists are able to enjoy. But, as scientists, once we know that we live in a state of uncertainty, we ought to admit it both to ourselves and to others. As Richard Feynman said in *The Joy of Finding Things Out*, "It is of great value to realize that we do not know the answers to difficult questions. This attitude of mind—this attitude of uncertainty—is vital to the scientist, and it is this attitude of mind which the student of science must acquire."[786]

Once scientists develop this attitude, they can never again retreat into certainty. Physicists have to live with the reality of quantum uncertainty, biologists do not. And this fact creates different mind-sets towards belief systems. It can make what appears to a biologist to be an act of intellectual high treason seem to a physicist just a normal acceptance of uncertainty.

It is rather odd that religion demands a certainty of belief that is shared by evolutionists, although the certainty is about different things. It is that certainty of belief that conflicts with a physicist's view of science. My key philosophy of science is that accepted knowledge is only the best guess I can make at this time. A new fact can change my view. As a scientist, I live in a state of perpetual uncertainty. Impartial observations decide the validity of a scientific assertion, but ultimately there are no absolute truths: I can only fail to disprove a hypothesis, I can never show it to be absolutely true. Religion deals with questions such as "would it be right to do this thing?", which are outside the competence of science, and then it makes pronouncements that are not allowed to be questioned. A physicist questions everything.

Western civilization is founded on two pillars: First, the scientific spirit of curiosity—the observation of the hidden mysteries of nature and science, the attitude that anything and everything may be questioned within the enforced humility of uncertainty, and that all assertions should be tested. And second, the ethics of Christianity—the brotherhood of all men, the value of the individual, and the importance of love in motivating actions.

Logically, there should be no conflict between these two founding principles. Science simply says "What will happen if I do this?" and makes no judgment on the morality of the action. Ethics says "Should I do this?" and has no view on the practically of what is to be done.

But is logic enough? To follow an idea, it must first engage your heart. You must be inspired. But to reason it through, to understand and apply it, you must question, analyze, and doubt. Where do you seek for a source of strength and courage to persevere in this daunting search for truth? Traditionally, religion provided that inspiration, while science's role was to provide the working tools to understand and share insights. But in modern society, this accommodation is seriously weakened. Let me consider why.

In my view, religion is based on two metaphysical concepts and one pragmatic one. The first is that there exists a personal God to whom you pray in order to influence his actions. Secondly, this God had something to do with creating the universe. And thirdly, the practical consequence is that the words of this God are intended to guide you in your morals. To profess a religion, you must accept all three views without question—yet a physicist must question, because she or he is uncertain.

The conflict between religion and science arises when the ethical and inspirational qualities of religion are claimed as a monopoly by those who express an absolute faith in the metaphysical aspects. No scientist can do this. I do not believe it is possible for religious theology to discover a set of metaphysical ideas that can be guaranteed not to come into conflict with the ever-advancing and always-changing ideas of science as it continues to probe the unknown. But this conflict only occurs in the class of questions concerning "What happens if I do this?" or "Does this particular entity exist, and how does it interact with me?"

What Is Man?

Let me give an example. The universe is extremely large. Lie on your back on a clear night in a field well away from the city lights, and you cannot fail to be impressed with the number and beauty of the stars. Then consider that what you are seeing is merely the local stars of our own galaxy. There a more galaxies in creation than there are stars in our galaxy; each galaxy contains hundreds of millions of stars, and there are billions of other galaxies. Some are so far away that their light takes billions of years to reach us. Our sun is but a tiny particle whirling among a hundred thousand million other suns in our own Milky Way.

Now think about the wondrous brotherhood of the life forms in our fragile biosphere. Every single one of the millions of species of life which exists, or has existed in our planet's past, is made up of an immortal mix of carbon, hydrogen, and oxygen atoms, stitched together by the complex codes of DNA that make up the great plan of life. Man is a late arrival in this vast evolving drama. It seems unlikely that the whole four-billion-year enterprise was set in motion just to allow him to become Lord of Creation, or that it will end with him.

The atoms from which the stars, the Earth, the human race, and my socks are all created appear to follow immutable laws. Nothing can escape these laws: Stars become novas because of them; tidal waves rise up and swamp the land because of them; and my brain is able to think because of them.

It is a great adventure to imagine the universe beyond the limited reach of man. Think of the vast majority of beautiful and strange places that we see through our telescopes. They have never known the footfall of a human. Once you have considered this enormous panorama of mystery and wonder, turn back and look at the transient patterns of matter that make up the human race. Life is part of a universal mystery of tremendous depth. It is brief dance of transient coupling by promiscuous, yet immortal, particles of matter. Truly I can bring nothing into this life and surely take nothing from it, for I cannot even own, let alone control, the atoms that make up my body. As my cells grow, mature, and die, they are replaced by new cells containing different atoms.

So what am I? I am nothing more than a temporary and shimmering pattern of atoms that choose for a brief moment to stay with each other before moving on to dance with new partners. The carbon that is such an important binding agent in my DNA is nothing more than the waste matter of an ancient hydrogen furnace that exploded into a supernova billions of years ago. Romantically, we are formed from stardust. Prosaically, we are made of atomic waste. Yet religion would have me accept unconditionally that such preposterous creatures as we humans are the sole preoccupation of the majesty of the Cosmos, or, as I prefer to call It, the Great Architect of the Universe.

Ultimately, a scientific view of creation ends in awe and mystery, in the contemplation of the vast expanses of the Universe, or in the nature of the subatomic zoo that blossoms when we try to shake the quarks out of our nuclei. At each end of the scale, science melds into an uncertainty that is deep and impressive. But it is hard to accept that this has all been simply arranged for a personal God to preside over man's struggle with good and evil.

Now, if a person's ethical and moral views are based in religion, these insights of science can pose enormous problems. If morality is based only on the instructions of a personal God, and you begin to doubt that such a limited and parochial God could be responsible for the vast scope of creation, you begin to entertain doubts about the value of the ethical teaching which he is said to promote. That is where Freemasonry offers a way forward.

To become a Freemason, you only need to express a belief in the existence of an order at the center of creation. This is metaphorically expressed as a belief in a Supreme Being, the nature of which is not questioned but left to each Mason's own conscience. Masonry leaves me free to believe in the immutable, but statistically uncertain, laws that govern the interactions of atoms, without forcing me to ascribe human characteristics onto the Great Architect of the Universe. I can stand in awe of the GAOTU, and expect fair and impartial treatment from It without having to pray to It.

A QUESTION OF SOUL

Freemasonry has developed into a mechanism for experiencing the power of storytelling. The basic myths are powerful, and reach deep into our need to understand our own stories. And the Lodge gives us a chance to act them out. I suspect it began when Masons who had been inspired by the power of stone to capture myths during the building of Roslin Chapel took this knowledge to Aberdeen and used it for their own betterment and inspiration.

Freemasonry tells stories to help its followers understand themselves and the world they live in. At the final audit, all we have are our stories. We come into the world as patterns of potential, nothing more. The collection of matter that comprised me when I was born has long since dispersed, and the *me* of the present is a totally different collection of material. All that connects them is my story of myself. The whole problem of self-consciousness is to explain the question of *me*. How do I explain *me* to myself? I tell myself *my* story, and it is only *my* story which connects the *me* of last week with the *me* of today. But is *my* story what a religious person would call a soul?

If there is such a thing as the soul, I think it is whatever it is that instigates the collapse of a multi-particle Schroedinger wave function (i.e., one that is describing entangled states). It is the thing that makes quantum measurement possible, or the observer that forces the haze of probability to collapse into a particular particle set of positions, or momentums (depending on which it chooses to measure). As far as I can see, the question of what is the human spirit is the answer to the puzzle of what measurement means, and what this observer thing is doing that fixes the result of the measurement (or the choice of world-path, if you prefer the Everett-Wheeler world-splitting model of quantum reality).

As I see it, the problem of measurement in quantum mechanics is this: When do the entangled states of many possibilities collapse down to just one observation, and how does it happen? Is it when the pointer on the dial moves, when the particle creates a path in the bubble chamber, when a charged particle hits the phosphor of a display screen, when the optic nerve of the observer pulses, or when the self-conscious awareness of the observer registers that the event has taken place?

If you buy into the Everett-Wheeler proposition, then collapse never happens; instead, the whole range of possibilities all continue, but your consciousness only perceives one of the outcome paths, and the observer that is you splits as well. This implies that each version of the observer sees one of the possible outcomes that the Copenhagen interpretation assumes is created by the wave function collapse. At each split, a whole infinity of world outcomes is split off from your observation. Does this mean that your self-aware spirit is the self-conscious system which traces the path of highest probability through the range of possible wave function collapses?

Whichever interpretation you favor, part of the world of possibilities dies each time you make a measurement. You either shed part of your spirit at each split, or many versions of you die, and only one lives on to observe another event, when the whole process happens again.

The third degree of Freemasonry ritual tells you:

> The Secrets of nature and the principles of intellectual truth were unveiled before
> you and to the man whose mind has thus been modeled by virtue and science,
> nature presents one grand and useful lesson more, the knowledge of yourself. She
> teaches you, by contemplation, to prepare for the closing hours of your existence;
> and when, by means of such contemplation, she has led you through the intricate
> windings of this, your mortal life, she finally teaches you how to die.
>
> Such, my dear Brother are the peculiar objects of this, the Third Degree in
> Freemasonry.

Part of you, the essential self-conscious observing you, either dies or is forever exiled down another world path every time you observe something, and by doing so collapse a mess of entangled wave functions into a fixed state. As a physicist, I find this the deepest mystery in postulating a theory of quantum cosmology. Do we, the observers, have to die each time we measure or observe, and is this the mystery which, if solved, will reconcile relativity with quantum wave collapse?

Behold the Unspeakable Glory of Planck's Constant

We may have to die not just every day, but every time we make an observation. But when I die, my story is complete as far as my impact on it is concerned. It passes into the public domain, so that others can change and interpret it. It can grow or it can wither, but if it is a story of the type which appeals to the hooks in other people's minds, it can continue to grow and change. Whether I become a myth or a nonentity depends on the appeal of the story I created while I was alive in the minds of the individuals who hear and retell the story.

The ritual of Templar Masonry sums this mystery up when it says:

My brother, the initiate is he who possesses the lamp, the cloak, and the staff.

The lamp is reason enlightened by science; the cloak is liberty, or the full and entire possession of one's self, which isolates the sage from the currents of instinct; and the staff is the assistance of the eternal forces of nature.

The lamp lights the past, the present, and the future, which are the three sides of the triangle. It burns with a threefold flame; the cloak is in three folds; and the staff is divided into three parts.

... To attain the Holy Empire, that is to say, the science and power of the Magi, four things are indispensable: an intellect enlightened by study; an audacity which nothing checks; a will that nothing can conquer; and a discretion that nothing can corrupt or intoxicate. To Know, to Dare, to Will, to be Silent—these are the four words of the Magus.[787]

But this modern ritual still carries with it the roots of its beginnings in the belief systems of the Daughters of the Neolithic Revolution. Look at this speech, taken from the same Masonic Templar degree:

Prepare, now, for admission to the inner mysteries.

My brethren, the power of darkness has prevailed over the Prince of Light. The earth mourns, and is wrinkled with frost. The leaves drop from the trees; snow shrouds the mountains, and cold winds sweep over the shuddering skies. All nature laments; and we share the common sorrow. Excellent Senior Warden, let prayers be offered up in the tabernacle for the return of light and the re-ascension of the Sun, and of that moral and spiritual light of which he is the type.

All the nations of the earth do fast and pray. Our ancient taskmasters on the banks of the Nile mourn for Osiris. The Chaldeans lament for Bel, and the Phoenicians for Thammuz. The Phrygian women clash their cymbals and weep for Atys; on the Syrian hills and over the Etruscan plains the virgins lament for Dionysus; while far in India the Brahmans pray for the return of Cama; and in Persia the Magi predict the resurrection of Mithras. The dead will rise again, as the wheat grows from the grain; and all the world will then rejoice.

We, like our ancient masters, mourn Osiris—the type to us of the sun, of light, of life. The scorpion and the serpent rule the winter waves, on which the frail ark tosses that contains his body. Weep, my brethren, for Osiris! Weep for light lost, and life departed, and the good and beautiful oppressed by evil! Man hath fallen from his first estate, and is lost, as the sun hath sunken into the icy arms of winter. Weep for Osiris, type of the good, the true, the beautiful! How shall his body be recovered from the embraces of the hungry sea; and earth again be gladdened by his presence?

Brethren, behold a new Priest of the Tabernacle, to be instructed and prepared to fulfill all his duties as a Prince of well-doers in this frail Tabernacle of life, that he may be raised on the great day of account, a shining monument of God's glory, in the tabernacle of eternity.[788]

While rituals such as this continue to be worked (performed in Masonic Temples by Lodges of Masons) the belief system of Gilgamesh lives on. He has achieved in death the immortality he so craved in life. The degree of Scottish Trinitarian, the 26th grade of the Ancient and Accepted rite, explains how the Mason should approach the problem of reconciling different belief systems:

Behold, the darkness is past, and the true light now shineth. My brother, you have before this been brought to light in Masonry, when the Worshipful Master, with the aid of the brethren, first made you a Mason. You have been taught to believe in the true God. You have passed through degrees intended to remind you of the Essenian and Hebrew mysteries; and in this you have heard described those practised by the first Christians. As you were not required to profess a belief in the tenets of the Essenes or the Pharisees, so neither here are you required to believe in the divine mission or character of Jesus the Nazarene. We shadow forth the secret discipline of the early Christians, as we do the other Mysteries, as the diverse and often eccentric forms in which Masonry has developed itself in the different ages of the world. Masonically, we know not whether you be Christian, Jew, or Moslem.

If you be Christian, you will see in this degree a Christian ceremony; and so you have the right to interpret it. Your brethren will respect your faith, as they have a right to demand that you shall respect theirs. If you be not a Christian, you will see in it a mere historical allegory, symbolizing great truths, acknowledged alike by you and them.

While you were veiled in darkness, you heard repeated by the voice of the great past its most ancient doctrines. No one has the right to object, if the Christian Mason sees foreshadowed in Krishna and Sosiosch, in Mithras and Osiris, the divine Word, that, as he believes, became man, and died upon the cross to redeem a fallen race. Nor can he object if others see in the Word that was in the beginning with God, and that was God, only the logos of Plato and Philo, or the uttered thought or first emanation of light, or the reason, of the great, silent, uncreated Deity, believed in and adored by all.

We do not undervalue the importance of any truth. We utter no word that can be deemed irreverent by any one of any faith. We do not tell the Moslem that it is only important for him to believe that there is but one God, and wholly unessential whether Mahomet was his prophet. We do not tell the Hebrew that the Messiah, whom he expects, was born in Bethlehem nearly two thousand years ago; and as little do we tell the Christian that Jesus the Nazarene was but a man, or his history the revival of an older legend. To do either is beyond our jurisdiction. Masonry, of no one age, belongs to all time; of no one religion, it finds its great truths in all.[789]

Here is the justification from the ritual itself of why I should be free to believe in my Physicist's Trinity of God the Father, whose laws govern the relativistic depths of space; God the Son, whose clockwork Newtonian mechanics oversees both the coding and decoding of strings of DNA and the forces which hold navigation satellites in orbit; and God the Holy Spirit, whose statistical uncertainty makes the void a reservoir of energy and quarks which bind themselves into the atoms of my body. Perhaps my Most Holy and Ever Blessed Trinity is the great, silent, uncreated Deity, but so what? As a thinking tool about the basic mysteries of life and consciousness, the myth of the Great Architect, expressed as an equilateral triangle, helps motivate and inspire me. If that is intellectual high treason, then I plead guilty.

If "non-materialists" cannot appreciate the sheer inspirational beauty in a physicist's thoughts, that does not invalidate them. I am free to wonder why it is that the Planck distance defines a measure that is beyond the scope of any scientific instrument to view. I can ask why the smallest tool we can use to look at small objects is the electron. I can speculate that bouncing electrons off objects the size of the Planck distance in order to create an image we can see is rather like trying to thread a needle wearing boxing gloves.

If "non-materialists" cannot see that I can use a term such as "the veil of Planck's constant" to express my awe at the mystery of quantum mechanisms and the uncertainty that is an inherent part of understanding them, it is a shortcoming they can address by reading more about physics. I can liken seeing through the veil of Planck's constant to perceiving the unspeakable glory of the goddess, and probably dying of ecstasy as a result. To me, this veil is a physical limiting factor that prevents me from fully understanding the structure of subatomic particles. It is the major unknown area in modern physics, and as such is a constant source of wonder and curiosity about the nature of the GAOTU, as well as an inspiration for theoretical striving. And I take this inspiration from Freemasonry.

The Old and the New

A nice visual metaphor for how I feel about the relationship between Science and Freemasonry can be drawn from the close proximity of the Niels Bohr Institute to the home of Danish Freemasonry on Blegdamsve, Copenhagen. They represent the New and Old Testaments of science. And perhaps they may, at some time in the future, cooperate to understand the human mind and its role as the observer that collapses the wave functions of quantum possibility. Freemasonry has evolved a spiritual system of studying the human mind that does not have the superstitious baggage of most religions. Blind Mother Nature, as Richard Dawkins calls the Most Holy and Ever Blessed Trinity, has used a kind of intellectual sieve to create brains and intelligences that are increasingly competent to deal with the laws of nature.

And Freemasonry offers a route to study this inner mystery of human conscious-ness in a way that is totally compatible with the quantum uncertainty of physics.

In the nineteenth century, scientists rejected Freemasonry's science of the human spirit and Freemasons turned away from physics, as it seemed to be deny-ing the need to know your self, which lies at the center of the Masonic system. But relativity and wave mechanics changed everything. Both give the observer a key role in defining the nature of a system. So now the scene is set for revisiting the secret science of Masonic Initiation, as an alternative means of approaching the problem of the self-conscious observer with an independent spirit.

I believe that Freemasonry offers an inspirational spiritual path to scientists that is totally free of the superstitious-metaphysical certainty which characterizes so much religious thinking. And it also offers training in the use of neutral sym-bolic language to discuss with all religious traditions the real questions of exis-tence without causing offense. For me, it is a calculus of the human spirit. Scientists need spiritual inspiration as much as the next person, but they don't need to be told that they must abandon their questioning uncertainty and accept a blind faith in impossible things to obtain it. Perhaps the time has come for Freemasonry to start to welcome back its prodigal scientist children into its Lodges. As it says in its own ritual:

> No evil hath so afflicted the world as intolerance of religious opinion; the human beings it has slain in various ways, if once and together brought to life, would make a nation of people, which, left to live and increase, would have doubled the popula-tion of the world; among which civilized portion it chiefly is that religious wars are waged.[790]

My final conclusion is that the tolerant Masonic degrees of Templar Mason and Craft are an accidental creation of a family that was seeking political power, but instead became immortal legends and is remembered, at least by some writ-ers, as the "High Sinclairs." William St. Clair, the builder of Roslin Chapel, created not just a stone structure but a mythical story which has been visited and revis-ited over the ages, and at each retelling has grown in its ability to take hold of the public mind. From the beginning, it drew on timeless motifs which gripped pub-lic perceptions and inspired belief. Over the centuries, its central themes have been refined, retold, and reused. It was fashioned as a political tool to inspire love and loyalty, and it continues to do so, growing with each retelling.

The St. Clair motives were base, self-seeking, and political, but they inspired a spiritual system which has evolved into the most tolerant and inclusive means of spiritual development in the world: Freemasonry. I can only leave you with the observation that often the best and most beautiful of flowers grow out of the largest dunghills.

BIBLIOGRAPHY

BOOKS AND JOURNALS

Aberdeen Burgh Records (1483), vol. I, no 39. University of Dundee Digitized Archives.

—— (1493), vol. I, no. 52. University of Dundee Digitized Archives.

Adamnan (ed. John Marsden, trans. John Gregory) (1995), *The Illustrated Life of Columba*, Floris Books, Edinburgh.

Ammerman, A.J., and L.L. Cavalli-Sforza (1979), "The Wave of Advance model for the spread of agriculture in Europe," in *Transformations: Mathematical Approaches to Culture Change*, Academic Press, London, pp. 201–202.

Baigent, M., and R. Leigh (1989), *The Temple and The Lodge*, Corgi, London.

Baillie, M. (1999), *Exodus to Arthur*, Batsford, London.

Barber, M. (1978), *The Trial of the Templars*, Cambridge University Press, Cambridge.

—— (1994), *The New Knighthood*, Cambridge University Press, Cambridge.

Barber, R.W. (1975), *The Knight and Chivalry*, Rowman and Littlefield, Totwa NJ.

Bardarson, I. (ed. F. Jonsson) (1930), *Description of Greenland in the Fourteenth Century*, Copenhagen, Bergen.

Barker Cryer, N (2006), York Mysteries Revealed, self-published, York.

Bede (trans. L. Sherley-Price) (1955), *A History of the English Church and People*, Penguin, Harmondsworth.

Bernard of Clairvaux (trans. C. Greenia) (1977), *The Works of Bernard of Clairvaux* , The Cistercian Fathers Series: no. 19, vol. 7, Cistercian Publications, Kalamazoo, Mich.

Berresford-Ellis, P. (1992), *Celtic Inheritance*, Constable, London.

Berrill, N.J. (1961), *Man's Emerging Mind*, Scientific Book Guild, London.

Booker, C. (2004), *The Seven Basic Plots—Why We Tell Stories*, Continuum, London.

Boyd, E. J. (1994), *A Brief History of the Knights of the Temple and of the Preceptory and Priory of St. George Aboyne*, Langstane Press, Aberdeen.

Brown, D. (2003), *The Da Vinci Code*, Corgi, London.

Bussel, F.W. (1918), *Religious Thought and Heresy in the Middle Ages*, Scott, London.

Butler, A., and J. Richie (2006), *Rosslyn Revealed: A Library in Stone*, O Books, Ropley.

Byrne, P. (2001), *Templar Gold, Discovering the Ark of the Covenant*, Symposium, Nevada City, CA.

Cann, R., *et al.* (1984), "Polymorphic sites and mechanisms of evolution in human mitochondrial DNA," *Genetics*, 106, pp. 479–99.

Cann, R., M. Stoneking and A. Wilson (1987), "Mitochondrial DNA and human evolution," *Nature*, 325, pp. 31–6.

Carlile, R. (1825), *Manual of Freemasonry*, William Reeves Ltd, London.

Cawthorne, N. (1996), *Sex Lives of the Popes*, Prion, London.

Childe, V.G. (1925), *The Dawn of European Civilisation*, Routledge, London.

—— (1939), "The Orient and Europe," *American Journal of Archaeology*, vol. 43, p. 10.

—— (1958), "Retrospect," *Antiquity*, vol. 32, p. 70.

Concise Dictionary of National Biography (1990), Oxford University Press, London.

Dawkins, R. (2006), *The God Delusion*Bantam Press, London.

de Curzon, H. (1888), *La Maison du Temple de Paris: Histoire et description*, Hachette, Paris.

Dennett, D.C. (2006), *Breaking the Spell—Religion as a Natural Phenomenon*, Allen Lane, London.

Diakonoff, I.M., and N.B. Jankowska (1990), "An Elamite Gilgamesh Text from Argistihenele, Urartu," *Zeitschrift fur Assyriologie* , vol. 80, no. 1, pp. 102–20.

Diamond, J. (1999), *Guns, Germs and Steel*, Vintage, London.

—— (2005), *Collapse: How Societies Choose to Fail or Survive*, Penguin, London.

Drummond, J. (1994) *Sculptured Monuments in Iona and the West Highlands*, Felinfach, Llanerch (originally published Edinburgh, Society of Antiquaries of Scotland, 1881).

Dutton, D. (2005), "Are There Seven Basic Plots?," *Washington Post*, May 8.

Edwards, B. (1987), *Drawing on the Right Side of the Brain*, Fontana/Collins, London.

Edwards, G.P. (1985), "William Elphinstone, His College Chapel and the Second of April," *Aberdeen University Review*, 1i, pp. 1–17.

Eeles, F.C. (1934), "The Monymusk Reliquary or Brecbennoch of St. Columba," *Proceedings of the Scottish Society of Antiquities*, vol. 69, May 14, p. 436.

Ellis Davidson, H. (1993), *The Lost Beliefs of Northern Europe*, Routledge, London.

Feynman, R.P. (1999), *The Pleasure of Finding Things Out*, Allen Lane, London.

Finlay, I. (1979) *Columba*, Victor Gollancz, London.

Foote, P.G., and D.M. Wilson (1970) *The Viking Achievement*, Sidgwick and Jackson, London.

Gimbutas, M. (1999), The Living Goddess, University of California Press, Los Angeles.

—— (2001), *The Language of the Goddess*, Thames and Hudson, London.

Gould, R.F. (1886), *The History of Freemasonry*, Caxton Publishing, London.

—— (ed. D. Wright) (1931) *Gould's History of Freemasonry*, Caxton Publishing, London.

Grand Lodge of Antient, Free and Accepted Masons of Scotland (1986), *Historical Sketch of the Grand Lodge of Antient, Free and Accepted Masons of Scotland* , Grand Lodge, Edinburgh.

Hale, R.B. (1976.) *The Magnificent Gael*, MOM Printing, Ottawa.

Hallam, E.M. (1980), *Capetian France 987–1328*, Longman, London.

Hamill, J., and R. Gilbert (1998), *Freemasonry: A Celebration of the Craft*, Greenwich Editions, London.

Hay, G. (1993), *The Prose Works of Sir Gilbert Hay*, vol. II, Scottish Text Society, Edinburgh.

Hay, R.A. (ed. J. Maidment) (1835), *Genealogie of the Saintclaires of Rosslyn, including the Chartulary of Rosslyn*, Stevenson, Edinburgh.

Heath, R. (2007), *Alexander Thom—Cracking the Stone Age Code*, Bluestone Press, Cardigan.

Hedges, J.W. (1992), *Tomb of the Eagles*, Tempus Reparatum, Oxford.

Henderson, M. (2002), "Scratches that Trace the Ascent of Man", *The Times*, Friday, Jan 11, p. 5.

Hibbert, C. (1968), *Charles I*, Weidenfield and Nicolson, London.

Holmes, A. (1981), *Principles of Physical Geology*, 3rd ed., Nelson, London.

Humphrey, N. (1996), *Soul Searching*, Vintage, London.

Jacobs, J. (1968), *The Economy of Cities*, Pelican, London.

Jarman, A.O.H. (1959), "Geoffrey of Monmouth," in A.J. Roderick ed., *Wales through the Ages*, vol. I, Christopher Davies, Llandybie.

Jones, G. (2001), *A History of the Vikings*, Oxford University Press, Oxford.

Jones, G., and T. Jones (1949), *The Mabinogion Translated*, Everyman Library, Dutton, London.

Kaku, M. (2004), *Einstein's Cosmos*, Weidenfeld & Nicolson, London.

Keighley, T. (1837), *Secret Societies of the Middle Ages*, London.

Kenyon, K. (1956) "Jericho and its setting in the Near Eastern history," *Antiquity*, vol. 30, p. 184–97.

—— (1957), *Digging Up Jericho*, Ernest Benn Ltd, London.

Kerr, A. (1877), "Rosslyn Castle: Its Buildings Past and Present," *Proceedings of the Edinburgh Society of Antiquaries*, December 10, p. 415.

Liden, K. (ed. A. Freeman and K. Sutherland) (1969), "From Pagan Sanctuary to Christian Church: the excavation of Maere Church, Trondelag," *Norwegian Archeological Review*, 2, pp. 23–32.

Lodge, D. (2003), *Consciousness and the Novel*, Penguin, London.

Lomas, R. (1994), private journal notes, unpublished.

—— (2003) *Freemasonry and the Birth of Modern Science*, Fair Winds Press, Rockport MA.

—— (2005), *Turning The Hiram Key*, Fair Winds Press, Rockport MA.

—— (2006), *The Secrets of Freemasonry*, Constable and Robinson, London.

Lomas, R., and C. Knight (1996), *The Hiram Key*, Century, London.

—— (1997), *The Second Messiah* , Fair Winds Press, Rockport MA.

—— (2001), *Uriel's Machine*, Fair Winds Press, Rockport MA.

Lyon, D.M. (1873), *History of the Lodge of Edinburgh embracing an account of the Rise and Progress of Freemasonry in Scotland*, William Blackwood, Edinburgh and London

McClenachan, C. (1867), *The Book of the Ancient and Accepted Scottish Rite of Freemasonry*, Masonic Publishing and Manufacturing, New York.

MacDonald, I. (1993), *Saint Magnus*, Floris Books, Edinburgh.

Mackey, A.G. (1870), *Encyclopedia of Freemasonry*, Griffin, London.

MacLennan, M. (ed. J. Grant) (1979, reprinted 1995), *A Pronouncing and Etymological Dictionary of the Gaelic Language*, Acair, Stornoway, and Mercat Press, Edinburgh.

Marsden, J. (1994), *The Tombs of the Kings: An Iona Book of the Dead*, Llanerch Publishers, Lampeter.

Mellaart, J. (1965), *Earliest Civilizations of The Near East*, Thames and Hudson, London.

—— (1967) *Çatalhöyük*, Thames and Hudson, London.

Mithen, S. (2003), *After the Ice*, Weidenfeld & Nicolson, London.

Newberg, A., E. d'Aquili and V. Rause (2002), *Why God Won't Go Away: Brain science and the biology of belief*, Ballantine, New York.

Nicholson, H. (2001), *The Knights Templar: A New History*, Sutton Publishing, Stroud.

Orkneyinga Saga: The History of the Earls of Orkney (1978) (trans. H. Palsson and P. Edwards), Penguin, London.

Piggott, S. (1957), "The Radiocarbon Date from Durrington Walls," *Antiquity*, vol. 31, p. 74.

Pinker, S. (1994), *The Language Instinct*, Penguin, London.

Pohl, F.J. (1967), *Prince Henry Sinclair. His Expedition to the New World in 1398*, Nimbus Publishing, Nova Scotia.

Popper, K.R. (1969), *Conjectures and Refutations: The Growth of Scientific Knowledge*, Routledge & Kegan Paul, London.

Preston, W. (1746), *Illustrations of Freemasonry*, William T Wilkie, London.

Public Record Office, HO 42/47, f. 51.

Renfrew, C. (1973), *Before Civilization*, Penguin, London.

—— (1973a), "Problems in the general correlation of archaeological and linguistic strata in prehistoric Greece: the model of autochthonous origin," in R.A. Crossland and A. Birchall (eds.), *Bronze Age Migrations in the Aegean*, Duckworth, London, p. 271.

—— (1987), *Archaeology and Language*, Jonathan Cape, London.

—— (2001), "From molecular genetics to archaeogenetics," *PNAS*, April 24, vol. 98, no. 9, pp. 4830–32.

Renfrew, C., and P. Bahn (1998), *Archaeology, Theories, Methods and Practice*, Thames and Hudson, London.

Robinson, C.E. (1920), *A History of England, 1485–1688*, Methuen, London.

Schumpeter, J.A. (1954), *History of Economic Analysis*, Nelson, London.

Skinner, A. (1999), *Analytical Introduction to the Wealth of Nations*, Penguin Classics, London.

Smith, A. (1999), *The Wealth of Nations, Books I–III*, Penguin, London.

Smith, C., and J. Ritchie (2006), "The Writing's on the Walls," *The Scotsman*, Mon., May 22.

Smyser, H.M. (1965), "Ibn Fadlan's account of the Rus," in J.B. Bessinger Jr and R.P. Creed (eds) *Franciplegius: Medieval and Linguistic Studies in Honour of Francis Peabody Magoun*, London, Allen & Unwin.

Somerville, J. (ed. Sir Walter Scott) (1815), *Memorie of the Somervilles; being a history of the baronial house of Somerville*, Constable, Edinburgh.

Stevenson, D. (1988), *The Origins of Freemasonry*, Cambridge University Press, Cambridge.

Stringer, C., and C. Gamble (1993), *In Search of the Neanderthals*, Thames and Hudson, London.

Stringer, K. (ed.) (1985), *Essays on the Nobility of Medieval Scotland*, John Donald, Edinburgh.

Sykes, B. (2001), *The Seven Daughters of Eve*, Bantam, London.

Temple, R. (1991), *He Who Saw Everything*, Rider, London.

Thompson, W.P.L. (1987), *History of Orkney*, Mercat Press, Edinburgh.

Thouless, R.. (1971), *An Introduction to the Psychology of Religion*, Cambridge University Press, Cambridge.

Torrington, F.W. (1974), *House of Lords Sessional Papers, Session 1798–9*, Oceana Publications, New York.

Walker, W.W. (1790), *Pilgrim and Knight Templar*, privately published, Ayrshire.

Wallace-Murphy, T., and M. Hopkins (1999), *Rosslyn—Guardian of the Secrets of the Holy Grail*, Element, Shaftesbury.

—— (2004), *Templars in America*, Weiserbooks, Boston.

Ward, J.S.M. (1921), *Freemasonry and the Ancient Gods*, Simpkin, Marshall, Hamilton, Kent & Co., London.

Wickham-Jones, C.R. (1997), *Scotland's First Settlers*, Historic Scotland, Edinburgh.

Wilson J.F., D.A. Weiss, M. Richards, M.G. Thomas, N. Bradman, and D.B. Goldstein (2001), "Genetic evidence for different male and female roles during cultural transitions in the British Isles," *PNAS*, April 24, vol. 98, no. 9, pp. 5078–83.

WEBSITES

http://catal.arch.cam.ac.uk/
http://classics.mit.edu/Aristotle/
http://concise.britannica.com/
http://freemasonry.dept.shef.ac.uk/
http://library.wustl.edu/
http://links.jstor.org/
http://marshall.thefreelibrary.com/
http://robertlomas.com/
http://sinclair.quarterman.org/
http://www.aberdeencity.gov.uk/
http://www.aberdeen-treasures.org/
http://www.adamsmith.org/
http://www.amphetameanies.co.uk/
http://www.babynamefinder.blogspot.com/
http://www.bartleby.com/211/0708.html
http://www.battlefieldstrust.com/

http://www.brad.ac.uk/acad/mancen/lomas/seminars.html
http://www.bradford.ac.uk/webofhiram/
http://www.britannica.com/
http://www.catalhoyuk.com/
http://www.catholic.org/
http://www.catholic-forum.com/
http://www.colourcountry.net/
http://www.constitution.org/
http://www.cushnieent.force9.co.uk/CollegiateChurches/index.htm
http://www.dailygrail.com/
http://www.dsl.ac.uk/dsl/
http://www.edinburgh.gov.uk/
http://www.ewtn.com/
http://www.fordham.edu/
http://www.gale.pwp.blueyonder.co.uk/
http://www.greatprioryofscotland.com/
http://www.imagesonline.bl.uk/britishlibrary/
http://www.iona.org.uk/
http://www.irish-freemasons.org/
http://www.journals.uchicago.edu/
http://www.kilmartin.org/
http://www.lib.rochester.edu/
http://www.lordbothwell.co.uk/
http://www.newadvent.org/
http://www.nms.ac.uk/monymuskreliquary.aspx
http://www.poemhunter.com/
http://www.princeton.edu/
http://www.rampantscotland.com/
http://www.rosslynchapel.org.uk/history
http://www.rosslyntemplars.org.uk/
http://www.royal.gov.uk/
http://www.sacred-texts.com/
http://www.savegaelic.org/
http://www.scotlandspast.org/
http://www.scotsconnection.com/
http://www.spartacus.schoolnet.co.uk/
http://www.spl.org.uk/poets_a-z/ransford.html
http://www.templarhistory.com/
http://www.thepeerage.com/
http://www.users.zetnet.co.uk/ahamilton/sinclair.htm

ΠΟΤΕ S

1. Nicholson, H. (2001), *The Knights Templar: A New History*, Sutton Publishing, Stroud, p. 246.
2. *Ibid.*, p. 240.
3. *Ibid.*, p. 240.
4. http://freemasonry.dept.shef.ac.uk/?q=papers_8 (accessed September 25, 2006).
5. *Ibid.*
6. *Ibid.*
7. *Ibid.*
8. http://www.spartacus.schoolnet.co.uk/PRpeterloo.htm (accessed September 25, 2006).
9. http://www.spartacus.schoolnet.co.uk/PRcarlile.htm (accessed September 25, 2006).
10. http://freemasonry.dept.shef.ac.uk/?q=papers_8 (accessed September 25, 2006).
11. *Ibid.*
12. Carlile, R. (1825), *Manual of Freemasonry*, William Reeves Ltd, London, p. 1.
13. *Ibid.*, p. 139.
14. *Ibid.*, p. 141.
15. *Ibid.*, p. 147.
16. *Ibid.*, pp. 146–47.
17. *Ibid.*, p. 147.
18. *Ibid.*, p. 147.
19. *Ibid.*, pp. 147–48.
20. *Ibid.*, p. 158.
21. *Ibid.*, p. 148.
22. *Ibid.*, p. 148.
23. *Ibid.*, pp. 148–49.
24. *Ibid.*, pp. 158–59.
25. *Ibid.*, p. 159.
26. *Ibid.*, pp. 80–97.
27. *Ibid.*, p. 148.
28. http://www.greatprioryofscotland.com/history.htm (accessed September 24, 2006).
29. Walker, W.W. (1790), *Pilgrim and Knight Templar*, privately published, Ayrshire, p. 3.
30. *Ibid.*, p. 4.
31. *Ibid.*, p. 4.
32. *Ibid.*, pp. 4–5.
33. *Ibid.*, p. 5.
34. *Ibid.*, p. 5.
35. *Ibid.*, p. 6.
36. *Ibid.*, p. 7.
37. *Ibid.*, p. 15.
38. *Ibid.*, p. 17.
39. *Ibid.*, p. 19.
40. McClenachan, C. (1867), *The Book of the Ancient and Accepted Scottish Rite of Freemasonry*, Masonic Publishing and Manufacturing, New York, pp. 146–8.
41. http://www.fordham.edu/halsall/source/urban2-5vers.html (accessed October 13, 2006).
42. http://www.fordham.edu/halsall/

source/urban2-5vers.html (accessed October 13, 2006).

43. Barber, M. (1994), *The New Knighthood*, Cambridge University Press, Cambridge, p. 6.
44. *Ibid.*, p. 6.
45. *Ibid.*, p. 8.
46. *Ibid.*, p. 10.
47. Lomas, R., and C. Knight (1997), *The Second Messiah*, Fair Winds Press, Rockport MA, p. 73.
48. Barber (1994), p. 14.
49. *Ibid.*, Cambridge, p. 14.
50. *Ibid.*, p. 18.
51. *Ibid.*, pp. 20–21.
52. *Ibid.*, Cambridge, p. 40.
53. http://www.newadvent.org/cathen/02498d.htm (accessed September 25, 2006).
54. http://www.newadvent.org/cathen/02498d.htm (accessed September 25, 2006).
55. Barber, (1994), p. 11.
56. Nicholson (2001), p. 22.
57. Barber (1994), p. 11.
58. *Ibid.*, p. 12.
59. *Ibid.*, p. 41.
60. Quoted in Nicholson (2001), p. 36.
61. Nicholson (2001), p.37.
62. http://www.newadvent.org/cathen/02498d.htm (accessed September 25, 2006).
63. Nicholson (2001), p. 26.
64. *Ibid.*, p. 26.
65. *Ibid.*, pp. 26–27.
66. http://www.catholic.org/featured/headline.php?ID=980 (accessed September 25, 2006).
67. Nicholson (2001), p. 37.
68. *Ibid.*, p. 36.
69. Quoted in Barber (1994), pp. 15–16.
70. Barber (1994), p. 16.
71. Nicholson (2001), p.153.
72. *Ibid.*, p. 149.
73. *Ibid.*, p. 153.
74. *Ibid.*, p. 153.
75. *Ibid.*, p. 153.
76. http://www.fordham.edu/halsall/source/urban2-5vers.html (accessed September 25, 2006).
77. Nicholson (2001), p.152.
78. *Ibid.*, p. 160.
79. *Ibid.*, p. 161.

80. *Ibid.*, p. 161.
81. *Ibid.*, p. 170.
82. *Ibid.*, p. 163.
83. *Ibid.*, p. 163.
84. http://www.imagesonline.bl.uk/britishlibrary/controller/subjectid-search?id=10175&startid=35611&width=4&height=2&idx=2 (accessed November 5, 2006).
85. Nicholson (2001), p. 163.
86. *Ibid.*, p. 162.
87. *Ibid.*, p. 164.
88. *Ibid.*, p. 164.
89. *Ibid.*, pp. 187–88.
90. *Ibid.*, pp. 192–93.
91. Diamond, J. (2005), *Collapse: How Societies Choose to Fail or Survive*, Penguin, London, p. 185.
92. Nicholson (2001), p. 197.
93. *Ibid.*, p. 192.
94. *Ibid.*, p. 181.
95. *Ibid.*, p. 4.
96. *Ibid.*, p. 146.
97. *Ibid.*, p. 149.
98. *Ibid.*, pp. 47–48.
99. Barber (1994), p. 281.
100. Nicholson (2001), p. 152.
101. Lomas and Knight (1997).
102. http://www.fordham.edu/halsall/source/gildas.html (accessed 7 Oct 2006).
103. http://www.fordham.edu/halsall/basis/nennius-full.html (accessed 7 Oct 2006).
104. http://links.jstor.org/sici?sici=0149-6611(195303)68%3A3%3C196%3AGOMHRB%3E2.0.CO%3B2-2 (accessed September 25, 2006).
105. http://www.lib.rochester.edu/CAMELOT/geofhkb.htm (accessed September 25, 2006).
106. Jarman, A.O.H. (1959), "Geoffrey of Monmouth," in A.J. Roderick ed., *Wales through the Ages*, vol. I, Christopher Davies, Llandybie, pp. 145–52.
107. *Ibid.*, pp. 146–50.
108. *Ibid.*, pp. 147–48.
109. Jones, G., and T. Jones (1949), *The Mabinogion Translated*, Everyman Library, Dutton, London.
110. http://marshall.thefreelibrary.com/English-Literature-For-Boys-And-

Girls/7-1 (accessed November 3, 2006).

111. Barber (1994), p. 7.

112. Nicholson (2001), p.171.

113. Berresford-Ellis, P. (1992), *Celtic Inheritance*, Constable, London, p. 26.

114. http://www.princeton.edu/~lancelot/romance.html (accessed November 3, 2006).

115. http://library.wustl.edu/units/spec/manuscripts/mlc/boron/boron.html (accessed November 3, 2006).

116. Barber, R.W. (1975), *The Knight and Chivalry*, Rowman and Littlefield, Totwa NJ, p. 86.

117. Nicholson (2001), pp. 238–40.

118. *Ibid.*, p. 170.

119. http://www.newadvent.org/cathen/07265b.htm (accessed November 3, 2006).

120. Nicholson (2001), p. 244.

121. *Ibid.*, p. 240.

122. Hallam, E.M. (1980), *Capetian France 987–1328*, Longman, London, pp. 263–64.

123. Nicholson (2001), p. 163.

124. Barber (1994), p. 300.

125. Hallam (1980), p. 277.

126. *Ibid.*, p. 278.

127. http://www.newadvent.org/cathen/09368a.htm (accessed November 3, 2006).

128. http://www.catholic-forum.com/SAINTS/ncd02176.htm (accessed November 3, 2006).

129. Barber (1994), pp. 151–53.

130. Hallam (1980), pp. 275–7.

131. *Ibid.*, pp. 278–83.

132. Barber, M. (1978), *The Trial of the Templars*, Cambridge University Press, Cambridge, pp. 38–39.

133. *Ibid.*, pp. 40–41.

134. Cawthorne, N. (1996), *Sex Lives of the Popes*, Prion, London, p. 112.

135. Hallam (1980), p. 282.

136. http://www.newadvent.org/cathen/02429c.htm (accessed November 3, 2006).

137. http://www.newadvent.org/cathen/04020a.htm (accessed November 3, 2006).

138. Barber (1978), pp. 14–16.

139. Bussel, F.W. (1918), *Religious Thought and Heresy in the Middle Ages*, Scott, London, p. 36.

140. Nicholson (2001), p. 164.

141. de Curzon, H. (1888), *La Maison du Temple de Paris: Histoire et description*, Hachette, Paris, p. 84.

142. Barber (1978), p. 47.

143. Barber (1978), p. 54.

144. Nicholson (2001), p. 192.

145. Barber (1994), p. 301.

146. Barber (1978), p. 45.

147. Nicholson (2001), p. 192.

148. Keighley, T. (1837), *Secret Societies of the Middle Ages*, London, pp. 288–89.

149. *Ibid.*, p. 285.

150. Barber (1978), p. 62.

151. Keighley (1837), p. 297.

152. http://www.newadvent.org/cathen/08026a.htm#II (accessed November 3, 2006).

153. Keighley (1837), p. 298.

154. *Ibid.*, p. 298.

155. *Ibid.*, pp. 300–303.

156. *Ibid.*, p. 305.

157. Barber (1978), p. 178.

158. Keighley (1837), pp. 321–22.

159. http://www.newadvent.org/cathen/08026a.htm#II (accessed November 3, 2006).

160. Barber (1978), p. 45.

161. Keighley (1837), p. 325.

162. *Ibid.*, p. 326.

163. *Ibid.*, p. 326.

164. Nicholson (2001), pp. 244–46.

165. Boyd, E. J. (1994), *A Brief History of the Knights of the Temple and of the Preceptory and Priory of St. George Aboyne*, Langstane Press, Aberdeen, p. 5.

166. *Ibid.*, p. 18.

167. *Ibid.*, p. 24.

168. *Ibid.*, p. 25.

169. http://freemasonry.dept.shef.ac.uk/?q=papers_6 (accessed 27 Sept 2006).

170. *Ibid.*

171. *Ibid.*

172. Public Record Office, HO 42/47, f. 51.

173. http://freemasonry.dept.shef.ac.uk/?q=papers_6 (accessed 27 Sept 2006).

174. Torrington, F.W. (1974), *House of Lords Sessional Papers, Session 1798–9*, Oceana Publications, New York, vol. 1, pp. 199–218.

175. Lyon, D.M (1873), *History of the Lodge of Edinburgh embracing an account of the Rise and Progress of Freemasonry in Scotland*, William Blackwood, Edinburgh and London, pp. 266–67.
176. http://www.greatprioryofscotland.com/history.htm (accessed 27 Sept 2006).
177. *Ibid.*
178. *Ibid.*
179. Boyd (1994), p. 28.
180. *Ibid.*, pp. 28–29.
181. *Ibid.*, pp. 31–32.
182. *Ibid.*, p. 33.
183. http://www.greatprioryofscotland.com/history.htm (accessed 27 Sept 2006).
184. *Ibid.*
185. *Ibid.*
186. Gould, R.F. (1886), *The History of Freemasonry*, vol. III, Caxton Publishing, London, p. 75.
187. Gould, R.F. (ed. D. Wright) (1931) *Gould's History of Freemasonry*, vol. V, Caxton Publishing, London, p. 254.
188. *Ibid.*, p. 255.
189. *Ibid.*, p. 253.
190. http://www.yorkrite.com/roos/info.html (accessed 27 Sept 2006).
191. Gould (1931), vol. III, p. 255.
192. http://www.greatprioryofscotland.com/history.htm (accessed 30 Sept 2006).
193. Gould (1931), vol. III, p. 259.
194. *Ibid.*, pp. 259–60.
195. *Ibid.*, p. 147.
196. Ward, J.S.M. (1921) *Freemasonry and the Ancient Gods*, Simpkin, Marshall, Hamilton, Kent & Co., London, pp. 299–300.
197. *Ibid.*, p. 300.
198. *Ibid.*, p. 301.
199. Mackey, A.G. (1870), *Encyclopedia of Freemasonry*, Griffin, London, p. 132.
200. Gould (1931), vol. V, p. 279.
201. *Ibid.*, p. 279
202. Barker Cryer, N (2006), *York Mysteries Revealed*, self-published, York, p. 135.
203. *Ibid.*, p. 270.
204. *Ibid.*, p. 269.
205. Ward (1921), p. 298.
206. Barker Cryer (2006), p. 273.
207. Gould (1931), vol. IV, p. 254.
208. *Ibid.*, p. 255.
209. *Ibid.*, p. 256.
210. Ward (1921), p. 282.
211. *Ibid.*, p. 148.
212. *Ibid.*, p. 270.
213. *Ibid.*, pp. 270–71.
214. *Ibid.*, p. 288.
215. *Ibid.*, pp. 286–88.
216. *Ibid.*, pp. 298–99.
217. Nicholson (2001), p. 240.
218. Gould (1931), vol. III, pp. 146–47.
219. *Ibid.*, p. 147.
220. Gould (1886), vol. II, p. 295.
221. *Ibid.*, pp. 295–96.
222. *Ibid.*, p. 296.
223. *Ibid.*, p. 296.
224. *Ibid.*, p. 388.
225. *Ibid.*, p. 392.
226. *Ibid.*, p. 392.
227. Gould (1931), vol. V, p. 252.
228. *Ibid.*, p. 253.
229. *Ibid.*, p. 253.
230. *Ibid.*, p. 255.
231. *Ibid.*, p. 255.
232. Lomas, R. (2006), *The Secrets of Freemasonry*, Constable and Robinson, London, pp. 226–48.
233. Gould (1886), vol. II, p. 296.
234. http://www.rosslynchapel.org.uk/history/history-pt1.htm (accessed November 3, 2006).
235. http://www.edinburgh.gov.uk/libraries/historysphere/roslin/roslin.html (accessed November 3, 2006).
236. MacLennan, M. (ed. J. Grant) (1979, reprinted 1995), *A Pronouncing and Etymological Dictionary of the Gaelic Language*, Acair, Stornoway, and Mercat Press, Edinburgh.
237. http://www.savegaelic.org/page/basic-gaelic.php (accessed November 3, 2006).
238. http://wwwbabynamefinder.blogspot.com/2006_06_27_wwwbaby-namefinder_archive.html (accessed November 3, 2006).
239. http://www.rosslynchapel.org.uk/history/history-pt2.htm (accessed November 3, 2006).
240. Thompson, W.P.L. (1987), *History of Orkney*, Mercat Press, Edinburgh, p. 107.

241. *Ibid.*, pp. 107–25.
242. http://www.brad.ac.uk/acad/man-cen/lomas/seminars.html (accessed November 3, 2006).
243. Stevenson, D. (1988), *The Origins of Freemasonry*, Cambridge University Press, Cambridge, p. 14.
244. *Ibid.*
245. Stevenson (1988), p. 24.
246. Edwards, G.P. (1985), "William Elphinstone, His College Chapel and the Second of April", *Aberdeen University Review*, 1i, pp. 1–17.
247. Stevenson (1988), p. 24.
248. http://www.aberdeencity.gov.uk/ACCI/web/site/LocalHistory/NC/loc_ArchKirkNicholas.asp (accessed November 3, 2006).
249. Gould (1886), vol. I, p. 422.
250. Aberdeen. Burgh Records (1483), vol. I, no 39. University of Dundee Digitized Archives.
251. Gould (1886), vol. I, pp. 422–23.
252. Stevenson (1988), p. 15.
253. Gould (1886), vol. I, p. 423.
254. Stevenson (1988), pp. 15–16.
255. http://www.dsl.ac.uk/dsl/.
256. Aberdeen Burgh Records (1493), vol. I, no. 52. University of Dundee Digitized Archives.
257. Gould (1886), vol. I, p. 423.
258. http://www.rosslynchapel.org.uk/history/history-pt2.htm (accessed November 3, 2006).
259. Ward (1921), p. 801.
260. Barber (1994), pp. 319–20.
261. Wallace-Murphy, T., and M. Hopkins (2004), *Templars in America*, Weiserbooks, Boston, p. 17.
262. http://www.kilmartin.org/main.html (accessed November 3, 2006).
263. http://www.rosslyntemplars.org.uk/kilmartin.htm (accessed November 3, 2006).
264. Baigent, M., and R. Leigh (1989), *The Temple and The Lodge*, Corgi, London, p. 24.
265. *Ibid.*, pp. 26–27.
266. *Ibid.*, pp. 101–102.
267. Adamnan (ed. John Marsden, trans. John Gregory) (1995), *The Illustrated Life of Columba*, Floris Books, Edinburgh, p. 72.
268. Hale, R.B. (1976.) *The Magnificent Gael*, MOM Printing, Ottawa, p. 180.
269. Marsden, J. (1994), *The Tombs of the Kings: An Iona Book of the Dead*, Llanerch Publishers, Lampeter, pp. 20–109.
270. http://www.iona.org.uk/abbey/main.htm (accessed November 3, 2006).
271. Bede (trans. L. Sherley-Price) (1955), *A History of the English Church and People*, Penguin, Harmondsworth, p. 143.
272. Adamnan (1995), pp. 217–18.
273. *Ibid.*, p. 221.
274. *Ibid.*, p. 186.
275. Drummond, J. (1994) *Sculptured Monuments in Iona and the West Highlands*, Felinfach, Llanerch (originally published Edinburgh, Society of Antiquaries of Scotland, 1881).
276. Baigent and Leigh (1989), p. 24.
277. Drummond (1994), pp. 25–28.
278. *Ibid.*, pp. 23–24.
279. *Ibid.*, pp. 23–24.
280. Gould (1886), vol. I, p. 422.
281. *Ibid.*, p. 422.
282. *Ibid.*, pp. 422–23.
283. *Ibid.*, p. 423.
284. *Ibid.*, p. 423.
285. http://www.aberdeen-treasures.org/stmachar_cath.shtml (accessed November 3, 2006).
286. Gould (1886), vol. I, p. 425.
287. *Ibid.*, p. 425.
288. *Ibid.*, pp. 425–26.
289. Lomas (2006), pp. 130–47.
290. http://sinclair.quarterman.org/sinclair/templars/index.html.
291. http://sinclair.quarterman.org/who/henry.html (accessed November 3, 2006).
292. Wallace-Murphy and Hopkins (2004), p. 15.
293. Nicholson (2001), p. 192.
294. *Ibid.*, p. 243.
295. Wallace-Murphy and Hopkins (2004), p. 17.
296. Nicholson (2001), p. 192.
297. Jones, G. (2001), *A History of the Vikings*, Oxford University Press, Oxford, pp. 229–31.
298. *Ibid.*, p. 231.

299. Wallace-Murphy and Hopkins (2004), pp. 9–10.
300. *Ibid.*, p. 11.
301. Jones (2001), p. 231.
302. *Ibid.*, p. 231.
303. Ellis Davidson, H. (1993), *The Lost Beliefs of Northern Europe*, Routledge, London, p. 48.
304. *Ibid.*, p. 126.
305. Liden, K. (ed. A. Freeman and K. Sutherland) (1969), "From Pagan Sanctuary to Christian Church: the excavation of Maere Church, Trondelag", *Norwegian Archaeological Review*, 2, pp. 23–32.
306. Wallace-Murphy and Hopkins (2004), pp. 11–12.
307. http://www.newadvent.org/cathen/06410a.htm (accessed November 3, 2006).
308. http://www.journals.uchicago.edu/AJHG/journal/issues/v66n2/990488/990488.html?erFrom=-5776591175096581422Guest (accessed November 3, 2006).
309. Wallace-Murphy and Hopkins (2004), pp. 12–13.
310. *Ibid.*, p. 7.
311. Diamond (2005), p. 180.
312. *Ibid.*, p. 181.
313. Jones (2001), p. 202.
314. A full translation of the Song of Rig can be found at http://www.gale.pwp.blueyonder.co.uk/midnite_gale_13.htm (accessed November 3, 2006).
315. Jones (2001), p. 197.
316. Smyser, H.M. (1965), "Ibn Fadlan's account of the Rus," in J.B. Bessinger Jr and R.P. Creed (eds) *Franciplegius: Medieval and Linguistic Studies in Honour of Francis Peabody Magoun*, London, Allen & Unwin, p. 69.
317. Jones (2001), p. 183.
318. *Ibid.*, pp. 187–89.
319. *Ibid.*, p. 191.
320. *Ibid.*, p. 195.
321. *Ibid.*, p. 196.
322. *Ibid.*, p. 198.
323. *Ibid.*, p. 90.
324. *Ibid.*, p. 269.
325. *Ibid.*, p. 270.
326. *Ibid.*, p. 273.
327. *Ibid.*, p. 277.
328. *Ibid.*, p. 292.
329. *Ibid.*, pp. 295–96.
330. *Ibid.*, pp. 295–99.
331. Foote, P.G., and D.M. Wilson (1970) *The Viking Achievement*, Sidgwick and Jackson, London, p xxii.
332. Jones (2001), p. 298.
333. *Ibid.*, p. 299.
334. Diamond (2005), pp. 206–207.
335. *Ibid.*, p. 208.
336. *Ibid.*, p. 208.
337. *Ibid.*, p. 209.
338. *Ibid.*, p. 209.
339. *Ibid.*, p. 209.
340. *Ibid.*, p. 213.
341. *Ibid.*, p. 236.
342. *Ibid.*, pp. 275–76.
343. *Ibid.*, p. 276.
344. Jones (2001), p. 307.
345. Pohl, F.J. (1967), *Prince Henry Sinclair. His Expedition to the New World in 1398*, Nimbus Publishing, Nova Scotia.
346. *Ibid.*, pp. 86–87.
347. *Ibid.*, pp. 128–30.
348. *Ibid.*, p. 10.
349. *Ibid.*, p. 10.
350. *Ibid.*, p. 1.
351. http://www.users.zetnet.co.uk/ahamilton/sinclair.htm (accessed November 3, 2006).
352. Thompson (1987), p. 92.
353. *Ibid.*, pp. 97–98.
354. *Ibid.*, pp. 98–99.
355. *Ibid.*, p. 99.
356. *Ibid.*, p. 100.
357. *Ibid.*, p. 101.
358. Wallace-Murphy and Hopkins (2004), p. 173.
359. *Ibid.*, p. 173.
360. Diamond (2005), p. 187.
361. *Ibid.*, p. 243.
362. *Ibid.*, p. 235.
363. *Ibid.*, pp. 240–49.
364. *Ibid.*, p. 267.
365. Bardarson, I. (ed. F. Jonsson) (1930), *Description of Greenland in the Fourteenth Century*, Copenhagen, Bergen.
366. Thompson (1987), pp. 97–98.
367. Diamond (2005), p. 270.
368. *Ibid.*, p. 270.

369. *Ibid.*, p. 270–71.
370. Byrne, P. (2001), *Templar Gold, Discovering the Ark of the Covenant*, Symposium, Nevada City, CA, p. 378.
371. Butler, A., and J. Richie (2006), *Rosslyn Revealed: A Library in Stone*, O Books, Ropley, p. 79.
372. Gould (1886), vol. I, p. 382.
373. Lomas (2006), pp. 295–98.
374. Gould (1886), vol. I, p. 383.
375. *Ibid.*, p. 383.
376. *Ibid.*, p. 384.
377. http://freemasonry.dept.shef.ac.uk/ ?q=seminars_stevenson. (accessed November 5, 2006).
378. Stevenson (1988), p. 25.
379. *Ibid.*, p. 27.
380. *Ibid.*, p. 27.
381. *Ibid.*, p. 28.
382. Calendar of State Papers relating to Scotland, 1581–3, 13 vols, HMSO, London, 1910–59, quoted in Stevenson (1988), p. 28.
383. Calendar of State Papers relating to Scotland, 1584–5, 13 Vols, HMSO, London, 1910–59, quoted in Stevenson (1988), p. 28.
384. Stevenson (1988), pp. 32–33.
385. Grand Lodge of Antient Free and Accepted Masons of Scotland (1986), *Historical Sketch of the Grand Lodge of Antient Free and Accepted Masons of Scotland*, Grand Lodge, Edinburgh, appendix 1.
386. Somerville, J. (ed. Sir Walter Scott) (1815), *Memorie of the Somervilles; being a history of the baronial house of Somerville*, Constable, Edinburgh, vol. 1, p. 63.
387. Gould (1886), vol. I, p. 411.
388. *Ibid.*, p. 412.
389. *Ibid.*, pp. 411–12.
390. Stevenson (1988), p. 167.
391. *Ibid.*, p. 53.
392. *Ibid.*, p. 47.
393. *Ibid.*, p. 54.
394. *Ibid.*, p. 54.
395. *Ibid.*, p. 54.
396. *Ibid.*, p. 54.
397. Hay, R.A. (ed. J. Maidment) (1835), *Genealogie of the Sainteclaires of Rosslyn, including the Chartulary of Rosslyn*, Stevenson, Edinburgh, p. 42.
398. Gould (1886), vol. I, pp. 398–410.
399. Hibbert, C. (1968), *Charles I*, Weidenfield and Nicolson, London, p. 26.
400. Robinson, C.E. (1920), *A History of England, 1485–1688*, Methuen, London, p. 45.
401. Preston, W. (1746), *Illustrations of Freemasonry*, William, T Wilkie, London, p. 207; see http://robertlomas.com/preston/padlock/book4/index.html for full text (accessed November 5, 2006).
402. Stevenson (1988), p. 48.
403. Hamill, J., and R. Gilbert (1998), *Freemasonry: A Celebration of the Craft*, Greenwich Editions, London, p. 22.
404. Stevenson (1988), p. 49.
405. *Ibid.*, p. 57.
406. *Ibid.*, p. 54.
407. *Ibid.*, p. 56.
408. Stevenson (1988), p. 56.
409. Lomas (2006), pp. 151–52.
410. Stevenson (1988), p. 51.
411. *Ibid.*, p. 62.
412. http://www.dsl.ac.uk/dsl/ (accessed November 5, 2006).
413. Stevenson (1988), p. 58.
414. *Ibid.*, p. 63.
415. *Ibid.*, pp. 67–72.
416. *Ibid.*, p. 59.
417. *Ibid.*, p. 60.
418. *Ibid.*, p. 60.
419. *Ibid.*, p. 64.
420. Gould (1886), vol. I, pp. 412–13.
421. http://www.rosslynchapel.org.uk/history/history-pt3.htm#1736 (accessed November 5, 2006).
422. *Ibid.*.
423. *Ibid.*.
424. Thompson (1987), p. 133.
425. Gould (1886), vol. III, p 48.
426. http://www.irishfreemasons.org/gl_history.htm (accessed November 5, 2006).
427. Preston (1746), pp. 259–60; see http://robertlomas.com/preston/padlock/book4/index.html for full text.
428. Gould (1886), vol. III, p. 48.
429. *Ibid.*, p. 49.
430. *Ibid.*, p. 48.
431. Gould (1886), vol. I, p. 397.
432. *Ibid.*, p. 410.

433. Gould (1886), vol. II, p. 116.
434. Gould (1886), vol. III, p. 49.
435. *Ibid.*, p. 50.
436. *Ibid.*, p. 49.
437. *Ibid.*, p. 50.
438. *Ibid.*, p. 51.
439. http://www.rosslynchapel.org.uk/history/history-pt3.htm#1736. (accessed November 5, 2006).
440. Gould (1886), vol. III, p. 50.
441. *Ibid.*, p. 51.
442. Stevenson (1988), p. 60.
443. Gould (1886), vol. III, p. 51.
444. *Ibid.*, p. 51.
445. *Ibid.*, p. 51.
446. *Ibid.*, p. 51.
447. *Ibid.*, p. 52.
448. *Ibid.*, p. 55.
449. *Ibid.*, p. 55.
450. *Ibid.*, p. 67.
451. http://www.rosslynchapel.org.uk/history/history-pt1.htm (accessed November 5, 2006).
452. Lomas, R. and C. Knight (1996), *The Hiram Key*, Century, London, pp. 301–309.
453. Lomas, R. (1994), private journal notes, unpublished.
454. http://www.rosslynchapel.org.uk/history/history-pt1.htm#1446 (accessed November 5, 2006).
455. http://www.newadvent.org/cathen/07423a.htm (accessed November 5, 2006).
456. http://sinclair.quarterman.org/who/seemly.html (accessed November 5, 2006).
457. http://www.royal.gov.uk/output/Page98.asp (accessed November 5, 2006).
458. http://www.royal.gov.uk/files/pdf/scottish.pdf (accessed November 5, 2006).
459. http://www.newadvent.org/cathen/09655c.htm (accessed November 5, 2006).
460. http://www.royal.gov.uk/output/Page 98.asp (accessed November 5, 2006).
461. http://www.newadvent.org/cathen/09655c.htm (accessed November 5, 2006).
462. http://www.bartleby.com/211/0708.html (accessed November 5, 2006).
463. http://194.203.40.17/output/Page 580.asp (accessed November 5, 2006).
464. http://www.scotlandspast.org/alexiii.cfm (accessed November 5, 2006).
465. http://www.edinburgh.gov.uk/ (accessed November 5, 2006).
466. http://www.lordbothwell.co.uk/roslinglen.html (accessed November 5, 2006).
467. *Ibid.*
468. *Concise Dictionary of National Biography* (1990), vol. III, Oxford University Press, London, p. 2754.
469. Wallace-Murphy and Hopkins (2004), p. 33.
470. http://www.constitution.org/scot/arbroath.htm (accessed November 5, 2006).
471. *Concise Dictionary of National Biography* (1990), p. 2756.
472. Thompson (1987), p 101
473. *Concise Dictionary of National Biography* (1990), p. 2754.
474. http://www.thepeerage.com/p10829.htm (accessed November 5, 2006).
475. http://www.rosslynchapel.org.uk/history/history-pt2.htm#1523 (accessed November 5, 2006).
476. http://www.rosslynchapel.org.uk/history/history-pt3.htm (accessed November 5, 2006).
477. http://www.rosslynchapel.org.uk/history/history-pt1.htm (accessed November 5, 2006).
478. Thompson (1987), p. 109.
479. Stevenson (1988), p. 54.
480. Gould (1886), vol. I, p. 383.
481. Pohl (1967), pp. 7–8.
482. *Ibid.*, p. 174.
483. Thompson (1987), p. 100.
484. Marsden (1994), pp. 11–12.
485. Finlay, I. (1979) *Columba*, Victor Gollancz, London, p. 17.
486. Eeles, F.C. (1934), "The Monymusk Reliquary or Brecbennoch of St. Columba," *Proceedings of the Scottish Society of Antiquities*, vol. 69, May 14, p. 436.
487. http://www.nms.ac.uk/monymuskreliquary.aspx (accessed November 5, 2006).
488. Hale (1976), p. 213.
489. http://www.rampantscotland.com/

ragman/blragman_index.htm (accessed November 5, 2006).

490. http://www.britannica.com/eb/article-9063869/Robert-I (accessed November 5, 2006).

491. http://www.battlefieldstrust.com/resource-centre/medieval/battleview.asp?BattleFieldId=28 (accessed November 5, 2006).

492. http://www.newadvent.org/cathen/07423a.htm (accessed November 5, 2006).

493. Lomas, R., and C. Knight (2001), *Uriel's Machine*, Fair Winds Press, Rockport MA, p. 233.

494. Lomas, R. (2003), *Freemasonry and the Birth of Modern Science*, Fair Winds Press, Rockport MA, pp. 127–28.

495. *Ibid.*, p. 132.

496. Baigent and Leigh (1989), pp, 158–59.

497. Wallace-Murphy, T., and M. Hopkins (1999), *Rosslyn—Guardian of the Secrets of the Holy Grail*, Element, Shaftesbury, pp. xii–10.

498. Wallace-Murphy and. Hopkins (2004), p. 200.

499. Brown, D. (2003), *The Da Vinci Code*, Corgi, London, pp. 564–65.

500. Lomas and Knight (1996), p. 324.

501. Thompson (1987), p. 108.

502. *Ibid.*, pp. 104–106.

503. *Concise Dictionary of National Biography* (1990), p. 2756.

504. Wallace-Murphy and. Hopkins (1999), pp. 12–14.

505. Thompson (1987), p. 101.

506. *Ibid.*, pp. 103–104.

507. *Ibid.*, pp. 104–105.

508. *Ibid.*, p. 105.

509. *Ibid.*, p. 105.

510. http://www.poemhunter.com/poem/the-argument/ (accessed November 5, 2006).

511. Thompson (1987), p. 57.

512. *Orkneyinga Saga: The History of the Earls of Orkney* (1978) (trans. H. Palsson and P. Edwards), Penguin, London, pp. 84–85.

513. *Ibid.*, pp. 89–90.

514. *Ibid.*, p. 92.

515. *Ibid.*, pp. 94–95.

516. *Ibid.*, p. 96.

517. MacDonald, I. (1993), *Saint Magnus*, Floris Books, Edinburgh, p. 11.

518. *Ibid.*, p. 10.

519. Thompson (1987), p. 57.

520. http://www.cushnieent.force9.co.uk/CollegiateChurches/index.htm (accessed November 5, 2006).

521. Stringer, K. (ed.) (1985), *Essays on the Nobility of Medieval Scotland*, John Donald, Edinburgh, pp. 231–2.

522. Thompson. (1987), p. 110.

523. *Ibid.*, p. 109.

524. *Ibid.*, p. 110.

525. http://www.scotsconnection.com/clan_crests/Boyd.htm (accessed November 5, 2006).

526. http://www.scotsconnection.com/clan_crests/Boyd.htm (accessed November 5, 2006).

527. Thompson (1987), p. 133.

528. Kerr, A. (1877), "Rosslyn Castle: Its Buildings Past and Present," *Proceedings of the Edinburgh Society of Antiquaries*, December 10, p. 415.

529. Lomas and Knight (1997), p. 30.

530. Lomas and Knight (1996), p. 324.

531. http://www.rosslynchapel.org.uk/history/history-pt2.htm (accessed November 3, 2006).

532. Thompson (1987), pp. 108–109.

533. http://www.amphetameanies.co.uk/Helen/currenttitles.htm#hayblurb (accessed November 5, 2006).

534. *Ibid.*

535. http://www.colourcountry.net/secretum/ (accessed November 5, 2006).

536. Hay, G. (1993), *The Prose Works of Sir Gilbert Hay*, vol. II, Scottish Text Society, Edinburgh, p. ii.

537. Thompson (1987), p. 109.

538. *Encyclopædia Britannica* Online (2006), "Hay, Sir Gilbert," retrieved from http://www.britannica.com/eb/article-9039634 November 5, 2006.

539. Kerr (1877), p. 417.

540. *Encyclopædia Britannica*Online (2006), retrieved from http://www.britannica.com/eb/article-9039634 November 5, 2006.

541. *Ibid.*

542. Lodge, D. (2003), *Consciousness and the Novel*, Penguin, London, pp. 96–97.

543. *Ibid.*, p. 97.
544. Smith, C., and J. Ritchie (2006), "The Writing's on the Walls," *The Scotsman*, Mon., May 22.
545. *Ibid.*
546. Butler and Ritchie (2006), pp. 54–55.
547. Pinker, S. (1994), *The Language Instinct*, Penguin, London, p. 15.
548. Feynman, R.P. (1999), *The Pleasure of Finding Things Out*, Allen Lane, London, p. 15.
549. *Ibid.*, p. 21.
550. *Ibid.*, p. 103.
551. Kaku, M. (2004), *Einstein's Cosmos*, Weidenfeld & Nicolson, London, pp. 22–23.
552. http://classics.mit.edu/Aristotle/poetics.1.1.html (accessed November 5, 2006).
553. *Ibid.*.
554. Dutton, D. (2005), "Are There Seven Basic Plots?," *Washington Post*, May 8.
555. Booker, C. (2004), *The Seven Basic Plots—Why We Tell Stories*, Continuum, London, p. 2.
556. *Ibid.*, p. 3.
557. Lomas, R. (2005), *Turning The Hiram Key*, Fair Winds Press, Rockport MA, p. 181.
558. Dawkins, R. (2006), *The God Delusion*, Bantam Press, London, p. 174.
559. *Ibid.*, pp. 174–75.
560. Dennett, D.C. (2006), *Breaking the Spell—Religion as a Natural Phenomenon*, Allen Lane, London, p. 262.
561. *Ibid.*, pp. 23–6.
562. *Ibid.*, p. 257.
563. Gimbutas, M. (2001), *The Language of the Goddess*, Thames and Hudson, London, p. 318.
564. Edwards, B. (1987), *Drawing on the Right Side of the Brain*, Fontana/Collins, London, p. 38.
565. *Ibid.*, p. 56.
566. Lomas (2005), pp. 228–29.
567. *Ibid.*, pp. 231–38.
568. *Ibid.*, pp. 239–40.
569. *Ibid.*, p. 239.
570. Renfrew, C., and P. Bahn (1998), *Archaeology, Theories, Methods and Practice*, Thames and Hudson, London, p. 535.
571. *Ibid.*, p. 536.
572. *Ibid.*, p. 536.
573. *Ibid.*, p. 536.
574. *Ibid.*, p. 537.
575. *Ibid.*, p. 537.
576. Wickham-Jones, C.R. (1997), *Scotland's First Settlers*, Historic Scotland, Edinburgh, p. 23.
577. Popper, K.R. (1969), *Conjectures and Refutations: The Growth of Scientific Knowledge*, Routledge & Kegan Paul, London, pp. 52–55.
578. Renfrew and Bahn (1998), p. 383.
579. Heath, R. (2007), *Alexander Thom—Cracking the Stone Age Code*, Bluestone Press, Cardigan.
580. Renfrew and Bahn (1998), p. 42.
581. Gimbutas (2001), p. xix.
582. *Ibid.*, p. 148.
583. *Ibid.*, p. 239.
584. *Ibid.*, p. 123.
585. *Ibid.*, p. 144.
586. Renfrew and Bahn (1998), p. 157.
587. Renfrew, C. (1973a), "Problems in the general correlation of archaeological and linguistic strata in prehistoric Greece: the model of autochthonous origin," in R.A. Crossland and A. Birchall (eds.), *Bronze Age Migrations in the Aegean*, Duckworth, London, p. 271.
588. Mellaart, J. (1965), *Earliest Civilizations of The Near East*, Thames and Hudson, London, p. 77.
589. *Ibid.*, p. 84.
590. Gimbutas, M. (1999), *The Living Goddess*, University of California Press, Los Angeles, p. 11.
591. *Ibid.*, p. 42.
592. Mellaart, J. (1967) *Çatalhöyük*, Thames and Hudson, London, p. 28.
593. http://www.catalhoyuk.com/archive_reports/1997/ar97_03.html (accessed November 5, 2006).
594. Gimbutas (1999), p. 16.
595. *Ibid.*, p. 165.
596. Lomas and Knight (2001), p. 227.
597. Gimbutas (1999), pp. 4–6.
598. Gimbutas (2001), p. 99.
599. *Ibid.*, pp. 151–58.
600. *Ibid.*, p. 151.
601. *Ibid.*, p. 163.
602. Gimbutas (1999), p. 43.

603. *Ibid.*, p. 45.
604. Lomas and Knight (2001), p. 173.
605. Lomas (2005), pp. 217–20.
606. Lomas and Knight (2001), pp. 226–27.
607. http://catal.arch.cam.ac.uk/catal/goddess.html (accessed November 5, 2006).
608. Hedges, J.W. (1992), *Tomb of the Eagles*, Tempus Reparatum, Oxford,
609. Renfrew and Bahn (1998), pp. 157–62.
610. Kenyon, K.M. (1957), *Digging Up Jericho*, Ernest Benn Ltd, London.
611. Mellaart (1967).
612. Smith, A. (1999), *The Wealth of Nations, Books I–III*, Penguin, London.
613. Childe, V.G. (1925), *The Dawn of European Civilisation*, Routledge, London, p. 6.
614. Childe, V.G. (1958), "Retrospect," *Antiquity*, vol. 32, p. 70.
615. Childe, V.G. (1939), "The Orient and Europe," *American Journal of Archaeology*, vol. 43, p. 10.
616. Piggott, S. (1957), "The Radiocarbon Date from Durrington Walls," *Antiquity*, vol. 31, p. 74.
617. Baillie, M. (1999), *Exodus to Arthur*, Batsford, London, pp. 14–30.
618. Renfrew, C. (1973), *Before Civilization*, Penguin, London, p. 83.
619. *Ibid.*, p. 133.
620. Jacobs, J. (1968), *The Economy of Cities*, Pelican, London, p. 27.
621. Mellaart (1965), p. 83.
622. *Ibid.*, p. 84.
623. Renfrew and Bahn (1998), p. 384.
624. Hedges (1992).
625. Berrill, N.J. (1961), *Man's Emerging Mind*, Scientific Book Guild, London, p. 182.
626. *Ibid.*, p. 183.
627. *Ibid.*, p, 184.
628. *Ibid.*, p. 185.
629. Mellaart (1965), p. 78.
630. Jacobs (1968), pp. 36–37.
631. Renfrew and Bahn (1998), p. 356.
632. Jacobs (1968), pp. 28–29.
633. *Ibid.*, p. 34.
634. Renfrew, C. (1987), *Archaeology and Language*, Jonathan Cape, London, p. 56.
635. Ammerman, A.J., and L.L. Cavalli-Sforza (1979), "The Wave of Advance model for the spread of agriculture in Europe," in *Transformations: Mathematical Approaches to Culture Change*, Academic Press, London, pp. 201–202.
636. Renfrew (1987), p. 86.
637. Renfrew and Bahn (1998), pp. 156–57.
638. Hedges (1992), pp. 174–90.
639. Smith (1999), p. 8.
640. Renfrew (1973), p. 60
641. Kenyon, K. (1956), "Jericho and its setting in the Near Eastern history," *Antiquity*, vol. 30, pp. 184–97.
642. Renfrew (1973), p. 61.
643. *Ibid.*, p. 62.
644. *Ibid.*, p. 68.
645. Holmes, A. (1981), *Principles of Physical Geology*, 3rd ed., Nelson, London, p. 30.
646. Skinner, A. (1999), *Analytical Introduction to the Wealth of Nations*, Penguin Classics, London, p. 12.
647. http://www.adamsmith.org/smith/tms/tms-p3-c5.html (accessed November 5, 2006).
648. Skinner (1999), p. 24.
649. Smith (1999), p. 483.
650. Schumpeter, J.A. (1954), *History of Economic Analysis*, Nelson, London, p. 185.
651. Smith (1999), pp. 479–84.
652. Skinner (1999), pp. 26–27.
653. *Ibid.*, pp. 34–35.
654. Gimbutas (1999), p. 3.
655. Sykes, B. (2001), *The Seven Daughters of Eve*, Bantam, London, p. 165.
656. Stringer, C., and C. Gamble (1993), *In Search of the Neanderthals*, Thames and Hudson, London, p. 26.
657. Sykes (2001), p. 15.
658. Cann, R., *et al.* (1984), "Polymorphic sites and mechanisms of evolution in human mitochondrial DNA," *Genetics*, 106, pp. 479–99
659. Sykes (2001), p. 336.
660. Cann, R., M. Stoneking and A. Wilson (1987), "Mitochondrial DNA and human evolution," *Nature*, 325, pp. 31–6.

661. Henderson, M. (2002), "Scratches that Trace the Ascent of Man", *The Times*, Friday, Jan 11, p. 5.

662. Sykes (2001), pp. 251–53.

663. *Ibid.*, pp. 264–72.

664. *Ibid.*, pp. 273–87.

665. *Ibid.*, pp. 288–98.

666. *Ibid.*, pp. 299–308.

667. *Ibid.*, pp. 309–18.

668. *Ibid.*, pp. 319–30.

669. *Ibid.*, p. 330.

670. Smith (1999), p. 483.

671. *Ibid.*, p. 105.

672. *Ibid.*, p. 481.

673. Wilson J.F., D.A. Weiss, M. Richards, M.G. Thomas, N. Bradman, and D.B. Goldstein (2001), "Genetic evidence for different male and female roles during cultural transitions in the British Isles," *PNAS*, April 24, vol. 98, no. 9, pp. 5078–83.

674. *Ibid.*

675. *Ibid.*

676. Renfrew, C. (2001), "From molecular genetics to archaeogenetics," *PNAS*, April 24, vol. 98, no. 9, pp. 4830–32.

677. *Ibid.*

678. Hedges (1992).

679. Gimbutas (1999), p. 11.

680. Jacobs (1968), p. 42.

681. Mellaart (1965), p. 84.

682. *Ibid.*, p. 92.

683. Gimbutas (1999), p. 11.

684. *Ibid.*, p. 16.

685. *Ibid.*, p. 16.

686. Kenyon (1957), p. 29.

687. http://concise.britannica.com/ebc/article-9043547/Jericho (accessed November 5, 2006).

688. Kenyon (1957), pp. 56–57.

689. Mithen, S. (2003), *After the Ice*, Weidenfeld & Nicolson, London, p. 62.

690. *Ibid.*, p. 27.

691. Hedges (1992), pp. 174–90.

692. *Ibid.*, p. 107.

693. Berrill (1961), p. 194.

694. Diamond, J. (1999), *Guns, Germs and Steel*, Vintage, London, pp. 123–24.

695. Jacobs (1968), p. 35.

696. Diamond (1999), p. 120.

697. Jacobs (1968), p. 34.

698. Gimbutas (1999), p. 48.

699. Mellaart (1965), pp. 79–80.

700. *Ibid.*, p. 98.

701. Lomas and Knight (2001), pp. 195–96.

702. Gimbutas (1999), p. 50.

703. Temple, R. (1991), *He Who Saw Everything*, Rider, London, p. ix.

704. Lomas and Knight (2001), pp. 75–78.

705. *Ibid.*, pp. 190–201.

706. Temple (1991), pp. x–xi.

707. Diakonoff, I.M., and N.B. Jankowska (1990), "An Elamite Gilgamesh Text from Argistihenele, Urartu," *Zeitschrift fur Assyriologie*, vol. 80, no. 1, pp. 102–20.

708. Temple (1991), p. xi.

709. Lomas (2005), p. 65.

710. Temple (1991), pp. xiii–xiv.

711. *Ibid.*, p. xvii.

712. Gimbutas (1999), p. 28.

713. Mellaart (1965), p. 94.

714. Temple (1991), p. 2.

715. Mellaart (1965), pp. 92–93.

716. Gimbutas (1999), p. 12.

717. Temple (1991), pp. 2–3.

718. *Ibid.*, p. 5.

719. *Ibid.*, p. 6.

720. *Ibid.*, p. 7.

721. *Ibid.*, pp. 9–10.

722. *Ibid.*, p. 17.

723. *Ibid.*, pp. 18–19.

724. *Ibid.*, p. 25.

725. *Ibid.*, p. 11.

726. *Ibid.*, p. 15.

727. *Ibid.*, p. 17.

728. *Ibid.*, p. 26.

729. *Ibid.*, p. 30.

730. *Ibid.*, p. 31.

731. *Ibid.*, p. 32.

732. *Ibid.*, p. 37.

733. *Ibid.*, p. 37.

734. Gimbutas (2001), p. 43.

735. Temple (1991), p. 61.

736. *Ibid.*, p. 62.

737. *Ibid.*, p. 62.

738. *Ibid.*, p. 64.

739. *Ibid.*, p. 69.

740. *Ibid.*, p. 69.

741. *Ibid.*, p. 79.

742. *Ibid.*, p. 101.

743. *Ibid.*, p. 83.

744. *Ibid.*, p. 88.
745. *Ibid.*, p. 99.
746. *Ibid.*, p. 101.
747. *Ibid.*, p. 104.
748. *Ibid.*, p. 115.
749. *Ibid.*, p. 127.
750. *Ibid.*, p. 130.
751. *Ibid.*, p. 131.
752. *Ibid.*, p. 131.
753. *Ibid.*, pp. 2–3.
754. Booker (2004), p. 601.
755. A diagram of Wilmshurst's Tracing Board of the Centre can be found at http://www.brad.ac.uk/webofhi-ram/?section=walter_leslie_wilmshurst&page=Tracingboard.html
756. *Ibid.*
757. *Ibid.*, p. 601.
758. http://www.sacred-texts.com/ane/gilgdelu.htm (accessed November 5, 2006).
759. Dennett (2006), p. 98.
760. *Ibid.*, p. 112.
761. Mellaart (1965), pp. 87–88.
762. Kenyon (1957), p. 62.
763. Temple (1991), pp. 114–15.
764. *Ibid.*, p. 101.
765. Lomas (2005), p. 152.
766. Humphrey, N. (1996), *Soul Searching*, Vintage, London, p. 40.
767. Temple (1991), p. 103.
768. Thouless, R.. (1971), *An Introduction to the Psychology of Religion*, Cambridge University Press, Cambridge, pp. 60–62.
769. Newberg, A., E. d'Aquili and V. Rause (2002), *Why God Won't Go Away: Brain science and the biology of belief*, Ballantine, New York, p. 61.
770. Dennett (2006), pp. 278–79.
771. Bernard of Clairvaux (trans. C. Greenia) (1977), *The Works of Bernard of Clairvaux* , The Cistercian Fathers Series: no. 19, vol. 7, Cistercian Publications, Kalamazoo, Mich., Treatise III

772. Dennett (2006), p. 279.
773. Lomas (2005), p. 41.
774. http://www.brad.ac.uk/webofhi-ram/?section=ancient_accepted&page=29standrew.html (accessed November 5, 2006).
775. http://www.brad.ac.uk/webofhi-ram/?section=ancient_accepted&page=29standrew.html (accessed November 5, 2006).
776. http://www.brad.ac.uk/webofhi-ram/?section=royal_order_scot-land&page=heredom.html (accessed November 5, 2006).
777. http://www.brad.ac.uk/webofhi-ram/?section=royal_order_scot-land&page=rosy_cross.html (accessed November 5, 2006).
778. Lomas (2003), chapter 12.
779. Lomas and Knight (1996), p. 325.
780. Lomas (2005), p. 376.
781. *Ibid.*, p. 217.
782. *Ibid.*, p. 38.
783. *Ibid.*, p. 39.
784. http://www.dailygrail.com/node/1727 (accessed November 5, 2006).
785. Dawkins (2006), pp. 18–19.
786. Feynman (1999), p. 18.
787. http://www.brad.ac.uk/webofhi-ram/?section=ancient_accepted&page=24princetab.html (accessed November 5, 2006).
788. http://www.brad.ac.uk/webofhi-ram/?section=ancient_accepted&page=24princetab.html (accessed November 5, 2006).
789. http://www.brad.ac.uk/webofhi-ram/?section=ancient_accepted&page=26princeofm.html (accessed November 5, 2006).
790. http://www.brad.ac.uk/webofhi-ram/?section=ancient_accepted&page=30knightkadosh.html (accessed November 5, 2006).

İ Π D E X